J. Kent Clark is Profes...
California Institute...

'Doth any man doubt tha...
out of men's minds vain...
hopes, false valuations, imaginations as one
would, and the like, but it would leave the
minds of a number of men poor shrunken things,
full of melancholy and indisposition, and
unpleasing to themselves?'
Sir Francis Bacon, 'Of Truth'

'Extremely erudite and entertaining . . . full of
picturesque details'
Peter Quennell, *Sunday Telegraph*

'This book, written in an appropriately dead-pan
style, tells us more about late 17th-century
society than scores of political histories'
Christopher Hill, *Sunday Times*

'Professor Clark tells his story remarkably
well — so well, we are left asking for more'
N. H. Keeble, *Times Higher Education Supplement*

Goodwin Wharton

J. KENT CLARK

CARDíNAL

A CARDINAL BOOK

First published in Great Britain by Oxford University Press 1984
First published in Cardinal by Sphere Books Ltd 1989

Copyright © J. Kent Clarke 1984

All rights reserved.
No part of this publication may be reproduced,
stored in a retrieval system, or transmitted, in any
form or by any means without the prior
permission in writing of the publisher, nor be
otherwise circulated in any form of binding or
cover other than that in which it is published and
without a similar condition including this
condition being imposed on the subsequent
purchaser.

Reproduced, printed and bound in Great Britain by
The Guernsey Press Co. Ltd, Guernsey, Channel Islands.

ISBN 07474 05506

Sphere Books Ltd
A Division of
Macdonald & Co. (Publishers) Ltd,
27 Wrights Lane, London W8 5TZ

A member of Maxwell Pergamon Publishing Corporation plc

To
James Stephen Diemer

PREFACE

If Goodwin Wharton had not existed, he could not have been invented. No historical novelist, however steeped in seventeenth-century lore, could have imagined the forces that shaped his career; no psychologist, however intuitive, could have confected the people and motives that formed him. If he had not written an autobiography for the enlightenment of an illegitimate son, whom he never saw, the strange story of his life could never have been told.

Again, if Goodwin Wharton had not met a genius named Mary Parish, he might not have deserved a biography. He would have been historically interesting, to be sure, as an alchemist, inventor, deep-sea diver, cavalry officer, MP, and Lord of the Admiralty; but without the talents of Mary Parish he would not have exorcised the evil spirits at Hounslow, pursued the Queen of England to Bath, outstared King James, recorded his erotic dreams, or volunteered for the assault echelon at Camaret Bay.

For biography, unfortunately, Goodwin Wharton's memoirs have a serious limitation. Though remorselessly truthful, they are by no means complete. Wharton wrote to explain marvels and spiritual adventures, not routine secular achievements—to record miracles, not parliamentary debates. For this reason, he often failed to record historic events he witnessed personally, and he did much less than justice to his accomplishments as MP, Sea Lord, and Whig tactician. He left such information to be dredged out of documents by scholars dull enough to care about committees of the Commons, resolutions, votes, and speeches.

On the other hand, Wharton was sometimes obliged to record the mundane in order to explain the marvellous; and sometimes his hidden life and his public life overlapped. When, for example, he led diving expeditions to Tobermory, joined the Prince of Orange at Henley, tried to destroy Jean Bart, and explained the Glorious Revolution to Queen Mary, he was at once performing public services and obeying secret revelations; he found it worthwhile, therefore, to recount the episodes. Similarly, his relationships with his family were freighted with moral significance. These he described with a candour raw enough to satisfy the most determined Freudian.

Mary Parish, Wharton's versatile partner, creates a special set of biographical problems. Among the most resourceful women of her time, or any other time, she was also a consummate story-teller—capable of constructing characters and kingdoms, re-arranging theological systems, devising intricate plots, and defending the indefensible. Gifted with rare abilities and accustomed to living by her wits, she seldom troubled herself with truth, especially where it conflicted with survival. She had perceived very early that there exists in human nature a bizarre and inextinguishable need for illusion—a need that is proof against mere reason—and she had learned to improve upon reality with enviable skill. This artistry, which transformed the life of Goodwin Wharton, is a source of constant trouble to his biographer, since it involves the complex, and often impossible, task of unsnarling threads of fact and fiction.

Aside from the difficulties caused by the imagination of Mrs Parish and the preoccupations of Goodwin Wharton, the problems of reconstructing Wharton's life are the generic tasks of historical scholarship—finding the right documents, experts, and places and correcting for the systematic diffraction of passing time. This process is theoretically endless, of course, and in practice it has involved many years of research. It has also placed me, as an author, under formidable obligations; I have acquired vast, unpayable debts, both foreign and domestic.

Among the many people in England who have made the biography possible are Mr Walter Garner, Mrs Irene Garner, and Mr Brian Wheals of Bourne End and London; Mrs Mary Gilbey, Revd G. Denis Staff, Mrs Ingrid Taylor, Mr Alan Taylor, and Revd Norman White of Wooburn; Revd Charles Ash of Turville; Mr James McNab and Mrs Elsie Maclean of Tobermory; Mrs Barbara de Veulle, Mrs Joan Stevens, and Mr Robin Cox of Jersey and the *Société Jersiaise*; Mr Graham Garner of Emsworth and the Temple; Mr Philip Burchardt, late of Gray's Inn, now of Western Australia; Revd Gordon Taylor and Mr Peter David Wheatland (Verger) of St. Giles-in-the-Fields, London; and Dr Evelyn Cruickshanks of the University of London.

Among Americans who have supplied invaluable criticism,

research, and encouragement are Dr James Diemer, Mrs Mary C. Hayes, Mrs Jane Evans, Mrs Jerry Davis, Mr Elliott Davis, Dr Lucyle Hook, Dr David Elliot, Dr Beach Langston, Dr George Mayhew, Dr Robert Oliver, and Dr Hallett Smith. Absolutely essential has been the work of Mrs Mary Ellis Arnett, my secretary, who has managed a voluminous correspondence, handled technical details, and worried with me through all phases of the work. I am also hopelessly indebted to my wife, Joanne, who transcribed the letters of Goodwin Wharton's tutors, helped chase Wharton through Caen, Camaret, Paris, Amsterdam, London, Bucks, Bath, and Oban, and showed heroic patience in what must have seemed an interminable illness.

Among professional librarians and archivists, I must thank the staffs of the British Public Record Office, the British Library (particularly the Department of Manuscripts), the Bodleian Library, the Guildhall Library, the Berkshire Record Office, the Algemeen Rijksarchief (s'-Gravenhage), and the William Andrews Clark Memorial Library of Los Angeles. To the staff of the Henry E. Huntington Library, both past and present, from director to page, I am deeply grateful. Of the battalions who have helped me I will mention, as symbolic, Miss Mary Isabel Fry, Mrs Eleanor Tolles Gernert, Mrs Doris Smedes, Mrs Diana Wilson, and Mrs Mary Wright. I am also grateful to the late John C. Pomfret, Director, for the original financial support of the Wharton project; and I wish to thank successive chairmen of the Humanities Division of the California Institute of Technology —Hallett Smith, Robert Huttenback, Roger Noll, and David Grether—for their generous support of a long, costly enterprise.

Finally, in some separate category I must acknowledge the multitudinous talents of research expert and editor Mrs Carol Brunner Pearson, who did everything for the book except write it—transcribed the half-million words of Wharton's autobiography, found and checked sources and references, transformed the text into OUP style, and indexed the final version. In the abbreviations of Goodwin Wharton, she can be classified as Ds of Sleuths, Ps of Style, and Qn of Editors.

Pasadena, California   J. KENT CLARK

CONTENTS

LIST OF ILLUSTRATIONS

NOTE ON SOURCES AND STYLE

The basic document for the study of the life of Goodwin Wharton is his holograph autobiography, BL, Add. MSS 20,006–7. This remarkable narrative, begun in February 1686 and continued as a journal until shortly before his death in October 1704, contains 530 closely written folio pages—approximately 500,000 words. Other primary sources of Wharton papers include Carte MSS 79, 80, 81, 109, and 233, and Rawlinson MSS 49–54 in the collection of the Bodleian Library.

In the text of this biography, I have modernized the spelling and punctuation of material drawn from seventeenth-century sources. My thought has been to make the narrative as clear as possible for the general reader and to avoid any suggestion that Goodwin and his contemporaries were either quaint or uneducated. For the benefit of literary scholars, I have retained original spellings in the notes, except for quotations from the autobiography, which I have modernized for the sake of consistency. Unless otherwise indicated, English (Old Style) dates are used throughout, except that new years begin on 1 January.

1

The Slough of Despond

As Goodwin Wharton, second son of Philip, Lord Wharton, approached his thirtieth birthday, 8 March 1683, he was in no mood to celebrate. He was in fact sliding into something very like despair. Somehow, through no fault of his own, everything had gone wrong; all of his carefully contrived projects had collapsed, one after another. Now the hands of all men, and of at least two women, were turned against him; he was alienated from his family, his friends, dozens of creditors, and most especially from James, Duke of York, soon to be King James II.

All this misfortune, Goodwin knew, was diabolically unfair. No man in England had struggled harder to improve himself morally and spiritually. In spite of fearful temptations, including those offered by the Court of Charles II, he had fought through to a religious faith that allowed him to despise the vanities of a foolish world. Nor had any man tried harder to improve his fortunes through his own efforts. Not content to be a parasite, dependent upon his wealthy father, he had applied himself to the useful arts: mechanics, deep-sea diving, and alchemy. To these he had added the more theoretical studies of astrology, theology, and medicine, in all of which he had acquired a more than gentlemanly competence. And yet, in spite of his virtue, his recondite studies, and his many talents, none of his affairs had flourished. Clearly he had a right to despair and to suspect some malign influences behind the course of events. Clearly, too, he needed help.

In that gloomy March of 1683, Goodwin Wharton was not alone in needing help. The whole Whig party, of which he was a junior member, a former MP from East Grinstead, was collapsing after its frantic effort to exclude the Duke of York from succession to the Crown. Its leader, the Earl of Shaftesbury, had fled to Holland and was lately dead, and the Tory reaction was in full cry. Though the revelations about the conspiracy known as the Rye House Plot and the bloody executions of

Whig notables would not occur until the following summer, it
was already clear to Goodwin that Whig politics were more
likely to lead to oblivion than to fame and fortune. Far from
involving himself in plots, he was busily trying to forget that he
had become an enemy of the Stuarts. He preferred to recall that
in earlier, happier times, Charles II had received him with easy
familiarity and made him some 'of the fairest promises that ever
were broke'.[1]

One fact, however, he could not forget. In the famous
Exclusion Parliament of 1680, he had attacked the Duke of
York in a speech that was inflammatory and slanderous, even by
current Whig standards. In a combination of assertion and
innuendo, he accused James of complicity in the burning of
London, of sacrificing English ships to save French ships during
the Dutch wars, of thirsting for the blood of Scots Covenanters,
of lying to protect the perpetrators of the Popish Plot, and of
doing 'his utmost endeavour' to ruin the nation. Such a prince,
Goodwin hinted broadly, was more deserving of a headsman's
axe than succession to the throne of England. Nor was this all.
Besides implying that James was a traitor to England, which he
was not, Goodwin had called James stupid, which he was. 'I do
not think it possible', Goodwin had said in an unfortunately
memorable phrase, 'that any person that hath been . . . weak
enough . . . to turn papist should ever after be wise enough to
turn Protestant.'[2]

By early 1686, when he sat down to write his autobiography for
the education of his illegitimate son, Goodwin had persuaded
himself that his notorious speech had been merely an attack
upon corruption in high places; but in March 1683, with the
phrases still echoing in his head, he feared some sort of Stuart
vengeance. Obviously, it was a time for caution, a time to step
quietly out of history—to hope that James had a short memory.
The road to success through politics was closed for the
immediate future, perhaps forever.

Another road closed, at least temporarily, was the favour of
Goodwin's family, and particularly the favour of his father,
Lord Wharton. To many people in England—and to practically
all sober and sincere Puritans—Philip, Lord Wharton, was the
model of a Christian gentleman. Strikingly handsome, as his
elegant portrait by Van Dyck shows, and endowed with artistic

tastes, like his friend Andrew Marvell, he was nevertheless modest, serious, and devout. He was also a leader in Puritan political causes, both in and out of Parliament.

During the revolution against Charles I, he served as a colonel in the Parliamentary Army, a lord lieutenant in the northern counties, a peace negotiator, and a spokesman for the Presbyterian peers. After the Restoration when Puritan fortunes were desperate, he rescued dispossessed ministers from poverty, sheltered Dissenters, and worked tirelessly to promote religious toleration. At last he helped to put together the Whig coalition that vied with Charles II for the control of England—an effort which once cost him a term in the Tower of London.[3]

The public admiration for the virtues of 'the good Lord Wharton' was shared by his children—Tom, Goodwin, Henry, William, Elizabeth, Anne, Margaret, Mary, and Philadelphia. His children, like everyone else, recognized true piety when they saw it, and they also recognized his almost obsessive concern with what he regarded as their welfare. Unfortunately, they found him easier to honour than to obey, easier to obey than to love, and easier to love than to please.

For Goodwin, Lord Wharton was especially difficult. Even at the best of times Goodwin found him cool, formal, and unapproachable. He could never speak to his father without feeling somehow inadequate and unworthy; and his most cherished religious experiences appeared frivolous when measured against Lord Wharton's granite Calvinistic faith and his long record of charitable works. And if Lord Wharton seemed chilly even when he was not actively displeased, he could be formidable indeed when he was disappointed or crossed. By 1683, it was Goodwin's misfortune to have spent most of his adult life displeasing his father.

To begin with, Goodwin had made great difficulties about giving up his right to a substantial share of his mother's property. His mother, Jane Goodwin Wharton, sole heir of Colonel Arthur Goodwin, had brought to her marriage with Lord Wharton extensive holdings in Buckinghamshire. Among these properties was the manor of Wooburn, then as now one of the loveliest sites in southern England. It was an estate that Lord Wharton eventually came to prefer above his many other rich holdings.[4]

Before Lady Jane died, in 1658, she and Lord Wharton drew
up a property settlement which specified that Wooburn should
descend after Lord Wharton's death to her second son Goodwin
rather than to her eldest son Tom. Lady Wharton's reasoning
was clear enough. Tom would inherit the manor of Winchendon
in Buckinghamshire, as well as the extensive and hereditary
Wharton properties in Westmorland, Cumberland, and York.
Even without Wooburn, he would be able to support the
Wharton family and title in great splendour. Meantime, she
decided, the manor of Wooburn would provide handsomely for
her namesake Goodwin.

Lord Wharton, however, came to regret this decision. After
Lady Jane died, he moved his family from Winchendon to
Wooburn and began to improve the old manor house. Unfortunately for Goodwin, the more Lord Wharton improved the
great house at Wooburn, and the more he embellished it with his
remarkable collection of Vandykes and Lelys, the more he was
convinced that the estate should descend intact to Tom.[5]
Wooburn, he reasoned, would not only add lustre to the
Wharton title, but also help him negotiate a richer marriage for
his heir. By 1672, when he was bargaining hotly for a wealthy
heiress, he decided to break the entail and transfer the
inheritance to Tom.

Breaking the entail, however, proved to be no easy matter. As
Lord Wharton's lawyer informed him, Wooburn was 'knitted in
so strong a manner to Mr Goodwin Wharton' that it could not
be transferred without endangering the entire settlement of Lady
Jane's property.[6] Moreover, no transfer was possible without
the consent of Goodwin himself. Unabashed by the difficulties,
Lord Wharton persisted. But Goodwin, to the surprise and
anger of his father, refused to cooperate. Instead of replying
with his usual 'Yes, Father,' he produced another memorable
phrase: 'I had rather live really a beggar', he said, 'than give the
world a real ground to count me a fool.'

'After some days' confinement and threats', Goodwin was
persuaded, on the advice of his own lawyers, to agree to
surrender Wooburn in exchange for a firm settlement of some
other properties and a yearly allowance of £200. This settlement,
later altered by Lord Wharton to Goodwin's disadvantage,
ended the brief and violent battle;[7] but the scars were never

completely healed. To Lord Wharton, Goodwin had become a headstrong, disobedient child. To Goodwin, the episode was a graphic demonstration of how much his father preferred his older brother.

Unfortunately, the battle of Wooburn proved to be only the first of Goodwin's financial misadventures. Others followed in discouraging succession, and each brought fresh disapproval from Lord Wharton, who usually found himself saddled with the unpaid bills. One of these promising but costly enterprises involved the invention of 'the first tolerably efficient fire-engine'.[8] Goodwin, like his contemporaries, had learned at least one lesson from the Great Fire of London: existing methods of fire fighting were practically useless against large fires, and anyone who could produce an effective machine would deserve, and probably make, a fortune. In late 1676, Goodwin found what he believed to be the answer to London's problems.

An ingenious Dutchman named Theodore Lattenhower had devised an engine capable of pumping and spraying water 'in greater quantity with much more force and facility than any yet extant'. With this machine, as witnesses testified, Lattenhower had saved St. Thomas's Hospital during the huge Southwark fire of 26 May 1676. He then presented one of his engines to the Mayor and Aldermen of London, who ordered several more and gave him 'a gratuity of one hundred pounds'.

Excited by the performance of the engine, Goodwin and a partner named Bernard Strode bought the rights to Lattenhower's invention and proceeded, on 6 January 1677, to get a patent for the new device.[9] The triumph, however, was short lived. The Aldermen of London had fought Goodwin's attempt to patent the engine; and when he succeeded in obtaining his patent over their opposition, they refused to deal with him. Revoking their previous orders, they chose, as Goodwin sadly remarked, to risk huge fire losses rather than allow the patentees to make a profit. At the end of a bitter struggle, 'the whole business fell to nothing'; and the partnership collapsed under a blizzard of bills.[10]

Only slightly less frustrating and even more expensive were Goodwin's attempts to turn a profit from deep-sea diving.[11] This infant art, he was convinced, needed only a few mechanical improvements to yield fabulous returns. As early as 12

November 1675, in concert with some 'ingenious artists', he had invented several 'engines and instruments' for raising sunken ships and for conveying air to submerged divers. On that date, Goodwin and two partners, William Perkins and James Innes, were granted a patent on the new equipment;[12] and for several years thereafter they tried to exploit their technical advantages. But although Goodwin invested several hundred pounds, his diving project, to his 'very great grief', eventually foundered on the ruinous cost of operations and the reluctance of cowardly divers to risk their lives.

When Goodwin was forced to abandon diving operations, he left one particularly attractive project unattempted. This was the wreck of a Spanish galleon sunk at Tobermory Bay in the Isle of Mull. In 1588 this vessel, thought to be the *Admiral of Florence*, the carrier of treasure for the fleeing Armada, had blown up while at anchor. The relatively undamaged after-section of the ship, including the captain's cabin and presumably the treasure, now lay under eight to ten fathoms of clear water 'in a very good road land-locked betwixt a little island and a bay'. Successive earls of Argyll, the legal owners of the wreck, had employed people to fish for salvage with grappling-hooks and diving-bells; but although a number of scattered cannon, bones, and trinkets had been retrieved, the vital part of the wreck, which was buried under mud and broken timbers, remained untouched.

In 1680 Archibald Campbell, the ninth Earl, contracted with Goodwin to salvage the wreck during the following summer. Goodwin was to have for his pains the 'fifth part of all cannon, iron, brass, silver, and gold recovered' by him. He was to begin work by 15 April 1681 and continue all summer.[13] But the project failed to come off. In the spring of 1681 Goodwin was unable to raise money for the expedition, and history intervened before he could get another chance. The Earl of Argyll, charged with treason during the Stuart reaction, fled to Holland, lucky to escape with his life. To Goodwin, the collapse of the diving project was simply one more example of his persistent misfortune. To Lord Wharton, it was another expensive demonstration of the hazards of having a 'projector' for a son. Neither of them could foresee that after the English Revolution Goodwin would lead two full-scale diving expeditions to Tobermory, nor that the expeditions would have the support of the Royal Navy and several supernatural powers. For the moment, and for several years after 1681, the diving business remained one of Goodwin's more costly mistakes.

But not his most costly mistake. This distinction was reserved for his adventures in alchemy. For several years, Goodwin poured much of his energy and most of the money he. could borrow into the search for the philosophers' stone. Nor was he alone in his pursuit. The new science of the seventeenth century, far from destroying alchemy, actually sparked a renewed interest. If nature indeed worked on rational mechanical principles, what could be more logical than that all metals might be reduced, by heating, to one basic substance and then reconstituted by the addition of proper chemicals? Why, given correct procedures, should it not be possible to reach a primal form? And why, with the addition of a potent chemical, variously and traditionally described as a 'stone', a 'powder', or a 'sulfur', should it not be possible to produce a different substance? In short, why should it not be possible to transmute tin or lead into gold? Until methodical bores like Dalton established the atomic theory on a firm foundation, these questions went unanswered, and attempts to transmute metals proceeded briskly—even among scientists like Newton and Boyle.[14]

Goodwin began his alchemical investments modestly enough by trying to buy the crucial additive from established adepts. After unsuccessful negotiations in Paris and Frankfurt, he was finally able to acquire in England a small quantity of 'the true powder of projection'. Half a grain of this precious substance, suitably applied to molten metal, was reputed to produce an ounce of gold. Unfortunately, Goodwin's equipment proved unequal to the process; his furnace fell apart and his crucibles were broken by 'the strength of the medicine'. This amateurish technical failure led to an obvious conclusion. Besides proper chemicals, he needed the services of an experienced professional alchemist.[15]

The man he chose, an Englishman named Broune, seemed admirably equipped to produce a fortune. Educated abroad under a 'true master', he had not only learned the secrets of chemistry but also acquired 'a very graceful, affable, kind, and insinuating behaviour'. These accomplishments he had taken to

Paris where he lived for a time in great splendour under the name of Count de Moras. Returning to England after some readily explainable reverses, he set about establishing a reputation for occult lore. To Goodwin, for whom he expressed a respect 'above all he had yet met with', he seemed 'a man sent from heaven'.[16]

When Broune agreed to help, Goodwin formed a syndicate to underwrite operations, bringing in a number of friends who were as eager as he to profit from a synthetic gold-mine. Among these was Major John Wildman, already noted for his plots against Cromwell and Charles II and soon to be famous for his plots against James II. The fact that Wildman's reputation for tight-fisted shrewdness with money equalled his reputation for political guile gave the project an additional touch of financial respectability.

In the new venture, Goodwin personally supervised the all-important heating of the crucibles. For some nine or ten months he took care to have five heating lamps burning at all times. He was able to verify for himself the progress of the work and see that it was being brought 'in a wonderful manner and a right way' to its conclusion.

Then came disaster. A mysterious fire broke out in the laboratory and spread through Broune's house. Within minutes a year's alchemical work and a large investment had been reduced to ashes, and Broune himself seemed to have narrowly escaped being burned. After the initial shock, Goodwin and his friends scraped together what money they could raise in the hope of resuming the experiment or financing Broune in some less ambitious project. This money Broune took, and then dropped out of sight; it was soon evident that he had fled the country. In the investigation that followed, it appeared that Broune himself had set fire to the laboratory in order to conceal the fact that he could not complete the experiment.

To Goodwin the blow was devastating. Having exhausted his credit to finance Broune, he now moved about in imminent danger of being arrested for debts that ran into hundreds of pounds. Besides ruining himself, he had damaged many of his friends and completely disgusted his father, who had disapproved of the project before it started. In no mood to pay off another batch of Goodwin's debts, Lord Wharton contented himself with giving Goodwin several lectures and leaving him to retrieve his disasters in his own way.

If Goodwin's troubles with his father and family had been limited to financial misfortune, he might have retrieved the Broune fiasco. He might have sought help from his wealthy sisters Mary and Margaret or his brother Tom. But his family was 'possessed against' him for other reasons—all of them women.

As early as 1664, while Tom and Goodwin were being educated in France, their father had begun looking about for suitable matches for them. With the aid of a small platoon of Dissenting ministers, he began to sort out prospects who met his high standards for wealth, moral character, and piety. Though Tom was not quite sixteen at the time and Goodwin barely eleven, the investigations went methodically forward. The emphasis, of course, was upon the interests of Tom, the Wharton heir; but there was always a chance that some young lady not rich enough for Tom might be adequate for Goodwin, who (as one agent expressed it) might be brought in 'by a side wind'.[17]

The early negotiations bore no immediate fruit. It was not until 1673 that Lord Wharton's tireless calculations paid dividends. In that year, he outmanoeuvred Tom's rivals for the hand of Anne Lee,[18] co-heiress to the opulent estate of Sir Henry Lee and niece to the Earl of Rochester.[19] The young lady, then fourteen, brought with her a dowry of £10,000 and an annual income of £2,500. Although by that time Tom had acquired a formidable reputation for chasing women, Lord Wharton had good reason to congratulate himself.

Goodwin, however, had little cause for joy. Tom's marriage had cost him Wooburn and weakened his position in the marriage market; and it made Lord Wharton, who had also scored triumphs the previous year with the rich marriages of two daughters, less anxious to pursue Goodwin's interests. Half-hearted negotiations with a young lady in Exeter came to nothing, and succeeding prospects all suffered from defects in beauty, character, or fortune that made them unsuitable for marriage.[20]

It is not certain that a well-arranged marriage, seventeenth-century style, would have kept Goodwin out of romantic difficulties. And it is not certain that Lord Wharton and the rest of the family would have totally approved of Goodwin had he married a wealthy saint. What is certain is that without any marriage at all, Goodwin managed to entangle himself in situations which alienated his family and complicated his life.

The first of these involved a boyhood crush on his stepmother, Lady Wharton.[21] This may have begun as early as 1661, when Anne Carr Popham, widow of Admiral Edward Popham, was brought to Wooburn as the new wife of Lord Wharton and the new mother of the already large Wharton brood. Although Lady Wharton had been a widow for ten years and brought with her two children, Letitia and Alexander, both older than Goodwin, she was still a comparatively young woman. She was also very handsome. To the eight-year-old Goodwin, who had been cared for by household servants since his mother's death three years earlier, she seemed an angel of deliverance.

But the new family arrangements did not last long. In June of 1663, shortly after Goodwin's tenth birthday, Goodwin and Tom were sent to France to be educated under the strict eye of the Puritan scholar Theophilus Gale and of his only slightly more lenient successor Abraham Clifford. There they remained for three years, first in Caen, a stronghold of French Protestantism, then (after a brief tour of Belgium) in the Saint-Germain section of Paris. In all this time, during which both Tom and Goodwin contracted smallpox, the two boys were kept carefully insulated from any corrupting influences. The little expedition, which also included Lord Wharton's faithful and pious servant John Perkins and the boys' French tutor Jacques Le Fevre, formed a small monastic community.[22]

When Goodwin returned to Wooburn, he found still another rival for his father's attention. This was his young half-brother William, whom Lady Wharton had borne in June 1662.[23] Now the child was obviously Lord Wharton's favourite; and Goodwin, already half-submerged by the vivid personalities of the other Wharton children, seemed in danger of sinking out of sight. Again Lady Wharton helped to rescue him—this time by allowing him to share in the attention she paid her own children. She served, in addition, as an intercessor between him and his father, and as an object of adolescent adoration.

As Goodwin grew older his feelings became more complicated. He began to have disturbing thoughts about his handsome stepmother, and he began to develop an uneasy sense of guilt about her. The notion occurred to him that the attention she paid him might be motivated by something stronger than kindness, and that she might be leading him deliberately towards a situation 'which in such a relation would have proved infamous'. He felt himself drifting closer and closer toward some fearful yet irresistible temptation.

Before Goodwin's attachment could betray itself in overt action, it dissolved in a family quarrel. Lady Wharton became involved in a dispute with her son Alexander over her handling of his father's estate. Goodwin would have been well advised to stay out of the argument, but he could not resist Alexander's appeals for help. Alexander had been born a deaf mute; and although he showed remarkable adaptability, he was an object of concern to the whole Wharton family. Once persuaded to take Alexander's side, Goodwin did so with characteristic thoroughness. From his lawyers, he got expert opinions, and to these he added some 'reflections' upon Lady Wharton's treatment of her son. All his conclusions, legal and moral, he embodied in a document which he then presented to Alexander for use against his mother.

Lady Wharton was incensed. Whether or not she suspected Goodwin of illicit inclinations, she resented his interference in her affairs, and she found his 'reflections' both slanderous and ungrateful. At once she was transformed from an ally into an enemy. And her counter-attack was crushing. Besides complaining bitterly to Lord Wharton, she denounced Goodwin to the rest of the family. Even if Goodwin had not been handicapped by a lively sense of guilt, he would have been powerless against her opposition. Her influence with Lord Wharton and the Wharton clan far exceeded his own; he was placed, as he later recalled, 'under such a heavy and remediless lash as is impossible to conceive'. For years after the explosion, which occurred about the time he came of age, Goodwin felt himself 'generally hated and slighted' by his family.

Goodwin's infatuation with Lady Wharton turned out to be disastrous. He later became enmeshed in an affair that was even more serious—an intrigue with his sister-in-law Anne Lee Wharton, the wife of his brother Tom. The stage for this alarming misadventure was set when Lord Wharton negotiated the match between Tom and Anne. By that time, Tom, then twenty-five years old, was rapidly achieving notoriety as 'one of the most gay and gallant men of his times'.[24] Although he was willing to endure a marriage of convenience, he was not willing to devote himself exclusively to his young wife. Anne was an attractive young lady, with imagination and wit; but had she been twice as attractive and witty she might still have lost the battle for Tom's affections. Besides the task of competing with his wily mistresses, she had to compete with his other interests, at least as formidable.

The first of these was politics. In 1673, the year of his marriage, Tom was elected to Parliament for the first time. He had not yet demonstrated the genius that was to make him a prince of the Whigs, but the passion for politics was already evident.[25] When he was not attending parliamentary sessions, he was entertaining his cronies and allies at Winchendon and Chelsea. Anne found herself cast as a bystander at a series of political caucuses.

Then there were the horses.[26] As owner and rider of an increasingly famous string of racers, Tom contested matches all over England. In addition, he possessed a race-track of his own at Quainton Meadows near Winchendon. Again Anne found herself deserted while her husband pursued his interests, or obliged to play hostess to a troop of horsemen.[27] Nor was she cheered by the growing perception that in the competition with his mistresses, his political cronies, and his horses, she was finishing a distant fourth.

Faced with these odds, Anne might have faded quietly into the background. Instead she began to construct a life of her own based on her literary interests and connections. In this effort she had the support of her uncle John Wilmot, Earl of Rochester, himself one of the most gifted poets, and dissipated rogues, of the Restoration period. She also had the friendship and encouragement of Edmund Waller, now elderly but still one of the century's foremost lyricists.[28]

By the time Anne was twenty-one, she had established a considerable reputation as a poet.[29] Her poems in manuscript had a wide circulation, first among Whig intellectuals and clergymen, who admired her rendering of biblical themes, and then among the literary élite, who praised her lyrics, elegies, and classical translations. More important, she had established an identity apart from her husband's. In the first seven years of her marriage she had grown from an adolescent girl to a woman to be reckoned with; she had acquired what Goodwin was to call a 'desperateness and greatness' of spirit.

One thing she did not acquire, however, was Tom's serious attention, now more likely than ever to be engaged by political dramas such as the Popish Plot and the Exclusion Crisis. An heir might have helped, but as the years went by it became apparent that Anne, whose health was uncertain, would never bear children. Her battles would be fought without the help of a family; and she was getting ready to fight in earnest.

It is not clear when or how consciously she began paying off her husband in his own coin, nor why of all men she should have chosen her brother-in-law Goodwin for a lover, except perhaps that he was available, and obviously susceptible.[30] But by the late summer of 1680 Goodwin had begun to meet Anne secretly and had fallen desperately in love with her, though he still prayed vigorously that his actions 'should be abstracted from a lustful intention', and thanked God every time he left her that he had not committed a 'fact' for which he would have hated himself forever.

Anne eased the crisis temporarily by spending the winter in Paris. There, removed from the day-to-day frustrations of her marriage, she devoted herself to writing and to reviewing her situation. Her first decision, wrong as it turned out, was to seek a rapprochement with Tom. She wrote him witty and affectionate letters, two of which are still extant, professed herself delighted by a brief visit he made her, and posed for a time as an 'obedient wife and humble servant'.[31] Her second decision, perhaps triggered by news of some fresh infidelity, was to break off sexual relations with her husband and scrap what remained of a mangled marriage. Her third decision was to complete the task of seducing Goodwin. By the time she returned to England, in the early summer of 1681, she could announce to Goodwin that she and Tom 'had parted as to her bed', and that far from ending her affair with Goodwin, 'she could be content to be damned rather than not have her desires.'

Meantime, Goodwin's high principles had altered. He had temporarily convinced himself that sexual relations with a woman separated from her husband were not cognizable under the Seventh Commandment. If he had not yet managed to rationalize the ethical propriety of lying with his brother's wife, he had at least fatigued his conscience into a convenient sleep. In short, he considered himself ready to make love to Anne at the first opportunity.

The first opportunity presented itself soon after Anne's return. After only token resistance, Goodwin yielded to temptation. But the excitement and tension proved too strong. Before he could consummate the act, he suffered what he later termed an 'ejection' of 'seed', and immediately 'grew incapable' of further action. Since the clandestine meeting was too brief to allow for his recovery, the couple found themselves saved in spite of themselves. They could only plan for the future.[32]

Another occasion was not long in coming. Goodwin and Anne visited Wooburn at a time when Tom could not be present. There, away from the household servants at Chelsea or Winchendon, they expected to find opportunities to make love. They reckoned, however, without the state of Goodwin's nerves, which seemed to come unstrung in the familiar atmosphere of his father's house. Goodwin plotted, as agreed, to arrange a tryst, but he manœuvred with all the conviction of a man arranging his own execution. When he finally managed to meet Anne alone, after several missed opportunities, he found himself more relieved than frustrated to learn that her menstrual period had just begun. 'Out of kindness' to him, she suggested they wait for a better day; she had no wish to defile him.

The better day never came. Goodwin retreated from Wooburn in disorder, half-pleased with himself for avoiding disaster, half-disgusted with himself for his fears and his sudden 'cold indifference', and wholly aware that he had cut a pusillanimous figure before Anne. Later he would attribute his narrow escape to the intervention of God, but at the time he could not be sure whether he had been saved by conscience or cowardice.

After this anticlimax, the intrigue died a natural death. There seem to have been a few half-hearted attempts to retrieve it, but the couple never again ventured so near the brink. Anne's health was deteriorating rapidly.[33] Although her spirit still flamed, she was subject to increasingly long illnesses. By late 1682 she was much more anxious to conceal her former intrigue with Goodwin than to pursue it further. About that time she persuaded Goodwin, who was an inveterate note-taker and diarist, to burn all his previous journals—incidentally depriving historians of a treasure more valuable than the Tobermory galleon. And before March of 1683, the two of them had decided to go their separate ways. Two and a half years later, in October 1685, Anne was dead, at the age of twenty-six, leaving Goodwin with an abiding sense of loss and guilt, only partially relieved by singularly vivid dreams in which he again resisted her charms and was assured that his rectitude had saved both their souls.

Goodwin's affair with Anne completed his alienation from the Whartons. Although his family could only suspect, not prove, suspicion alone was enough to mortify Goodwin. He could hardly explain his heroic wrestling with temptation and his fundamental, though shaken, integrity. More especially, he could not bear the sight of Tom, whom he avoided as much as possible; nor could he bear with patience the sheer injustice of his plight. Tom, an open and flamboyant scapegrace, could be forgiven everything by his selectively blind family; whereas Goodwin, who had actually committed no sin, could be suspected of everything and forgiven nothing.

Thus, in the spring of 1683 as he surveyed the wreckage of his life, Goodwin had a right to despair. The collapse of his alchemical project had left him almost friendless and hundreds of pounds in debt. The collapse of the Whig party had left him without a political future and in danger of royal revenge. The disgust of his father and the ill will of his family had removed all hope of retrieving his disasters through their help. God alone knew what indignities he had endured and how much he needed recognition and love. Only his often battered but never broken faith could save him from sinful and perhaps fatal despondency.

Specifically he needed a miracle. He needed the help of a genius who could penetrate the mysteries of the natural and spiritual worlds and bring back the riches that awaited such knowledge. He needed someone, no ordinary projector or plodding merchant, who could make his fortune and vindicate his life in a single dramatic coup. Beyond this, he very obviously needed the help of a good woman. It was his fortune, shortly before his thirtieth birthday, to find the genius and the good woman combined in the same person. Her name was Mary Tomson Boucher Lawrence Parish. She was one of the most imaginative and versatile women that England has ever produced.

Mary Tomson Boucher
Lawrence Parish

ON first meeting Mary Parish, Goodwin Wharton was not immediately impressed. Nothing in her surroundings or her appearance marked her as extraordinary, or even respectable. He knew in advance he must seek her out in a seedy section of London, but he was dismayed when he found her in 'a sorry little lodging in a poor beggarly alley and a very ill house'[1]—a place where no self-respecting young aristocrat would care to be seen. As he looked about him, Goodwin was glad he had taken the precaution of throwing a greatcoat over his expensive clothes and of wearing a wide-brimmed hat which could be pulled down low over his face. Now he took the further precaution of not giving his right name.

Except for the intelligence in her eyes, Mrs Parish seemed little more attractive than her surroundings. She looked, in fact, more like a middle-aged derelict than a woman of wisdom, medical skill, and occult learning. She had recently suffered a broken leg, which had barely healed, and she still moved about with difficulty; but more generally, as Goodwin soon learned, she suffered from 'an ill habit of body' caused by light eating and heavy drinking. For the past year she had often neglected food in favour of large quantities of brandy, and this practice 'had almost cost her her life'. Now it disguised the fact that her face was naturally well shaped, 'without any ill feature', and made her look every bit of her age, which was fifty-two years and nine months, the exact age of Charles II.[2]

Mrs Parish had been recommended by an 'honest, well-meaning, and ingenious man' who had shared with Goodwin a remarkable discovery—a method, which he had found among his father's papers, for conversing with good angels. This method, unfortunately, involved some technical problems, and while Goodwin was trying to solve these, his friend suggested that he should consult a certain Mary Parish, who had a

reputation for wisdom in abstruse matters and who might know
easier methods of summoning angels than those in the papers.
At the very least, she could furnish rare secrets in medicine.

But as Goodwin sat in a squalid apartment looking at Mary
Parish, ill and bedraggled, he thought that his friend had been
misled. She was far more likely, he thought, to be a cheap
fortune-teller and quack than a woman of penetration and skill.
For this reason, and also because he had just been fleeced by a
smooth, plausible alchemist, he conducted the interview with all
possible scepticism. Though he listened to Mrs Parish politely,
he did not 'immediately give faith' to what he heard.

There emerged, however, several strong points in her favour.
First was her obvious competence in arcane studies. Whether the
subject was astrology, alchemy, buried treasure, pharmacology,
or the making of lucky charms, Goodwin found that she gave
'very smart answers' to all his questions. These answers she
illustrated with anecdotes from what was clearly a vast
experience, and they coincided with many of Goodwin's own
conclusions. Moreover, her calm, matter-of-fact way of speaking
was itself reassuring, as was the unmistakable tone of piety that
ran through her conversation. Without cant or dogmatism, she
managed to convey a simple Christian faith, tested by much
adversity.

The interview ended on a hopeful note. Mrs Parish, Goodwin
decided, had proved worthy of further investigation. Without
risking any substantial sum, he could check out her claims with
a simple experiment. He had long been interested in finding a
charm that would enable him to win at gambling. Mrs Parish
assured him that she had made such devices. She had in fact
helped several gentlemen to make their living at play. There
were two such charms: one, the elaborate and foolproof play-
piece, was a piece of gold or silver cast in a cuttle shell, marked
with appropriate signs, and consecrated by a priest; the other,
usually effective, was simply a periwinkle leaf, gathered at a
proper astrological hour to the accompaniment of a special
incantation. She would be happy, she said, to provide him with
either of these devices. Goodwin chose the simpler and less
expensive model; and having got her promise that she would
proceed quickly, he left the first meeting with the feeling that he
had conducted the affair very artfully.

The test of Mrs Parish's skill proved to be unavoidably delayed. The periwinkle could be profitably gathered only on Friday, at 'Venus's hour'; and on the Friday after the first meeting when Mrs Parish went to Leicester House, where she had formerly found periwinkles, she was unable to find any. The next Friday was similarly lost when her sore leg prevented her from gathering the plants that had been located on Old Street. Meantime, however, nothing prevented her from meeting Goodwin several times, both at her lodgings and abroad, and giving him the outlines of her remarkable background—a story so impressive and so self-consistent that after 'comparing circumstances one with another' Goodwin began to credit what was told him. He also perceived that if he expected frankness from her he must give openness and honesty in return. Accordingly, he told her his name, his family background, and some of his own experiences. She immediately rewarded his good faith by entrusting him with secrets which she had never shared with another human being. Among these was the startling fact (which Goodwin already suspected) that she had found a method for communicating with the spirit of 'an honest man deceased'; and it was to this ability, she admitted candidly, that she owed much of her former greatness.

This last revelation took place on Goodwin's thirtieth birthday. It was a date that Goodwin could not help regarding as significant, and the secret itself pleased him 'infinitely'. Along with the other secrets which Mrs Parish had told him, it promised a way to wealth and personal vindication; for as Goodwin followed the narrative of her accomplishments and misfortunes, he could make out a consistent pattern. While she had evidently achieved a splendid mastery of the arcane arts, she had seriously mismanaged her gifts. Besides being much too generous and naive for her own good, she had been frequently victimized as a woman in a male society. What she needed, Goodwin saw clearly, was an honest, prudent, and worldly-wise man to manage her affairs and exploit her amazing gifts—a man like himself, learned in the more difficult sciences. If she would place herself under his protection and detach herself from the lowly people who sought her advice and 'hunted on all occasions after her as after a goddess', he would make a fortune for both of them.

When Goodwin proposed this arrangement, Mrs Parish consented, even though it meant sacrificing an independent livelihood, however humble. She had found from the very first, she said, that Goodwin had 'dealt fairer' with her 'than ever anybody had done, first or last'. Furthermore, during their brief acquaintance she had become unaccountably willing to trust him 'in everything whatever' and to make him master of all her secrets. For herself, she assured him, she did not want wealth. When she had made him rich she would be content 'to live quietly and serve God' without being distracted with her troubles. As for Goodwin, who had just received his allowance, he was confident that he could support himself and Mrs Parish until he turned some of her vast knowledge to account. After relieving her immediate wants 'with a little money', he began to plan future operations on a scale that made mere gambling charms appear trivial.

In assuming the management of Mrs Parish's affairs, Goodwin proceeded in a commendably systematic way. Since everything depended upon a proper understanding of her life and art, he took voluminous notes and 'lost not a tittle of what she said'. By the time of his birthday he had heard and recorded most of her intricate history—both the relatively prosaic public life which she could tell the world and the marvellous secret life which (like all great adepts) she could share with only one or two faithful disciples. In telling her story to Goodwin, she mixed the astonishing with the commonplace, and Goodwin later recounted the whole in chronological order. Here, for the sake of clarity, Mary's two lives, public and private, will be summarized separately.[3]

Mrs Parish began her prosaic life, she said, on 29 May 1630, in the village of Turville, Buckinghamshire, only a few miles from Wooburn. Her maiden name was Mary Tomson. On her father's side she was descended from an old family of Lincolnshire gentry, and on her mother's side from a Turville family of yeoman farmers named Cox. According to her account, her father was a near relation of Jane Goodwin Wharton, Goodwin's mother. A handsome gentleman from a large family, he had married somewhat beneath his social station for the sake of an attractive property settlement.

This property had descended through Mrs Parish's maternal

grandmother Mary Cox, who had acquired it at the death of her first husband. Widowed early and left with one daughter (Mrs Parish's mother), Mary Cox later married a man named Richard West, a former soldier who soon improved the family holdings so substantially that he was suspected of receiving supernatural help. Richard West proved to be a kind stepfather, and when his wife's daughter came of marriageable age, he provided her with an ample dowry and made her his heir—an arrangement which induced Mr Tomson to marry her.[4]

The Cox-Tomson alliance proved unusually fruitful. Mary was the eldest daughter in a family that ultimately included seventeen children. The family was also unusual in being Catholic—a fact that was to have much significance in Mary's later career.[5] Young Mary, whose intelligence and wit marked her out as destined for something beyond a farm in Turville, managed to become the family favourite. Accordingly, at the age of nine or ten she was sent to stay with her uncle John Tomson, a man of great learning in medicine and other arts. There she remained for about two years, becoming so proficient as a 'housewife' that her uncle, a widower, turned over to her the management of his household. Then, for her further education, she was sent to a boarding-school in Hackney.[6]

While at Hackney, she suffered the first of a long series of misfortunes. To the school one day came a man named Boucher, dressed in the height of fashion and wearing a periwig—one of the first she had ever seen. 'Blinded with the sight of his periwig', the thirteen-year-old Mary failed to discern that he was not a fine young gentleman but rather a London tailor almost old enough to be her grandfather. Boucher at once began to court her and with little difficulty persuaded her to marry him secretly. By this imprudent marriage, which was soon discovered, she alienated her father and uncle, who at first made some half-hearted efforts to break up the marriage and then disowned her.

Mary Tomson's marriage to Boucher lasted seven years and produced seven children, all daughters. It also taught Mary the tailoring trade—the arts of buying and selling cloth, keeping accounts, and managing an establishment which included several journeymen tailors. By the time of her husband's death, about 1650, she had become a capable business woman and an expert in the ways of London; she had also managed, in between duties, to acquire some knowledge of medicine.

For the first few years of her widowhood, her affairs flourished, even though her husband, a free spender, had left her with substantial debts. Besides continuing the business with a full complement of employees, she began to dispense medical advice; she was able, in Goodwin's idiom, to set up for physic. She could not, however, pay off all Boucher's creditors, and after five or six years, some of these, fearing that the debts would soon be legally uncollectable, had her arrested and thrown into Ludgate prison.

During her prison term, which lasted about a year and a half, two very important men entered her life. The first was one George Whitmore, a gentleman debtor who befriended her and performed many services for her. Her gratitude toward him had begun to mix with thoughts of a possible marriage when suddenly he was thrown into Newgate on charges of highway robbery. These charges, he soon confessed, were only too true. After an exemplary apology to her and a sincere repentance that clearly removed him from any danger of damnation, he was publicly hanged. He was not, however, dismissed from her mind; he became, in fact, more important to her after his death than during his life.

Unfortunately for Mary, the other man who entered her life was not hanged; he lived instead to marry her, to father thirteen children in eleven years, to bring his paramours home to bed, and to beat her bloody whenever the fancy seized him. This man, one Mr Lawrence, was not a prisoner, but a gentleman from Berkshire, whom Mary Boucher had known before her first marriage. When she met him again, during one of her occasional liberties from Ludgate, she found that he had become a widower, with three children of his own. A handsome man, though 'lame by a shot', he had been a soldier during the Civil Wars and was currently a seaman. Mary fell in love with him at once, and they were married six months before her final release from Ludgate.

When she was freed from prison, Mary added a new and difficult speciality to her activities in medicine and the cloth trade; she began to give professional counsel to people who faced difficult personal decisions or who had lost valuable objects. This counsel, which she was careful to distinguish from ordinary fortune-telling, was designed to solve 'doubtful' problems, such as the location of buried treasure or the suitability of proposed marriages.[7] Nor was counselling the only talent she discovered during the late 1650s and the early 1660s. In the intervals between producing daughters (sometimes twins or triplets), she began to experiment with alchemy. Her progress in this intricate study, along with a sound preparation in astrology, rounded out her education in the difficult arts.

But her professional triumphs were soon marred by a series of personal disasters. The bubonic plague, which raged through London in 1665, swept away fourteen of her children. This calamity almost obliterated her large brood of girls; along with the loss of four children from normal seventeenth-century hazards, it reduced a family of twenty children to a mere two. Then, in the next year, the Great Fire of London destroyed most of Mary's property and forced her, after more than twenty years in London, to start all over again with little more than the clothes on her back.

About two years later, after she had recovered some of her wealth, her family was further reduced by the death of her husband Lawrence. Although Lawrence had been a grotesquely bad husband, squandering his sea-pay on liquor and women, insulting his wife in public and beating her in private, Mary had borne her injuries with a forbearance that Griselda herself might have envied. Lawrence was, after all, 'the only husband she ever loved so as to be in love with'; and now she mourned his death sincerely.

Left a widow with only two daughters to support, Mary completed her enfranchisement by marrying one of her daughters to 'a gentleman in Cornwall' and allowing the other to stay with her own former guardian, her uncle John Tomson. With her new freedom she finished restoring her fortunes, and she began to attract serious admirers. One of these was a man named Thomas Parish, 'a Suffolk gentleman of a good estate'. On 14 June 1669 they were married.[8]

When she married Parish, then an 'old man' of fifty, Mary planned to retire from her multitudinous enterprises and live the life of a country gentlewoman. But when she arrived at his country estate, she found a household full of enemies. Though

Parish, a widower, had no children of his own, he had nephews who were determined not to share their expectations with an interloper. More important, he had a housekeeper-mistress who had dominated him for several years. From the first, Mary fought a losing battle. Parish would not turn away his nephews or his mistress, and he would not prevent them from insulting and flouting his wife. When she perceived that her condition was not likely to improve and that she had been 'sold a slave' to 'a revengeful, imperious, ill-bred whore', she gave up the contest and returned to London.

Once again she established a reputation in alchemy and medicine; and in time these skills brought her to the notice of Sir Thomas Williams (the newly appointed Chemical Physician to Charles II[9]), who persuaded her to join him as a technical advisor and as manager of his household at Whitehall. The new alliance, however, proved to be a mistake. Sir Thomas, it turned out, had designs on Mary's professional secrets; he was constantly trying to pry out of her the formulas for transmuting metals. Worse yet, he had designs on her body; she was compelled more than once to fight off his attempts to seduce her.

In spite of such roguery, Mary remained with Williams for more than two years. During this time, according to her account, she often exhibited her talents in medicine. With access to the royal laboratories she concocted some 'most delicate waters and spirits' for Charles II and 'came in great favour with the King and all the Court'. But court favour could not compensate for the constant machinations of Williams; and finally, without collecting all the money owed her, she slipped away quietly from Whitehall and returned to an independent life.

This time when she attempted to resume private practice, she failed to prosper. The long absence from her old clients and a series of misfortunes and mistakes brought about her gradual decay. Settled in a little house in Long Acre, she 'continued several years still growing less and less'. Finally, her reverses, along with illness and accidents, forced her to give up her house and move to the beggarly alley where Goodwin found her. This move, which occurred in early 1682, marked the low point in her fortunes. Her clientele, which had once included rich merchants and even princes, now consisted of a shabby crew of 'little acquaintances'. By the time Goodwin met her, she was well on the way to ruining a capacious brain by heavy drinking. Like Goodwin himself, she badly needed help.

If the 'ordinary' life of Mary Parish included extraordinary episodes, the secret life that was interwoven with it included rare episodes indeed. The first of these—an event which actually occurred before Mary was born—was a remarkable discovery by her stepgrandfather West. One day in the woods at Northend (near Turville), while Richard West was digging a pit for burning charcoal, he found a large iron pot filled with gold and silver. Upon cleaning the pot, he discovered a legend engraved around the rim: 'Where this pot doth lie, there stands a better by.' This writing, as well as 'several old fine medals of gold', convinced him that he had stumbled upon fairy treasure. When he searched the pit for the 'better' treasure, however, he was unable to find anything. He was obliged to content himself with the small fortune in hand, which he invested so shrewdly that his increased wealth drew the envy and gossip of the neighbourhood.

Richard West guarded his secret carefully, but when Mary, his favourite granddaughter, was six or seven years old he showed her the treasure site and explained to her in an oblique way the details of the discovery. Soon she began to slip away from home to scrabble about in the pit and to listen for the sound of fairies. Finally, when she was about eight years old, she saw the fairies—'a great many of them altogether in an orchard of her aunt's dancing'. She was 'mightily pleased' by this experience, but it proved to be unrepeatable; she was not to see fairies again until much later in life. Meantime, a year or two after her unique vision, she was sent off to live with her uncle John Tomson.

Mary's stay with her uncle laid the foundation for her future greatness. John Tomson, she discovered, was not only a physician but the possessor of a spirit advisor—a Spanish lady who had been his mistress during her lifetime. Before her death, the lady had instructed him in the art 'of conversing with one deceased'. Now she visited him frequently and brought him valuable information. With her help he was able to solve problems for 'people of quality' and, over the years, to acquire a comfortable fortune.

Many years after Mary had left his household, John Tomson gave Charles II a splendid private exhibition of an extraordinary power. One night, according to Mrs Parish's account, 'he walked perfectly on foot without any device or trick over the Thames straight from Whitehall without being any otherwise wet than his feet a little.' The King was highly impressed by this 'eminent and strange' performance—as well he might have been. He showed his appreciation by making Tomson a knight.[10]

Naturally enough, John Tomson did not share with his ten-year-old niece his secrets of walking on water and communicating with dead ladies. He did, however, show her that such arts were possible and he whetted her appetite for occult studies. In addition, he gave her valuable basic training in both 'physic' and surgery, especially in the 'practic part'. It was this training, along with some very advanced knowledge acquired from another source, that ultimately allowed Mary to set up a medical practice.

During her stay with her uncle, Mary met another expert in the arcane arts—an elderly German gentleman who possessed resources that even Tomson lacked. From Germany, traditionally the home of the secret sciences, he had brought not only a headful of rare formulas but also a large book containing the quintessence of Continental lore. Written in several languages, the easiest of which was Greek, the book brought together all the choicest secrets in medicine, alchemy, spiritualism, and biology. The old German, who took a fancy to the young girl, explained to her some of the treasures that his book contained, and then (secretly plotting to take her back to Germany with him) entrusted the book to her keeping. But his scheme was discovered and he was forced to flee to Germany without her—and without his priceless book. Thus, young Mary became the possessor of a book which, in Goodwin's phrase, 'was worth more than the world itself'.

Mary's education in 'things not common' was seriously interrupted by her marriage to Boucher. Learning the cloth trade, raising seven daughters, and managing a business left her little opportunity for adventures with fairies or spirits. In one respect, however, she prepared herself for greater things. With enviable prudence and precaution, she found translators for portions of her treasured book. By the time of Boucher's death she had mastered several sections dealing with medicine. Armed with this formidable lore, she was prepared to effect cures well beyond the reach of the doctors of her time, or of any other time.

She was able, for instance, to cure breast cancer and cancer of the uterus without surgery. She could also cure hereditary syphilitic blindness, both in children and in adults, and successfully treat advanced consumption. With 'the bare touch' of a water she had manufactured she could perfectly cure sores and ulcers—'running, stinking, old and thought incurable'. Nor were her treatments limited to mere physical disorders; she developed a potion which cured raving lunacy within a few days and which prevented several 'foaming and roaring' patients from 'being carried to Bedlam'. More spectacularly, she could diagnose and treat cases of diabolical possession. In one particularly dramatic case, she routed an evil spirit 'visibly out' of its victim—a feat which brought her great renown as a healer.[11]

The next major step in Mary's extraordinary career occurred during her stay in Ludgate. By this time, she had learned from her book the difficult art of conversing with spirits; she had learned that acquiring a spirit-confidant depends upon finding a living person of 'sense' and 'courage', who will agree to return after his death. Obviously such arrangements are not easy to make. Few friends can be depended upon to die at a convenient time, and fewer still wish to spend their days in the spirit world at the beck and call of a mere mortal. At Ludgate, however, Mary found in George Whitmore, gentleman felon, the perfect candidate for the role of departed spirit. Since he had been condemned to death for highway robbery, there would be no waiting around for him to die; since he was basically an excellent man, there was no danger of his becoming an evil spirit; and since he loved Mary sincerely, there could be little question of his willingness to serve her. When she approached him on the subject, he agreed to her proposals with enthusiasm. He would meet her immediately after he was hanged and attend her thereafter, at her discretion, for the rest of her life.

George Whitmore was as good as his word. After a memorable repentance and a moving exhortation to the crowd, he submitted calmly to his execution. Then he betook himself to

Moorfields to keep his appointment with Mary. Mary was pleased to note that he looked 'just as he formerly did'. At first, indeed, he complained of being somewhat weak and found his speech 'a little imperfect', but he soon recovered from these inconveniences. Within a few days he had mastered all the techniques of communication, including the art of appearing to Mary without being seen by anyone else.

The possession of a reliable spirit gave Mary immense advantages, particularly in personal counselling. Invisible, wide-ranging, and privy to all manner of secrets, George provided her with invaluable information upon the true characters of the people who consulted her and of the people they dealt with; he was especially adept at finding long-buried caches of money and jewellery. He could listen to the living and talk with the dead. In short, he could produce for Mary the kind of results that ordinary psychics only dream of achieving.

Never greedy, Mary was very modest in exploiting her twin sources of power—her precious book and her friendly spirit. She was indefatigable, however, in carrying on rare scientific experiments. In alchemy, for example, she found 'a way of fixing of quicksilver into good gold in three weeks' time'. She also found a method of turning copper into a white substance indistinguishable from silver. With this method she transmuted her household copper 'so that her very andirons and tongs' appeared to be perfect silver. Both methods required, of course, an alchemical laboratory, but Mary provided for these require-ments with no particular difficulty. Disguising her operations as medical experimentation, she continued for many years to produce a modest but steady supply of gold and silver.

Even more spectacular was an experiment in biology, which aimed at producing from 'chaos' a living human being—a 'homunculus'. Begun several years after Mary's success with metals and carried on in her alchemical laboratory, the experiment continued for three and a half years. It had proceeded so far as to produce 'the figure and proportion of a man with a crown on his head' when an accident shattered her equipment and terminated the operation.

Some of Mary's experiments required the addition of a little natural magic. The most dramatic of these involved 'a certain pea'. Planted at the proper astrological hour, raised under carefully prescribed conditions, and consecrated by competent authority, the pea possessed a wonderful virtue. When it was placed in the mouth, it rendered its owner invisible. Like a true artist, Mary contented herself with preparing only one such pea, which she never thought of using for any utilitarian end. After demonstrating the soundness of the method and frightening a few of her friends by appearing and disappearing before their eyes, she lost the pea and never bothered to make another.

Not so dramatic but clearly valuable was a later experiment with frog bones. With proper astrological and biological preparation, a frog bone could be transformed into 'a lodestone of love and hatred'. Applied in one fashion to the skin of the beloved, the bone evoked instant love towards its possessor. Applied in another fashion, it dispelled unwanted love and invoked enmity. This device had such obvious utility that Mary could hardly keep from applying it from time to time. Once she applied it 'positively' to her estranged husband Parish, who responded by taking her to bed and getting her pregnant. Later, after she sued unsuccessfully for separate maintenance, she applied the bone 'negatively' and chilled his affection for good. In general, however, she used the bone impersonally to cure sick marriages and to reconcile parents with their children.

Mary would have been perfectly contented with the secret powers conferred upon her by her book and by the spirit of George Whitmore, but shortly after her separation from Parish she acquired, without conscious effort, still another source of secret knowledge and power. While on an errand of perfect charity to a woman who lived near Hounslow Heath, she rediscovered the fairies and began an association that made her thoroughly familiar with a new realm of surpassing wealth and splendour.

The fairies, according to her graphic account, had their principal colony under the ground in the area between the town of Hounslow and King John's Palace in Colnbrook,[12] with subsidiary colonies in Cornwall and at Shirburn Castle, Oxfordshire. The entrance to their principal realm was located on the third heath northwest of Hounslow. It was here that Mary had been directed by the woman she had helped, and where she had stamped, half in jest, and called to the fairies 'to come out if they were there'. And it was to this spot that she was directed to return by an emissary from the fairies, who appeared in her room one night shortly afterwards. The entrance at Hounslow was 'a kind of door', perfectly concealed in the earth. Beneath it lay a spiral path which led down to a level plain, upon which stood the elegant royal palace with its many marble-paved courts.

On her first visit to the 'lowlands', Mary was dazed by her surroundings and somewhat fearful of her unusual hosts, though they treated her with great deference and presented her with 'jewels and gold amounting to several hundred pounds'. Subsequent visits, however, accustomed her to the country and to the ways of the fairies. She became intimately acquainted with the King and Queen and with the prominent courtiers, especially with one Father Friar, the old and trusted spiritual advisor of the King; and she carefully observed the characteristics which distinguish fairies from ordinary mortals.

Perhaps the most striking distinction was one of size. Normally, the fairies appeared to be delicate creatures 'not above a yard in height', and their horses 'seemed no bigger than masty dogs'. Besides unusual size, the fairies had the ability to fly (though they often preferred to ride on horses or in coaches) and the ability to appear and disappear at will; they could also open any door or casement, an art which allowed them to appear to anyone in any place. Finally, because of a low body temperature (a 'cold nature'), they matured slowly and some-times lived to a great age. Father Friar, for instance, 'the oldest lowlander in the world', was about seventeen hundred years old at the time Mary met him. The fairies, unfortunately, paid for their cold natures and long lives with a relative infertility and a very low rate of reproduction. Both men and women were inclined to look for lovers among hot-blooded uplanders— sometimes with unfortunate results.

In other respects, as Mary gradually learned, the lowlanders were much like other mortals. In religion, they favoured a form much resembling the Catholic, with ornaments and music of the sort Mary was used to in her own chapel. Their church, headed by a pope, was in some respects more conservative than the Catholic, since it preserved some crucial rituals and practices from the Mosaic Law. In government, the lowlanders maintained a traditional monarchy, with descent through both the male and female lines, as in England, but without the parliamentary and legal machinery of the English system. Although the government was subject to arbitrary decisions and court intrigue, the King and Queen were remarkably generous. For several years they presented Mary with gifts so valuable that she needed no other source of income.

Mary's profitable relationship with the lowlanders might have continued indefinitely had it not been for her own indiscretion. The fairies, understandably, wanted their existence and their powers kept secret from ordinary uplanders. Mary, however, with her naturally open nature, could not help telling her friends about her commerce with the fairies. Although warned from time to time, she continued to violate the lowland code—a practice which especially angered the King. When the Queen, her most loyal protector, suddenly died, Mary immediately found herself excluded from the lowlands. The gates were tightly shut, and no calling, stamping, or entreaties could bring the least response.

Mary's exclusion by the fairies marked the beginning of her dramatic decline from affluence. It was soon followed by the accidental destruction of her alchemical equipment, the mistaken alliance with Sir Thomas Williams, and the loss of her genteel clientele. To these misfortunes, Mary added a pair of catastrophic blunders. The first of these involved an argument with George Whitmore. Enraged because George had failed to warn her of the treachery of a thieving maidservant, she berated him soundly and dismissed him from her service, 'not without some curses'. Thus, in one violent outburst, she cut herself off from the spirit world. Then, pressed by debts, weakened by illness, and 'desperate of all things', she began pawning her property 'to get bread'; and she ended by pawning her priceless and irreplaceable book. By this astonishing blunder she lost the complex formulas that had formed the true foundation of her arts. In effect, as Goodwin shrewdly observed, she had pawned the world itself 'for under five pounds'. She had forever condemned herself to squalid houses in beggarly alleys.

But as Goodwin heard the tragic end of Mary's round unvarnished tale, he was undismayed; he conceived, in fact, a dazzling hope. Obviously Mary had despaired too soon. True she had been abused and maltreated by a series of worthless men, and true she had mismanaged unexampled powers. But all was not lost. Even without external aids, she was still more deeply learned than any other person in England; she still remembered enough of her old lore to make a dozen fortunes. Nor was there any evidence that her losses were permanent. Her magnificent book, after all, was merely in pawn; its present holder could be traced and the book redeemed. Furthermore, with suitable apologies on Mary's part, the spirit of George Whitmore might be recalled and reconciled. Finally, with the aid of George, fairyland itself might be retrieved and its treasure exploited.

In fact, as Goodwin reviewed Mary's remarkable career and prepared to direct her affairs, he was inclined to see the hand of God in her strange reverses. Perhaps she had been brought down so that she would throw herself upon the mercy of Goodwin Wharton and so that together they could reach heights to which singly they could never aspire. Perhaps too his own misfortunes had been a necessary prologue to unimagined glories. Now the future, lately hopeless, bubbled with possibilities. With Mary's art and his own wisdom, he would obliterate the past, humble his family, and confound a hostile world. And it would all be simple. He could readily conceive a dozen profitable designs, each of which seemed 'as easy as getting a dinner when one hath money in one's pocket'.

3

George Whitmore and the Lowlanders

To a detached observer the alliance between Goodwin Wharton and Mary Parish might have seemed like the merger of two bankrupt corporations. To Goodwin, however, it seemed a miracle. Delivered from despair and filled with schemes, he resolved to waste no time in putting Mary's great gifts to profitable use. Obviously there were three operations of the highest importance: to retrieve Mary's book, to recall George Whitmore, and to re-establish friendly relations with the fairies. There were, however, lesser projects which could yield an immediate profit. Of these the simplest was the gambling charm that Mary had promised to produce, and it was this operation that Goodwin decided to undertake first.

On Friday, 9 March,[1] the new partners found periwinkles in Old Street, and at the proper astrological hour Mary prepared one of these with the necessary incantation. Since Goodwin had been instructed in the procedure, he could see for himself that the ritual had been correctly performed and that he was receiving a bona fide charm. He was now prepared to gather the first fruits of his new knowledge.

But the new partnership, instead of scoring its first triumph, suffered its first reversal. When Goodwin tried out his lucky charm at the gaming table, he found that it would not work for him. Instead of winning as he expected, he lost all the money he had brought. This disappointment gave him 'a little shock'; he found himself doubting some of the things Mary had told him. When he discussed his failure with Mary, however, he was soon put at ease. She 'seemed to wonder with so much innocency and did protest so seriously the truth of what she said, naming particular people' to whom she had given the charm, that Goodwin could not help believing her. He remembered too that she had never claimed infallibility for the periwinkle, that she had always preferred the play-piece cast from gold or silver, and that the operation of charms might be thwarted by secret causes. On sober second thought, therefore, he refused to be daunted by what was, after all, a trifling reverse; he would press on to more important things.

He did not, of course, abandon his search for an effective gambling charm. In fact, he procured a cuttle shell and some 'clean gold and silver' and endeavoured to cast an infallible play-piece. But since he had no private laboratory and was not 'practiced in that way', he bungled the casting. This mischance meant a long delay, for the operation demanded certain favourable astrological aspects. Meantime, Mary promised to recover a play-piece which she had made for one Mr Glover, an eminently successful gambler who had been killed 'in a quarrel'.[2]

Of much greater moment was the search for Mary's book. This task, which Mary undertook by herself, began with a remarkable piece of luck. Though the pawnbroker who held the book had moved, Mary met him by sheer accident on a London street, and he seemed willing to part with the book as soon as he received the five pounds he had lent her. But a snag developed. Mary, who had only twenty shillings at the time, could not redeem the book on the spot; and her eagerness made the man suspect something of the true nature of the document. He accused her of being a conjurer and attempted to raise his terms. When she refused to be bullied, he haled her and the book before a justice of the peace. The Justice, however, laughed at the charges of conjuring and said that he would hold the book until it was redeemed at the original price. At this point one of Mary's friends, a certain Mrs Seymour, stepped forward with five pounds. She redeemed the book on Mary's behalf and promised to keep it for her until Mary could raise five pounds of her own.

Goodwin had reason to be pleased. With the precious book in the hands of a reliable friend, all that remained was to pay her five pounds and reclaim it. Nothing could be simpler. But as Goodwin soon learned, nothing in fact could be more difficult. Mrs Seymour proved herself to be as elusive as the philosophers' stone. Not only did she move from lodging to lodging, always one step ahead of Mary's attempts to track her down, but she began to spend long periods deep in the country. In these twists and turns she was motivated, Mary concluded, by a 'flippiting' disposition and by fear of her creditors. As March faded into April and April into May, the book, which had seemed within easy reach, began to seem farther away than ever.

Meantime Goodwin urged forward the vital project of recalling George Whitmore. In this, the new partners were considerably more successful. On 25 March, after two hours of calling, Mary was able to summon George and persuade him to speak with her. When he appeared, he complained, naturally enough, of her former ill-usage and expressed surprise that she should now recall him after dismissing him forever. He was not, however, disposed to be bitter or to forget his devotion to Mary. He soon agreed to put himself again at her service.

Goodwin lost no time in suggesting that Mary should ask George to appear to him directly. If she would 'make him over to' her partner, then Goodwin could consult him at any time and carry on the partnership's business with the greatest efficiency. Mary quickly and unselfishly agreed to share George's talents. George, on the other hand, objected strongly to the arrangement. Placing himself under Goodwin's command, he argued, would add many years to his earthly commitments. Mary, who was almost fifty-three, might die within a few years; but Goodwin, who was barely thirty, would not die for fifty years. It was unreasonable, George complained, to extend his service so far.

Although Mary was resolute in pressing Goodwin's case, Goodwin wanted to conduct the argument himself, and since there was no reason why he should not speak to George, even though he could not see him, he persuaded Mary to arrange a meeting in her chambers. In the debates that ensued, Goodwin found himself at a great tactical disadvantage. Since he could not see George (although Mary announced George's presence and indicated that he was 'standing before her'), Goodwin was forced to launch his arguments at the apparently empty air. Then, since George refused to talk with him directly, he was obliged to leave the room while George made his answers, which could sometimes be heard, indistinctly, through the door and which Mary later repeated for Goodwin's benefit.

Undismayed by this clumsy procedure, Goodwin argued his

case 'mightily'. In three or four days, he persuaded George to a grudging compromise. George agreed to appear to Goodwin, but only during Mary's lifetime, and only when he approved of the tasks assigned. With this agreement Goodwin was satisfied, and he looked forward eagerly to the time George set for his first appearance.

But at the appointed hour, after Goodwin 'perceived something like a sudden wind or a puff' arise near Mary, George explained privately to Mary that he could not yet appear because Goodwin had not prayed for him. This objection Goodwin considered grossly unfair. Raised in a religion that frowned upon prayers for the dead, he had not dreamed that prayers were required. He agreed, nevertheless, to perform the proper rituals, and George professed himself satisfied. In two successive meetings, however, George found that he could not yet bring himself to appear; he could only propose a highly attractive plan. If Goodwin and Mary would meet him at Moorfields upon the spot where he had first shown himself to Mary and upon the anniversary and hour of his death, he would make himself visible. Since the anniversary date was only three or four days away, the partners agreed; and at the appointed time Mary led Goodwin to the fateful site at Moorfields—a grassy area near a path. Goodwin observed, with admiration, that 'there was a round spot' more than a yard in diameter where, as Mary explained, the grass had 'remained russet' ever since the original meeting.

In spite of this clear sign, Goodwin was ultimately disappointed. A small April shower had fallen, and this seriously impaired George's ability to become visible.[3] He did indeed appear briefly to Mary, long enough to explain that he would recruit his strength and try again in two hours, but before that time had passed, the rains came down in earnest and Goodwin had the frustration of watching his chance of seeing George washed away.

During Goodwin's early difficulties with George, he managed to solve the vexing problem of Mary's lodgings. Nothing important could be accomplished at her beggarly dwelling, where she was never free from a swarm of low acquaintances. For this reason Goodwin insisted that she should leave, and on 26 March he paid off her old lodgings and got her safely moved to a house in Shire Lane.[4] The new quarters, not far from Goodwin's own room at the Temple,[5] provided the partnership with a refuge from prying eyes and sharp ears. Here Goodwin was free to carry on his debates with George and plot strategy with Mary. He was also able to make overtures to the fairies.

Sometime around 10 April, Goodwin proposed that George should go to Hounslow, speak with the fairies, and begin negotiations for their appearance to the partners. George was glad to go, he explained to Mary, not only because the fairies were a religious people but also because Father Friar had long possessed a familiar spirit of his own. George set off at once, therefore, and returned the same evening with good news. The fairies, he reported to Mary, had cheerfully 'embraced the proposition' of appearing to Goodwin and renewing their acquaintance with Mary. Very soon a party of them, including the King (who had forgiven Mary's old indiscretions) and the new Queen, would visit Goodwin in his chamber at the Temple. The Queen, George added, was a 'very understanding wise person', who had in addition to native intelligence the advantage of communication with a spirit named Sisery.

Along with the good news, George reported one complication. The Queen requested that Goodwin should leave off his endeavours to see George until after he had seen the fairies. This request, she had explained, was not simply a matter of respect for royalty but a reasonable token of regard for the lowlanders as a people. As mortals, like Goodwin himself, they deserved to take precedence over spirits.

Although the Queen's request had a certain logic, Goodwin felt 'a little obstinate'. He had been making steady progress, he believed, in his efforts to see George. Since the Moorfields incident, he had reached a point where he could remain in the room while George conversed with Mary. As yet he was obliged to turn his back while George was speaking and he 'could not well understand' what was said; but there was every reason to hope that within a day or two communication would be complete. Under the circumstances, he felt justified in protesting any further delay—reasonable or not.

When George conveyed Goodwin's protest to the Queen, her response was firm. If Goodwin would not show her people such a courtesy, she said, he would never see any of them. This reply, when relayed from George to Mary to Goodwin, ended the protest. Goodwin agreed to desist from endeavouring to see George. He consoled himself with the Queen's repeated assurance that she would visit him 'suddenly'. This meant that if all went well he would see both George and the fairies within a week.

While Goodwin negotiated with the Queen, he also strove to produce a magic pea—a process which demanded a proper site, a proper seed pea, favourable astrological aspects, and a proper sacrificial animal. (This last—either 'a black bone cat'[6] or a hedgehog—was to be planted along with the pea.) In carrying out the operation, Goodwin discovered that finding, catching, and transporting black bone cats was no trifling occupation and that finding a hedgehog around London was difficult indeed. Nevertheless, he persevered until 'with great pains' he had captured three black cats, and Mary, 'by great providence', discovered a hedgehog. After setting these in the ground at carefully selected sites 'at the right time', he was finally able to pronounce the task finished. Nothing remained but to wait for the autumn when the peas would be ready to harvest.

Meanwhile, by tracking down the mistress of Mr Glover, the dead gambler, Mary managed to recover the properly-cast, foolproof play-piece she had made for him; and in early April she handed it over to Goodwin. At the gaming table, unfortunately, the new charm worked as badly as the periwinkle. Again Goodwin lost his money, and again he came home 'discontented'. This time, however, there was an obvious explanation, soon supplied by George. The play-piece had been made and consecrated specifically for Mr Glover; it could have 'no applicative virtue' to Goodwin until it had been reconsecrated to his use. This process involved finding a Catholic priest and persuading him to perform the necessary ritual; and this meant in turn that Mary, herself a Catholic, was once more put in motion to make arrangements.

Finding a Catholic priest in London in April 1683, though not as difficult as finding a hedgehog, was no routine matter. The town, still sullen from the aftermath of the Popish Plot and from the prospect of a Catholic succession, was inclined to take very seriously the penal laws which forbade priests to reside in England unless attached to a foreign embassy. Priests who defied these laws stayed carefully out of sight. Nevertheless, Mary soon found one. But there her luck ended. The priest, obviously reluctant to consecrate the charm, procrastinated until he had effectively halted the project—until the partners became so thoroughly involved with the fairies that they had no time for mere charms.

During the vicissitudes of his lesser projects, Goodwin's arrangements for meeting with the lowlanders went forward rapidly. The Queen obviously intended to honour her promise to visit him, and she sent Father Friar and his attractive daughter Madam Friar to confer with Mary. Appearing freely during Goodwin's absence, this pair set a firm date for the first appointment and outlined procedures for receiving the court. Thus, about 15 April, Goodwin was instructed to prepare himself and his room for the arrival of his lowland guests. They would come, he was told, sometime during the night.

Since he had been informed that fairies 'mightily loved neatness',[7] his first concern was to make sure that all things, including his clothes, should be orderly and tasteful. He was also careful to provide new candlesticks, 'delicate' candles, clean linens, fresh herbs, and fresh flowers. After completing his arrangements by preparing a good charcoal fire, he sat down, Bible in hand, to wait for the Queen and her entourage. From time to time as the night wore on he consulted his Bible, and he occasionally prayed that God would prosper his designs. But though excitement kept him constantly alert, warding off the fatigue of a busy day, no lowlanders came. When dawn finally arrived, and then broad daylight, he was obliged to admit defeat.

Much troubled, he hurried over to Shire Lane to learn the reason for his disappointment. By the time he arrived, George had already given Mary an explanation, simple and complete. The fairies had cancelled their visit because the Queen had fallen ill. Luckily the illness did not appear to be serious; the Queen, in fact, had such confidence in a speedy recovery that she wished to make another appointment only two nights away.

This explanation satisfied Goodwin, who could hardly argue with illness or gracefully complain of what was obviously God's providence. Stifling his frustration, he looked forward to the next appointment. On the designated evening, he again put himself and his chamber into proper order, and he again waited and watched throughout the night. Again no one came.

Exhausted by his vigil and feeling ill used, he plodded back to Mary's lodgings. There, after a short wait while George returned from Hounslow, he received a reasonable explanation. The King had suddenly fallen ill—so ill that the whole court had been frightened. Fortunately, the illness proved to be 'only a sudden fit'. By dawn the King was recovering nicely, and the Queen could assure George that in two more days she would be able to keep her promise to Goodwin.

The 'fresh hopes' offered by the Queen 'allayed the grief' of Goodwin's disappointment, as did the Queen's solicitude. Understanding that he had sat up two nights waiting for his guests, she sent instructions that hereafter he should 'lie abed' while he waited. Nor was this concession the only sign of her concern. In her chagrin at the repeated delays, she had sworn a solemn oath: Goodwin should see none of her people until he had first seen her.

To Goodwin the logic of the Queen's oath was something less than compelling. It was not obvious why forbidding him to see her subjects should be construed as a mark of her grace. Nor was it clear why she wished to route her messages to him through George and Mary instead of through her own messengers. On the other hand, he could not take the oath unkindly, since apparently it was meant to show her 'civility and favour'. Only a churl would criticize a Queen who expected, in any event, to visit him within two days.

For his next appointment with the fairy court, Goodwin settled himself in bed as ordered. Propped up on his pillows and sometimes reading from his Bible, he managed to stay awake to hear the clock strike one, two, three, and four. Then, much against his will, he 'fell into a fast sleep'. The sleep did not last long; he woke early in the morning and soon betook himself to Shire Lane, where he was stunned to learn from George and Mary that the Queen and her court had come while he was asleep, arriving in his chamber about five o'clock. Seeing him fast asleep and obviously exhausted (George had explained to Mary), 'they thought it a pity' to wake him. And so they had gone back to the lowlands after seeing only one side of his face.

After this 'seeming casualty', which frustrated and troubled Goodwin more than the previous mischances, Madam Friar brought word to Mary that the Queen had devised a more elegant plan for meeting. For the present she would leave off trying to visit Goodwin at the Temple. Instead, she would receive Mary and Goodwin at Hounslow. The fairies customarily celebrated St. George's Day, 23 April, with a great festival on Hounslow Heath. If the partners would present themselves on that occasion, only four or five days hence, they would be suitably welcomed with gifts and then escorted into the lowlands. Meantime, there were a few facts about the fairies that might prove useful.

First, the fairies always referred to themselves as *lowlanders*—a name which distinguished them from ordinary uplanders and emphasized their basically human nature. Second, the lowlanders were indeed able to appear and disappear at will, but this ability implied no supernatural gift. It was merely a matter of state policy. Lowland governments knew how to make magic peas, and they simply issued one to each lowlander. Similarly, the ability of lowlanders to open doors and casements came from the possession of a magic leaf, also produced (by very secret methods) and distributed by the government. Finally, as to the lowlanders' ability to fly, this was a special skill taught to each lowlander from early childhood. Although unusual, this accomplishment too had a sound basis in natural principles.

Taken altogether, the new information strongly confirmed Mary's impression and George's conviction that the lowlanders were as human as uplanders. With their pseudosupernatural abilities explained away, they became readily comprehensible. There remained, of course, much to learn about them. There was, for instance, the matter of their size. Several incidents in Mary's experience with them (and several authentic stories of sexual encounters between lowland women and upland men) suggested that they might assume 'normal' size if they chose.[8] This fact, if it was a fact, had yet to be explained.

There was also the matter of their religion, in which some of the practices seemed strange—the custom, for example, of burning alive any woman taken in adultery. This appeared, to say the least, an over-zealous application of the Mosaic Law, as did the strict observance of laws regarding the 'purification' of women—an observance which was soon to give Goodwin more trouble than all the Ten Commandments combined. These oddities, along with other lowland customs, Goodwin fully intended to explore. For the present, however, he was highly satisfied with the information at hand.

By the eve of St. George's Day, the partners were handsomely equipped for their expedition. Besides providing themselves with fine clothes, they had bought presents for the lowlanders —such little things as the lowlanders 'most fancied'. When they parted to go to their separate lodgings, they had nothing left to do but wait 'with impatience' for the morning. But about five o'clock, before the appointed hour to rise, Goodwin was aroused by a frantic knocking. When he opened his door, he saw Mary, who rushed inside and burst into tears. 'We are all undone,' she said, 'for the Queen hath been taken sick this night, and George is come with all speed to tell us. All the court is in an uproar, and the whole expectation of the day is lost.'

Though staggered by the message, Goodwin rallied with a spirit worthy of an English nobleman. Pulling himself together and comforting Mary, he insisted that George should be dispatched 'in civility' to the Queen, offering sympathy and inquiring after her health. He was even able to bear the additional salt rubbed into his wounds when George returned from Hounslow and described the 'great presents' the Queen had intended to give him. Luckily, George also brought a measure of comfort. The Queen had expressed more concern for Goodwin than for herself. Furthermore, she was confident that by May Day, only eight days hence, she would be well enough to hold the festival as planned.

In spite of his courage, Goodwin could not help wondering, uneasily, why he 'had been all this while without yet making any advantage of anything'. The partnership, he reflected, had been in operation for nearly two months, and so far it had not produced a penny. Financially, in fact, it had been a continual drain. Besides the losses from gambling and the expense of maintaining two establishments, there were such operating costs as new candlesticks, new clothes, presents for lowlanders, and travel by coach and water. The money with which he had launched the partnership had almost disappeared. Turning occult knowledge into cash, he had discovered, was much more difficult than he had supposed—not at all like ordering a dinner.

And there were other worries. He was now farther away than ever from seeing or speaking directly with George. In recent

days, because of the thin walls at Shire Lane and the danger that
George might be overheard, Goodwin had been forced to
suggest that George should give up speaking aloud and
accustom himself to speaking softly in Mary's ear. Although this
strategem made it unnecessary for Goodwin to leave the room
or turn his back while George was speaking, and although it
allowed George to speak with Mary 'though in never so much
company', it effectively removed Goodwin one step farther from
direct communication. Now he could not even hear George's
voice.

There was a problem too with Mary. Before May Day,
Goodwin was again obliged to find new lodgings for her. Too
many of her lowly, time-wasting friends had 'found her out' at
Shire Lane, and she was too good natured to snub them.
Goodwin resolved to remove her bodily. Shortly before the end
of April, he found chambers for her in the Arundel Buildings,
very near the Temple. The move, however, was not without its
difficulties. Goodwin's funds had run so low that he could not
completely pay off Mary's old lodgings without jeopardizing his
coming expedition to Hounslow. In the end, the partners
retreated from Shire Lane in the debt of the landlady.[9]

As May Day approached, Goodwin, determined to make the
journey to Hounslow in a style befitting a Wharton, 'bespoke' a
coach and four horses. With this additional preparation the
partners once more made ready to meet the Queen. But shortly
after Mary arrived at Goodwin's room in the early morning of
May Day, George brought a message so strange and delicate
that though its immediate effect was to postpone the meeting, it
intrigued Goodwin almost as much as it disappointed him.

The Queen, George announced, had 'fallen ill'—not ill in the
sense of being 'sick', but ill with the 'monthly natural concerns'
of women. She had begun her menstrual period. Among upland
women, of course, such an event would be no cause to postpone
an important meeting, much less a national festival; but among
lowland women (as George now explained), it was a compelling
cause to postpone everything. For according to the lowland
interpretation of the Mosaic Law, menstruation rendered a
woman 'unclean'. During her period and for eight additional
days of purification, she could not touch men or even speak with
them face to face. At best she could communicate with them

through a speaking tube, as the Queen was accustomed to do with the King and the Pope. The purification laws applied equally to Queen and peasant, and violations were punishable by death. For this reason the Queen could not possibly meet with Goodwin.

Naturally, the collapse of the meeting at Hounslow made Goodwin 'very melancholy'. He would have been still more melancholy if he had been able to foresee how many times in the next two or three years he would be prevented from seeing the Queen by her delicate ovarian system and her unpredictable cycles. But all this lay in the future. For the present the partners, left in a 'very musing' financial condition, laboured to shorten the Queen's illness and to hasten the next appointment. Here Mary's medical knowledge was useful. She dispatched Goodwin to the 'physic garden at Westminster'[10] where he gathered some 'stinking aridge'.[11] This she made up with Frontignac wine and produced a potion which she sent to the Queen with such happy results that the Queen's period was significantly shortened and a new meeting scheduled for Holy Thursday, 17 May.[12]

Meanwhile, Goodwin was receiving further essential information about the court of the lowlanders. The King, he learned, was named Byron. Though formerly a great warrior, he had never been reckoned 'a great headpiece', and in recent years he had grown 'old, debauched, and something doting'. The Queen, by contrast, had shown herself to be extremely wise. Her maiden name was Penelope LaGard, and like the wife of Charles II she was Portuguese—the sister, in fact, of the reigning lowland King of Portugal. The couple had been married for nine years without producing an heir, and recently they had been at odds over a matter of policy. During his marriage to the former Queen, the King had admitted to the lowlands some seven uplanders besides Mary—all of them (except for one gentleman named Gifford) 'of mean education and extraction'. The new Queen, distressed at the quality of this 'beggarly crew', had finally succeeded in excluding them, on the grounds that only aristocrats should be received at court. Her success, however, had not gone unresented by the King, who had a fondness for low companions, and this resentment was about to produce an explosion.

Unfortunately for the partners, the explosion occurred in the early morning of 17 May, just before they were to set off for Hounslow. The King, having 'a cup too much in his head', suddenly balked at admitting Goodwin. He had resolved instead to admit a journeyman tailor who had long solicited for entry to the lowlands. The Queen, taken by surprise, objected strongly, reminding him of their many promises to Goodwin, but her objections only enraged the King, who ordered the gates to the uplands to be locked. Since the Queen too had a 'very passionate' nature, she became equally enraged, and the dispute rose to a flame that alarmed the whole court. Eventually the Queen, who had both wit and justice on her side, was able to prevail in the argument. The explosion, however, had effectively cancelled the meeting of 17 May, and (as George reported to Mary) the Queen wisely decided to let injured feelings mend for a few days before scheduling another.

But while Queen Penelope was restoring domestic tranquillity, the partners suddenly found themselves facing a crisis much more serious than any battle among princes. This incident, which began innocently enough as a simple illness, quickly developed, before Goodwin's panic-stricken eyes, into a matter of life and death.

For some time Mary had been slightly ailing, in spite of Goodwin's efforts to see that she ate regularly and stayed away from brandy. Now about 20 May, she said that she needed a purge and asked Goodwin to prepare it for her. This task was routine for Goodwin, who prided himself on his medical lore. He not only prepared a purge for Mary but, while he was about it, concocted an extra dose for a friend. Unfortunately, he mixed both doses in the same glass and left the glass, full of medicine, on the window sill. When Mary saw it, she picked it up and, ignoring Goodwin's shout of warning, gulped down the entire potion.

When Goodwin explained what she had done, she sent for some sack and prepared herself an emetic. But the combination of emetic and purge proved extremely powerful; once she began vomiting, she could not stop. Soon her retching broke a vein, and she began spewing large quantities of blood. It quickly became evident to Goodwin that she was in great danger of bleeding to death; and Mary herself, when she finally stopped vomiting, confirmed this opinion. She plainly told him that 'she thought she could not recover.' For though her spasms of retching ceased, the internal bleeding did not, as evidenced by the blood that she continued to cough up.

Mary proceeded without panic. She directed Goodwin to bring comfrey and nettle-seeds, specifics against internal bleeding. Then, at Goodwin's suggestion, she dispatched George to seek additional advice from Father Friar and Sisery, who recommended adding a few grains of spermaceti to the medication. She also declared that midnight was the crucial time. If the bleeding stopped by then, she would recover; if not, she must die.

As Goodwin sat beside Mary's bed, comforting his wise and good friend, he had a clear perception of the hideous loss he faced. Without Mary, he realized, he was nothing. All his hopes depended upon her 'honesty and knowledge'. At her death they would vanish without a trace. George Whitmore, the lowlanders, the book, the magic pea, the play-piece, and much unattempted treasure would be gone like a tantalizing dream. He would be left alone with his debts, his family, and his troubles.

To Goodwin's admiration, Mary not only understood his anxiety but seemed more concerned for his condition than for her own. Although she 'expressed no manner of sorrow' about dying, she expressed great regret that she might leave him with 'nothing perfected'. She attempted, therefore, before midnight, to help him as much as possible. She wrote a note authorizing him to receive her book from Mrs Seymour; she made George 'promise and swear' that he would appear to Goodwin; and she swore 'over and over' that she herself would come to him after her death.

For herself Mary asked only that she should be buried at St. Sepulchre's, beside her children and her husband Lawrence.[13] Beyond this, she seemed to have no other concerns. 'She said she was not at all afraid to die,' Goodwin wrote later, 'for she thanked God she had never in her life wronged man, woman, nor child, and never had injured anybody but herself; and though all her friends and relations had forsaken her and often abused her, yet she forgave them all.'

At this expression of courage Goodwin wept. His tears, however, did not prevent him from doing everything possible. He insisted that to conserve her strength Mary should stop speaking. He held his hand against the place where she could feel pain and where the broken vein seemed to throb. He thanked her for her kindness and offered her encouragement. Most of all, as the critical hour drew near, he prayed for her—both for her life and for her soul.

When midnight finally arrived, the crisis passed. By that time the blood had ceased to flow and the coughing had diminished. Though weak, Mary seemed to be out of danger. The partners, now back on firmer ground, felt confident enough of her recovery to offer thanks to God 'for this mercy'. After hours of grief and anxiety, it only remained for Goodwin to finish out the night watching over Mary and guarding against a possible relapse.

Although the medical effects of the crisis were over within a week or two, other effects were permanent. Goodwin would not forget Mary's courage and devotion in the face of death. He would not forget that for an agonizing time he and Mary had not been a partnership to acquire wealth but an alliance against disaster. And he would not forget the promises she had repeated 'over and over'. He would recall them twenty years later in an even more serious crisis. For the present, the partnership which had shown signs of cracking in disappointment and irritation had become more strongly knit than ever.

4

Sex and Buried Treasure

GOODWIN and Mary arrived in Hounslow on the afternoon of 30 May 1683, not knowing that the little town, at the junction of the Bath and Salisbury roads, was to become a permanent base of operations for dealing with lowlanders and launching searches after buried treasure. They knew, of course, that Hounslow lay on the eastern edge of the vast Hounslow Heath and that it was conveniently near the entrance to the lowlands,[1] but they had not intended to stop there at all. Originally they were to meet the lowland court at Brentford and to ride back with the Queen, through Hounslow, to her dominions. But at Brentford, they were instructed to continue on to Hounslow and wait there for the royal cavalcade. When they reached Hounslow, however, it began to rain heavily, and it became evident that no meeting would be possible that day. The partners were obliged to find an inn where they could spend the night and await the meeting that had been rescheduled for the next morning.

Of five Hounslow inns, Goodwin chose the one that lay farthest west—the one nearest the lowlands.[2] In this establishment he was pleased to find that 'the best and quietest room above stairs had two beds in it'—an arrangement that offered obvious advantages. Sharing a room would enable the partners to discuss and conduct their business with the greatest possible efficiency, and it would help Goodwin to save money. This was now vital. Unable to afford the coach fare for the current expedition, he had been forced to make the journey from London to Brentford by water. And even with these economies, he was down to his last few shillings. Mary, like Goodwin, could see nothing compromising in sharing a room. She was, after all, twenty-three years older, and the two of them had been together almost constantly for three months without any hint of sexual involvement. This record, along with the consciousness of pure intentions, made the plan seem natural. Intended as a one-night expedient, it was to become a standard practice throughout a long, disappointing summer.

The disappointments began immediately. All through the night of 30 May the rain continued to fall 'most vehemently'. Part of a storm which had continued for more than a fortnight,[3] the rain flooded the low-lying portions of Hounslow Heath, covered the entrance to the lowlands with a layer of mud and water, and obliged the Queen to postpone meeting the partners until the gates could be opened without flooding her domains.[4] After two more days of steady rain, when it became evident that the lowlands would be 'drowned up' for at least another week, Goodwin used the last of his money to pay his reckoning, and the partners went back to London to wait for dry weather.

To finance the next expedition to Hounslow, Goodwin was obliged to pawn some of his clothes, and it was mid-June before he and Mary were reinstalled at their inn. There they soon learned that their arrangements for meeting the lowland court had collapsed. The Queen felt herself obliged to accompany some of her Portuguese relatives to their ship at Rye, where adverse winds detained the party for more than a week. This time, however, the partners made a discovery which greatly reduced their disappointment. Not far from their inn they found the site of a buried treasure.[5]

Goodwin had been hoping for this ever since he had heard of George's ability to locate treasure. His first opportunity came when he was walking on a common just outside Hounslow. There he noticed 'four great mighty trees set by themselves all alone, with a mount of earth cast up between them'. This configuration struck him as unnatural and somehow significant; and when George investigated, he found that the site, significant indeed, concealed a 'vast treasure', buried during the reign of King John and attended by no less than thirteen guardian spirits—spirits of the people who had buried it. Of these, George reported, five were good (eager to part with their treasure) and eight were miserly and depraved.

At this point a less sophisticated man might have attacked the treasure site with a pick and shovel; but Goodwin was too wise to proceed with ill-considered haste. He knew, in the first place, that the four trees were on a common and very much exposed to public view; any direct attack would attract a host of spectators.

He knew, in addition, that the evil spirits might be troublesome and should be banished or otherwise neutralized while the treasure was being secured. And finally, he knew that adepts had ways of opening the ground without resorting to entrenching tools.

When he explained his reasoning to Mary, she agreed that secret methods must be employed. She herself well remembered a way of opening the earth—a secret which she had learned from her book and verified experimentally by opening 'a little hill'. Essentially simple, the method required only three items: a parchment properly marked with astrological characters and two hazel sticks, both gathered at 'a right planetary hour'.[6] There was, however, a small technical difficulty. Although one of the sticks could be taken from the 'common smooth' hazel plant, the other was to be taken from a rare female species which Mary described as 'the right *she* witch-hazel'. Finding this species, Mary conceded, might take considerable time.

The partners began their search by returning to London, where Mary had found the right she witch-hazel many years before. With the help of George and some herb women who said they knew the plant, they explored Highgate Woods, Stoke Newington, Charter House Gardens, Tyburn Road, and an area along the New River. But though they looked through many copses and gardens, their search ultimately failed. After an exhausting effort and a near calamity, when Mary fell from a horse,[7] they went back to Hounslow to plot further strategy and to await the return of the King and Queen from Rye.

On 22 June, at Hounslow, they discovered 'at the end of the town' a house that to Mary's practiced eye appeared to be haunted, perhaps by a spirit guarding buried treasure. From the landlady at the inn, they learned that the spirit of the former owner, a man named Nicholson, had indeed been seen in the area; and from George, sent to investigate, they learned that shortly before his death Nicholson had buried near his house a small hoard consisting of £250, a fine saddle, and a silver cup. Now a good spirit, Nicholson agreed to let the partners have the treasure if they could get possession of the property. Goodwin decided, therefore, to find the present owner and try to rent the house.

During the next few days it became evident that the partners would have plenty of time for hunting treasure. On 24 June, the King and Queen returned to their domains much too tired to receive the partners, and early next morning, George arrived in all haste with the word that the King 'had waked very sick and was taken with great vomitings'. This illness, brought on by the King's drunken debauchery at Rye, was extremely serious. Naturally, no one could be admitted to the lowlands until the King was out of danger.

During the King's illness, Mary discovered that Father Friar was an expert on buried treasure, that he had often opened the earth, and that he knew the right she witch-hazel when he saw it. He could tell, for example, that some witch-hazel the partners had gathered near Hounslow was not the proper female variety but its male counterpart. At the time, however, he did not know where to find the correct species; and Mary's recollection that she had seen the right she witch-hazel at Cliveden proved to be mistaken, though George did not inform her of this fact until the partners had got as far as Slough on their way there.[8]

Fortunately, the partners' inability to open the earth did not prevent them from conversing with the good spirits at the four trees. One of these, a woman dressed in the habit of a nun, once appeared above ground (though invisible to Goodwin) and spoke to Mary in 'a loud shrill voice', which Goodwin could hear. In general, however, the spirits remained with their treasure under the earth, and this policy made conversation difficult. Goodwin could sometimes hear voices when he put his ear to the ground, but never distinctly. In the end, the partners found it simpler to carry on their conversations through George than to struggle with such difficulties.

Had Goodwin been less frustrated by the continual delays, he might have considered himself lucky to be spending his time at Hounslow. London had suddenly become extremely unhealthy for Whigs. One after another his old acquaintances were being arrested for complicity in the Rye House Plot. The first proclamations were issued on 23 June, the day after he had last left town, and throughout late June and early July, grim events succeeded each other almost daily.

On 26 June Algernon Sidney, Lord William Russell, and John Wildman were sent to the Tower. Three days later proclamations were issued for the Duke of Monmouth, Lord Grey, Sir Thomas

Armstrong, and Robert Ferguson. On 8 July Lord Howard of Escrick, Lord Brandon, and John Hampden were arrested; and two days later the Earl of Essex was also sent to the Tower. On 13 July Lord Russell and three less prominent men, Thomas Walcott, John Rouse, and William Hone, were convicted of treason, and the Earl of Essex committed suicide. On 20 July Walcott, Rouse, and Hone were hanged, and the next day Lord Russell was beheaded.

While his friends were being executed, gaoled, or driven from the country, and while his brother's house at Winchendon was being searched for arms,[9] Goodwin remained safely at Hounslow, engaged in dramas of his own. The first of these was a distressing battle with Mary.

One evening at 'the right planetary hour' he captured a frog from which he asked Mary to prepare one of her magical lodestones of love and hatred. Mary was standing before the open window of their room as she cut the flesh away from the bone—the first step in the preparation—and when she finished, she began to throw the flesh out the window onto the highway below. Surprised and vexed at her thoughtlessness, Goodwin gave a warning shout and seized her by the arm. At this she flew into a hysterical rage, delivered herself of a screaming, incoherent tirade, and then rushed out of the room, down the stairs, and out into the night.

By the time Goodwin, who had been half-undressed, struggled into his clothes and got outside, Mary had vanished. Fearing that she would go to Brentford, catch a boat, and escape to Essex to live with her uncle John Tomson (as she had sometimes threatened to do), Goodwin ran down the Brentford road until he was sure she had not gone that way; then he doubled back to the inn. There, to his great relief, he found Mary walking alone in the garden, apparently recovered from her sudden hysteria. He approached her cautiously, full of apology; but she immediately took the blame on herself. She had been 'so often abused' by others, she explained, that when he had shouted and caught her arm, she had believed he was about to strike her. Her fear that frustration would goad him to blows had been building up for some time, she now realized; and it was this fear that had triggered her outburst.

Goodwin insisted upon sharing the blame. His repeated

disappointments and his financial worries had made him snappish. Furthermore, his experiences of being cheated had made him 'very incredulous' and suspicious—especially fearful that Mary might desert him under their continuing hardships. It was also clear that the Devil had been cunning in sowing divisions between them. These explanations Mary understood perfectly, and the partners, though bruised, became 'very good friends again'.

One morning shortly after her quarrel with Goodwin, Mary saw an apparition that looked like her husband Parish. Puzzled, she consulted George, who informed her that her husband was dead. This news was not entirely unexpected. In mid-April Mary had told Goodwin of being summoned to the bedside of Parish, then at his City residence at Aldgate. Seemingly near death, he had apologized for his conduct and affirmed Mary's right to a jointure of eighty pounds. He had then rallied sufficiently to be removed to his country home, but Mary had predicted that he could not live much longer. Now her prediction was confirmed.[10]

At first, the death of Parish made little difference to the partners. Mary did not pretend grief for her long-estranged husband, nor did she try to collect her jointure—a process that might involve several weeks in London and interrupt vital operations in Hounslow. In the long run, however, Parish's death became significant. By making Mary a widow rather than the alienated wife of a living man, it rendered her as free from legal obligations as Goodwin himself and removed her from the purview of the Seventh Commandment. These changes, which Goodwin barely registered at the time, were to become important before the summer ended.

While the partners struggled with their personal problems, their business affairs remained in suspense. Except for a brief excursion to London, where Goodwin managed to borrow a guinea, the pair stayed in Hounslow waiting for the King of the lowlands to recover. Finally, on 24 July, the partners were summoned to come to the lowlands with all possible speed. The King, George reported, had suffered a frightening relapse, and the Queen hoped that the medical skills of Mary and Goodwin might save him. Immediately they set off for the entrance to the lowlands, walking as fast as possible; but when they arrived at the third heath, within half a mile of their goal, George brought word that the King was dead.

This message stopped the partners in their tracks. It meant, of course, that for the present they could not enter the lowlands. And for Goodwin it meant profound discouragement. To be halted almost at the gates of the lowlands seemed to imply divine intervention—'as if God had said, "You shall not go."' In the following days, however, Goodwin came to realize that the King's death had actually simplified matters. He was no longer at the mercy of the King's whims and humours. The Queen, who had inherited the royal power, was now free to follow her own favourable inclinations. After a decent interval for the King's burial, which would take place in his native Cornwall, she would bring Goodwin into her domains.

Meanwhile the financial situation remained desperate; Goodwin found himself in 'an agony' for want of money. And he had other reasons to complain. He had not yet seen George or any of the lowlanders, and he had not found the proper witch-hazel. Now, after five months of broken promises, he could not forbear 'fretting'. Mary too had grievances. Goodwin, who had promised to support her, refused to apply to his father for help, and he always postponed borrowing from others until he was down to his last shilling. His grumbling, moreover, seemed to imply mismanagement on her part—a monstrous imputation. Made edgy by poverty and failure, both partners had become prone to 'disputes and jangles'; they seemed to be moving towards another full-scale battle.

About bedtime on the night of 2 August, Goodwin was in a particularly combative mood. Irritated with Mary for nagging him about money and determined to vex her, he began pacing up and down their room without any clothes on. Mary seemed unperturbed. Already settled in her bed, she merely warned him that he might catch cold and advised him to go to sleep. When he persisted with his pacing and fretting, she repeated her advice. Finally, 'being the best natured woman in the world', she held up the coverlet to her bed.

'You will certainly catch your death,' she said. 'If you must talk, . . . cover yourself with this.'

At this invitation, given in perfect innocence, Goodwin lay down beside her. Up until that time, as he later swore, he had never considered making love to Mary, nor did the thought cross his mind when he first climbed under the coverlet. But soon 'nature' began to suggest many thoughts. Clearly she was defenceless. Clearly she was too fond of him to resist. Certainly he could arouse a woman of such strong passions. Thoroughly excited, he threw off the rest of the bedclothes and lay hold of her. For a few moments, as he brought her 'farther' within his 'power', he thought she was acquiescing—that she saw no moral problem in sex between a bachelor and a 'free woman'. But just as he sensed that he had brought her 'absolutely' within his power, she began to protest. The deed was unlawful, she pleaded. Goodwin hesitated, hoping that her pleas were a matter of form, but she continued to make 'such entreaties and such complaints against it' that he was compelled to stop. With an effort at self-control that he could only regard as heroic, he disentangled himself from Mary and stumbled back to his own bed.

The next morning Mary rose early and sent for Father Friar. As the oldest living lowlander and as an accomplished theologian, he was the obvious man to resolve the moral dilemma that now confronted the partners. When he arrived, she described the case in detail. As for herself, she added, she loved Goodwin so well that it was torture to deny him. Yet she was determined at all costs to be 'mistress of herself' and to do no violence to her conscience. She would leave him, if necessary, to save herself from sin.

Father Friar's reply, which she repeated at length to Goodwin, solved the problem very neatly. Goodwin, he began, had shown himself superior to 'base lust or mean viciousness'. In an unparalleled example of self-control, he had not only mastered his passions but he had shown a noble respect for a conscience weaker than his own. As for Mary, Father Friar continued, her performance had been equally heroic. In obedience to conscience, 'she had done violence to nature and all her passions'; she had overcome 'that love and affection which is almost in all women unconquerable'.

In view of this, Father Friar concluded, the partners had proven themselves worthy of special consideration. 'Though you are both undoubtedly justified in what you did,' he said to Mary, 'yet if you keep true to him, and he likewise to you—not having been at first led on and conquered by vice and evil thoughts, which you have both overcome—you will not undoubtedly offend God, and you need not therefore offend your conscience in what you do.'

Father Friar's words, which Goodwin found to be in accordance with reason, nature, and the Mosaic Law, convinced Mary that her scruples were unnecessary. As she candidly admitted to Goodwin, she now considered herself free to lie with him. This she proceeded to do the same evening, and Goodwin made love to her 'without her resistance'.

The happy solution to Goodwin's moral problems and sexual frustrations pleased him immensely. He was further delighted the next day when Mary announced that she was pregnant. Her condition, she explained, had been easy to diagnose, since she had been pregnant many times before. Furthermore, she said, she knew the child would be a boy, since she had learned 'by a maxim' how to produce children of either sex. To make doubly sure of her conclusions, she had checked them with George, who affirmed that she was pregnant and that the small spirit within her was indeed male.

To Goodwin, Mary's pregnancy was not merely a sign of God's blessing upon the union but something of a miracle in itself. At fifty-three Mary seemed very unlikely to produce children. Although not so well stricken in years as the biblical Sarah, she was well beyond the normal age of childbearing. If not miraculous, her conception was at least a prodigy. And only two nights later, she reduplicated the feat. After another bout of love-making, she announced that she had again conceived, of another boy.

And Mary soon made a different kind of contribution to the partnership. As the burial ceremonies for the King and the subsequent menstrual period of the Queen delayed Goodwin's entrance into the lowlands, Mary outlined an attractive project. She remembered very well, she said, the place at Northend where her Grandfather West had found fairy treasure. She remembered too that a richer cache, undiscovered by her grandfather, lay nearby. Now she would undertake to lead Goodwin to the spot and help him get the treasure.

Leaving their landlady unpaid, the couple took a coach as far as Slough and there rented a horse for the jaunt to Northend, some eighteen miles away. It was already late when their horse, doubly loaded, brought them to Turville; but Goodwin, 'unwilling to lie short of the place', insisted upon pushing forward for the remaining two miles. Within minutes, they were lost 'in a dark stogy wood', where they stumbled about for hours before they reached a clearing near Northend and found shelter with 'a neat charcoal man' and his wife.

The next morning Mary led Goodwin to a spot in the woods that George identified as the treasure site. There she knelt down, put her head to the ground, and asked the spirit-guardian to speak to her. This he did, in a 'great hollow voice' which Goodwin, who had been ordered to stand back a little, could sometimes hear. After conversing with the spirit for several minutes, Mary suddenly began to struggle, as if she were being pulled about by the hood of her cloak. Moments later, she called for help, and Goodwin ran to her side and 'caught her up'.

The spirit, she explained, had begun pulling her to keep her from attacking the treasure site with her bare hands. He had told her that he had to contend with an evil co-guardian and that he could deliver up the treasure only on Mondays, when his evil companion was away. Although he would gladly give Mary the money any Monday afternoon at six o'clock, he could do nothing at present. This news, which meant a delay of six days, had angered her. Knowing that she and Goodwin could not remain in Northend for almost a week, she had threatened to start digging at once—a threat which had provoked him to pull her about.

When Goodwin understood the situation, he apologized to the spirit for Mary's excessive zeal, thanked him for his kindness, and agreed to return on a Monday as instructed. In answer, the spirit told Mary to stoop down and receive a sign of his power. When she stooped, he pushed 'a great stone through the ground, as clean as if it had been new wiped'. Encouraged by the demonstration, the partners again thanked him and then set out on the road to Hounslow.

On the journey back their overburdened horse stumbled in the road and rolled 'over and over' with them, knocking Mary unconscious and severely shaking Goodwin. The accident did not prevent them, however, from completing a vital project. On their way to Northend they had noticed 'a most delicate tree' which Mary positively identified as the right she witch-hazel. Now returning, they were careful to reach the tree at the proper planetary hour and to cut a number of branches from it—enough to make several earth-opening sticks.

Once back in Hounslow, the partners hastened to try their new resource. Without waiting for help from Father Friar, they made their way unobserved to the four trees and carefully laid their hazel sticks and parchment in proper order. Then, very deliberately, Mary took up the right she witch-hazel and three times struck the earth, commanding it to open. Nothing happened. The ground did not even quiver. Goodwin could hardly believe his eyes. Such inexplicable failure put him in 'a maze'.

When Father Friar arrived, he diagnosed the trouble at once. He pointed out to Mary that in her haste to try the sticks she had forgotten to have them consecrated. This oversight he remedied himself, taking the sticks away that night and returning them two days later, properly consecrated and ready for use. But again the partners acted too hastily. Without consulting the attendant spirits, they hurried to the four trees and performed the ritual. Again the ground failed to open. Again Goodwin was amazed. The explanation, however, was relatively simple. When questioned by George, the spirits said that delivery of the treasure depended upon precise timing. When the treasure had been hidden, it had been 'so tied' that it could only be delivered 'just at the point of time of the new moon'. Hence there was only a minute or two in every twenty-eight days when the ground above the treasure could be opened, and it could remain open only an hour.

Luckily for the partners, the time of the next new moon was the following Sunday, 12 August. And this time, to prevent any mistake, Mary invited Father Friar to come along and perform the ritual himself. Widely experienced and invisible to chance passers-by, he would prevent mishap. Mary's decision, though perfectly logical, turned out to be wrong. At the proper moment, while Goodwin and Mary remained at a respectful distance, Father Friar struck the earth, opened it, and went inside. But he soon came out, 'as it were in a huff, and struck his rod and the earth immediately closed'. The spirits, he told Mary, had refused to give him anything; they would deliver their treasure only to the partners. Angered by the rebuff, he had impulsively closed the earth. A moment later he regretted his thoughtless action, but the error was irretrievable; the ground could not be opened again until 10 September.

Though 'much troubled' by his first disappointments at the four trees, Goodwin found reason for optimism. The soundness of the method had been well demonstrated, and the errors were readily avoidable. Meanwhile, there was the treasure at Northend, less closely 'tied', which could be collected any Monday afternoon. He was further encouraged by a remarkable piece of luck. When he went to London to borrow money, he was lent five pounds by a man he had never seen before. This sum not only sufficed for a month of operations but enabled him to rent a horse and a light carriage.

As Goodwin looked ahead he could see only one flaw in the brightening picture. Queen Penelope continued to be inaccessible. He had hoped that her new powers would make everything easy, but apparently they made everything difficult. For one thing, the strain of royal authority seemed to affect her menstrual cycle, bringing on frequent periods and condemning her to many days of purification. Then there was the matter of royal hospitality. Twice during August, unexpected visitors (nobles from Cornwall and Brittany) compelled her to cancel appointments with Goodwin. Finally, royal power seemed to make the Queen abrupt and imperious. When Goodwin protested, for example, that there was no reason why he should not be introduced to her visitors, she simply dismissed his protests without comment.

On the other hand, her expressions of regret for his troubles and her promises of rich rewards grew steadily more fervent. As relayed by Mary, the Queen's messages no longer stopped with the offer of opulent presents; they hinted ever more strongly that she intended to marry him and make him the new king of the lowlanders. Here, obviously, was a prize worth waiting for—a recompense more than adequate for all his disappointments.

Meanwhile, Princess Ursula LaPerle, the sister of the Queen and reputedly the most beautiful woman in the world, entered Goodwin's life. The Princess, recently returned from Italy, came to Hounslow one day in mid-August, made herself visible to Mary, and declared that she had come to find out whether Goodwin was really as charming as the Queen had said. Then, clapping her magic pea in her mouth and following Mary into

Goodwin's room, she approached him within arm's length (as he played the recorder) and studied him intently—concluding, as she later said, that he was 'the handsomest man that she ever saw'.

Impetuously, Princess Ursula began to woo Goodwin for herself. Early the next morning, after kissing Goodwin while he slept, she laid her case before Mary. The Queen, she argued, was 'a very cunning, subtle woman', who would wear Goodwin out with 'humours and tricks'. Furthermore the Queen, now 350 years old, was beyond the normal age of childbearing among lowland women; whereas she herself, only 50, was in the prime of youth. She would be happy, she said, to live above ground with Goodwin and make him the richest man in England, or she would take him back to Italy if he preferred. She would also defy the Queen's oath and appear to him at once if he would trust her and risk the Queen's displeasure.

When Mary had repeated the Princess's speech, Goodwin felt obliged to reject the proposal. He could not, within a few minutes, agree to marry someone he had never seen or to betray the trust of the Queen, whose promises were even more dazzling. With all possible assurances of good will, he conveyed his thanks to the Princess and his decision to honour his commitments.

During the succeeding weeks, Goodwin often regretted his decision. Although the Princess continued to intrigue against the Queen for Goodwin's favour, she did not repeat her offer to appear to him. He had missed his chance, she said, and now he could not see her until he had decided once and for all to abandon her sister. The Queen, meanwhile, continued to suffer one misfortune after another; try as she would, she could not break through the diplomatic problems and female disorders that plagued her. However, she gave him a very sensible token of her love—a demonstration that left no room for doubt about her intentions towards him.

During the latter part of August, Goodwin had been much troubled by a chronic backache. This he attributed at first to the bone-jarring fall he had suffered returning from Northend, but as time went on, this explanation seemed inadequate. An injury which involved no broken bones, he reasoned, should get better, yet his back continued to grow worse. He also noticed that his

condition seemed aggravated by his sexual bouts with Mary—
that he felt 'half-dead' afterwards. It seemed, then, that his
backache had some connection with love-making. And yet this
too appeared unlikely, since he had performed with judgement
and restraint—well within the normal capacity of a 'young and
strong' thirty-year-old man.

While mulling over these facts, he happened to recall a
passage from Mary's life among the lowlanders. The King had
once informed Mary that if he wished to do so he could make
himself invisible, enter her room, and lie with her while she was
asleep; nothing could restrain him, he said, except his own
honesty. Upon recalling Mary's story, Goodwin began to
suspect that he might be the victim of some unscrupulous
lowland woman. He begged Mary to ask George whether
'something of this kind might be in the wind'.

After only a short pause to consider the matter, George gave
the partners a shocking reply: Goodwin had been assaulted by
Queen Penelope herself. Ever since mid-June, she had occasionally slipped into his bed and taken her pleasures with his
defenceless body. Inspired by the 'greatness of her passion' and
by 'raptures and joys' she had never dreamed possible, she had
increased the number and intensity of the encounters with each
passing week. At last, about the first of September, exceeding all
reasonable bounds, she not only made love to him three times,
'without ever quitting' his body, but the third time at the
moment of climax she had 'sucked up her breath' so violently
that she had drawn 'the very substance of the marrow' out of his
bones. In her thoughtless ecstasy, she had almost killed him.

Although George's account solved the problem of Goodwin's
back, it raised ugly questions about deceit and treachery. Why,
for example, had the Queen taken by stealth what she might
have had by permission? Why had she not made herself visible
to him? One simple appearance would have cancelled her oath
and enabled him to converse with her people. Nor was George
without blame in the affair. Why had he allowed 'a thing of such
great moment' to continue without giving Goodwin any
warning? Why had he remained silent until Mary had dragged
the truth from him? George's excuses—that he never volunteered
information and that he had forgotten about the Queen's sins
until Mary had 'put him in mind' of them—were highly

unsatisfactory, but he refused to elaborate. He did promise, however, to atone for his errors by helping Goodwin with a plan to trap the Queen at her next adventure in love-making.

Instructing George to watch the Queen and to warn him when she left the lowlands for Hounslow, Goodwin intended to wait in his bed until she was within his grasp, then seize her and hold her until she made herself visible and explained her proceedings. He knew, of course, that before leaving home the Queen would send Sisery, her attendant spirit, to make sure that Goodwin was fast asleep and that he must therefore actually be asleep during Sisery's scrutiny; but he also knew that George and Mary would wake him when the Queen started for Hounslow.

Up to a point the strategem worked perfectly. Goodwin passed Sisery's inspection and was wakened from his sleep by Mary, who relayed George's message that the Queen was flying straight into the trap. But the Queen was delayed 'a pretty while', and although Goodwin struggled to keep his 'eyes and senses open', he was asleep again when she arrived. Nevertheless, he partially registered her presence. 'When she had slipped off her nightgown and was got within the clothes and beginning her worthy trade', he caught hold of her 'and began to wake'. He had almost come to his senses when she perceived her danger and slipped away from him. In a few moments she was gone.

The attempt to trap Queen Penelope brought the whole affair out into the open. Aware that her barbarous conduct had been discovered, she sent Goodwin a flood of excuses. She had never meant to hurt him, she explained; she had simply been carried away by an uncontrollable passion. Reasons of State had prevented her from appearing honestly and openly to him, but she would reward him for his patience. If he would forgive her, he would receive treasures worth seven years of waiting.

Goodwin found it easy to accept her apology. Though openly condemning her misconduct, he could hardly remain angry at a woman who had found him infinitely attractive. Nor could he give up the wealth of the lowlands because of an aching back. In the end, he was content to give her a soft answer. He would overlook her lapse from grace, he said, and regard it merely as 'a sign of her love'.

Unfortunately, the effects of the Queen's folly did not end with apology and forgiveness. On 22 September, Goodwin learned that she had suffered a miscarriage. The foetus, already identifiable as 'a fine boy', was clearly the result of her concealed love affair with Goodwin. Then on 15 October, she miscarried again, of still another boy, and suffered an illness that proved nearly fatal. The Queen's double miscarriage, her illness, and the long purification rites that followed confined her to her palace for the rest of the year and prevented Goodwin from seeing her. In effect, her unbridled passion had wrecked the Hounslow campaign of 1683. Along with strange disappointments at the four trees and at Northend, it eventually forced the partners to retreat to London, where they would plan new strategies and seek additional help.

5

John Wildman and the Angels

THE Queen's miscarriages, enough in themselves 'to break a heart of flint', turned out to be only a prelude to the misfortunes which frustrated Goodwin through the fall and winter of 1683–84. They were followed by a series of maddening reverses. Time after time Goodwin saw his bright hopes baffled, not only through the folly of men and lowlanders but also through a combination of trivial accidents. It seemed as if he were a sailor continually 'beat off the shore' and fated to drown within sight of land. Worse yet, it seemed as if Mary, now pregnant with twin boys, would drown with him.

Typical of Goodwin's frustrations were his defeats at the four trees. Perfectly equipped with hazel sticks and parchment, the partners made plans at each new moon to open the earth, and each month they were baffled by some circumstance or other. On 10 September 1683 the mischance involved their landlady's cow. As ill luck would have it, the landlady normally passed close to the four trees when she went to milk. To the partners, this homely fact presented a severe tactical problem, since the time for opening the earth, 5.55 p.m., was about the normal time for milking and they could not let the landlady see them at their work. An inquisitive, gossiping woman, who already suspected them of being conjurors, she would have called them conjurors indeed if she had seen them kneeling at the trees, striking the ground with sticks.

To solve this delicate problem of timing, the partners offered to keep her company if she would do her milking early—an offer which she gladly accepted. But the strategy was ruined by the cow, which broke loose from her mistress after the milking and went charging off across the common. Goodwin, who could not decently refuse to help, joined the landlady in the pursuit, and when it was over, September had been lost; the moment for opening the earth had passed.

In October, the time of the new moon proved to be

unpropitious for treasure hunting. The critical hour, which occurred between two and three o'clock in the morning, was 'an ill time to pretend business' on a Hounslow common. In November, however, all the omens were favourable. The partners arrived at the trees at the appointed time, 1.20 p.m. Goodwin laid the sticks and parchment in proper order, prayed to God that the ground would open, and struck the ground twice. Before he could strike a third and final time, Mary spied a horseman riding toward them on a nearby road. Panic-stricken at the danger of being observed, she caught up the sticks and thus aborted the whole operation. This startling turn of events crushed Goodwin, who was sure that he 'had heard the ground crack at the second stroke' and that he had been within a minute of a vast fortune. Now he would be obliged to wait for at least another month.

December brought heavy rains, which discouraged spirits and changed the texture of the earth so that it could not respond to spells, even at the time of the new moon. Nor was January any better. The most severe winter in living memory had begun about 15 December. By 7 January the Thames was completely frozen over,[1] and at the four trees the partners found the earth so solidly frozen that it 'could not perform its work'. The bitter cold, sometimes so severe (as Goodwin observed) that lowlanders were unable to fly, continued into February; and even on 6 March, when the partners came to Hounslow at their appointed hour, they found the ground still frosted from the 'long and grievous cold'. The treasure, which had seemed only seconds away in November, now seemed to the discouraged Goodwin to be more remote than ever.

Equally discouraging were the frustrations Goodwin suffered in trying to get the treasure at Northend. The original expedition of 6–7 August 1683 had been highly successful, in spite of a stogy wood and a stumbling horse. The partners had located a great treasure, which the attendant spirit had promised to deliver up on any Monday afternoon they might choose. Apparently nothing remained to be done but to hire another horse and make a timely arrival at the treasure site. But misfortune haunted the enterprise. Less than two weeks later, as the partners were nearing Maidenhead, Mary began to complain of severe pains in her head, and just before they reached Marlow she fell from the horse in a faint. Examination showed that she was suffering from a dangerous abscess in her ear. The partners were compelled to remain at an inn in Marlow until the 'impostume' had broken and drained; then they returned to Hounslow to recruit Mary's strength.

Their next expedition began on Sunday, 16 September, when they again journeyed as far as Marlow (this time in the little one-horse carriage Goodwin had rented). There they took lodgings at an inn and dispatched George to confer with the attendant spirit at Northend. But Monday, 17 September, proved to be one of the blackest days in the history of the partnership. To begin with, George arrived early in the morning with the information that the expedition would have to be postponed. The attendant spirit at Northend, one Bromka, had suddenly remembered a previous engagement. Bromka, the partners learned, was Jewish and very strict about ceremonial observances. He was particularly strict in observing the anniversary of his own death, which had occurred in a battle on 17 September. Though he regretted his earlier failure to check the date, he could not possibly work on such a day.

While Goodwin was digesting this news. Mary presented him with another problem. She pointed out that from Marlow it was only three or four miles to Wooburn. She also pointed out—what was obvious—that the partnership was desperate for money. Goodwin, in fact, did not have enough left to pay the bill at the inn. It would be wise, she hinted broadly, if Goodwin swallowed his pride and sought help from his father.

Goodwin demurred. Though he had nowhere else to turn and though he could not afford to be 'pawned' at an inn within a few miles of his home, he cringed at the thought of exposing himself 'so meanly' to his father. All summer he had struggled to avoid just such debasement. But Mary was not to be refused. When he hesitated, she 'flew into a passion'. Then she slipped away from the inn and disappeared. It was only after a frantic and exhausting search throughout Marlow that he found her again—back at the inn. By that time he had decided that he would rather face Lord Wharton than go through another crisis with Mary. Accordingly, he agreed to set out next morning for Wooburn.

At Wooburn, in one last effort to avoid ignominy, Goodwin

attempted to borrow forty shillings from his widowed sister Margaret Wharton Dunch,[2] then visiting at the family home. But instead of lending him the money, Margaret reported the episode to Lord Wharton, who summoned Goodwin before him. At last, then, after all his plans and projects, Goodwin found himself standing before his father pleading for help. To Goodwin's temporary relief, Lord Wharton behaved with something like graciousness. He gave Goodwin forty shillings and even apologized for not having more money about the house. Along with the money, however, he could not resist giving Goodwin a 'lesson and a severe heart cutting'. And as Goodwin left Wooburn, he was mortified at 'the mean things' he had been forced to do. He would not go through such an experience again for all the gold at Northend. In the future he would not go near Wooburn, or Northend, until he was reasonably solvent. Unfortunately, he did not become solvent until November, after the rains and cold had made it impossible for Bromka to deliver treasure through the earth. And he did not make another expedition to Northend until the following summer.

The pattern of defeats that wrecked the treasure-hunting campaigns of the fall and winter of 1683–84 was repeated in Goodwin's dealings with the lowlanders. Here again, bad luck and human folly combined against the partners. The fundamental problem, of course, was the illness of the Queen, which kept her immured in her domains until the beginning of January. But the Queen's arbitrary decisions, for which illness was no excuse, became problems as well. She could not be persuaded, for example, to send Goodwin the legacy the King had willed him—1,000 marks in gold and a valuable ring. She sent him instead a series of implausible excuses.

He was similarly frustrated in his attempt to get a workable magic pea. In late November he harvested the peas that had grown from his careful planting of the previous April. Most of the peas, he now realized, were worthless, since the black bone cats had been buried at the wrong time. There were several peas, however, derived from the hedgehog setting, that were excellent. The most perfect of these he clapped into his mouth, expecting to disappear immediately. But he remained stubbornly visible. Magic peas, he learned, could not operate without proper consecration. Like hazel sticks and play-pieces, they required the services of a priest.

At this point, the Queen made a kindly suggestion. If Goodwin would give up trying to get his own peas consecrated, she would deliver to him the already consecrated magic pea and magic leaf that had belonged to the King—the most delicate and effectual charms in existence. To this proposition Goodwin cheerfully agreed, only to find that he was once more at the mercy of the Queen's unaccountable whims. The delivery of the King's pea, like the delivery of the legacy, was postponed month after month.

Equally distressing were the machinations of Princess Ursula, who attempted all through the latter part of 1683 to supplant her sister in Goodwin's affections. Finally, in early January, just at the time when the Queen was permitted to leave her domains, the Princess went too far. Suspecting that the Queen intended to meet Goodwin even though she was beginning her menstrual period, she denounced her sister to the Pope, who in turn charged the Queen with breach of the Mosaic Law and put her on trial for her life. After a delicate and intricate investigation, the Queen managed to clear herself of the charge, but she could not forgive the Princess for bringing it. Determined to punish this treachery and put an end to all plots, she had the Princess arrested and confined in an upper room of the palace.

These events, faithfully narrated to Mary by George, had the effect of postponing Goodwin's meeting with the Queen. And there was worse to come. Towards the end of January, in a hazardous and unsuccessful effort to escape, the Princess fell down into a marble courtyard with a 'considerable squelsh' and injured herself severely. Then about 8 February, in total despair, she attempted to commit suicide by stabbing herself; and when she seemed to be in a fair way to recovery, she pulled the plaster off her wound and suffered a near-fatal relapse. Inevitably such disasters further delayed Goodwin's entrance into the lowlands, for however much the Queen might resent her sister's plotting, she could not receive company when the life of the Princess was in danger.

The misfortunes that buffeted Goodwin throughout the autumn and winter of 1683–84 might have shattered his hopes and faith if they had not been countered by other forces. The first of these was Mary's pregnancy. Sometime in early May, Mary was scheduled to produce twin sons, and it ill behoved a father who was about to be so miraculously blessed to yield to unmanly despair. For her part, Mary conquered some black moods that afflicted her in November and resolved to bear whatever trials the Lord put upon her. Luckily too she was able to conceal her pregnancy from prying and censorious eyes. During the summer of 1683 she had grown fat, and the added weight effectively disguised her condition. Not once in all the time of her pregnancy, Goodwin noted gratefully, did she arouse suspicion.

Another circumstance that helped to keep Goodwin afloat was the easing of his financial agonies. In late September, not long after his frightful embarrassment at Wooburn, Goodwin ventured to appear at his father's town house at St. Giles-in-the-Fields. There, without any solicitation, his father relieved his immediate distress with a gift of ten pounds. Then, sometime in late October or early November, Goodwin received another instalment on his allowance—a sum which enabled him and Mary to stay at Hounslow until bad luck and bad weather drove them back to town. Although his allowance could hardly make a dent in his debts, it did permit the partners to afford tolerable quarters on Vere Street in London and, for the time at least, to avoid the crises that had harassed them throughout the summer of 1683. It reduced despair to mere anxiety.

A final source of strength that allowed Goodwin to 'swim still after so many baffles' was the vast increase in his arcane knowledge. Financially, the partnership had been disastrous. After a year, Goodwin had not made a shilling from his enterprises. Philosophically and spiritually, however, the alliance had proved rich in wonders. He now knew more, both theoretically and practically, about the lowlanders than any man alive. From Mary's detailed descriptions he knew the characters and personalities of each member of the Queen's entourage and of all the leaders in the subordinate colonies. He knew, for example, the Duke and Duchess of Brittany, the Duke of Lorraine, the Duke of Hungary, the Duke of Cornwall, the Duke of Ireland, and the Duke of Turenne. He even knew the depraved confessor of the Princess (one Cottrell), the laundry-woman of the Queen, and the palace bellman.

Similarly, his knowledge of the spirit world had increased immeasurably. Although he had never seen George Whitmore, he had communicated with him, through Mary, almost every day for nearly a year. From George he had learned the powers and limitations of spirits, as well as the mistakes of both Catholics and Protestants in dealing with the spirit realm. Through George, furthermore, he had made overtures towards the spirits of some of his dead friends and relatives—his brother-in-law Major Dunch,[3] the famous Israel Tonge,[4] one Mr Trott,[5] and most of all his mother, Jane Goodwin Wharton. For various reasons, none of these spirits actually spoke to him or made themselves visible, but all of them sent him friendly messages. And his mother, whom George first spoke to in late December, sent assurances that she would eventually appear to him.

In spite of the forces that helped to sustain him, it was a much-sobered Goodwin Wharton who approached his thirty-first birthday in March 1684. For 'almost a twelvemonth', the spirits and the lowlanders had consistently failed him; and although their promises remained as fervent as ever, there was little reason to suppose that they would be any better fulfilled. It was now time, Goodwin saw, to insure against continued misfortune and to seek help from a source more powerful and reliable than mere spirits. He must try to find a financial backer for the partnership; and, if possible, he must talk to the angels.

Finding a financial backer, Goodwin realized, was a matter of great delicacy. First of all, the position demanded a personal friend. No stranger could be trusted with the momentous secrets of the partnership. Next, of course, it demanded that the friend should be wise, discreet, and faithful; a fool or a babbler might betray operations to the outside world and expose the partnership to odium, ridicule, or outright danger. Finally, the position required some antecedent knowlede of the obscure arts. No ordinary layman could be expected to understand, much less invest in, projects that involved alchemy, charms, or other deep philosophical lore.

The man Goodwin finally selected for the delicate task of helping the partnership was one of the most remarkable men of a remarkable age. His name was John Wildman,[6] although he was usually called Major Wildman because of a Commonwealth army commission, and he was ultimately to become Sir John

Wildman when he was knighted by William III. Wildman was sixty-one years old in the spring of 1684 when Goodwin called upon him for help. He had long since become legendary for his political craft and his plots against successive governments; he had likewise earned a substantial reputation for business acumen. He had become, in fact, that rarest of seventeenth-century species—a chronic conspirator who not only survived but grew rich in the process.

The key to Wildman's tortuous political career was his conviction that England should be turned into a democratic republic. This view made him a Leveller, in seventeenth-century terms, and a dangerous radical to most of his contemporaries. For a few glorious months after the defeat of Charles I, Wildman hoped to use Cromwell's New Model Army to establish a democratic constitution. In support of this aim he not only wrote tracts[7] but also argued the case among the troops and before the General Council of the Army. Unfortunately for Wildman, his proposals seemed too radical for Cromwell and the other 'grandees' of the army, and the chance of establishing a democratic constitution slipped away. In defeat, however, Wildman continued to agitate for his views and to plot against any version of a commonwealth that moved counter to his ideal of individual liberty and popular elections. He was as unhappy with the military dictatorship of Cromwell as he had been with the would-be absolutism of Charles I.

To most of his contemporaries, both royalist and republican, Wildman's religious views were as distressing as his politics. Dangerously sceptical by the standards of his age, he scandalized Cromwell and his colonels by arguing that the Old Testament could produce no useful precedents for the government of England, and by preferring worldly common sense to prayer in arriving at political decisions. He irritated Anglicans as well as Presbyterians by insisting on a strict separation between Church and State and by denying that religion can be established by law. And he was as little charmed by the rule of the Saints as that of Archbishop Laud.

Inevitably, Wildman's attempt to install the nineteenth century two hundred years early landed him in gaol several times. Inevitably too it made him an expert in the laws of England. Without formal legal training he became in effect a professional lawyer, qualified not only to outwit government prosecutors but to administer estates and transfer property. During the Interregnum he used his legal knowledge, along with a canny eye for business, to make a comfortable fortune from the buying and selling of properties 'sequestrated' from royalists. For himself he acquired, among other properties, the estate of Becket in Berkshire, a town house on Queen Street in London, and the Nonsuch Tavern in Covent Garden.[8] In succeeding years Wildman proved as adept at keeping his money and property as he had been in acquiring them. Whether in or out of jail, he managed to protect his estates through every shift of the political wind and through many suits in Chancery. Nor did he allow his political aims to affect his business judgement. He never invested large sums of his own money in his conspiracies, however promising.

By an odd turn of events, the Restoration of Charles II in 1660 made Wildman *de facto* Postmaster General of England.[9] In the seventeenth century the Post Office was a money-making enterprise, customarily farmed out to the highest bidder, who then became Postmaster General. At the Restoration Wildman helped to purchase the office for his friend Colonel Henry Bishop and volunteered to supervise operations. Bishop was more than willing that Wildman should do the actual work; and at first the new government could see no harm in the arrangement. Wildman, after all, had been a notorious enemy of Cromwell's; he had been imprisoned twice by republican governments; and he had even dabbled briefly in a royalist conspiracy.

By October of 1661, however, the government began to suspect that Wildman, who loved to hobnob with radical theorists and old soldiers of the Commonwealth, was using his position to construct and conceal plots against the monarchy. And in November, alarmed by charges that Wildman was intercepting official dispatches, the government arrested him and sent him to the Tower. He was a ringleader, the Crown alleged, in a republican conspiracy. But the Stuart government was no luckier than its predecessors in obtaining hard evidence against him. It soon became clear, as the Crown's case evaporated, that Wildman would be freed on a writ of habeas corpus. To prevent such embarrassment, the government removed him to the Scilly Isles, well out of the reach of the London courts; and there he was held for six years—until it was deemed safe to allow men of his views and talents to be at large.

Many years later, after the Revolution of 1688, Wildman would again become Postmaster General—appointed *officially* by William III. In 1667, however, when he emerged from confinement, he could see no prospect of power for himself or his friends; Charles II was firmly in the saddle, and a constitutional republic had become a distant dream. The best Wildman could do was ally himself with the Duke of Buckingham in an attempt to gain legal toleration for Dissenters, and even this modest goal proved unattainable. The alliance involved Wildman with the Duke's business affairs and improved his knowledge of chemistry, but achieved nothing politically.

In the late 1670s, however, the pro-French policies of Charles II and the chilling prospect of a popish successor to the throne changed the face of English politics, turning good Englishmen into Whigs and brightening immeasurably the hopes of old republicans. In the crises that followed the Popish Plot, it seemed likely that the Whigs could change the succession or reduce the successor to a cypher. Naturally, Wildman joined with Buckingham and Shaftesbury to promote the Whig cause; he even managed to get himself elected to the last Exclusion Parliament.

Then came the Tory reaction. After dissolving the Oxford Parliament and depriving the Whigs of their legal base of operations, Charles II rallied the conservative forces of England to his side—Anglicans who hated Dissenters, country squires who hated bourgeois upstarts, and many moderate men who feared a new civil war more than they feared royal absolutism. He then began to move against Whig leaders and the town corporations that supported them.

Predictably some of the bolder Whigs began to hold 'consults' about the feasibility of armed rebellion, and naturally these discussions involved Wildman, who still had links with old army men, and whose genius for plotting was well known. Whether the Whig 'consults', if left undisturbed, would have ended in full-scale insurrection will never be known. Before any master strategy had been concerted, the government intervened. Aided by informers and 'trepanners' (*provocateurs*), the government 'discovered' the Rye House Plot, an alleged conspiracy to kill the King and the Duke of York.[10] Within a few days the most active Whig leaders were either in exile or in gaol. Among those taken up in the government's net was John Wildman. On 26 June 1683 he was arrested and, for the third time, lodged in the Tower of London.

All through the latter part of 1683, while Goodwin was campaigning at Hounslow, Wildman was fighting for his life, and as usual he won. The government had found two rusty cannon in his cellar, but could not prove that they were intended for use against the King's forces, or even that they were serviceable. Although it could produce a squad of informers to give hearsay evidence against him, it could not find two credible witnesses who would offer direct testimony. Wildman kept his mouth shut, as did the Whig 'martyrs' who might have implicated him. While the government threshed about in its attempt to bring him to the gallows, he was conducting his private legal affairs from his room in the Tower. Finally, on 12 February 1684, the government gave up; it freed him without a trial, dismissing the charges for lack of evidence.

To Goodwin, looking desperately for a financial backer, the fact that Wildman had 'but newly got out of the Tower' did not matter in the least. What did matter was that he was rich, that he was legendary for his wisdom and secrecy, and that he had an interest (unsuspected by any but his most intimate friends) in the arcane arts.

Wildman, Goodwin knew, loved 'designs in chemistry', like his old patron Buckingham. He had suffered, along with Goodwin, from the pretences of the false alchemist Broune; but he had not blamed Goodwin nor allowed the experience to weaken his faith in alchemy. In addition, Wildman shared Goodwin's enthusiasm for medicine. Though he had achieved nothing so spectacular as Mary's greatest cures, he prided himself upon his knowledge of diagnosis and treatment. With such interests and training, he was obviously well qualified to understand Goodwin's secret projects.

In late February, then, Goodwin went to Wildman and began to explain, in a general way, the business of the partnership. Wildman was interested. He agreed to meet with Goodwin and Mary for further discussion. The more he heard, the more interested he became. Soon he had been 'prepared and fitted' to serve the partnership and had promised faithful cooperation. By 12 March, a government spy detailed to keep Wildman under surveillance reported to his superiors that Wildman was appearing two or three times a week at a house on Vere Street, where he remained two or three hours at a time with a mysterious young man who seldom or never 'stirred abroad'.[11] Wildman, the spy noted, was careful to leave his coach and servants 'in the next street' and to conceal his identity from the other lodgers in the house. The spy, of course, suspected the worst—that Wildman and his young friend were hatching another plot against the government. He would have been relieved to know that the young man was Goodwin Wharton and that the pair was hatching nothing more serious than a plan to transmute mercury into gold and to dig up a treasure buried at Somerset House.

The alliance with John Wildman solved Goodwin's immediate financial problem. Though Wildman's money sometimes came from him 'hard like blood', he was willing to back the partners in their most important projects. There remained, however, a more basic problem. A year of continual disappointment had shaken Goodwin's confidence in the reliability of spirits and lowlanders. No doubt they meant well; no doubt they controlled great wealth; no doubt they possessed rare powers. But somehow they never delivered. What Goodwin needed, he now saw with great clarity, was an infallible supernatural power which could guarantee results. In short, he needed the help of the angels. Wildman might keep the partnership afloat temporarily, but only the angels could bring it safely, and gloriously, to shore.

A method of getting in touch with angels had been suggested to him by the kindly gentleman who had first directed him to Mary Parish. But the method had required a virgin intermediary; and, as Goodwin had quickly learned, the task of finding mature, discreet, and wise virgins presented great difficulties. Now, shortly before his thirty-first birthday, he hit upon a brilliant idea. It occurred to him that 'there might be such a thing in nature' as an 'imputative virginity'. Mary was now pregnant with two obviously virgin sons, and since 'the influences that children have upon their mothers is undeniable', it might be possible, he reasoned, that she had derived from her sons the powers and purity of regular virginity. When Goodwin explained his theory to Mary, she found it highly probable and agreed to put the matter to the test. In accordance with the instructions he had received from his old friend, she would attempt to summon 'the blessed angel Uriel'.

The day chosen for the experiment was Goodwin's birthday, 8 March 1684. The place was the house on Vere Street, where (for the sake of propriety) Goodwin and Mary occupied separate rooms. The method was simplicity itself. Goodwin procured a glass of clean water and placed it before Mary; then, repeating a formula he had learned, he asked that Uriel should appear to her. The result was sudden and dramatic. No sooner had Goodwin finished the invocation than Mary saw Uriel in the glass—'first making, as it were, a cloud in the water, and then showing himself perfect in all the beauty and proportions of a youth, but with the splendour of an angel of light and happiness'.

At his first appearance, Mary noted, Uriel was not permitted to speak with her; he could only make signs. But within five days, he was not only free to converse with her, in a 'perfect and plain' voice, but to explain many things of great moment. He explained, first of all, that his name was indeed Uriel and that he 'had the happiness to behold the face of the Lord in heaven'. In biblical times he had transmitted God's messages to several men, including Gideon and King Ahab, and he was still able and willing to come 'to good men if they rightly desired it of him'. Hereafter he would come to Goodwin, through Mary, whenever he was summoned, unless otherwise engaged in the service of the Lord. The simple formula, 'Pray, Uriel, come', would suffice to bring him. For the present, of course, he could not be audible or visible to Goodwin—who had no claim to imputative virginity—but sometime soon he might be granted a special dispensation to appear to Goodwin as he had appeared to others 'in the old time'.[12]

There was a good, natural reason, Uriel explained further, for his appearing in a glass of water. Water, being 'more substantial' than air, 'and yet transparent', rendered the extremely thin angelic essence more discernible to mortal eyes. Without such help, even a clear-sighted virgin might be unable to sense the presence of an angel of Uriel's rank—unless of course God had specifically empowered him to appear. There were indeed orders of angels so powerful that they might routinely dispense with aids of any kind and appear without difficulty to non-virgins. These, however, seldom left heaven. In general, Uriel told Mary, the business of communicating with men was left to angels like himself who spent most of their time near the earth.

With the appearance of Uriel, Goodwin's hopes became immeasurably brighter. Vast realms of spiritual knowledge now stretched before him, and the temporal success that had so far eluded him was clearly at hand. Assured of divine favour, he could throw himself into all his projects with renewed energy. Even the restriction on his ability to see angels seemed about to be lifted. In mid-March, Uriel told Mary that within four weeks he hoped to speak with Goodwin and within seven weeks to become visible. He promised, furthermore, that the new alchemical project being launched by Goodwin and Wildman would prosper; by the middle of April, he said, the experiment would produce 'perfect gold' and by 22 April all Goodwin's troubles would be over.

Then about 1 April, to Goodwin's delight, Uriel brought with him the angel Ahab, who appeared in the glass and introduced himself to Mary. He had formerly been a man, he said, but had become an angel of great power. Not limited like Uriel, he could appear more readily to ordinary mortals and he would soon appear to Goodwin. Meanwhile he would add his powerful services to those of Uriel in seeking the prosperity of the partners.

It was a renewed partnership, then, that began its second year of operation in the spring of 1684. Subsidized by Wildman, instructed by the angels, and educated by wonders and misfortunes, Goodwin and Mary could look forward to a fresh scene. Goodwin had every reason to suppose that within a short time he would produce gold from base metals, marry the Queen, retrieve the treasure at Hounslow, and become the father of twin boys.

6

Delivery and Execution

THE first major project undertaken by the new, expanded partnership was an alchemical experiment designed to produce gold from mercury. This operation Goodwin launched with great optimism. Besides the combined expertise of the partners themselves, he had formidable resources at his disposal. Through Mary, he could call upon Father Friar, generally conceded to be the most talented alchemist among the lowlanders, and upon the spirit of a Jewish philosopher-adept named Mr Abab, who had been during his lifetime the finest chemist among uplanders. This dazzling array of experts seemed to justify Uriel's flat prediction that the partners would achieve perfect gold by the middle of April.

As the work went forward, however, some unexpected difficulties developed. Father Friar was immensely helpful, actually delivering to Mary an 'excellent vinegar' and a 'certain stone' that lowlanders used in alchemy, but he was also very absent-minded. He sometimes forgot the chemical formulas he had once employed and he sometimes forgot appointments with the partners. Such lapses were pardonable in a lowlander 1700 years old, but they were nevertheless troublesome. The metallic mixture bubbling away in the crucible might very well lack some vital ingredient.

Mr Abab likewise suffered from a troublesome defect. Although he cheerfully came to Vere Street from Montpelier, France (where he had died), he could not make himself intelligible when he arrived. He spoke a barbarous mixture of Hebrew, German, and French[1] which Goodwin (who could sometimes hear him) could not unscramble; and his attempts at English were hopeless. Though eager 'to improve himself', he would obviously require months to achieve adequate communication.

In spite of the defects of their advisors, the partners struggled on with their experiment, and at length, about the middle of

April, they produced 'one ingot of metal' which to the sight and touch appeared very much like gold. Tests showed, however, that the metal was not genuine gold; and there was no escaping the fact that the project—and Uriel's promise—had failed. The partners had not produced 'perfect gold', and Goodwin's troubles were by no means over.

For this shocking situation—an obvious error by a holy angel—Uriel's explanation was direct and simple: the project had failed, he told Mary, because of the will of God. This pronouncement Goodwin found unarguable. As he well knew, God's ultimate will might be unknown to the highest order of angels and might contravene the most confident predictions. In this case, as in all others, God's will was to be cheerfully accepted—in the serene faith that ultimately a greater good would ensue.

Meanwhile God's inscrutable will seemed to be working against Goodwin's attempts to see and hear Ahab. All through April, this powerful angel tried to communicate with Goodwin, only to find that, contrary to all his previous experience, he could neither succeed nor find the reason for his failure. He suspected, of course, that some sort of restraint was being laid upon his power, and in early May this theory was confirmed by Uriel, who told Mary that for the present God had forbidden Goodwin to see angels or spirits.

Goodwin was equally unfortunate in trying to see the Queen of the lowlanders. Twice, in late March and early April, he journeyed to Hounslow, only to be turned back at the last moment when Queen Penelope received unexpected visitors. These journeys were not totally wasted, however, since Goodwin was allowed, for the first time, to see the exact spot where the entrance to the lowlands was located—an entrance so cunningly concealed in the earth that it was indistinguishable from the terrain about it. Goodwin noted its position carefully so that he might sometime return, if necessary, without a guide.

But before the next appointment at Hounslow Heath, Mary fell violently ill, apparently poisoned by some uncleaned spinach. When her own remedies brought her no relief, she allowed John Wildman, against Goodwin's advice, to 'give her a vomit'. Wildman's therapy, though derived from a good understanding of medicine, proved almost fatally mistaken.

Once Mary started vomiting, she could not stop, and the vomiting was accompanied by fever and diarrhea. Nothing that Goodwin or Wildman could do had any effect, and although this time Mary did not break a vein, she weakened so rapidly that Goodwin feared she could not survive—especially since she was now 'near her time'. During her illness, furthermore, she had a vision of Death (who appeared as a 'skeleton'); and Ahab, interpreting the visitation, declared that either she or one of her sons must die.

The crisis arrived four or five days after the original attack and after Mary had vomited 'many hundreds if not thousands of times'. As a last resort Goodwin and Wildman prepared 'a great glass of hot spirit of aniseeds and cherry brandy'. If this measure failed to help, they conceded, Mary would not live through the night. To Goodwin's great joy the remedy worked. Mary's vomiting stopped. 'By degrees' she began to recover. She would not regain her full strength for several weeks, but she had survived a terrible ordeal, Goodwin noted gratefully, 'without breaking her vein, and without miscarrying'. Furthermore, she had endured her suffering without divulging, even to Wildman, the fact that she was pregnant. Though she was several times 'light-headed' with fever 'so as to talk of all manner of things', she never once mentioned her children.

During the worst of Mary's illness, the time came for Goodwin to see the Queen. This appointment Mary advised him to keep, in spite of her own danger. Repeating her promises of the previous year, she assured him that if she died in his absence she would return to him after death. As for the children (who could only be saved by post-mortem surgery if she died), they might be safely entrusted to God's providence. Impressed by this reasoning, Goodwin agreed to make the journey; he asked only that George should be sent to him and permitted to speak to him (though invisible) if Mary's condition worsened or if the Queen could not see him as planned.

On the morning of 22 April, in his one-horse carriage, Goodwin reached the gates of the lowlands without hearing from George. As he drew up at the entrance to the Queen's kingdom, he expected to see open gates, or at least a few lowland courtiers sent to meet him. But there was no sign of an opening in the earth and no evidence of anyone in the area except himself. Goodwin got down from his carriage and tied up his horse. Sure that he was upon the exact site that Mary had indicated, he walked back and forth across it several times, 'stamping and calling'. Still he saw and heard nothing. As far as he could tell, he was all alone on the deserted heath, stamping on solid ground and shouting into empty air.

Convinced at length that his efforts were 'all to no purpose', Goodwin drove back as far as his inn at Hounslow. It was possible, he reasoned, that the gates had been closed because of some unforeseen and temporary difficulty, or some misunderstanding about the time of the appointment. He would wait two or three hours and then try once more. But when he returned to the site, the heath was as blank as ever. His stamping and calling brought no response. There was no sign that his presence was heeded by anything except his horse. At last, 'melancholy and almost in despair', he set out 'all alone' on the long road to London.

When he got home, after dark, Mary was able to explain what had happened. While he was *en route* to Hounslow, she said, Queen Penelope had received an unscheduled visit from the Duchess of Brittany. In a characteristic 'fret and humour' the Queen had commanded that the gates of the lowlands should be tightly closed and no one admitted until further orders. George had attempted to carry this information to Goodwin, but his voice had been drowned out by the noise of the carriage wheels. Once again, Mary concluded, Goodwin had been victimized by the Queen's whims.

During Mary's convalescence from her physical crisis, she suddenly found herself faced with a spiritual crisis which changed her relationship with her church. The trouble arose, Mary said, because she had not been to confession since her misfortunes. Though she had often attended the Catholic chapel at Wild House,[2] she could not bring herself to confess to the priest there, whom she disliked personally. Now that priest had assigned her a severe penance to atone for her long neglect. For three consecutive days, in spite of the unseasonable heat and her own ill health, she was to walk to Tyburn and back without stopping for food or water.

Goodwin, who learned of her trouble when she returned home one day looking 'almost as one quite dead', was outraged when he observed the effects of her first journey. He argued that the penance was unreasonable and that if she continued it, she would 'murder herself and her children'. Mary agreed to one day's respite, but she insisted on continuing the penance, and when she returned from her second journey, she looked so bad that Goodwin 'thought truly she would have almost died'. And she brought back a story that filled him with 'amazement and fear'.

On her way to Tyburn, she said, she had met a personage who called himself her father and instructed her to go back where she came from. He said that she had 'committed all sorts of wickednesses' and that she was 'mad', but that she had 'a great spirit'. Hereafter, he said, she should 'be no more subject to the priest'. Afraid that the stranger might be a devil sent to tempt her from her duty, Mary had ignored his instructions and continued on her journey. Now, shaken and exhausted, she was still uncertain what to make of her strange experience.

When Mary regained her composure, she summoned Ahab for advice; but when Ahab appeared in the glass, he brought with him the archangel Gabriel, bearing direct 'orders from the Lord'. Her encounter on the road to Tyburn, Gabriel declared, had been a visitation from the Lord, who had decided that she should no longer be subject to any priest. Therefore, she was now commanded to tell the priest at Wild House that 'he had dealt wickedly by her' and that 'she would renounce his church forever.' As for herself, Gabriel added, 'she was a poor disconsolate woman, and fitter for heaven than this world.'

Mary immediately obeyed the orders from Gabriel. After berating the priest at Wild House, she began attending prayers at St. Paul's, Covent Garden. There she was met by another angel, who further explained the Lord's command. All Christian religions are good, the angel said, but not equally good for all people. For her the Catholic religion was unsatisfactory because she did not understand it. Protestantism, on the other hand, would be more helpful because 'she would understand it best.' Accepting this latitudinarian doctrine, Mary remained a Protestant for the rest of her life; 'she never returned to the Church of Rome.'

While Mary struggled with her health and her religion, Goodwin worried about her delivery, which was clearly imminent, since she had conceived in early August. As the middle of May drew near, he 'daily enquired' of the angels just when the delivery would take place, but on this subject he could get no definite answer. Meanwhile, the partners grappled with the problem of how she could be 'delivered without suspicion'. So far, by occupying separate rooms on different floors, they had kept their liaison secret from the other lodgers at the house on Vere Street. Now they faced the task of getting Mary safely away to a midwife and back again for her recovery without betraying her condition. For this purpose, they decided that Goodwin should take additional lodgings in a strange neighbourhood and occupy them until after Mary's confinement. They planned that Mary would call at the new lodgings 'just before her time' and that Goodwin would take her from there to the midwife.

Unfortunately, their best calculations of Mary's time proved to be wrong. In the very early morning of 17 May, a day or two before the date Mary had finally set, she awoke (as she later reported to Goodwin) with the first stirrings of labour pains. As she dressed herself, she realized that she had forgotten the exact address of Goodwin's new lodgings, that she was without money, and that she had not made final arrangements for her delivery. Without wasting any time trying to send for Goodwin, she gathered up 'a little linen' and pawned it for six shillings; then continuing on to Old Fish Street, she collected fifteen shillings more from a man who owed her a debt. Finally, having 'bethought herself of a midwife she knew', she headed for the midwife's house at Long Lane. By the time she arrived at Long Lane, 'looking like death', she was ready to be delivered. About eleven o'clock, after less than a hour of hard labour, she produced two fine boys.

Mary's problems did not end with the birth of her sons. She noted immediately that one of the infants (in accordance with Ahab's prediction) seemed 'ready to die'. Sending for a minister in all haste, she had the sickly child christened Charles and arranged for his burial in case he could not be saved. She instructed the minister to christen the healthy child Peregrine, a name that Goodwin had selected as appropriate for a young 'stranger'. Then she set about making arrangements for the care of her children—since it was impossible for her to bring them home and look after them herself.

Providentially, 'a most wonderful, good nurse' was visiting the midwife at the time Mary was delivered. This woman, highly recommended by the midwife, agreed to take young Peregrine home and bring him up 'by hand'. No doubt she would have cared for Charles also had he looked capable of survival, but it became obvious that he could scarcely live through the day and that he must be left to the ministrations of the midwife and the clergyman.

As for herself, Mary refused to remain in bed. With the last of her small stock of money, she took a coach back to Vere Street, where Goodwin, almost ill with worry, had come to look for her. Alighting after a jolting ride, she crawled up 'two steep pair of stairs' and made her way to Goodwin's chamber. There, 'being just spent', she finally collapsed on the bed—ending a series of events that evoked Goodwin's awe and admiration. There were 'few wonders in the world', he later remarked, greater than her ability to 'do so much and yet live'.

During the next fortnight it became evident that Mary's recovery would be as remarkable as her delivery. For two or three days she was obliged to 'keep her bed a little', but her indisposition seemed so slight that the lodgers on Vere Street never suspected its cause. By Wednesday, 21 May, four days after her delivery, she felt so well that she allowed Goodwin to make love to her. And she was able to announce, shortly afterward, that she had become pregnant with another boy—a blessing which restored her imputative virginity and, of course, her ability to see angels. Finally, on 30 May, she completed her recovery by conceiving of a second son.

Goodwin's joy in these blessings was only slightly tempered by the fact that young Charles had died as predicted. Peregrine, at least, had been saved and lodged with an excellent nurse, who realized from his delicate beauty that he was no ordinary child. For the time being, of course, it was essential to conceal the child's identity, even from the nurse; and for this reason it was also essential to keep Goodwin at a safe distance from Peregrine, since anyone seeing the two together would have infallibly guessed the relationship. These necessities Goodwin accepted with good grace. Knowing that he could soon arrange to see the child, if only from a distance, he financed its care without complaint. Eventually, he would write his autobiography for Peregrine's instruction.

During Mary's rapid return to complete health, Goodwin looked for a project that would recompense John Wildman for the temporary failures in alchemy; and in early June, Mary announced that George had found such a project—a rich treasure buried in a private garden at Somerset House.[3] George, she said, had marked the place where the treasure lay, and she herself had visited the site and seen the mark.

Following Mary's instructions, Goodwin and Wildman found the garden and George's mark without difficulty, but they also found a hopeless problem in tactics. Somerset House was owned by Catherine of Braganza, Queen of England, and the garden in question belonged to 'an earl of the Court'. Since the treasure could only be approached through the middle of Somerset House or through the earl's house, there was no way of digging it up and carrying it away unobserved; and Goodwin and Wildman were unwilling to risk discovery 'for twice the money in that place'. The project, they decided, could wait until Goodwin received the magic pea, which would allow him to work invisibly. Meantime, Wildman was to share in the treasure at the four trees when it was retrieved and enter the lowlands as soon as Goodwin established himself there.

At the four trees, unfortunately, Goodwin, Wildman, and Mary were defeated by a rainstorm, but when the partners returned to London, Goodwin's prospects for meeting Queen Penelope looked brighter than ever. The Queen, now perfectly healthy for the first time in weeks, had decided to take the initiative herself. On 6 June, rather than wait for Goodwin in her own domains, she would drive to London in her coach, pick up Goodwin and Mary, and transport them to Moorfields, where the lowlanders had a colony under the command of the Duke of Hungary. At Moorfields, the royal party would find the lowland Pope, who would finally perform the long-delayed marriage ceremony between Goodwin and the Queen.

To Goodwin the Queen's plan 'looked wondrous well' (as it did to John Wildman when it was explained to him); and on the morning of 6 June, Goodwin and Mary, dressed in their most elegant clothes, betook themselves to an inn on Piccadilly to wait for the Queen's party. With the help of the angels (who frequently appeared in Mary's glass) Goodwin was able to follow the progress of the Queen's coach almost mile by mile as it made its way, 'fine and gently', from Hounslow Heath, through Brentford and Hammersmith, towards London. At Knightsbridge, however, a complication developed. In a narrow portion of the road, the Queen's coach locked wheels with a vehicle driven by an ill-natured carter. The result was a sharp jolt, not violent enough to cause injury but severe enough to frighten and upset the Queen, who alighted at the nearest inn to refresh herself with a glass of wine. Then, feeling herself 'a little heavy' and being determined to keep herself well, she decided to take a nap and pass the heat of the day in the safety of the inn.

Goodwin bore the suspense as well as he could; but as the Queen slept on through two, three, and four o'clock in the afternoon, he could not help finding himself 'a little upon thorns'. It occurred to him that the Queen's inn at Knightsbridge was less than a mile from his own, and that by simply hiring a coach he could be with her in a few minutes, ready to greet her when she awoke. Accordingly, when the angels told Mary that the Queen would awake presently, the partners set out in a coach for Knightsbridge. Almost within sight of the goal, Mary suddenly asked Goodwin to stop. George, she said, had arrived with terrible news. The Queen had awakened from her nap to find herself beginning her period. 'Very ill', she had been rushed by her women into her coach and was now on her way back to Hounslow. In tears she had instructed George to send her regrets to Goodwin. 'Certainly', she had said, she was 'the most unhappy woman in the world'.

But Goodwin was in no mood to stop. Now that he was in motion, his fighting blood was aroused. The Queen's coach, he argued, could hardly be more than a quarter of a mile ahead. With fast driving he could overtake it. At the very least, he could finally catch sight of the Queen and end more than a year of frustration. George, however, quickly pointed out that there was no chance of overtaking the royal coach and six, now driving at full speed; nor, if this were possible, was there a chance of seeing the Queen, who had made herself invisible. Reluctantly, Goodwin found himself compelled to yield to this remorseless logic. Halted just short of the unlucky inn at

Knightsbridge, he made the return journey along Piccadilly in great 'trouble' of spirit.

While Goodwin was suffering these staggering reverses, a deadly train of events was beginning in Holland.[4] Sir Thomas Armstrong, one of the Rye House plotters and an old acquaintance of Goodwin's, was seized in Leyden by an English agent (with the connivance of a Dutch official), carried aboard an English yacht, and spirited away to England. By 11 June he was loaded with irons and locked in Newgate.[5]

The government hated and feared Sir Thomas. A bold and hot-tempered soldier, once commander of the King's guards, he was obviously well fitted to lead a military coup; and as a trusted lieutenant of the Duke of Monmouth, he was seen as a sinister force pushing the Duke towards treason. On top of all this, Crown officials believed that Armstrong had plotted to murder Charles II and his brother James. The government, however, was not so sure of its evidence that it wished to give Armstrong a jury trial, especially when it could find a good pretext for hanging him without one. During his absence in Holland, he had been declared an outlaw, which meant (the government contended) that the Crown could proceed as if he had already been convicted of treason. In accordance with this strategy, Armstrong was brought before Judge Jeffreys at the King's Bench on 14 June and asked to show cause why he should not be punished as an outlaw.

Although not allowed counsel, Armstrong pleaded very cogently, pointing out that he was still within the year of grace allowed to outlaws for surrendering themselves and that legal precedent was in his favour. In theory, perhaps, outlaws might be hanged without trial, but in practice they were allowed to appear before a jury. Predictably, Jeffreys brushed Armstrong's pleas aside. Agreeing with Sir Robert Sawyer, who argued the case for the Crown, he ruled that Sir Thomas had no right to a trial and that he should be hanged, drawn, and quartered at Tyburn on the following Friday—20 June.[6]

After the Revolution of 1688, a Whig House of Commons, which included Goodwin, condemned Jeffreys's decision as judicial murder and expelled Sir Robert Sawyer for his share in the proceedings. But to Sir Thomas Armstrong the dim prospect of future vindication furnished little comfort. His present concern was to cleanse his soul and steel himself to face the executioner without flinching.

It was in the preparation of Armstrong's spirit that Goodwin now took a hand. Having served in Parliament with him, Goodwin was well aware of Armstrong's moral failings. He knew that Sir Thomas had been 'an ill liver and an ill man' and that he would need a dramatic infusion of faith if he was to merit salvation and 'make a good end'. Goodwin also knew that if Sir Thomas could achieve a state of grace before his execution, he would be eligible to return to Goodwin as a good spirit. And if he agreed to return, Goodwin would at last have a spirit of his own—one that he could actually see.

Goodwin, of course, could not visit Armstrong in Newgate. His attack on James during his days in Parliament had already marked him as an enemy of the government, and he could not afford to be seen with a condemned traitor. It was even dangerous to let his name be mentioned at Newgate, since Sir Thomas might be forced, or tempted, to implicate his friends. In this delicate situation, Goodwin approached Sir Thomas through George, who could appear at any time to men doomed to death and who was cautioned not to reveal who sent him.

George did his duty admirably. In three visits to Newgate, he encouraged Sir Thomas to trust God and explained the 'mysteries' involved in returning after death. At first Sir Thomas 'startled a little' at seeing a spirit, but he made great progress towards faith and salvation. There remained, nevertheless, a few dregs of uncertainty until the very morning of the execution, and to remove these, Goodwin assigned George to accompany Sir Thomas in the sledge from Newgate to Tyburn and to stay with him through the execution. At the last moment he was to entrust Sir Thomas with Goodwin's name, as the benefactor to whom he was to return.

Having made these arrangements, Goodwin stationed himself on Holborn Street where he could watch the condemned man and his cavalcade of guards pass by. When Sir Thomas came in sight, he was standing stoically in the sledge, apparently absorbed in a devotional book. Goodwin could see that he had overcome his fears and that his bearing was 'very grave and manly'. And when Goodwin ventured up close to him to wave a last farewell and signal encouragement, Sir Thomas acknowledged the gesture with 'a little blush' and politely removed his hat.

Throughout the execution, which Goodwin did not attend, Armstrong remained courageous and devout. At the gallows, as one observer noted, he 'preserved a becoming and heroic countenance' while he knelt in prayer, first with Dr Thomas Tenison and then alone. Finally he arose, put off his periwig, accepted the hood given him by the hangman, and firmly mounted the executioner's cart. His lips were moving in prayer as the cart pulled away, and for a time they continued to move 'even whilst he hung.'[7] When he was pronounced dead, half an hour later, even his enemies conceded that he had died very well. He had behaved himself, as Gilbert Burnet wrote later, with the serene deportment of a Christian gentleman.[8]

After George returned from the hanging, he reported to Mary and Goodwin that everything had gone as planned. He had stood beside Sir Thomas throughout the ordeal, exhorting him to have faith in God. Then just as the hangman's cart began to move, he had revealed Goodwin's name. There could be no doubt that Sir Thomas had died in a state of grace, and there was much reason to hope that he would be willing to appear to Goodwin. This hope, unfortunately, was frustrated. When George consulted with Armstrong's spirit, after a proper interval, Sir Thomas politely declined to visit Goodwin. He preferred (George reported) to see Goodwin's brother Tom or the Duke of Monmouth—friends more intimate and more powerful than Goodwin. This decision Goodwin accepted without complaint. He had done something, after all, more important than acquiring a spirit for himself. He had made Sir Thomas a hero and saved his damaged soul.

Goodwin's success with Sir Thomas Armstrong was his only victory during a month of bitter defeats. With the disappointments at the four trees, Somerset House, and Knightsbridge, his affairs were once more assuming the familiar pattern of failure. And by the middle of June, his patience was exhausted. More and more the repeated delays seemed outrageous—no matter how carefully they were explained by Mary. Particularly galling were two chronic and unreasonable frustrations—the angels' failure to appear to him and the Queen's failure to send him the small legacy from the King.

Then, about the time that George was visiting Sir Thomas in

Newgate, affairs suddenly took a happy turn. The Queen announced that Goodwin should have the legacy at once. If he would go to a certain inn at Brentford, he would be met by the Duchess of Plymouth and Father Friar, who would give him the gold and jewels. Moreover, the Queen said, she was now convinced that she could legally dispense with the famous oath which had forbidden Goodwin to see any of her people. Thus, the Duchess of Plymouth and Father Friar would be permitted to make themselves visible to Goodwin and hand him the legacy in person.

Concurrently, Goodwin received more important news. For a month the angels had been trying to appear to him—and failing, even though they believed that God had lifted the restraint on their ability to become visible. Goodwin did not understand why Ahab and Gabriel, two of the most powerful angels in heaven, could not manage a simple appearance, or why angels should be as unreliable in their promises as spirits. Now, however, Gabriel and Ahab declared that they would appear to Goodwin at Brentford, just as they regularly appeared to Mary. There was nothing tentative about this promise, the angels said; they would appear to him 'without peradventure'.

When Goodwin set out for Brentford, then, he was 'satisfied' in his 'expectations'. And when he and Mary arrived at the inn without receiving any contradictory messages, his hopes rose even higher. He alighted from his carriage, engaged a room, and bespoke lunch for himself and Mary and two possible guests. Then he settled himself in his room, set up the glass of water for the angels, and prepared to receive visitors.

But instead of the Duchess of Plymouth and Father Friar, he received a message from George, who had just arrived from Hounslow. On the verge of leaving the lowlands, the Friar and the Duchess had been stopped by the sudden death of the palace bellman. This gentleman, an old retainer, was a general favourite at court, and no one could decently leave the lowlands on the day of his death. For this reason, the delivery of the legacy would be postponed for at least one more day.

At another time, Goodwin might have received 'this strange news' with patience; he might have marvelled at the odd turns of Providence. But now he was sick of disappointments and in no mood for excuses, however ingenious. Suddenly, at a blow no worse than a hundred others, he felt his 'constancy' begin to 'stagger'. He found himself wishing, 'almost', that he was dead and 'out of the world'.

He tried to collect himself and look forward to the appearance of the angels—a blessing vastly more important than a legacy. Still, as he watched Mary peering into the glass, he could not feel any real optimism. And as the afternoon wore on, events began to take on a familiar, ominous rhythm. At the proper time, Mary announced that all three angels had appeared to her. They promised, Mary said, that 'in a little time' they would also appear to Goodwin. But as the minutes dragged by, the 'little time' lengthened into 'a great deal of time' and still Goodwin could discern nothing in the glass. Finally, as if to fulfil his growing resentment and foreboding, the angels confessed, through Mary, that they could not now appear or speak 'at all'.

At this, Goodwin exploded. Overwhelmed with 'trouble, anguish, grief, doubt', and anger, he began to spew forth the frustration accumulated over months of constant defeat. 'Fretful passions' poured out in a torrent of words (as he later admitted) too swift and violent to recall. In volleys of abuse—some of which Mary remembered verbatim—he berated Uriel, Ahab, and Gabriel for fraud and deception. They had told him 'nothing but lies', he said; and he would never believe Gabriel again—not even if he repeated promises 'a thousand times'.

When at last Goodwin's passion had spent itself, Mary quietly pointed out what he had done. The angels, she noted, had disappeared from the glass. It was now doubtful that they would ever come back. Though she understood Goodwin's feelings, she was obliged to recall to him the enormity of what he had said. It now appeared that after all they had suffered together, he had decided to throw away his chances. If so, she would not complain for herself. But if not, he must speak immediately to recall the angels and apologize for his conduct.

Goodwin hesitated. With his anger only half-settled, he was still full of self-justification. He had been cruelly wronged; he deserved to *receive* apologies, not offer them. And yet, even as he seethed, he had the uneasy feeling that he might be guilty of 'folly and rashness'. In contrast with Mary's calm acceptance of misfortune, his own response had been that of a petulant child. Now, as he gained control of himself, one thing was certain: he could not face the complete wreckage of his hopes. At the very least he would ask the angels for explanations.

The angels, however, did not return. For five bleak days, Goodwin was left to reflect upon his obvious error. The angels, he soon saw, could not be blamed for failing to appear to him. Though endowed with great powers, they could not know 'the secret will of God or how far it restrained them'. No doubt they had themselves been deceived about their own unaided strength. Mary, indeed, had seen Ahab 'strain himself' to speak with Goodwin, 'as if a man should strive to call out for help'. Viewed in this light, Goodwin conceded, his fault had been monstrous. Without justification, he had insulted and alienated the blessed angels; and if he was now abandoned, he had only himself to blame.

Finally, on the fifth day, Uriel and Ahab appeared successively to Mary. Goodwin, they explained to her, had 'done very ill' in his behaviour towards them and, especially, towards Gabriel. They had been impressed, nevertheless, by his sincere repentance and were now willing to forgive him. Similarly Gabriel, who appeared the next day, declared himself willing to forgive Goodwin—though Goodwin's rashness had 'reflected upon God'.

At last, then, Goodwin became reconciled to the angels—and to his strange misfortunes. 'This heat', he later recalled, 'became cool again, and after the storm' there appeared 'a fair calm as before'. Moreover, the results of his unseemly temper tantrum taught him a valuable lesson: whatever the provocation, he must not be 'hasty nor rash with the spirits in heaven'. They could lose nothing by his anger, but he could lose everything.

The Exorcists

GOODWIN recovered his faith in the angels just in time. By the latter part of June, John Wildman was threatening to defect from the partnership, and Goodwin needed all of his own optimism to prevent the alliance from breaking up. Wildman was particularly discouraged by the failure of a new alchemical project, which shared the defects of the old one. In the interval from April to June, neither Father Friar's memory nor Mr Abab's English had improved significantly; and the partners were unable to obtain an exotic foreign vinegar which the new experiments required. After a month of hard work, they again managed to produce a metallic compound, but they could not produce gold.

Wildman was further discouraged by 'the failing of promises in other things'. Inexperienced in dealing with spirits and angels, he could not understand how the information they provided could be wrong; he was sometimes inclined to doubt that their knowledge came from God. Meanwhile, he began to complain about expenses; his necessities, he said, were so pressing that he might be compelled to leave England.

Goodwin intended to remain 'faithfully cordial' to Wildman, and he scorned to fabricate any 'great pretence' that might prompt Wildman to give him a large lump sum of money. In view of Wildman's weak faith, however, there was one minor pretence that he felt obliged to keep up. He had not admitted to Wildman that he had never actually seen George, Uriel, and Ahab; he had led Wildman to believe, in fact, that he could see spirits and angels almost as well as Mary could. This small deception helped him to explain with more authority the limitations of supernatural powers and gave him a great advantage over his friend. It was easier, Wildman found, to argue with Crown prosecutors than with a man who could see Ahab.

And Goodwin had other powerful weapons at his disposal.

The treasure at the four trees, which he had offered to share with Wildman, was only one lucky new moon away; and recently Queen Penelope had shown strong evidence of good faith. Besides rescinding her unfortunate oath, she had finally sent the King's magic pea and magic leaf. These arrived in Goodwin's room about 24 June and proved to be 'most delicate things'. They needed reconsecration, of course, but Father Friar agreed to take care of that. These priceless objects, which Wildman could see for himself, represented the key to the treasure at Somerset House and to much else.

With such inducements, along with the promise to take Wildman to Northend as soon as possible, Goodwin managed to keep his friend in line. Wildman grumbled, but he paid. Mary, meantime, undistracted by two more conceptions (making four in all), set about forwarding the designs that would make the investments profitable. The most immediate of the projects, of course, was Goodwin's marriage to the Queen, which after many postponements was finally and firmly scheduled for Monday, 30 June, at the royal palace below Hounslow Heath.

The day before, however, as the partners were having lunch at their inn, they suddenly heard a great noise and felt a concussion that shook their 'very room'. A powder mill, located on the heath a mile or two west of Hounslow, had blown up, along with all its stores of gunpowder.[1] Goodwin feared the worst. The powder mill, he knew, lay above one part of the Queen's domain. No doubt the explosion had wrought extensive damage among the lowlanders, and very probably it had caused another delay in his own plans. George, sent to investigate, reported that the damage was indeed extensive. The explosion had knocked down statuary in the Queen's chapel, demolished part of the old monastery where Princess Ursula was confined, and caused great 'mischiefs' throughout the lowlands. Nevertheless, George said, there were no deaths, and the Queen, contrary to all expectation, had not begun to menstruate. Though 'much discomposed by her fright', she was still bent on proceeding with the marriage. She would send for Goodwin on Monday afternoon.

Earlier in the month, Goodwin had succeeded in renting Nicholson's house[2]—the haunted house that Mary had discovered the previous summer; and on Monday morning as the partners waited for the Queen's messengers, Goodwin explored the interior of the house while Mary walked around the grounds outside. Emerging from the house after a time, Goodwin found Mary 'flat on her face upon the ground' in what first appeared to be a swoon but what proved to be a trance—so deep that even when she regained consciousness she found herself still 'in a maze'. And the account she gave of her experience was equally amazing.

Gabriel had appeared to her, she said, in a glory bright as the sun, bringing her a message from God. In response to Lord Wharton's prayers, God now commanded that Goodwin should go at once to Wooburn and spend fifteen days there. This mission, Gabriel said, would relieve Lord Wharton's mind and convince him that his son was not 'in an evil course', and it was so important that 'nothing could thrive' with Goodwin until he had completed it. At Wooburn, Gabriel promised, Goodwin would have nothing to fear; God would incline Lord Wharton's heart to kindness.

Goodwin realized at once that God's command postponed his wedding to the Queen, cancelled the next attempt at the four trees (scheduled for 2 July), and separated him from Mary for the first time in more than a year. Nevertheless, he did not protest. He had recently learned that he must never argue with angels, and he did not dream of disputing the will of God. After sending word to the Queen that he had been commanded home, he exchanged 'good and kind wishes' with Mary and set out for Wooburn.

To Goodwin's relief, Lord Wharton seemed genuinely glad of the visit, and he did not ask embarrassing questions. Goodwin had not yet worked out a plausible explanation for his relationship with Mary; and without one he found it difficult to give his father any creditable account of his activities. For this reason, he was delighted when Lord Wharton, without cross-examining him, accepted his assurances that he was not spending his time 'idly nor foolishly'. He realized that God had softened his father's heart, as promised.

In other respects, Goodwin's fifteen days at Wooburn seemed oddly vacuous. He saw no sign of Queen Penelope or the angel Ahab, both of whom had promised to visit him; and he did not see the spirit of his mother, who hoped to meet him at Wooburn and show him where she had hidden some jewels for his benefit.[3] His affairs stood still, in fact, until he returned to London, where Mary gave him excellent news. The time had finally come, she said, when they could go to Northend, with John Wildman, and collect the treasure they had located many months before.

During the previous summer Goodwin and Mary, riding double on a 'gouty' nag, had reached Northend from the east, via Marlow and Turville. This time, riding stylishly in Wildman's coach, they arrived from the west, via Henley and Watlington. On the way, they dispatched George to ask the Duke of Lorraine (the nobleman who ruled the lowland colony at Shirburn Castle) to send to Northend a crew of servants who could transport large quantities of gold from the treasure site to their coach, which had to be left some distance away. This favour the Duke readily granted. Thus, when the partners reached the treasure area (about 5.30 p.m., on Monday, 28 July), they were fully prepared.

At a safe distance from the actual site, Mary set up a glass of clear water and summoned Ahab, who informed her that the Duke's servants had arrived at a strategic position close by the woods and that Rumbonium, the evil co-guardian of the treasure, had departed on schedule, leaving the site entirely to Bromka, the good spirit. At six o'clock, therefore, the partners might safely enter the pit and collect their treasure.

But when they came within a few feet of the site, Mary stopped suddenly, obviously startled. 'O Lord,' she said, 'what is that just at the brink of the pit?' Goodwin and Wildman, who could see nothing unusual, stopped also. 'I see something like a fiery dragon,' Mary added, 'and [it] looks as if it would devour me.'

Then Mary seemed to collect herself. 'I fear it not,' she said, 'and if it please God, I will do my business.'

Once more she began to move forward, but Goodwin caught hold of her. By this time he was accustomed to being unable to see the things that Mary saw, and he had learned much about invisible danger. He would not allow her to advance another step until she had again consulted Ahab. It would be foolhardy, he knew, to proceed further without better information.

So Mary recalled Ahab, who explained that the partners had

almost fallen into a devilish trap. The evil Rumbonium had indeed left the area, but he had cunningly arranged to substitute a worse spirit in his place. This spirit, named Accoron, was no ordinary depraved ex-human but a powerful devil, one of four that haunted the woods at Northend. He had concerted his plot with Rumbonium so skilfully that Ahab himself had suspected nothing until Accoron suddenly appeared as a dragon. And now if Mary went on, 'she might perhaps lose a limb, if not her life.'

In spite of Ahab's warning, Mary boldly declared that she would defy Accoron and brave any danger rather than accept defeat. Goodwin and Wildman were obliged to restrain her by force, telling her flatly that they would 'by no means' allow her to take such risks. Ultimately, cool reason prevailed. Goodwin dispatched George to dismiss the Duke of Lorraine's servants, and he asked Ahab to draw up a plan for exorcizing devils. Then retreating from the gloomy woods of Northend, he led Mary and Wildman back to the coach and conducted them to the safety of an inn at Henley.

At Henley, Ahab arrived with much information and an excellent plan. There were indeed four devils at Northend woods (he explained): Rumbonium, Accoron, Rismin, and Osmindor; and the last of these, Osmindor, ranked third after Satan in the hierarchy of devils. In addition, at the four trees in Hounslow there were three devils: Gabetius, Hyadromicon, and Belsacanom. These three, mixed in with the eight lost souls of ordinary men, had no doubt impeded the partners' efforts to gather the treasure there. Luckily, however, there was an infallible method of exorcizing devils—of banishing them forever from any place and confining them in hell where they belonged.

The method, Ahab explained, was simple. Calling by name the devil to be banished, the exorcist three times circled the devil's dwelling place, commanding him 'in the name of the great God Jehovah and by all the powers of heaven forthwith to depart and be thrown forever into Gaharell (which is hell)'. This ritual, performed at the proper time with 'strong faith', would exorcize any devil, no matter how powerful. And there was a similar method of dealing with the evil spirits of men—spirits not yet sentenced to final damnation. Here, since Christian charity demanded that the spirit should not be sent to hell but only banished temporarily from the area it haunted, the ritual specified a time and place of banishment.

The proper time to banish the devils at Northend, Ahab continued, was on a Friday afternoon at two o'clock (Mercury's hour), and the time to banish the devils and evil spirits at the four trees was on Saturday at 4 p.m. Ahab strongly advised that the partners should return to Northend on the following Friday (1 August) and then proceed the next day to the four trees at Hounslow. In a single weekend they could exorcize all four of the devils at Northend and two of the three devils at the four trees, thus laying the groundwork for a successful summer campaign.

Following Ahab's strategy, Goodwin, Mary, and Wildman reached Northend well before the appointed hour. Although Mary complained of feeling ill, she bravely traversed the rough and hilly terrain between their coach and the treasure site. Then at two o'clock, led by Goodwin, the partners performed the rituals of exorcism. Circling the pit three times and calling the four devils by name, they banished Rumbonium, Accoron, Rismin, and Osmindor to hell. Goodwin heard 'a terrible humming noise' as Rumbonium departed, but Accoron, Rismin, and Osmindor, for all their power and malice, left the woods without so much as a sound. Within minutes the partners had rid Northend of four devils who had infested the place for years. And they did not stop with banishing devils; while they were about it, they also exorcized 'all other evil spirits whatever from the woods', clearing the whole area of evil influences and removing all impediments to collecting treasure. Although the gruelling hike back to the coach exhausted the 61-year-old Wildman and almost caused Mary to miscarry (as she secretly confided to Goodwin), the little band of exorcists drove back to Henley in triumph.

Next day, the partners pushed on to Hounslow to banish Hyadromicon and Belsacanom from the four trees. Goodwin performed the rituals with such strong faith that both devils fled before he had finished circling their lair. Belsacanom left without protest, but as Hyadromicon passed by John Wildman, Wildman heard something 'whizz by his ear and hum with a great noise'—a sound which both 'frighted' and 'confirmed him' in the seriousness and reality of the enterprise. The exorcism provided a fitting climax to a weekend of great work. As the partners returned to Henley, they could congratulate themselves upon having banished six major devils in two days. Only Gabetius and a few evil spirits remained at Hounslow; and at Northend Bromka guarded his treasure alone with no diabolic interference.

On Monday, 4 August, the partners, completely rested and fit for hiking, were again at Northend and again provided with servants by the Duke of Lorraine. At the treasure site, Mary knelt down confidently, greeted Bromka, and asked him to put forth the gold and silver. But after thanking her for banishing the devils and removing his 'troublesome guests', Bromka sorrowfully explained that she had arrived 'half an hour too late' to collect his treasure. Nevertheless, he added quickly, he could offer splendid compensations: 'I will show you', he said, 'where a great deal more treasure is in this wood than mine is, which you shall have.'

Following Bromka and followed in turn by Goodwin and Wildman, Mary set off to find the new site, about a half a mile from Bromka's pit. When she knelt down and put her ear to the ground, the attendant spirit of the new hoard, a Jew named Ruben Pen Dennis, promptly hailed her as the 'Lady of the Woods' and promised that next week at six in the afternoon he would deliver up his treasure. (This treasure, as Ahab later explained, consisted of £27,000 in gold and the priceless biblical seer stones, the Urim and Thummim, which Pen Dennis and his good friend Hezekiah had rescued from Vespasian's sack of Jerusalem and brought to Northend for safekeeping.)

After relaying the messages of Pen Dennis to her partners, Mary followed Bromka to another site nearby, kept by the spirit of Hezekiah. As the partners approached the place, a pit gouged into a bank, they heard the spirit say aloud, almost in Wildman's ear: 'Here it is.' Wildman was 'mightily pleased' at hearing Hezekiah speak and at learning that his treasure amounted to £41,000 in gold—a sum much greater than Bromka's hoard, which amounted to a mere £11,000. Although for the present the partners were compelled to dismiss the Duke's servants once again and return to the coach empty handed, the new discoveries inspired 'great hopes'; and they retired to London in good order.

In London, between expeditions, Mary was occupied with a
new project. During the latter part of July, she had remembered
a way, described in her book, of making magic purses; and with
the help of Uriel, she set about making three of these—one for
herself, one for Goodwin, and one for Wildman. Properly
constructed and blessed, a magic purse generated money,
producing each week the sum requested by the owner and
granted by the angels. In making her own purse, Mary at first
asked for only three and a half crowns per week—a sum the
angels declared inadequate and raised to ten guineas a week. For
John Wildman Mary recommended ten guineas, and for
Goodwin she requested the opulent sum of a hundred pounds a
week. These requests were soon granted in principle, though
there remained several steps in procedure before the purses
could become fully operative.

Although important to long-range plans, the magic purses
were trivial compared with the immediate prospects of treasure
at Northend and Goodwin's marriage to the Queen, now
rescheduled for 12 August. As the partners set out from London
on Saturday, 9 August, they hoped to achieve both of these
major goals in a single expedition. They felt particularly certain
about the treasure at Northend, since a day or two earlier Ruben
Pen Dennis had appeared to Mary at Vere Street and promised
faithfully to deliver up his treasure, including the Urim and
Thummim, when the partners appeared at his site.[4]

The expedition began on a note of triumph. On their way to
Northend the partners stopped at Hounslow to exorcize the
devil Gabetius. As they approached the four trees, Mary saw
something 'like a black great dog grinning at her'—an apparition
she instantly recognized as Gabetius, who believed himself much
too powerful and firmly rooted to be displaced. But Mary was
completely unafraid of his 'great huffs', and at four o'clock he
was sent, 'in spite of his teeth', to join his fellow devils in hell.

With Gabetius disposed of, the partners headed towards
Northend and a series of agonizing mischances. Fearing that
they had been seen too often on the road between Watlington
and Northend, where an elegant coach was a prodigy, they
decided to abandon the long, easy route through Oxfordshire
and take the shorter, rougher route through Marlow and
Turville. This decision proved disastrous. Trouble began even

before the partners reached Turville, where they were obliged to rest their 'harassed' horses for two or three hours. Thereafter, through a long afternoon in the 'dreadful wood' between Turville and Northend, they found themselves struggling with too-narrow roads, tree stumps, and branches—ending up finally, after a long detour and a mistaken short cut, in a lane so overgrown that 'it almost tore the coach to pieces'. Then, as the last of their precious time leaked away, they abandoned their coach and hurried off on foot to the site guarded by Ruben Pen Dennis.

After Mary knelt down and consulted the spirit, she gave her partners a cruelly disappointing message. They had arrived just fifteen minutes too late. Though grieved, Pen Dennis could not give them his gold. Goodwin did not accept this bitter news without a struggle. Later he would see that the intricate pattern of accidents was the work of Providence, but for the moment he felt only outrage. He could not recall precisely why a good spirit, unimpeded by devils, should not deliver up a treasure at any time, nor why a delay of fifteen minutes should be fatal to 'a great and weighty matter'. He was anxiously aware too that John Wildman had received nothing for all the money he had invested. In the jumble of such feelings, Goodwin was disposed to quarrel. He told Pen Dennis, 'a little roughly', that he did not believe the message, which seemed a mere excuse for not handing over the treasure.

Pen Dennis had the 'modesty and goodness' not to resent Goodwin's outburst. After expressing his sorrow for the misfortune, he allowed Goodwin time to regain control of his temper. This difficult task, after a sharp internal struggle, Goodwin accomplished. Having 'recollected' himself, he apologized to Pen Dennis and humbly acknowledged his own error. He had relied, he now saw, upon human calculation and foresight, and God had given him a demonstration of 'how vain the wit of man is.'

After the repulse at Northend, the partners went to Colnbrook, where Goodwin was to meet the Queen's messengers. There, a few miles from the lowland gates, Mary and Goodwin tried to part with Wildman, who was supposed to take the coach and continue on to London. But Wildman did not want to go. He wished to stay with his partners and accompany them into the lowlands. This attitude, Goodwin felt, showed a deplorable distrust. Goodwin had promised faithfully that at an appropriate time he would bring Wildman into his lowland kingdom; but Wildman obviously suspected that once Goodwin had achieved wealth and power he would let his partners 'sink like a millstone in the sea'. Wildman could hardly be persuaded that for the moment his presence could only complicate arrangements with the Queen.

After much argument Wildman reluctantly agreed to go. Before he left, however, he gave another sign of distrust and duplicity. Heretofore he had dealt with Mary through Goodwin. Officially, at least, he had treated Goodwin as the head of the organization and Mary as the trusty technical advisor. Now, in a manœuvre that Mary quickly reported to Goodwin, he attempted to deal with her directly. As he was leaving the inn at Colnbrook, he whispered to her 'that he would give a hundred pounds for half an hour's talk with her'. Wildman's offer shocked and insulted Goodwin. It could only mean that Wildman regarded Mary as the real head of operations and that he was prepared to consult her behind Goodwin's back. At the very least it was treachery that wronged Goodwin and 'offended God'.

While Goodwin was absorbing this lesson on the duplicity of false friends, he also received a lesson on the feather-brained wilfulness of the Queen. She would not meet him as promised, he learned; she was hurrying off instead to Moorfields to watch the lying in of a noble lady—a relative of the Duke of Hungary, ruler of the Moorfields colony. She was anxious, she said, to see a woman in labour—a comparatively rare event in the lowlands.

Naturally the Queen's folly brought complications. The labour proved longer than expected, and the Queen fatigued herself with watching. Then she decided to remain at Moorfields an additional eight days, until the child, a little boy, was circumcised. Finally, she attended the circumcision, became ill at the sight of blood, and brought on another of her untimely menstrual periods. As a result, then, of what was essentially a whim, she succeeded in trapping herself in Moorfields throughout the rest of August.

Along with his personal frustration, Goodwin felt a strong concern for the Queen's safety. He suspected that the Duke of

Hungary, who was heir presumptive to the lowland throne and obviously eager to prevent a marriage between the Queen and Goodwin, had lured the Queen to Moorfields for some sinister purpose; he might, in fact, be plotting to murder her. Yet the Queen could not be brought to see the potential danger, and without concrete evidence Goodwin could only fret and fume.

Meanwhile at Hounslow, where he waited vainly for the Queen's return, his soft heart prevented him from retrieving the small treasure at Nicholson's house. When he had first rented the house, in June, he had learned that the spirit of Nicholson had become loath to part with the treasure. Now in August, at the proper astrological hour (with the moon in Capricorn), when Goodwin arrived at the site with a mattock, he 'heard such a groaning' from Nicholson's spirit, obviously in 'an intolerable torment', that in an unparalleled example of charity towards a misguided soul he left the treasure undisturbed.

With the evil spirits at the four trees Goodwin was not so tender. On the evening of Saturday, 16 August, with Mary and John Wildman, he went to the treasure site to exorcize the eight evil spirits that remained after the banishment of the three major devils. Repeating the ritual eight separate times, he drove the spirits one by one from their old home and confined them for six months in Windsor Forest. These spirits—Samuel Storton, Richard Barnely, Ralph Sharpe, Thomas Phelps, John Carmell, Ann Carmell, Thomas Owen, and Fondon Barwick Jacobs—departed from the four trees without a sound; and the site was finally left to its five good spirits—William Spensely, Ann Spensely, John Abram Trevers, Robert Jackson, and Ralph Chivens.

Although completely exorcized, the evil spirits were still capable of revenge. In leaving the four trees, they had 'bound' the treasure under a spell that could not be removed in less than three separate expeditions. For the present, however, the partners were unaware of this obstacle. As they returned to London, they took comfort in the fact that their triumphs in exorcism had allowed them to salvage something important out of what had been, in general, a series of disasters.

There were other disappointments to come. Goodwin soon learned that the next expedition to Northend would be postponed for several weeks while Bromka, Hezekiah, and

Ruben Pen Dennis were involved with religious celebrations. He also learned that the Queen had again reversed herself on the subject of her oath and that she would not allow him to see Father Friar—the lowlander most useful to his projects. She did, however, give Father Friar permission to consecrate the late King's magic pea for Goodwin's benefit, and about 20 August, the old lowlander (unseen by Goodwin) reported to Mary at Vere Street and set about the project.

The consecration of the magic pea depended ultimately upon the power of prayer. The pea was placed, to begin with, on one edge of a clean, folded napkin, which in turn was placed upon a table. Then, through the prayers of Father Friar, the pea moved, 'of itself', across the napkin. This movement occurred 'by degrees' or jumps rather than by smooth increments, and it took place in the night following Father Friar's prayers, not during the prayers themselves. At the end of the process, which required about ten days, the pea, having traversed the napkin, was to fall off onto the table, thus signifying that the consecration was complete.

Goodwin observed that as a result of the first day's work the pea had moved more than an inch and a half and that it had left a deep 'dint' in the napkin at the place where it had lain. On subsequent days, the pea made steady progress across the napkin, leaving behind a vivid train of dints. Father Friar, a veteran in such matters, told Mary that the pea 'had moved most wonderful well and he doubted not that it would be the finest pea . . . in the world'. And as the pea moved inexorably to the very 'brink' of the napkin, Goodwin could see for himself that all was well—that one more day and the taking of Communion would suffice to finish the consecration.

And yet as the work went forward Goodwin became increasingly worried about Father Friar's health. The poor old man had grown subject to migraines and fainting spells. One day indeed he fainted at Hammersmith, on the way from Hounslow, and was compelled to return home. Such symptoms, Goodwin concluded rightly, were ominous; and when Father Friar failed to arrive on the final day of consecration, the partners were hardly surprised to learn that he had fallen desperately ill and that he was summoning his daughter to his bedside. It was all too evident that the wise old gentleman, 'a man of worthy principles and of great sincerity', was going to die, and that his death would end the project of the consecrated pea, as well as all serious work in alchemy. And so it proved. About 31 August, after two days of illness, Father Friar died, leaving all the lowlands in mourning.

Fortunately, the magic pea, though invaluable, was only one charm among many. In early September, Ahab, who had once furnished Goodwin with a potent inscription against gunshot wounds, provided him with a whole series of quasi-divine formulas, including charms against gout, plague, witchcraft, thieves, vomiting, poisoning, kidney stone, fires, and explosions. Ahab also provided Goodwin with a charm for walking 'dry' upon water, a charm which Goodwin never found proper occasion to use. More importantly, Ahab promised that he would soon make Goodwin a priest and a prophet. These blessed offices carried with them, of course, the power to consecrate; they would enable Goodwin to take up the work left unfinished by Father Friar.

At Moorfields, the Queen began to reap the fruits of her folly. As she prepared to leave, the Duke of Hungary contrived to poison her with a dish of chocolate. Totally unsuspicious, the Queen would have died if she had not sent an account of her illness to Goodwin, who quickly diagnosed the trouble and sent her a mixture of viper wine and saffron, along with a poultice made from bryony roots, black soap, and salt. This antidote (recommended by Mary and Ahab) arrived in time to save the Queen's life, though not in time to prevent a long illness.

To guard the Queen against further treachery, Goodwin first sent for the Duke of Lorraine, who came to Moorfields with a band of armed retainers and arrested the Duke of Hungary. Goodwin then warned the Duke of Lorraine against a secondary plot worthy of Guy Fawkes. The Duke of Hungary had mined all four entrances to the Queen's palace with barrels of gunpowder and had instructed the sappers at each mine to explode their charges if the Queen attempted to leave. Forewarned, the Duke of Lorraine and his men surprised and overpowered three of the four crews and conducted the Queen to safety.

Once again, Goodwin had saved the Queen from destruction, and now only an accident prevented him from entering

Moorfields and marrying her. When the Duke of Lorraine's men attempted to reach the sappers at the main entrance, they were discovered too soon. The sappers fired their train, destroying the only passage that led from Moorfields to the uplands and imprisoning the Queen and her party underground. It would be two months before lowland engineers could clear the entrance.

Shortly before she was irretrievably cut off from Goodwin, the Queen (in partial atonement for her mistakes) formally pronounced Goodwin king of the lowlanders, asserting that after King Byron's death Father Friar had secretly married her to Goodwin—an assertion true in intent though false in fact. She further declared that she had borne Goodwin a son named Peregrine, now the only 'lawful heir' to the throne. By this convenient fiction, she established the succession and conferred a vast favour on Goodwin and Mary, who were happy to allow their child to pass for the son of a queen.

Queen Penelope's pronouncements, promulgated in the latter part of September, were shortly followed by great spiritual events. Ahab, according to his promise, ordained Goodwin a priest and a prophet. In a simple ceremony, during which Ahab remained invisible (though Mary saw him lay his hands on Goodwin's head), he conferred upon Goodwin the powers of healing, casting out devils, and consecration; and a few days later he conferred the powers of prophecy.

Goodwin's new powers came at a time when he was again desperate for money. The summer campaign, though unique in the annals of exorcism, had left him penniless, and his only live project was the spirit treasure at Northend. Accordingly, as soon as the Queen was out of danger and Pen Dennis, Bromka, and Hezekiah were finished with their religious observances, he organized another expedition. This venture Wildman agreed to subsidize, and he further agreed to reward the Duke of Lorraine's servants, who had been summoned three times to Northend, only to be sent back unemployed.

This time the pattern for the expedition was slightly varied. Since Wildman was obliged to visit his home in Berkshire shortly before the crucial date (22 September), and since there was no reason for returning to town, he arranged to meet his partners at Northend. Before leaving London, Wildman gave Goodwin enough money to finance the operation, including fifty guineas in gold for the Duke of Lorraine's servants. This sum (over £1,000 in modern currency) Goodwin considered no more than adequate; the partners, he felt, could not gracefully do less. Wildman, of course, thought the sum munificent. It was more than he would contribute to Monmouth's Rebellion or to the Glorious Revolution. It was a solid demonstration of his faith in Goodwin's projects and a handsome gratuity for deserving lowlanders.

As events turned out, Wildman's guineas never reached the Duke's retainers. They served instead to keep Goodwin from a long term in gaol. Wildman had barely left for Berkshire when two of Goodwin's creditors had him seized by bailiffs and carried off to prison. There he remained for four days, while his plans for Northend evaporated. Then, using Wildman's gold—more money than he had had in hand for 'some years'—he got bail for one of his debts and appeased his other creditor with a down payment of twenty guineas. At last, after a distressing period, he was free. Though deeply humiliated by the experience, he could see that he had been rescued 'by God's singular providence'. He could also reflect that with his new powers as priest, prophet, and king, he would never suffer such indignities again.

8

Crime and Punishment

LIKE a resourceful general after a bitter defeat, Goodwin reorganized his forces and prepared another campaign. His first precaution, on getting out of gaol, was to see that he was not arrested again. This strategy involved another negotiation with Lord Wharton, who finally agreed to pay one of Goodwin's larger debts.[1] It also involved moving from the house on Vere Street (now known to Goodwin's creditors) to 'more convenient' lodgings in another neighbourhood.[2] This time Goodwin did not bother to pretend that he and Mary occupied separate quarters; he simply moved himself and Mary into the new lodgings and arranged their belongings in the fashion best suited for the reception of angels. In particular, he set up in Mary's room a simple altar, where he could perform rituals and receive heavenly visitations.

All of Goodwin's immediate hopes now centered on the angels. With the Queen entrapped at Moorfields, with the treasure at the four trees 'bound' for several months, and with the operations at Northend suspended for the winter, Goodwin concentrated upon the powers the angels conferred and the projects they controlled. And in early October, he achieved a triumph of the first magnitude: direct communication. After months of trying to hear or see an angel, he began to hear the voices of the great archangels Gabriel and Michael. Michael, he observed, 'had a great manly deep voice' and Gabriel 'a high thin one'. Ordinarily, the angel voices were clearly audible to Goodwin as he knelt by his new altar; but sometimes he could not distinctly understand what the angels said and was obliged to ask Ahab, through Mary, to repeat the messages.

Aided by direct communications, the archangels confirmed the priestly and prophetic powers that Ahab had bestowed upon Goodwin. Throughout October, in a series of dramatic pronouncements, Goodwin was established in new prerogatives, and on 5 November he awoke to find himself officially anointed priest, prophet, and king. He was promised also that he should have everlasting faith, be greater than any king or prophet except Christ, and that he should see the Lord in glory. There were also physical signs of special grace. One morning 'before it was well light', Goodwin saw the canopy of his bed 'all covered as a sun with her beams playing about'. These marvellous flashes of light, which reappeared often in subsequent months, were manifestations (Ahab said) of 'the Lord's glory'.

Deeply grateful for his spiritual blessings, Goodwin tried not to be dismayed by his temporal failures. As the well-raised son of a staunch Puritan family,[3] he knew perfectly well that the riches of this world are empty vanities; and with the example of Job always before him, he also knew that the faithful are often severely tried. And yet, he found some of his failures difficult to bear. Particularly annoying was his inability to acquire usable magic peas for himself and his partners. Early in October after receiving permission from the angels to use his new priestly powers of consecration, he placed three peas on the edge of a napkin, repeated the appropriate prayers, and watched with satisfaction as the peas marched, day after day, towards the opposite edge. When at last they toppled off the napkin onto the table (the sign of completion), he took Holy Communion, the final step in the process. But although the angels declared the consecration valid and told him that his own pea would render him invisible to lowlanders as well as uplanders, he was strictly forbidden to put it to the test. He was ordered instead to wrap all the peas up carefully and put them away until further orders.[4]

He was similarly depressed about the magic purses, which could never be brought to function properly. Week after week, Wildman's purse and his own remained empty, and promised dates of completion were postponed. Mary's purse, on the other hand, was filled rapidly; it grew so heavy, in fact, that it wore a callous on her hip. But except for a few shillings which she was allowed to withdraw in the early stages of the operation, she was not permitted to use her money. As Goodwin ruefully observed, the partners 'lay in want in the midst of plenty'.

In late October, he received an explanation for his failures and for the broken promises of the angels. He was being tested, Gabriel said, more rigorously than ever before; the Lord, who had earlier tried his heart, was now trying his 'heart and reins'. If he remained faithful, the Lord would soon send him a covenant as a sign that all promises were 'certain and sure' and that all his affairs would prosper. To Goodwin it was not quite clear why God's promises needed to be reinforced with a covenant, but he did not presume to dispute the matter with Gabriel.

Meanwhile there were important family matters that needed attention. Goodwin was forced to invent a fiction that would explain Mary to Lord Wharton, who was beginning to hear gossip about his son and a middle-aged woman companion. A sure instinct warned Goodwin against telling his father the truth; Lord Wharton, he knew, would not be able 'to receive it'. He constructed, therefore, a plausible half-truth that exploited his father's desires to have him solvent and married. Mary, he said, was an expert matchmaker who was helping him arrange a marriage with a woman of 'great fortune'—a woman who insisted that her identity should be concealed until all details were settled.

This story Goodwin told with a relatively clear conscience, since Mary was indeed helping him to a rich marriage with the Queen of the lowlanders. Lord Wharton, unfortunately, showed little enthusiasm for the explanation. He questioned Goodwin many times about progress and often seemed dissatisfied that Goodwin would not name his fiancée. Nevertheless, he appeared to accept the main outlines of the story, and eventually, to Goodwin's relief, he became 'pretty quiet'.

Throughout the autumn and winter of 1684 Mary remained pregnant with the children she had conceived in May and June—a girl and three boys. In late November, her pregnancy, already extraordinary, was miraculously augmented by the conception of a fifth child. And in mid-January, when she feared that her multiple pregnancy was becoming noticeable, she was informed that through a 'wonderful work of the Lord' all five children had been reduced in size, without injury to the children or danger to the ultimate delivery. Goodwin noted thankfully that Mary seemed smaller in January than she had been in December and that she did not again become suspiciously large.

Goodwin's success with his unborn children was counter-balanced by his misfortunes in attempting to visit his son

Peregrine. During the busy summer of 1684, he had not tried to see the boy, but when he led his little troop into winter quarters, he began to take active measures. He knew, of course, that he must not be seen by the child's nurse—who would have recognized him at once as the boy's father. He knew also that the nurse frequently took the little boy out of town, to 'great houses of her acquaintance'. But both of these difficulties seemed trivial. It should be an easy matter, he reasoned, to have Mary pick up the child from its nurse and bring it to a private room in a nearby tavern. As the child's mother, Mary obviously had a right to take it anywhere she chose. Seeing Peregrine, he concluded, should be simply a matter of setting up an appointment while the nurse was in town.

Goodwin's simple plan proved unworkable. Somehow appointments could never be kept. Sometimes the child was 'abroad'; sometimes he was 'undressed'; sometimes his clothes were being washed; and sometimes he was suffering from a minor injury. At last Goodwin perceived that he was combating God's will; his failure, he saw, was not a matter of chance but of 'God's providence ordering it so', and he would not attempt to see Peregrine again until the Lord appointed a meeting. Meantime, without presuming to guess the Lord's reasons, he would go on sending money for the boy's support, comforting himself with the fact that Peregrine (already heir apparent to the lowland throne) was getting the best possible care.

By 1 December, the winter campaign, full of marvels and frustrations, was moving towards another crisis. Goodwin had many reasons to rejoice. He had often spoken with archangels; he had beheld many signs and portents; he had received vast spiritual powers. Perhaps most important, he had finally received the Lord's Covenant. This instrument, which was to guarantee the fulfilment of all God's promises, turned out to be an elegant scroll, beautifully ornamented, and inscribed with a copy of the Ten Commandments—written (Ahab said) by an angel.

And yet, in spite of such blessings, Goodwin found himself in doubt and confusion. The Covenant, he soon learned, could not end his troubles as he had been led to believe. It was only the First Covenant, and it could not take effect until the 'Second Covenant' was delivered. Goodwin could not help wondering why one covenant should not be enough; and a dismal intuition told him that another set of delays was stretching out before him. Even when the angels positively promised that the Second Covenant would be delivered on 7 December, he could not be entirely cheerful.

Goodwin was also troubled by a technical detail—an oddity that grew more worrisome as the weeks went by. From the very first, he had noticed that the voices of Gabriel and Michael had come from somewhere behind him as he knelt at the altar. He observed too that they seemed to come from Mary's direction, no matter where she might be kneeling or sitting. Neither voice, Goodwin noted, resembled Mary's 'ordinary voice', but every time one of the angels spoke, 'the voice came as if it were from her.'

The possibility that Mary was producing the voices—that she was carrying on a complicated hoax—was too hideous to contemplate. Other explanations leaped to Goodwin's mind. It was possible that the angels chose to speak through her, using her body much as evil spirits use the bodies 'of those they possess'. This theory would explain why he could sometimes see her lips move while the angels spoke. Or again, it was possible that while she was 'abroad' the angels told her what to say and ordered her to relay their messages in a vivid and dramatic way.

These explanations, though plausible, could not satisfy Goodwin completely. Although Mary had proved her honesty many times, he found a suspicion 'hatching and growing' inside him. He could not suspect that he had been duped in the general course of his operations, but he could suspect that he was being deceived in this particular matter. Once entertained, the suspicion was so poisonous that he could not mention it to Mary. Instead of questioning her, as usual, he allowed his melancholy humour to fester.

The crisis finally came on 7 December, while Goodwin was awaiting the delivery of the Second Covenant. Following orders, he had lit a bright fire and arranged seven candles for his angel guests, but as he knelt before the altar, the rhythm seemed wrong. Gabriel's coming was delayed beyond the appointed hour, and when he did come he seemed more disposed to talk than to produce a covenant. By the time Gabriel had spoken two or three times, Goodwin concluded, with disgust, that some further delay would be announced.

Meantime, he was watching Mary carefully. Whenever he heard Gabriel's voice, he turned his head to get a clear view of Mary, who was kneeling only two or three feet away. In the light of the candles he could see her lips moving in what seemed to be perfect synchronization with Gabriel's words. The sight proved too much for his self-control. At last, turning completely towards Mary just as her lips quit moving and Gabriel's voice died away, he let his suspicions burst forth.

'It was you who spoke to me now,' he said.

For a few moments Mary said nothing. Goodwin was left with the sound of his own voice ringing in his ears. Then, in a 'wondering' tone, she said, 'That's strange.'

Again there was a blank silence, this time not so long.

'So, now we are ruined,' Mary said.

The ominous words and the thought of his own rashness shook Goodwin. He waited for Mary to explain.

Gabriel was gone, Mary informed him, and he had said in leaving that 'he would come again seven years hence.'

In the dreadful silence that followed, Goodwin realized that he had made another unforgivable mistake—that he had yielded to folly and to 'the suggestion of the Devil'. Now, he perceived, all his hopes and projects were 'squashed'. This sense of guilt was deepened when he told Mary the cause of his outburst—that he had seen her lips moving. The explanation, he learned, was childishly simple. He had been misled by her piety and prayers. During the visitations of the angels, she conceded frankly, 'her lips indeed might go, for she was generally in prayer to herself.' Certainly on this occasion, during Gabriel's visit, she had been praying earnestly.

Once the mystery was explained, Goodwin recalled that during his conversation with the angels, Mary's hands had been devoutly joined, and he could see how grossly he had wronged her. For her part, Mary could not explain why the angel voices seemed to come from her direction; this fact baffled her as much as it did Goodwin. Still less could she account for Goodwin's fancy that her lips moved 'exactly at the very time' of Gabriel's words. These lesser mysteries were cleared up by Ahab two or three weeks later, after Goodwin's faith, completely restored, had made him 'unbelief proof'. Paraphrasing the Bible, Ahab pointed out that 'the spirit moves where it lists' and that angelic voices may come from anywhere. Appearing to come from Mary, they might serve to test Goodwin's faith, and in the future they would also remind him of his sin.

In view of Goodwin's sincere repentance, both Mary and Gabriel soon forgave him for his folly, but the effects of his crime lingered for many weeks. The delivery of the Second Covenant was delayed, and all his projects remained in suspense. His temporal affairs were so desperate, in fact, that he seldom ventured outside in the daytime; he remained within, hiding from bailiffs, while Mary conducted the business of the partnership abroad.

These misfortunes, which made the partners edgy and quarrelsome, soon tempted Mary towards a crime even more heinous than Goodwin's. One evening after an argument, Goodwin went into Mary's bedroom just in time to prevent her from stabbing herself. She had set the handle of a dagger against her bed and was in the act of 'thrusting her body' upon the blade when he rushed to her side and struck the weapon to the floor. She had chosen to die rather than live 'in such miseries'.

Unlike Goodwin's punishment for mistrust, which was lingering and subtle, Mary's punishment for attempted suicide was short and brutal. For three days she was marched to and fro about the London area—from the Neat Houses to Aldgate, from St. James's to Islington, from Tothill Fields[5] to the Pinner of Wakefield—without mercy for her bruised and swollen feet or her lamentable moans. Returning each night 'almost like a dead woman', she was harried forth the next day for further torture and for spiritual torments that 'thoroughly pierced' her soul. The angels had promised to make her weary of the life she had tried to take away violently, and that promise they punctually kept.

When Mary was pardoned, after three bitter days, there remained only one major worry. During her penance, she had been told by the angels that Charles II 'had not long to live'. She was ordered, therefore, to go to see the King, to tell him frankly of his faults, 'bid him amend his life', and warn him 'to repent and prepare for death'. Naturally, Mary was frightened at the prospect of appearing before Charles and delivering the angels' message. Goodwin was apprehensive too. 'Knowing the King's temper', he could not help fearing 'ill consequences'. Even in a good mood Charles would not be overjoyed to be told of his sins, and in a bad mood he might very well send God's messenger to gaol for impertinence and seditious libel. Goodwin thought Mary justified in begging to be excused from the task. Nevertheless, he did not wish to dispute the Lord's commands. If absolutely ordered to appear before the King, Mary must go; and if Mary could not muster enough courage, Goodwin would go himself, though his own danger in such an assignment would be much greater than Mary's.

In the end, the angels excused Mary from delivering the message; and Charles, who had less than two months left to live, was allowed to amble on towards death without any special preparation.[6] Goodwin was relieved, of course, to be excused from a dangerous task, but he learned later that Mary had been 'too refractory' and that several projects would be postponed because she had been derelict in her duty.

Before King Charles died, as prophesied, Goodwin and Mary were compelled to move again—this time to a flat on Long Acre Street, where they installed themselves on 12 January 1685. Here Goodwin entered a new phase of his spiritual development. Informed that his sin of mistrust had been completely expiated, he began to receive visible and tangible signs of God's favour. Almost daily throughout January and February, religious objects appeared upon his altar. These included, among other gifts, two three-dimensional scenes, picturing (Ahab said) the temple at Jerusalem; a hollow heart-shaped gem from which fresh blood sometimes issued; an elegant medal picturing Jesus, Mary, and St. John at the crucifixion; a tapered ivory rod made (Gabriel said) from 'a true unicorn's horn'; an ivory 'relic box' ornamented with a carved *pietà*; an elaborate seal, or signet, of coral set in gold and in the ivory from one of St. Joseph's teeth; and a great stick of 'fine' sealing wax to be used with the signet.

Unhappily, Goodwin's gifts did not include the Second Covenant, which would have guaranteed completion of his projects; and thus, although he 'was daily fed with the Lord's mercies', he continued to suffer agonies from his temporal misfortunes. And on 6 February 1685, he was dealt another fearsome blow. Shortly after noon, the disaster foretold by the angels came to pass. After an 'apoplexy' and four days of suffering, King Charles II died.[7]

Up until the end Goodwin had hoped to use his newly acquired powers of healing to rescue Charles from death, but he could not get Gabriel's permission. He would never be allowed near the royal bedchamber, Gabriel had declared, and in any case the King must die 'suddenly' as predicted. Goodwin was not surprised, therefore, though much dismayed, when Gabriel brought word to Long Acre that 'the King was dead, and had no breath nor sense'.

Most Englishmen shared Goodwin's distress at the death of Charles. Even Englishmen who deplored the King's pro-French policies and his taste in mistresses found him difficult to dislike, and in a crisis they preferred his cool and tolerant cynicism to the passion and self-serving rectitude of his opponents. In his later years, of course, the Whigs had opposed him fiercely, but they much preferred Charles to his papist brother James, whom they had tried desperately to exclude from the throne. To Whigs, the death of Charles meant that a persistent nightmare had become real. Their inveterate enemy was now King of England.

The death of Charles brought a special nightmare for Goodwin, as he hid from his creditors at Long Acre. He had villified James—now King James II—in Parliament, accusing him of dishonesty, treason, and stupidity. In vain Goodwin attempted to convince himself that his notorious speech had been a general attack upon corruption; the ugly suspicion that he was a marked man haunted his waking thoughts and sometimes worked its way into his dreams. To the certain knowledge that he was being sought by bailiffs was added the lively possibility that he was wanted by the King's officers.

Less anxiously and more scientifically, Goodwin was also concerned with King Charles's soul. Charles, the angels said, was at first a very uneasy spirit, unhappy about his dissolute life and sorry for the way he had mistreated Goodwin. Not long after Charles's death, rumours began to circulate about London that his spirit had been seen in several places.[8] Some of these rumours the angels confirmed. Charles was particularly active, they said, at the coronation of James (whom he distrusted). He cried 'Fire' in an audible voice, shook the royal canopy, and terrified one of the speakers by standing within arm's length and staring into the man's face.

Several times during the spring of 1685, Charles promised to appear to Goodwin, but Goodwin, who looked upon Charles as a likely candidate for damnation, did not take the promises seriously. A year and a half later, the King's spirit was allowed to perform a notable act of penance, Goodwin learned, and Charles was admitted to heaven after all. Much surprised, Goodwin sent congratulations by way of the angels. Charles, he said frankly, was now in a place where no one had ever expected to find him.[9]

Meanwhile, John Wildman continued to make Goodwin's life miserable. Understandably disappointed that the Northend journeys had been discontinued, that the magic pea and purses remained inoperative, and that new prospects at Holborn were unexploited, Wildman pressed constantly for the completion of at least one of the projects. He could not understand, he said, how promises given by angels could be broken or why God should put the partnership through so many excruciating tests.

Queen Penelope too gave Goodwin constant trouble. In November 1684 the lowland engineers finally succeeded in tunneling their way out of Moorfields; by December the damage wrought by the Duke of Hungary's land mines had been repaired, and the way was clear for the Queen to bring Goodwin into her domains. But week after week the Queen's delicate health and flighty disposition, along with a great deal of bad luck, continued to thwart Goodwin's attempts to establish himself upon the lowland throne. To make matters worse, the Queen failed to deliver the King's legacy or otherwise relieve Goodwin's financial distress. She likewise refused to let her sister Princess Ursula out of her genteel prison at Hounslow, where she had been held for more than a year.

Goodwin's misfortunes with Queen Penelope left him open, of course, to temptations from upland women; and in late February, Mary inadvertently furnished him with a seductive romantic interest. During her wanderings about London, Mary had formed a close acquaintance with an Irish gentlewoman and with the lady's niece, a certain Mrs Wilder. She often invited both women to the flat at Long Acre and to nearby taverns, where Goodwin had much opportunity to converse with Mrs Wilder and study her considerable charms.

Mrs Wilder, he observed, was 'graceful, handsome, and well bred', and her conversation was at once witty and sincere. She was also very unfortunate. She had been seduced by an Irish gentleman of 'great quality and estate', who had promised marriage but had basely deserted her when she became pregnant. Banished in disgrace from her father's house, she had taken refuge with an old priest at Wild House, a family friend, who now maintained her out of charity.

As Goodwin saw more of Mrs Wilder, it occurred to him that she was remarkably well suited for 'propagation' and that she might be induced to cooperate with him in a plan for producing children. Since neither he nor Mrs Wilder was married, there could be no question of adultery, which he could disdain as 'the worst of crimes'; nor were his motives tainted by a casual degrading lust. In such a situation, he was convinced, his plan of getting her with child was not only 'lawful' but laudable.

Goodwin was confident of his theology, but he did not proceed rashly. He prayed about the matter several times, begging the Lord to send him instructions, preferably through the voice of an angel. When he received no oral answer, he prayed for a non-verbal sign. The miraculous rod made of unicorn's horn was lying upon the altar at some distance from a letter which had been left there. He now asked that if his plan was approved the rod should be moved closer to the letter. The sign was not long in coming. One morning, he observed that the rod and the letter lay palpably nearer to one another. In studying the new configuration, he could not be sure whether the rod had moved or whether (as he rather suspected) the paper had moved; but he did not pause long over the ambiguity, which seemed more like a quibble than a problem. He now had a sign and was ready to proceed with his plan.

An opportunity presented itself when Mary was away from home. Mrs Wilder dropped in as usual, and Goodwin had no trouble in persuading her to cooperate in his scheme. She proved so cooperative, in fact, that she lay with him before he had fully explained all the details of his plan, including the sort of life he expected her to lead.

For a day or two, Goodwin was entirely satisfied with his

progress and with Mrs Wilder's talents for propagation. Then he began to worry. He thought he could detect in himself some symptoms of weakness and discomfort, conceivably the prelude to a venereal disease. When he confronted Mrs Wilder, however, she showed great surprise and dismay. She had been intimate, she said, with only 'one man in the world', and she had not seen him for many weeks. It was impossible that she had any other 'distemper' than 'that natural to women, of which she had not been then well long'.

Reassured, Goodwin immediately made love to Mrs Wilder again—only to find that his confidence had been hopelessly misplaced. Within a few more days, it became clear beyond doubt that he had not contracted a weakness but 'a real distemper', which not only attacked his 'blood and seed' but threatened to shatter the whole frame of his body. And now, besides his physical agony, he faced the problem of what to tell Mary and what to do about Mrs Wilder.

Planning to deal with Mrs Wilder first, Goodwin went to her lodgings to accuse her of treachery and tell her he would never see her again. There, unfortunately, he found Mary, who was sitting beside the bed conversing with Mrs Wilder. When she saw him at the door, she rose without a word and marched out into the street, obviously surprised and angry; and as Goodwin caught up with her, she told him to go back to his whore.

Goodwin realized that it would be folly to deny the facts, since Mary could learn everything from George or the angels. He could, however, plead in his own defence that he had acted upon a worthy plan and that he had received a sign of divine approval. Somehow these pleas, gently urged, seemed to increase Mary's sense of injury; she refused to listen to any more of what she obviously regarded as hypocritical nonsense, and she threatened several times to leave him and to expose their son Peregrine 'shamefully' to the world.

Though overwhelmed by Mary's rage, Goodwin was not convinced of his own guilt until a few days later when the angels explained the flaw in his reasoning. In the eyes of God, they said, he was married to Mary and to Queen Penelope, and he was required to remain strictly faithful to his 'two wives'. He was not free, as he had mistakenly supposed, to pursue other women, even though his intent to propagate children was entirely honourable.

Meanwhile, since he had sinned through ignorance, not lust, and since he had broken off the affair with the treacherous Mrs Wilder, Goodwin was forgiven both by the Lord and by Mary. He even found a blessing in his misfortune—God's official approval of his liaison with Mary. (In calling Mary Goodwin's 'wife', God had removed any doubt about the sanctity of the union.) Goodwin knew, nevertheless, that in a strict, technical sense, he had committed adultery and that he could not escape punishment.

Goodwin's physical punishment began immediately. His disease, virulent from the outset, soon proved to be unexampled; the 'very substance' of his body seemed to be melting away in abundant and strange discharges, and none of his own remedies, which included 'six or seven of the best sort of purges', taken daily, could abate the flow or 'give the least correction to the seed'. Even Mary's uncanny skill failed to halt the destruction. To Goodwin, 'almost raked away to nothing', it appeared that he was marked for death unless God intervened to save him.

Providentially, Mary escaped the infection, and this sign of mercy was followed by a gift from Gabriel—a divine formula, inscribed on paper, for the cure of Goodwin's disease. At the very sight of the paper, Goodwin could feel himself begin to mend. Sensible of the Lord's favour, he began to grow stronger and 'fatter'. He could not, indeed, conquer a certain amount of residual weakness which lasted for several months; but by the end of March, about a month after his original infection, he could give thanks for a signal demonstration of God's grace.

Goodwin's crime, unfortunately, could not be completely expiated by disease. On 14 March, Mary brought him a message from Uriel that God would take away all five of his unborn children. This punishment, Goodwin noted sadly, was particularly designed to fit his nature. Since children were what he loved 'most in the world', he was to be deprived of them; and since he had attempted to get children 'where they were not to be had', he was to lose the ones he had fathered legitimately.

Luckily, Goodwin began making significant progress in his temporal projects. On 13 March the long-promised Second Covenant was at last delivered. This Covenant—a heavy, square plate 'wrapped up and sealed in a piece of white paper'—was at present made of brass, the angels said, but it was to be taken away, turned into gold, and engraved by the finger of God. Removed again precisely on schedule, the Covenant was brought back, completed, on Sunday, 22 March. Goodwin was not yet permitted to open it, but he was allowed to leave it upon the altar, ready for unveiling the moment he received God's permission.

Goodwin was further heartened when the angels began giving Mary a guinea every week—a sum that she and Goodwin were permitted to spend. Granted to sustain the partners until their magic purses were perfected, the 'weekly guinea' was delivered to Mary at her flat or at St. Paul's, Covent Garden, every Thursday for ten weeks, beginning on 5 March. This money Goodwin found wonderfully comforting, both for its cash value and its symbolic worth. As the first gold he had ever received from his projects, it clearly augured a more prosperous future.

By the evening of 8 April, Goodwin needed all the comfort he could get. Mary's delivery, weeks overdue, could be postponed no longer; she must now deliver all five children, all marked for death, and Goodwin could get no firm guarantee that she would survive the delivery herself. He could not even get permission to accompany her to her midwife's house. He could only go as far as a tavern near their lodgings at Long Acre, and there she renewed her promise to appear to him after death and granted him the right to come to look for her if she had not returned home within a reasonable time. Then she trudged off into the dark.

After wrestling with his anxiety for perhaps an hour and a half, Goodwin set off to find her. At York Buildings (a street near Charing Cross), he eventually found the lodgings of one Mrs Martin, Mary's midwife. Mrs Martin, however, denied knowing anyone named Mary Parish; and Goodwin, 'in great trouble', was compelled to return home. There, after many tears and prayers, it occurred to him that there might be other midwives named Martin at York Buildings, or that Mary, intent upon secrecy, had given a false name. Once more he hurried down to York Buildings, determined to search the neighbourhood and to describe Mary fully to the midwife he had already seen. Again he was repulsed. Mrs Martin continued to deny any knowledge of Mary, and no one else in the area would admit having seen her. At last, almost ill with worry, he was forced to return to Long Acre.

To his great joy, he found her in bed—'extremely weak', of course, but obviously beyond any danger. The whole process of her delivery, Goodwin learned, had shown the special care of Providence. She had been easily delivered of all five children, who lived long enough to be christened and who were to be buried, 'by permission', in the churchyard of St. Martin's-in-the-Fields.[10] She had then set out for home in a sedan chair along St. Martin's Lane. At the junction of the Lane with Long Acre, she had left her chair and walked, 'wonderfully', up Long Acre, 'over a great kennel', into the house, and finally up the stairs to her bedroom. Even the timing of her return had been providential. The maid, already sent to bed, was safely out of the way so that she could not observe Mary's weakness. Goodwin was able to get everything necessary for Mary and to avert any suspicion of her true state, just as he had done the year before.

With the death of his five infant children, Goodwin's punishment came to an end. Perfectly reconciled with Mary and restored to God's favour, he could look forward again to the completion of his great works. The chastening he had received for his errors had left him humble, knowledgeable, and better able to resist temptation. Although he had paid dearly for the knowledge that he must not question the voices of angels or seduce women, the knowledge itself was invaluable.

9

Wildman's Rebellion

THE winter of 1684–85 had not been kind to John Wildman. With the death of Charles II, in early February, he had suffered a political misfortune almost as traumatic as Goodwin's. His enemy James II had succeeded to the throne without opposition; his Whig friends were scattered and powerless; and the prospects of old republicans, already dimmed by the Tory reaction, became even darker. Wildman's personal affairs were equally frustrating. Since the heady days of the previous summer when spirits had whizzed about his ears, he had encountered nothing but disappointment. His alchemical experiments had failed, and the trips to Northend had been continually postponed. He now had a consecrated pea that he was forbidden to use and a magic purse that could not be made to function. A year's work and the investment of two or three hundred pounds had so far yielded him three or four shillings. And when he complained of delays, he received lectures on his impatience.

In mid-February, Wildman suffered still another financial defeat. During the preceding autumn, Mary Parish had shown him a house in Holborn where a rich treasure lay concealed under a great stone in an entry between a shop and a kitchen. He had taken a lodging there, as advised, only to find that the entry was piled high with heavy chests and that the servants of the house seldom left the area unguarded. Persevering nevertheless, he at last succeeded in getting the entry cleared, and on 16 February he received permission from the angels to lift up the stone and take the treasure. When he prised up the slab, however, in the dead of night, he found nothing; the gold had vanished.

He soon learned from Goodwin and the angels that he had contributed to his own failure. He had often probed about the stone with a stick, thus alerting some evil spirits, who carried the gold away. Although he was promised that the spirits would be compelled to bring the treasure back, the damage turned out to be irretrievable. By the time the gold was returned, after several postponements, a combination of circumstances made its recovery impossible.

In the midst of his misfortunes, Wildman descried one glimmer of hope on the political front. From abroad he received word that the Earl of Argyll, exiled in Holland, was preparing a descent on Western Scotland, the stronghold of his formidable highland clan. Also in exile, Wildman knew, was the Duke of Monmouth, the illegitimate son of Charles II and once the idol of the Whig party. If he were to join fortunes with the Earl of Argyll, it was conceivable that James might be unseated before he could consolidate royal power. This possibility, Wildman thought, should be explored; at least he should send an agent to Holland to find out what Monmouth and Argyll were planning.[1]

As a veteran plotter, Wildman chose and instructed his agent—a man named Robert Cragg—through an intermediary. On the sound principle that an agent who has never met his employer can give only hearsay evidence against him, Wildman conducted all negotiations through Colonel William Disney, his cousin and political crony. It was Disney who met with Cragg, entrusted him with messages, told him where Whig agents were to be found, and sent him to Amsterdam about the end of February.[2]

Meanwhile, Wildman's partners found him unusually annoying. After his disappointment at Holborn, he became 'more excessively urgent than is imaginable' in demanding the completion of at least one project. He sometimes argued that broken promises could not come from God. 'The exercise of faith', he once said, 'was not to believe things against reason.' Goodwin was obliged to warn him against 'displeasing God' and to remind him that 'the whole course of Scripture' demonstrates that faith is superior to reason.

Finally, the angels intervened to soothe Wildman. On 8 March, they wrote him a letter and left it with his partners at Long Acre. The letter, subscribed 'This for thee: J:[ohn] W:[ildman]' and stamped with the holy seal, consisted of four lines of verse. It promised Wildman that he should 'surely see/The Great God in His Majesty' and warned him not to show himself ungrateful for God's mercy. Wildman was impressed by the writing itself; he was sure, he told Mary, that it was 'not the hand of any mortal'. And the message, which promised inestimable blessings, made complaints about financial difficulties seem infantile. For the moment Wildman was quieted.

But not for long. A few days later, his agent Cragg returned from Holland with the word that within a few weeks Monmouth would raise a rebellion in England while Argyll was invading Scotland. All the Duke needed, one of his fellow exiles had declared, was money for arms, ammunition, and ships; and he expected Wildman and a few other rich friends to raise it for him.[3] This message inspired Wildman with no enthusiasm at all. To exiles in Holland it might seem obvious that he should bet his life and fortune on Monmouth, but to Wildman himself it seemed merely stupid. Exiles might imagine a vast spontaneous uprising on behalf of the illegitimate Duke against the legitimate (though Catholic) King—a revolution that could be triggered by a few thousand pounds invested in ships and arms; but Wildman knew that without much careful recruiting of Whig gentry and grandees, the uprising had no chance of success and that even with such preparation, the venture was an unpromising gamble. He was willing to sound out his friends on the subject of financing a revolution, but he was unwilling to invest a penny of his own money.

Whether Wildman would have invested some of the Northend and Holborn treasure in the Monmouth conspiracy can never be known. In spite of his best efforts, he did not collect any treasure to invest. Similarly unrewarding were his preliminary consultations with his Whig friends, who were also loath to risk their money. There seemed a 'coldness and backwardness' among people in general and a reluctance to talk about a revolution. These conclusions Wildman transmitted through Disney to Cragg, who was to tell Monmouth that 'there was no likelihood of raising any money here [in London], especially in so short a time' and that he should 'not think of coming for England'.[4]

While Cragg journeyed abroad, Wildman had trouble getting the full attention of his partners. In the latter part of March, Goodwin, still fighting gonorrhea and negotiating for the all-important Second Covenant, could spare little time for such 'lesser concerns' as Northend and Holborn; while Mary (who had not yet delivered her quintuplets) was occupied with an exciting new project. On 16 March, she learned that great treasures lay hidden in St. James's Park and Leicester Fields. A few days later, she was promised that from 10 April she and Goodwin could collect thirty pounds every Friday at each of the caches; and twice in early April she took Goodwin to the sites themselves. Both places, he observed, were uncomfortably exposed to public view; the treasure at Leicester Fields lay 'in the open place' (near what is now the centre of Leicester Square), and the site at St. James's lay near the Mall. Nevertheless, Mary conversed with the attendant spirits, who told her that Goodwin would be allowed to collect the weekly allotments while she was recovering from childbirth. As a sign of good faith, the spirits at Leicester Fields scattered five shillings on the ground near their treasure site—a token that Goodwin received with satisfaction. To Goodwin's further satisfaction, Mary learned shortly afterwards that at Red Lion Fields there was still another rich and available treasure.

Meanwhile Robert Cragg returned from Amsterdam, bringing orders from Monmouth, who persisted in his invasion plans. Wildman and his friends were to send five or six thousand pounds immediately, and if they could not raise the cash themselves, they were to borrow it and guarantee the loan. These orders Wildman met with a flat refusal; he would neither send his own money nor guarantee loans. He complained instead of the mismangement of the enterprise. Not only were Monmouth's affairs being directed by misinformed exiles, but they were being launched without a declared goal. It 'looked like madness', Wildman declared, to ask men to risk their lives without telling them whether they were fighting for a republic or a new monarchy with an illegitimate Stuart as king.[5]

To reinforce his opinions, Wildman took the chance of instructing Cragg personally. Disguising himself in 'a great long coat', he met Cragg one very dark night in Lincoln's Inn Fields and (without giving his real name) talked for nearly a half hour, repeating his now familiar arguments. The exiles were ruining the Duke and their friends in England by their rash plans. Monmouth could not count on English support for his uprising; he would be much better advised to accompany Argyll on the expedition to Scotland.[6]

The advice that Monmouth should not invade England—the best advice that Monmouth ever received on any subject—was then reiterated by way of a second messenger, one John Jones. Shortly after Cragg left again for Holland, Disney sent Jones to Amsterdam to confirm Cragg's messages—to tell Monmouth that his friends 'would not by any means have him come for England'.[7]

Although too hard-headed to gamble money on Monmouth's cause, Wildman was willing to consult with Monmouth's agent Captain Edward Matthews (who identified himself with an 'indenture'—a serrated half-sheet of paper matching a half-sheet held by Wildman) and with Lord Delamere and Francis Charlton, Monmouth's trustworthy friends. Using the double-talk of conspiracy, he also continued to sound out possible sympathizers, including Gilbert Burnet; but he spoke 'in so remote a way' that no one could accuse him of 'treasonable discourse'.[8]

Wildman was similarly cautious in dealing with Goodwin. He had survived to the age of sixty-two by employing what a later generation would call the 'need-to-know' principle—confiding only in people who could be useful and giving them only as much information as they needed to carry out their assignments. Judged by these standards, Goodwin needed to know little. In the present state of his affairs, he had no influence among his old Whig friends, and less than no influence with his family. He was estranged from his brother Tom and barely tolerated by his father. There were, however, non-political ways in which Goodwin and Mary Parish might prove very helpful. In spite of all the delays, they might yet produce some of the treasure they had so often promised. Furthermore, they might learn from the angels what God thought of Monmouth's enterprise. And if they could not find out God's hidden purposes, they might at least advise their partner on his personal safety.

Without incriminating himself, therefore, or admitting that his interest was anything but general, Wildman asked his partners to solicit information from the angels. Through late March, however, and all of April, the angels seemed as cautious and evasive as Wildman himself. As early as 16 March, they left with Mary a letter about Wildman's 'business', but they did not give Wildman permission to read it. For a month and a half it lay on Mary's table, and finally, after being directed to Wildman at the wrong lodging, it vanished altogether.

In early May, Wildman received chilling information from Cragg, back from Holland: Argyll and his men had sailed for Western Scotland on 2 May; and Monmouth, undeterred by good advice, would sail for Western England shortly—perhaps within two weeks. The Duke had been furious at Wildman's refusal to send money (which he attributed to cowardice and chicane) and had declared that if Wildman would not fight for him, he would 'hang with him'.[9] He had then sent Wildman a batch of orders: he was to consult daily with his friends Colonel Henry Danvers and Matthew Mead and organize an uprising in London; he was to dispatch to the West 'five or six good horses' for the Duke's personal use; and he was to cooperate in setting up a printing press and two message centres for disseminating information and propaganda.[10]

The orders from Monmouth placed Wildman in a nerve-racking dilemma. It was one thing, he saw, to warn the half-wits in Holland to stay there, but it was another thing to refuse to help them when they insisted upon invading England. They included, after all, some of his old friends from the days of Shaftesbury, and some surviving remnants of the good old republican cause. Furthermore, there was always an outside chance that Monmouth would win. If this should happen, the personal fortunes of his henchmen would be made and the prospect of a republican form of government would brighten immeasurably. Monmouth might be wise enough to declare for a republic and to content himself with the office of chief magistrate; but even if he foolishly seized the Crown, the principle of monarchy would be gravely wounded. A bastard king of England would make the doctrines of divine right and 'legitimacy' doubly ridiculous. Balanced against these motives for helping Monmouth was the cold fact that the revolution stood little chance of succeeding; a man who engaged in it too deeply was probably committing suicide. In short, Wildman reasoned, he was much more apt to be hanged by his enemies than by his friends.

In resolving his dilemma, Wildman received no substantial help from the angels. Upon the vital matter of Monmouth's fate, the angels seemed unwilling, or unable, to make a pronounce-ment; and Mary (perhaps unaware of the urgency of the information) did not importune them in her usual manner.

During mid-May her time was taken up by more important affairs than the fate of Whig politicians. From the angels she learned that the Lord himself would soon appear to Goodwin and speak audibly—a miracle that would put all of Goodwin's projects on a new, sure footing. Immersed in planning for this overwhelming event, she had little interest to spare for the concerns of John Wildman.

Temporarily neglected by the angels and left to his own devices, Wildman prudently decided to hedge his bets. He would stay on the fringes of the revolution in case it should succeed, but he would remain as remote and unbetrayable as possible. One danger he was particularly anxious to avoid: he would not organize, command, or finance an insurrection in London. Mere carnal reason told him that he was too old for street fighting, that the 'consults' necessary to organize such an uprising would put his life in the hands of untrustworthy people, and that the process of buying arms would probably get him arrested. He would not appear at a London rising 'in person or purse'.[11]

On the other hand, Wildman was willing to keep in touch with Lord Delamere, who had been assigned to raise Cheshire for Monmouth.[12] Although the operation was hazardous, Delamere himself (Wildman reasoned, rightly) was a cool, courageous gentleman who would not betray his friends if the affair turned out badly. Wildman also professed himself willing to provide horses for Monmouth; he would arrange to have 'three or four led horses' meet the Duke in the West.[13] This modest gift (a hedge against unexpected victory) could help expiate his failure to provide real financial aid. The gesture, moreover, was safe. Horses, Wildman knew, were even more trustworthy than Lord Delamere.

On 18 May, word reached Whitehall that Argyll and his men had been seen in the Orkneys, and the English government sprang into action. Already alarmed by rumours of an Argyll-Monmouth invasion, King James's officers began to issue warrants and round up suspected collaborators. Naturally enough, one of their first acts was to order the arrest of John Wildman. Although they had not yet uncovered the Wildman-Disney-Cragg link to Monmouth nor the Wildman-Delamere connection, they were wise enough to know that they could not make a mistake by gaoling the most practiced plotter in the kingdom. On 19 May, therefore, the royal messengers were instructed to 'apprehend' Wildman, along with a dozen other likely suspects.[14]

But the King's messengers could not find Wildman. Warned somehow of the order for his arrest (or made cautious by the news from Scotland), he dropped quietly out of sight, leaving his pursuers to begin a search that would last for three months and produce absolutely nothing. He did not, however, vanish without a trace. His wife Lucy, his friend Colonel Disney, and his partners Goodwin and Mary were able to keep in touch with him.

Meanwhile, on Long Acre Street, 19 May produced an event of transcendent significance: Goodwin received his first audible revelation from God. This glorious episode was the culmination of many days of preparation. For several months Goodwin had glimpsed the strange flashes of light which marked 'the Lord's glory'. For several weeks, he had been promised, like Wildman, that he might soon behold 'the Great God in His Majesty'; and lately he had been led to hope that he might also hear God's voice. Of these great blessings, welcome at any time, Goodwin now stood in almost desperate need. Besides the frustrations at Northend and Holborn, there remained the continuous problem of the Second Covenant, which after two months was as closely wrapped and ineffectual as ever. There were also disappointments in the newest project, the promised treasures at St. James's Park and Leicester Fields. On Friday, 10 April, while Mary recovered from delivering her quintuplets, Goodwin went to both sites and made his presence known to the spirit guardians, but at neither place could he get the slightest response. In succeeding weeks, Mary herself failed to bring home the promised instalments, though she faithfully carried money-bags to St. James's and Leicester Fields every Friday.

Then, on Wednesday, 13 May, came a dazzling spiritual triumph. Shortly after nine o'clock in the evening, kneeling in his accustomed place, Goodwin heard the voice of Michael and saw a flash of the 'fire of the Lord'. 'Lift up thy eyes to the Lord,' Michael commanded, and as Goodwin obeyed, he 'saw as it were a mighty glorious sun within an oval compass'. For a few moments the bright image remained fixed; then as Goodwin 'worshipped' there followed more flashings of the Lord's glory, and Goodwin heard Michael say, definitively: '. . . God hath thrice shown his face unto thee, thou blessed man.'

The triumph of 13 May was followed six days later by a still greater miracle. After several notices from angel voices that he should prepare himself to hear God speak, and after Ahab told Mary that the time had come, Goodwin knelt at last, about 11.15 p.m., in his 'accustomed place', while Mary, who was not yet to hear God's voice, withdrew into the next room.

The voice of the Lord, accompanied by flashes of fire, spoke in verse:

> I am come unto thee to end thy misery;
> In twenty days, no more, thy bounties shall be o'er.
> The Lord is true and what He saith is sure;
> And that thou may'st it know, He to thee His face doth show.
> In twenty days and then thou shalt be the happiest of men.

The Lord's voice continued for several more verses, but of these Goodwin could retain only the last line:

> I have no more to say now.

When the revelation ended, Goodwin called Mary back to his chamber. From her own room, she said, she had seen him 'all on fire'. She was delighted with the Lord's message when it was recounted to her, and she soon summoned Ahab, who explained that Goodwin might rely completely on God's promise to end all his troubles in twenty days, since God's own words had never been known to fail.

Before Goodwin had quite digested these marvels, they were repeated. The next morning he again heard the voice of the Lord and was again promised that his troubles would end in twenty days. In the evening he received two more revelations, both assuring him that his business had been 'perfected' and the time set. With the new revelations Goodwin discovered a slight mystery. He could not 'perfectly understand' all of the Lord's words, which seemed to come from a considerable distance, and he was obliged to rely upon Ahab for a complete rendering of the messages. This minor difficulty, however, did not affect the sense of the communications. The Lord had seen fit to put an end to his suffering, and the Lord's promises were (in Ahab's words) 'as sure as if the thing said were already done'.

While Goodwin was waiting for his felicity to begin and Wildman was hiding from the King's officers, the agent John Jones arrived from Amsterdam with more orders from Monmouth. Reaching London on 27 May, he tried to see Wildman or Matthews, but he was informed by Colonel Disney that both men were 'out of town'. He entrusted his message, therefore, to Disney and asked him to transmit it to Lord Delamere. Monmouth, Jones said, would sail for England presently, landing at Lyme Regis, and he wanted Delamere to go to Chester at once to prepare a rising.[15] This message Disney passed to Delamere, who set out from London that night, under an assumed name, and by indirect roads hurried to Cheshire.

It is unlikely that Wildman was actually 'out of town' on 27 May. More probably, he was simply avoiding Monmouth's messenger. At any rate, the next day he was urgently soliciting advice from his partners and the angels on the subject of his personal safety. Upon this delicate matter, the angels deliberated from noon on 28 May until 8 a.m. on 29 May, when Goodwin finally received an audible message from a cherubin, who told him that Wildman 'must not stir' until 3 June.

The angel's advice that Wildman should remain hidden, at least temporarily, made admirable sense, and Goodwin did not try to dispute it. He knew that Wildman was 'involved in some trouble and danger' and that there was a warrant out for his arrest. He believed, nevertheless, that Wildman had been wrong to hide in the first place. Now, after ten days, his disappearance could be looked upon as a presumption of guilt. Wildman's mistake, Goodwin felt, was particularly annoying because he had acted against the advice of his partners. They had given him timely 'notice', but he 'chose rather his own way'.

A few days later, Goodwin was obliged to extend the term of Wildman's concealment, upon the advice of another angel, who said, audibly, that 'Mr Wildman had best not go in danger for fifteen days.' Naturally enough, Wildman heeded the warnings he received from the angels, especially since they coincided with his own judgement and with the grim outlook for the rebellion. Monmouth was delayed about two weeks by contrary winds—a delay which confused his supporters and gave the government time for countermeasures. Thus Delamere, who had gone to Cheshire hoping to raise 20,000 men, returned, much sobered, on 5 June to report that surprise was no longer possible and that the initiative had passed to the government. Wildman emerged briefly from his hiding place on 5 and 6 June to hold discouraged, 'cold' conversations with Delamere and Disney;[16] but otherwise, through the crucial month of June, he remained as invisible to his friends as to his enemies.

Meanwhile, twenty days after God's oral promises to Goodwin, the time came when his troubles were to be ended and his prosperity was to begin. Throughout the crucial day, 9 June, Goodwin received assurances from the angels that God was completing the business as promised. The next morning, however, Gabriel brought a sombre message. Certain evil spirits had now laid an accusation against Goodwin, alleging that his faith was not yet perfect and that if the Lord would subject him to another trial he would 'quite fall off'. This allegation the Lord consented to hear, since He sometimes allowed devils to make complaints 'against the sons of men', as He had done in biblical times. He consented, furthermore, to one more test for Goodwin—another postponement of his projects. Gabriel's message was later confirmed by the voice of the Lord, speaking audibly. 'The Lord is perfect and true,' the voice said to Goodwin, 'and what He doth is just. He will certainly do as He promised, but it shall not be thine but His own time.'

Goodwin bore his crushing disappointment with 'patience and submission', even when he learned that God's own time was indefinite and that God had assigned him to Wooburn for week-long sojourns, beginning 16 June. Determined to belie the evil spirits, who had not only impugned his faith but also accused him of neglecting his father, he left Mary behind in London to deal with John Wildman and the treasure sites and betook himself to Wooburn. There he remained, except for short respites at Hounslow, until 6 July—the day, coincidentally, that Monmouth's insurrection was snuffed out at Sedgemoor.

For his obedience, he was promised by Gabriel that he would be visited at Wooburn by at least one angel and probably by the Lord Himself. This promise was not kept; but Goodwin did receive two unpromised rewards. Lord Wharton accepted his latest excuse for the postponement of his marriage—that the mother of his intended bride was ill. And his presence at

Wooburn kept him insulated from the dangerous political events that swirled about London.

Monmouth had finally landed at Lyme Regis on 11 June, and when the word reached London, the government redoubled its efforts to find his allies. Wildman, of course, remained prudently concealed in accordance with his intuitions and angelic instructions. And since no government agent had ferreted out the connection between Wildman and his partners (perhaps because Goodwin had hidden so well from his creditors), neither Goodwin nor Mary was ever questioned on his whereabouts. Baffled as usual, the government was obliged to content itself with issuing warrants—including a warrant for seizing Wildman's horses.[17]

Wildman's friend Colonel Disney was not so lucky. Captured on 15 June, along with some printing apparatus and a batch of Monmouth's Proclamations, he was given a brief trial, and then hanged.[18] Disney, who was a brave man, died without betraying any of his friends; but his death seriously damaged the conspiracy, since he was the only reliable link between the London conspirators and Delamere and, of course, the only link with Wildman. Other arrests further disorganized the London group; many people, as Cragg observed, 'were taken up and kept in custody, and those that were not were hiding themselves'.[19] Among those obliged to hide was Delamere. The government pre-empted a rising in Cheshire by securing Chester Castle, raising the militia, and rounding up suspects; and on 25 June it issued warrants for Delamere's arrest.[20]

In spite of the discomfiture of Monmouth's friends and the appalling fact that in Scotland Argyll's little army was dispersed without a battle, Monmouth himself scored some early successes. After achieving a tactical surprise with his landing at Lyme Regis, he made his way to Taunton, gathering recruits as he went. Within a few days his army had swelled to some six or seven thousand men, and he felt strong enough to march on Bristol. For a time his fortunes appeared much brighter than cautious pessimists like Wildman had expected. Although the nobility and gentry remained opposed or aloof, Monmouth and his ragtag army of artisans and peasants became formidable. Under such circumstances, Wildman decided to risk a few words of support, even though his partners, meeting in Hounslow on

23–24 June, were still unable to get a pronouncement from the angels on Monmouth's fate.

During the last week of June, therefore, Wildman got in touch with his wife Lucy and told her to send a young man named Manley to the Duke with a message. Manley was to tell Monmouth that Delamere had gone into Cheshire 'to rise', that the London conspirators were 'ready to rise also', and that Mr Indenture himself [Wildman] was completely at the Duke's disposal.[21] The message, of course, was highly fanciful. Delamere was in hiding; the London conspirators were hopelessly disorganized; and Wildman himself, concealed from friend and enemy, was at no one's disposal. From Wildman's point of view, however, the gesture was important as another hedge against victory, and the danger was slight. An oral message entrusted to a discreet messenger who could identify the ultimate sender only as 'Mr Indenture' was not likely to prove fatal.

Before Manley could thread his way through the royal patrols to reach Monmouth, the attack on Bristol had bogged down, the royal forces dispatched to the West had combined, and Monmouth had begun a retreat toward Bridgwater. As it daily became more evident that the rebellion had been contained, the faint-hearted began to desert, and at Wells frustrated Puritans from the rebel forces plundered the cathedral. The news that was carried through Hounslow to London, always many hours after events in Somersetshire, grew progressively more gloomy.

In Hounslow, meanwhile, the angels, who had been silent in late June, brought Goodwin and Mary an important message on 1 July: Wildman (an angel told Goodwin audibly) was now in 'great danger'; he should not stir until further orders. This excellent advice Wildman followed faithfully, and when young Manley returned to London on 5 July with word from Monmouth that Wildman and his friends should stage a rising,[22] Wildman ignored the message. He was still safely hidden when news arrived from the West that Monmouth's army had been smashed at Sedgemoor on the night of 5–6 July and that the rebellion had been crushed.

Goodwin and Mary were again at Hounslow when the messengers clattered through with the news of Monmouth's defeat. Goodwin had been given a reprieve from Wooburn, where he had suffered severe defeats of his own. In spite of

Gabriel's promises he had neither seen nor heard 'anything at all'. Reunited now with Mary, he needed explanations for his own failures as well as the fate of Monmouth. When the angels finally spoke, they did not say why he had been deserted at Wooburn; they merely reminded him of his blessings and admonished him to 'continue to the end'. They did, however, provide the definitive explanation of Monmouth's defeat. The Duke had been persuaded to undertake the expedition by the spirit of his father, Charles II, who had appeared to him 'several times'. This meant, of course, that the rebellion had been handicapped from the start, since Charles II was a troubled, untrustworthy spirit. Nevertheless, the Lord had not doomed the insurrection until Monmouth had committed offences of his own. Monmouth had offended God, Ahab explained, when 'in despair he began to do mischief and demolish churches and plunder'. Then God had forsaken him.

For John Wildman, of course, no explanation of Monmouth's defeat could do any good. As the government began arresting and executing its enemies, Wildman's concerns narrowed down to the problem of staying alive. After Sedgemoor, the government saturated the port towns with its agents and conducted house-to-house searches in suspected areas.[23] Some major conspirators managed to slip through the net, and some lesser men not yet implicated by government investigation, including Robert Cragg, also escaped in time to Holland; but many more, including Monmouth, Grey, and Jones, were captured. To Wildman, the arrest of his friends was distressing in itself. Equally distressing was the knowledge that some of them might be induced to give evidence against him.

Two potential sources of danger were removed with the executions of Monmouth and Argyll. Although Monmouth had been urged to 'discover' his secret accomplices, he did not reveal anything the government did not know already, and he did not mention Wildman, whom he had once threatened with hanging. He spent the last hours before his execution, on 15 July, in exculpating his family. The Earl of Argyll was similarly uncooperative with the Crown. He went to his death, in Edinburgh, without incriminating any of his friends.

As Wildman was weighing his peril, his partner Goodwin was undergoing another crisis of his own. After a week's respite in

London, Goodwin was re-sentenced to Wooburn, his projects were again postponed, and he was ignored by the angels. He was 'greatly tempted', in fact, 'to fly into a passion' and curse his ill fortune. Unable to help himself, he could not for the present give Wildman anything beyond his standing orders to stay well hidden. Wildman did not grow rich as he worked on the problem of saving his life.

The problem soon became doubly complicated. Two major conspirators—Lord Grey, Monmouth's chief lieutenant, and Richard Goodenough, Monmouth's secretary of state—turned King's evidence. Captured after Sedgemoor and committed to the Tower, the two men decided to save their own lives at the expense of their friends.[24] Their confessions flowed copiously, not only about the Monmouth affair but also about the Rye House Plot two years before; and soon the government was issuing a new batch of warrants. On 25 July, Charles Gerard, Lord Brandon, was committed to the Tower, where he was joined by Lord Delamere, who surrendered in response to a royal proclamation.[25] Both men figured largely in Grey's confession, but neither so prominently as John Wildman, against whom Grey felt particularly resentful.

Although Wildman could not know the extent of the confessions, the rumours and the arrests were not encouraging. And he was soon forced to make a life-and-death decision. On 27 July, the government issued a proclamation summoning him to surrender within twenty days.[26] Failure to surrender, he knew, meant outlawry; it meant that he must get out of the country at all costs, leaving behind his property and his projects. Surrender seemed even more grim; for no matter how cleverly he had covered his tracks, he could never tell what witnesses the government could produce or suborn, or whether the best possible case could survive a trial before Judge Jeffreys and a packed jury. And if he could squirm out of the Monmouth affair, there was still the conspiracy of 1683 hanging over his head. On this matter, the testimony of Grey and Goodenough could almost certainly convict him.

As the days for making an irrevocable decision slipped away, Wildman at last received help from his partners. At Hounslow on 9 August, at 2 p.m., Goodwin received a long audible revelation from a seraphin, who gave the final word on the

Wildman case. 'Wildman will come off,' the angel said, 'if he will go to the King [though] with some trouble; if not, the Lord will not release him [from hiding] until October the latter end.' The seraphin's advice—possibly the most dangerous advice a seraphin ever gave to an Englishman—Goodwin sent along to Wildman, expecting that Wildman would 'trust God' and surrender himself. In this crisis, however, Wildman showed a lamentable want of faith. Tacitly rejecting revelation, he chose to rely instead on human calculation—which convinced him that the government would hang him if he surrendered. Having come to this conclusion, he waited quietly in hiding until he could find a safe passage out of England. Then he sailed away to Holland and exile.

Goodwin, scornful of Wildman's cowardice, was later pleased to note that Wildman reaped the punishment he deserved. For his rebellion against the angels, he was afflicted (Goodwin learned) with a chronic fear—'as bad as death and worse to a great mind'. Nor was this punishment the worst. In fleeing to Holland, Wildman sailed out of his partners' lives. Though Goodwin saw him in Amsterdam for an hour or so during the next summer, Wildman had forfeited his place in the partnership. Now he would never turn base metals into gold, collect the treasures at Holborn or Northend, meet Queen Penelope, or see 'the Great God in His Majesty'.

Nevertheless, Wildman's later career furnished a few consolations. In 1688 it was the turn of James II to flee the country, and Wildman accompanied the expedition that drove James into exile. Under the new regime, Wildman became Postmaster General of England; he was knighted by King William, against whom he conspired briefly and ineffectually; he was made an Alderman of London; and he served in the Parliament of 1689–90. Perhaps it was some further consolation to Wildman that his friend Delamere won acquittal after a dramatic trial[27] and that after all his own plots he did not end his life hanging at Tyburn along with some of his braver and less crafty comrades.

10

God and Lord Wharton

ON 10 August 1685, the day after Goodwin received the seraphin's message for John Wildman, he returned once more to Wooburn, where he was greeted with astonishing news.

'Sir,' a servant said, 'you are just come time enough to see my Lord before his going into France.'

Goodwin was shocked and distressed. 'The very word *France*' produced alarm and fear. Lord Wharton, at seventy-two, had already outlived most of his contemporaries, and to Goodwin he seemed too frail for travel on the Continent. Along with his fears Goodwin experienced a bleak sense of abandonment. He had avoided his father and had often trembled in his presence, but now he felt that he was being 'left, as it were, alone without any support or friend'.

As soon as he could trust himself to speak, he volunteered to accompany his father to Calais; and Lord Wharton, who seemed pleased with the offer, promised that Goodwin could travel with him as far as Dover. This kindly reception and Lord Wharton's business-like composure temporarily allayed Goodwin's anxiety, but the distress of the rest of the household, 'who were all almost in tears', and the knowledge that his father 'had settled his will and all things else as if he were going to die' upset him again. The next morning as he watched Lord Wharton say goodbye to the family, servants, and tenants at Wooburn, he found that he 'could hardly see'.

At Dover, where contrary winds delayed Lord Wharton's sailing for six days, Goodwin had further opportunity to demonstrate his concern. He was the only one of the eight Wharton children (as he noted proudly) to remain until the end, and he often repeated his offer to make the Channel crossing. Lord Wharton, on the other hand, showed little concern of his own. Ignoring sentiment and distant hazards, he concentrated stoically upon the business at hand, as if he routinely took dangerous trips to the Continent.

Lord Wharton's immediate business was to get out of England and to make his way to Aix-la-Chapelle. For this purpose, on 7 August, he had gone to Windsor and appeared before Sunderland and King James. His health, he told them, demanded an extended visit to the spas at Aix; he hoped he might be granted a formal passport, since he intended to present himself to the rulers of the places he visited.

Neither James nor Sunderland could see any reason for withholding the passport. The old nobleman was indeed 'lame';[1] a season at the spas was a sensible prescription for his ailment. There were no outstanding accusations against him, either in the Monmouth affair or the earlier Whig conspiracy. Sunderland, therefore, issued and signed a passport that authorized Lord Wharton to travel overseas with his wife, servants, horses, and goods.[2] King James himself wished him a safe journey and a speedy recovery.[3]

Understandably, Lord Wharton did not explain to James and Sunderland that he had other worries besides his health. The persecution of Dissenters, which had increased dramatically during the last three years of the reign of Charles II, threatened to increase still further in the wake of Monmouth's Rebellion. As a long-time patron of Dissenting ministers and as a spokesman for Puritan causes, Lord Wharton had so far been protected by aristocratic privilege and by his own cautious moderation; but such protection, he believed, was likely to vanish at any time.

Besides this anxiety (which he later recorded in a letter to Baron von Spaen),[4] Lord Wharton had a fear which he did not commit to paper. Like many of his Whig friends, he had been approached by the Monmouth conspirators; and though, like his sons Tom and Henry, he had been wise enough to remain aloof,[5] there was always a chance that his name would come up in the confessions now pouring out of English gaols. He could not feel safe until he reached the territory of a friendly Protestant prince. Meantime, to avoid any appearance of flight or any connection with the rebels in Holland, he would land in France and proceed to the German provinces of Mark and Cleves.

While Lord Wharton waited at Dover for a friendly wind, he was unusually kind. He did not nag Goodwin about his always-postponed marriage; he merely advised him to move as quickly as possible and gave him permission to leave at once in pursuit of his fiancée. As the time of departure drew near, he presented his son (who insisted upon remaining) with 'four little medals of gold' as a keepsake and promised that when his affairs became settled he would send him some money. And on the evening of 18 August, when Goodwin helped him aboard the packet-boat,[6] he shook Goodwin warmly by the hand and pronounced a blessing upon him.

Though Goodwin feared he might never see his father again, he had little time to brood. According to Mary's calculations, the days of trial God had assigned him on 10 June were to end on 20 August. The day before that, therefore, he hurried back to London, ready to complete his great projects. Few men, he believed, could have weathered so many disappointments. Not once during his seventy days of trial had he seen God or the angels; he had not even seen a lowlander. Queen Penelope, now insanely jealous of Mary, had failed to appear. Worse yet, she had twice been unfaithful to him. George had discovered her treachery and lust, of course, and she had been thoroughly chastened by the Lord. Her ill conduct, nevertheless, had wasted months of his time.

Against such reverses, which included many defeats at Leicester Fields and St. James's Park, there were encouraging signs. One of these was Mary's continuing fertility; she had conceived seven times since the delivery of her quintuplets, and although she had suffered three miscarriages, she still retained four children. More remarkable was a spate of gifts from the spirits and angels, who had begun to deliver their bounty in a new way. Earlier they had left their gifts (usually religious objects) in plain sight and trusted the partners to lock them safely in trunks; now they bypassed the partners and placed their treasures, often gold or jewels, directly into the trunks. As yet the partners were absolutely forbidden to use the treasures, or even to touch the trunks, without express orders, but they were comforted to know that their closet was being filled with wealth, including gold and silver from Northend.

Goodwin hoped, of course, that upon his return from Dover he could open his trunks and complete all his other projects. This hope, however, proved illusory. Nothing happened on 20

August, and a few days later a powerful, 'peremptory' angel named Anatch was sent to explain that Goodwin's time of trial had been extended until 1 January 1686. Meanwhile, Anatch said, beginning on 7 September the partners would be allowed to achieve a few goals: Anatch himself would appear to Goodwin (ending his inability to see angels); Queen Penelope too would make herself visible; and Goodwin would receive £2,000—enough to pay off all his debts.

By the end of September it became evident that these modest goals would not be met. Besides failing utterly in his attempts to show himself to Goodwin, Anatch proved wrong in predicting the appearance of the Queen. Most dismally of all, he failed in the simple task of producing £2,000. Though the trunks in the closet filled so rapidly that the angels brought new trunks to hold the overflow, Anatch could not give permission to open any of them. Meanwhile, Goodwin's little supply of money was dwindling inexorably, and the nearest reliable source of help, Lord Wharton, was in the town of Emmerich, beyond the Dutch border.

Lord Wharton had reached Emmerich in September after a token stop in Aix-la-Chapelle, where he arrived too late to take the waters. Emmerich, in the Duchy of Cleves, belonged to Frederick William, Elector of Brandenburg, a stalwart of the Protestant interest; and Lord Wharton hoped that the Elector's officers would protect him from English agents, prevent the serving of any official summons to return home, and allow him to slip over the border into the United Provinces if the English government tried to extradite him. To make sure of this arrangement, he carefully drew up a long statement on his life and politics for transmission to the Elector.[7]

Upon the point of personal safety, the news that reached Lord Wharton from England was satisfactory. As the months went by, there were no warrants (or rumours of warrants) for his arrest. The news from his family, however, was distressing. His son Henry, recently promoted to Captain in the Duke of Norfolk's regiment,[8] involved himself in three serious brawls—the beating of a coachman,[9] an assault upon the Tory Earl of Carnarvon,[10] and a fatal duel at a tavern. In 'a drunken rencontre at the Blue Posts', Henry killed Robert Moxam, a fellow army officer.[11] Along with reports of Henry's 'brangling broils' came word that Anne Lee Wharton, Tom's wife, lay critically ill at Adderbury (the home of her sister Eleanora, Countess of Abingdon).

The reports of Anne's illness, alarming to Lord Wharton, were not frightening at all to Goodwin, who saw the episode as a heaven-sent opportunity. It was well within his powers, Goodwin knew, to effect a miraculous cure, and he needed nothing but the permission of the angels to go to Adderbury and save her. Goodwin's love affair with Anne had nagged at his conscience for years. On 1 October, therefore, when the angels gave him permission to cure her, he saw a chance to expiate his crime—to free himself from a burden almost as galling as his debts.

For a few days, Goodwin's preparations progressed smoothly. The angels provided him with some holy oil, instructed him in the special prayer he was to use, and fixed the date of his journey for 7 October—a day (the angels foresaw) when Tom would leave his wife's bedside and go elsewhere. That morning, however, as Goodwin was waiting for 'his last dispatches', he heard from somewhere close behind him the voice of the Lord.

'Wharton,' the voice said, 'the Lord hath done thy business for thee.'

Goodwin understood the words perfectly; he also understood their general import—that the Lord would save Anne without his help. This interpretation was confirmed by Ahab, who told Mary that the Lord would restore Anne and that Goodwin must not go to Adderbury at all. It would be sufficient, Ahab said, for Goodwin to write Anne a letter and send her some drops of holy oil.

Goodwin never saw Anne again, except in dreams. On 29 October, she died. Her death, tragic in itself,[12] was particularly devastating to Goodwin because it seemed to mark the flat failure of a divine promise; the Lord Himself had promised to cure her. Mary, however, brought a complete explanation from the angels. During the worst of her illness, Anne had repented sincerely of all her sins and prepared herself for a better world. Unhappily, as she began to recover, she showed signs of relapsing into 'an ill temper', and 'the Lord in His mercy thought best to take her off whilst penitent.'

Anne, Mary explained further, had spent some of her last

moments reconciling herself with Tom and removing his suspicion that she had committed adultery with Goodwin. She testified to Tom 'upon the blessed Sacrament' that she had not committed the crime 'he suspected her guilty of'. Tom, who had tearfully repented of his own misconduct, had been 'convinced in his own conscience' of her innocence. It consoled Goodwin to know that Anne had vindicated his essential integrity. Although he did not attend her funeral, held at Winchendon on 10 November, he dreamed of her many times and eventually learned beyond doubt that God had forgiven both of them for what had seemed at the time a monstrous lust.

In early November, Mary was often assured that the business of the partnership would end on New Year's Day as Anatch had promised. On 10 November, she received less heartening information; until 1 January, neither she nor Goodwin would be allowed to use any of the riches accumulating in their trunks, and they would receive no usable treasure from other sources. In spite of the information, Goodwin could not bring himself to write to his father for money; and by December he was subsisting on the few shillings that Mary could get 'by pawning', or from treating an occasional patient. He had entered into a period of suffering 'beyond expression'.

But while Goodwin suffered from his temporal failures, his spiritual powers were marvellously augmented by a new method of communicating with God. On 7 December 1685 he was informed for the first time, by Gabriel and Michael, that if he lay down patiently in his own bed he could expect some divine revelation 'by vision or by dream'. He might, in fact, see and hear 'the Lord Christ'.

Heavenly instructions, Goodwin knew perfectly well, were often transmitted in dreams. It was the special mark of the prophet, he also knew, to receive significant visions, and it followed from his new prophetic powers that he should receive visions too. His first attempt, nevertheless, was only partially successful. He found it difficult to fall asleep in the daytime, as the method prescribed; noises from Long Acre Street distracted him, and random thoughts swirled through his head. At last when he drifted off into sleep and then into a dream, which seemed to be triggered by 'a small noise', he thought he saw 'the Lord in His glory' and heard several sentences; but when he awoke, the picture had grown dim and the conversation had vanished completely. Ahab, called to explain the partial failure, said that the new method required practice; like 'the prophets of old', Goodwin would need at least three sessions to become proficient.

As the weeks went by, in spite of occasional failures, Goodwin improved. By 1 January 1686 he could receive and recall dreams of great complexity, and a month later he had learned to distinguish between a vision and a dream. A dream, whether significant or trivial, is a product of a comparatively sound sleep: a vision is something radically different. As he wrote for the instruction of his son Peregrine,

. . . having a vision is not being asleep, for whilst my vision passed I heard distinctly other noises (that is, sometimes) of the world, as knocking, stamping, etc.; and when the vision goes off, you clearly find you awake not from a sleep; but the trance like a cloud goes over you—sleeping upon a vision being the enemy to it, because if you fall asleep upon it, you in sleeping forget the vision, generally.

During his training period, Goodwin learned another vital fact. The angels themselves cannot tell when divine communications are being transmitted or what they contain. Since visions are direct revelations from God to His chosen instruments, they can be hidden from any intermediaries. In short, Goodwin learned, he now possessed an independent source of heavenly information; he was freed, in a sense, from the tutelage of the angels and also freed, though he did not perceive it at the time, from complete dependence upon Mary.

While Goodwin was mastering the art of receiving visions, he received an even more important gift. On 10 December 1685 God took over personal direction of Goodwin's affairs. He began to speak to Goodwin, not merely on special and rare occasions, but on a frequent and sometimes daily basis.

The format for these communications seldom varied. Propping himself up in his bed at some appointed time and fixing his eyes upon the place where flashes of the Lord's glory often appeared, Goodwin waited for the Lord to speak. When the Lord's voice itself issued forth, it seemed always to come from outside the bedroom door, from a passage that led to the head of the stairs. Sometimes through the partially opened door Goodwin could see flashes of light in the passage outside and what appeared to be a shadow along the crack at the bottom of the door. These light and dark manifestations, however, served merely as accompaniment to the Lord's words, and it was upon these that Goodwin concentrated his most rapt attention.

The early messages Goodwin found difficult to understand and remember verbatim, not only because they seemed muffled by distance but also because they were spoken in prose. After the Lord's voice had ceased, he was frequently obliged to call upon Ahab to repeat the message. In January, however, the Lord began speaking regularly in verse—a form that Goodwin found easier to retain. Frequently he could dispense with Ahab's help entirely, and he was seldom obliged to question more than a verse or two of the messages that he carefully wrote down.

One of God's first speeches, delivered in prose on 14 December, Goodwin understood very clearly. 'Wharton,' the Lord's voice said, 'write as soon as may be a submissive letter to thy father, he not knowing how you live.'

This command Goodwin hastened to obey. Although the angels had promised many times that his financial problems would be solved on 1 January—long before a letter could reach Emmerich and bring help from Lord Wharton—and although confessing his misery to his father meant swallowing his pride once again, he cheerfully did what he was told.

Goodwin's hope of being rescued on New Year's Day was strengthened by a verse revelation of 31 December which seemed to confirm the angels' promises. The Lord instructed him to visit his obdurate family at St. Giles-in-the-Fields and cause 'their stiff-necked hearts to ache' with the innocence of his manner. This visit, the Lord seemed to imply, would prepare them for the imminent change in his fortunes.

> For when tomorrow thou has got a name [God's voice concluded]
> It shall be to thy family an everlasting fame.
> When they see that, they will their pardons crave
> And be much sorry for the ill that to thee done they have.

But a verse revelation of New Year's Day showed that Goodwin had slightly misinterpreted the Lord's meaning. He was indeed to receive a name, but the wealth and fame which he had been promised by the angels would be again postponed.

'I did promise thee yesterday thou should'st receive a name,'
the Lord's voice began:

> Thy name is *Hezekiah*,
> And then I to honour bring,
> An earl, a duke, a prince, and king,
> Then a[n] emperor thou shalt be,
> The highest that e'er was in that degree.

After a momentary pause, the Lord's voice continued, still in
verse:

> Though all this honour is to thee given,
> Thou must suffer nine weeks; so did the King of heaven.

Although somewhat cryptic, the Lord's message was essentially clear. Obviously God now intended to try Goodwin for
nine more weeks, until sometime in early March, probably until
his birthday. Meantime as a token of His affection He had given
him the special name *Hezekiah*. Goodwin was disappointed, of
course, yet this was not like his previous failures. This time he
was sustained by God's own words, which were further
reinforced next day by another verse revelation:

> Rise, Wharton, rise, do not be dismayed,
> Though I, the Lord, have this burden on thee laid,
> But in my time I'll make thee surely free
> And take thy yoke and burden off of thee.

The new order of 1686 transformed Goodwin's way of living.
Though he was still confined to his lodgings by his debts and his
political fears, his days and nights were filled with messages,
dreams, and visions. He learned, for example, that Mary, whom
the Lord described as 'Hezekiah Wharton's truest wife', had been
given the name *Lucretia*.[13] He also learned, in a memorable
vision, that he would be vindicated for his disastrous speech
against James II and for his misbehaviour with his brother's
wife.

Goodwin's visions and revelations spurred a project of the
highest importance. Ever since he had met Mary, he had taken
extensive notes on his strange experiences. Sometime, he knew,
he would wish to enlighten an ignorant world on these matters
and instruct his son Peregrine in the methods by which he had

become rich and glorious. This would involve turning his raw notes into a systematic narrative. Now, with the Lord's assurance that within a few weeks he would emerge into the brightest honour, Goodwin saw that his intended account had become an urgent project. By the middle of March he would be much too deeply immersed in worldly responsibilities to spare time for writing. Accordingly, he procured a folio-sized volume of excellent vellum and set to work. Addressing Peregrine directly, he launched himself into his autobiography. 'My life, my dear son, being now become most worthy of notice [he began], I thought fit to compile it together and . . . leave it you as the greatest and best of earthly legacies I can bequeath you. . .'.

Once started, in late January, Goodwin wrote at a furious clip.[14] In little more than two months, before he was interrupted by a long journey, he managed to write more than 200,000 words and bring his narrative up to the year 1685. Unknowingly, Lord Wharton contributed to the speed of composition by sending the money Goodwin had requested in December. This relief, which ended a period of financial desperation, enabled Goodwin to concentrate upon his notes and recollections. Although he could not pay his debts, he could eat regularly, fend off the landlady, and take occasional trips to Hounslow; he could survive until the Lord permanently ended his suffering.

Yet it appeared for a time that he might pay a fearful price for the prosperity which was soon to be his. Mary, the Lord said in two oral revelations, would die as soon as Goodwin achieved wealth and power. Mary was undismayed when the revelations were explained to her. She had always been willing, she said, to trade her life for Goodwin's glory, and she fully realized that in his days of power he could not have 'an old woman' for his wife. She also knew that she could not bear to see him married to Queen Penelope, whose jealousy and faithlessness had caused three years of frustration.

Fortunately, God's promises proved to be contingent rather than absolute. Although a date was set for Mary's death and although in early March she bade a formal farewell to the spirits at Hounslow, Goodwin learned in a later oral revelation that his prayers could save her. These prayers he offered at once, and Mary declared herself willing to postpone her heavenly reward and resume, for Goodwin's sake, a life that involved much 'trampling about' and offered 'no manner of rest nor quiet'.

Goodwin expected his worldly glory to begin on his thirty-third birthday, 8 March 1686, and on the morning of the crucial day a long oral revelation which compared his recent life to a tragic play and promised that he would blossom into greatness seemed to confirm this expectation. As the day wore on, however, he learned that his blossoming would take place in stages, beginning with spiritual gifts and ending, perhaps on Easter, with financial rewards, including the opening of his treasure chests.

Goodwin's spiritual improvement began with reconsecration. Three times during the next three days while he was asleep, he was reanointed by the Lord himself and pronounced 'priest and king' in oral revelations. And during the ensuing two weeks, his temporal prospects were also improved and clarified. A revelation informed him that Queen Penelope would soon die and be replaced on the throne by her sister Princess Ursula, who had always doted upon him. He learned further that his son Peregrine had been taken by his nurse to an elegant private home near Shirburn Castle, where he was treated with all possible deference. Finally, he learned through Mary and Ahab that the spirit of Cardinal Thomas Wolsey still walked the earth and controlled great treasures that Goodwin would be allowed to share. Wolsey (Mary reported, after meeting him for the first time) resembled his portraits, down to such details as his square cap and russet coat; he frequented an 'old house in the City' which still retained a cellar called by his name; and he was eager to meet Goodwin.

On 28 March, Goodwin's steady progress towards earthly glory was halted abruptly. The Lord's morning message, clearly audible, warned that another penance might be laid upon Goodwin. As yet, the Lord said, the issue was still in doubt; but the tone of the message suggested to Goodwin that the case was likely to be decided against him, as did a vision which showed him nailed upside-down upon a cross. The premonition was confirmed by a series of oral revelations, which announced that in answer to Lord Wharton's fervent prayers to see his son, God had determined to send Goodwin to Germany.

Goodwin's immediate response to the Lord's command was

relief. Going to see his father was preferable to being crucified upside-down, or to delivering a message to King James. Nevertheless, he found a journey to Emmerich hazardous enough, since he had no money for the trip and Mary was on the verge of delivering the long-overdue children she had conceived in April and May of 1685. Though only two children now remained of the four that she had carried through December— two children having 'pined away' because of her tribulations— Goodwin feared for her safety. He also trembled at the prospect of presenting himself to Lord Wharton. When he had parted from his father at Dover he had promised that within weeks he would be married to a rich heiress. To face Lord Wharton now, alone and still unmarried, took a kind of courage that he feared he might not possess.

Fortunately, Mary brought encouragement from the angels, who assured her that contrary to all appearances Lord Wharton loved Goodwin 'above all his children'. These assurances were placed beyond doubt by an oral revelation.

> Hezekiah, my true and well beloved son [the Lord said],
> Thy father's prayers, and sighs, and groans have come to me,
> Which made me take pity of his age and gravity.
> Thou art the only son of his heart,
> Though he to thee doth seem most tart.

The angels also declared that Goodwin's trip to Germany would be his last trial and that upon his return all his treasures would be 'laid open'. They promised further that he would not be left unattended. The Lord would see him 'face to face every day or every other day'. Mary herself would come to him 'in spirit every night'—a feat which she could perform in fifteen minutes, no matter where he might be. Meanwhile, God would soften Lord Wharton's heart and give him faith to believe whatever Goodwin told him.

Persuaded beyond cavil that his journey was necessary, Goodwin borrowed money from one of his rich sisters for the trip. On 14 April he set off for Holland and a series of baffling disappointments. For as he travelled towards Emmerich, through Rotterdam, Utrecht, and Arnhem, he 'heard not the least voice nor saw the least thing'; though he prayed and waited at inns and listened in coaches, neither God nor Mary spoke to him.

With every mile it became more evident that he would have to
face his father with no help at all. At Emmerich, he offered one
last prayer for 'instructions what to say', and when that too
failed he was compelled to undergo his trial alone.

Lord Wharton expressed great surprise when he saw Goodwin,
whom he had not expected 'in the least', and he immediately
proceeded to the question that Goodwin hoped most fervently
to avoid: 'Are you married yet?' Extemporizing desperately,
Goodwin tried to hedge. 'I am as good as married,' he said.
Then he tried to close the discussion by promising to give a full
account the next day. But Lord Wharton, who could see no
reason for postponing a simple answer to a simple question,
refused to be put off. He supposed, he said, that by this time
Goodwin was indeed married; 'I do believe you are,' he
repeated.

Having expected help on this problem, Goodwin had prepared
no smooth, plausible excuse. Nevertheless, in spite of his 'heat
and fluster', he produced an answer so convincing that it seemed
divinely inspired. His fiancée, he said, had accompanied her
mother, now gravely ill, to an English spa, where she planned to
stay until June, or until her mother died. The mother, Goodwin
explained, had 'fallen out' with him and withdrawn her consent
to the marriage. In view of her mortal illness, it seemed foolish
to risk a huge inheritance by marrying against her wishes.
Hence, Goodwin and his fiancée, though virtually married
already, were content to wait a month or two longer.

To Goodwin's intense relief, Lord Wharton found the
explanation 'greatly rational' and even suggested that Goodwin
should 'venture all' and marry the lady, with or without her
mother's consent. Goodwin did not attempt to argue with his
father's uncharacteristically romantic suggestion. Happy to find
Lord Wharton temporarily appeased, he escaped as quickly as
he could to fortify himself with a drink.

Though Goodwin had passed the crisis, his frustrations soon
returned. In early March Lord Wharton's last political anxieties
had been removed by a royal proclamation of amnesty for those
involved in Monmouth's Rebellion[15]—except for a few notorious
conspirators, including John Wildman. Lord Wharton, therefore,
felt free to move about Europe, and soon after Goodwin's
arrival he decided to tour the German states, beginning with two

weeks at Aix-la-Chapelle. This decision worried Goodwin. Without instructions from God or Mary he did not know what to do. His general orders called for him to remain abroad until 1 June, but whether they obliged him to stay with his father he could not be sure. In the end, after much agonizing, he decided to accompany Lord Wharton.

At Aix he was further dismayed by letters from Mary which told him that he must stay on the Continent until 21 June and, even more dismally, that Mary had lost the twins she finally delivered. Her letters did not explain why she had not appeared (although he later learned that she was too weak from childbearing to travel in spirit) or why he had received 'no intelligence at all' from God and the angels.

Fortunately, Goodwin's anxieties were occasionally relieved by attractive ladies. One of these, whom he met in his walks about Aix, was to affect his life for many months. At the time, the meeting seemed casual enough. Noticing 'a delicate fine woman', he took the opportunity, without waiting for an introduction, to pay her an elegant compliment. Aix-la-Chapelle, he said (in French), was indebted to her for his good word, for if he had not seen her he would have said that 'there had been never a woman perfectly beautiful' in the town. Shortly thereafter, before he could talk with her again, or even learn her name, she left town. It was months later that the angels identified her as Anne Gartwrott, a Spanish princess travelling incognito, and told him that she would soon come to England in search of him.[16]

On 2 June, Goodwin took leave of Lord Wharton, who was setting out for the German capitals[17] and who had not included him in his travel plans. The parting took place 'on very good terms'; Lord Wharton gave Goodwin a bill of exchange for £30,[18] enough to finance a leisurely journey home, and bade him a friendly goodbye. Thus, as Goodwin retreated to Holland, where he would serve out the rest of his sentence abroad, he had completed his basic mission. In spite of faith-bruising trials, he had brought comfort to his father in accordance with God's original commands.

In Holland, he had a delicate secondary mission; he was to find and encourage John Wildman, who was hiding somewhere in Amsterdam. This task made Goodwin hesitate. God had not positively commanded him to see Wildman but only promised to help find him. A visit to Amsterdam, on the other hand, involved political dangers. If Goodwin were seen with any of the English outlaws there, and especially with Wildman, he might find himself in serious trouble when he returned home. On this problem, he received no help from Mary (whose letters merely told him that Queen Penelope was dying on schedule) or from the Lord, who remained silent as always.

Then in Leyden on 13 June Goodwin received a short vision which not only resolved his dilemma but proved that God had not abandoned him. As he drifted into a trance on his way towards sleep, a clearly audible voice said, 'Thou must go.' The voice, unfortunately, did not say where Wildman was hiding, and though Goodwin went to Amsterdam at once and began discreet inquiries, the cautious Wildman 'lay so close' that it took Goodwin five days to find anyone who might possibly get in touch with him.

In his anxiety to conceal his own identity, Goodwin almost bungled his mission. Pretending to be a Frenchman, he addressed Wildman's contact in French and tried to persuade him to carry a letter to Wildman; but the agent refused to carry messages for a stranger who could not speak English or identify himself as Wildman's friend. Having aroused suspicion, Goodwin could not undo the damage. When he approached the man next day and addressed him in English, he made him even more suspicious. Goodwin had given up in despair when a marvellous coincidence, clearly the work of Providence, brought his mission to a triumphant conclusion. Unexpectedly Wildman's agent came to Goodwin with word that a mutual acquaintance had recognized Goodwin in an Amsterdam coffee-house and positively identified him. The agent was happy, therefore, to arrange a safe meeting with Wildman, who was anxious to see his ex-partner.

Accordingly, Goodwin met John Wildman 'in the dark' and proceeded to comfort him, as he would have comforted his 'own father'. Without mentioning Wildman's many failings, he recounted his own progress and assured Wildman that their projects were coming to a happy conclusion. He hoped too, he said, that they would both 'be the better' for their past suffering. Wildman replied that he hoped 'to be the better as long as he lived'. Finally, Goodwin asked Wildman to pray for him and to avoid being cast down; and Wildman said that he always prayed for Goodwin and that their meeting had prevented him from being cast down. On this conciliatory note the two men ended their last recorded conversation. Wildman returned to his hiding place and two more years of exile; and Goodwin, who had now completed his sentence and all the missions assigned him, returned to England and the rewards that awaited him.

11

Visions and Revisions

WHEN Goodwin reached London, on 3 July 1686, he found a scene much different from the one he had left in April. The lodgings on Long Acre Street had been pre-empted by a new owner, and Mary had moved herself and the precious trunks to a second-floor flat on Grafton Street.[1] Princess Ursula had succeeded Queen Penelope on the lowland throne. Hounslow and the heath beyond it had been taken over as a summer base for the royal army.[2] And King James, who had earlier alarmed his Tory Parliament by demanding a large standing army and refusing to dismiss the Catholic officers he had illegally appointed during the Monmouth emergency, had sent another shiver down the spines of his Protestant subjects. His judges had ruled, in the famous Hales case,[3] that the King might 'dispense' with the penalties for violating the Test Act—that he could retain his Catholic officers and appoint others if he chose.

In a few respects, however, Goodwin found the situation unchanged. Mary remained as fertile as ever, soon conceiving of a son who was to be named Hezekiah and a daughter to be named Susan; Goodwin's debts continued to confine him to his lodgings; and the promises of great wealth remained unfulfilled. At Grafton Street as at Long Acre, the orders for unwrapping the Second Covenant and opening the treasure trunks did not come. As if the Lord had forgotten His own words, the assurances of April silently lapsed. For this failure the angels could give no explanation, nor could they learn why God had not appeared to Goodwin in Holland; and when God Himself began to speak again in oral revelations, He spoke of new prospects rather than old promises. In particular, he spoke of Queen Ursula, Cardinal Wolsey, and rich treasures that lay hidden about London. It was to these prospects, therefore, that Goodwin turned his attention.

For a few days in early July it appeared that Queen Ursula might break the chain of misfortunes that had prevented

Goodwin from seeing a lowlander. Before the time of mourning for Queen Penelope had expired, Ursula planned to slip invisibly away from her court for a meeting with Goodwin at Isleworth. On the crucial morning, however, she carelessly left a chamber door unlocked and was trapped by an officious priest, who walked in to find her 'ready dressed'; she was obliged to talk fast to avert the suspicion that she intended to violate the stringent laws of mourning.

Queen Ursula's first failure to keep an appointment, though fully understandable, made Goodwin uneasy; and it was soon followed by a second misfortune—the death of the Pope, which threw the lowlands into another period of mourning. Goodwin was also distressed that although the lowlanders were no longer bound by the late Queen's oath and could legally appear to him at any time, none of them called at Grafton Street. This could only mean that Queen Ursula, who had been given his new address, had chosen to conceal it from her subjects.

Goodwin had begun to suspect the Queen's good faith when George revealed that she had suddenly conceived a mighty hatred for Mary and had tried to persuade George to remain in the lowlands out of Mary's reach. This message drew a cry of agony from Goodwin: 'Good God, what is woman?' he wrote to his son Peregrine. 'Is there none just but your mother?' Two days later, a clear vision confirmed by implication George's damning report and drew the obvious conclusion. 'The Princess's marriage', a voice in Goodwin's vision declared, 'shall be a scourge to thee.'

Naturally these revelations ended Goodwin's plans to marry Queen Ursula. He could not afford to break with her completely, however, since the angels predicted that she would help him to power. He continued to negotiate with her, carefully concealing the fact that he would never marry her. During the summer of 1686, she not only troubled his visions and dreams but even invaded his bedroom. In one symbolic vision, she appeared as 'a mad, curst cow with short horns' that blocked his entrance to the lowlands; in another dream, she became a beautiful woman who enticed him into love-making before he discovered that 'she had in her head only a few rotten loose teeth.' And one night in late August, making herself invisible, she crept into Goodwin's bed and assaulted his sleeping body. She was plying her arts for the second or third time, when Goodwin felt 'her endeavours' upon him and almost succeeded in catching her before she could 'melt away'.

In late September, seeing that she could neither marry Goodwin nor seduce him again in secret, Queen Ursula decided to make a long visit to her old home in Italy. With this decision Goodwin did not quarrel, since he suspected that without her obstruction he would find it easier to get into his lowland kingdom. What he did not suspect when she left, on 2 October 1686, was that she would never come back. During the following winter and spring, George (who had been sent along with her) occasionally returned to England, but in early summer the Queen was taken ill, and on 27 June 1687 she died.

During Goodwin's unlucky negotiations with Queen Ursula, Mary was engaged in the complex task of getting treasure from Cardinal Thomas Wolsey. Almost every day she went into the City to confer with him, usually in his cellar. This procedure involved a delicate technical problem. The Cardinal's Cellar, once part of a building that had been burned in the Fire of London, now underlay the Queen's Head tavern on (or near) Old Fish Street.[4] To visit the cellar, Mary had to pretend to use a toilet located there; and to carry on extended conversations, she was obliged to feign 'a violent looseness'.

An even more delicate problem was the Cardinal himself, whose character seemed to deteriorate almost as rapidly as Queen Ursula's. After beginning with grandiose promises, he soon found ingenious reasons for not keeping them. Obviously fond of exercising power, he seemed to take pleasure in running Mary about London, and he gradually evinced an unmistakable jealousy of Goodwin, whose spiritual eminence exceeded his own. When Mary lost patience and threatened to exorcize him if he did not hand over his treasure, he delivered only a token gift—a small amount of gold, which he locked in a trunk and 'tied' so that it could not be used without his permission. Thereafter, for several months, he evaded all commands and entreaties.

The Cardinal's obstructive power, unfortunately, extended beyond his own personal hoard of wealth. As Mary eventually learned after months of arguments with the spirits at St. James's Park, Leicester Fields, and Red Lion Fields, Wolsey was the

overlord of the treasures buried there, as well as at the great
central repository near 'the walk by the Pall Mall'. All these
treasures had been buried 'in the beginning of the turn in
religion' when Henry VIII seized the monasteries; and the
guardians, who had obeyed Wolsey in life, continued to obey
him after death.

Had Goodwin been able to conduct the negotiations himself,
his progress might have been faster. Mary was too warm-
hearted to take effective punitive measures. It was only after
extreme provocation over many months that she sentenced
Wolsey to four months' confinement under the Red Sea, and
even then she quickly relented and obtained his reprieve.
Similarly she showed undue tenderness to the spirits—ninety-
three in all—who served under him and who refused to deliver
anything while he lay imprisoned.

Mary had still another fault as a negotiator. Worn out from
her never-ending journeys about London, she developed the
habit of refreshing herself with brandy at taverns along her
route; not infrequently, she came home visibly 'disordered'.
Though Goodwin could not accuse her of being drunk on duty,
he could not help fearing that her efficiency was impaired and
that she might relapse into the deplorable state in which he first
found her. Plagued by these anxieties, he expostulated and
pleaded, but he succeeded only in provoking degrading arguments.

By mid-August Goodwin had almost decided to risk the
ultimate remedy: 'drowning an eel' in Mary's brandy—a
measure which sometimes caused 'a dangerous heartsickness'.
In this crisis God mercifully intervened by sending Mary a vision
of her own, warning her to 'leave off keeping company with the
rabble', and shortly thereafter the angels announced that her
tolerance for brandy had been reduced, making it impossible for
her to drink as much as four ounces a day. Thus she was able to
assure Goodwin that 'she had taken her leave of brandy', and he
was relieved of 'farther solicitude in the matter'.

During Mary's difficulties with brandy and Cardinal Wolsey,
she discovered two new treasure sites. The first was another rich
hoard at Red Lion Fields,[5] on the property of a recently
deceased gentleman named Sticestead. The second, located at
Ratcliff, was a house which not only contained vast wealth but
also held the key to an ancient system of communications with

the lowlands. From the house there ran underground passages, long since abandoned by the lowlanders themselves, to the colonies at Moorfields and Hounslow. This tunnel system had been in active use during the reign of King John, who had built King John's Palace in Colnbrook to facilitate his business with the lowlanders. Now, however, the old network, practically forgotten, had fallen under the control of a powerful lowland spirit named Thomas Shashbesh, who also commanded the guardian spirits at Sticestead's.

When Mary first visited Sticestead's and Ratcliff, the guardian spirits seemed tractable. The house at Ratcliff, with its musty tunnels and dark chambers, was frightening, to be sure, but when Thomas Shashbesh himself showed her his treasure, which included bags of pulverized philosophers' stone, there seemed no reason to doubt that he intended to share it. During her third visit to Ratcliff, however, she experienced true terror. Conducted to a dark corner of an underground treasure chamber (this time by a lesser spirit), she was instructed to take up a bag of the 'precious dust'. But through the gloom she perceived the place to be 'full of great monstrous serpents, snakes, and toads, which lay warbling and heaving and rolling one amongst another as if thousands of them were there'. For a few moments, even the intrepid Mary was shaken. Soon, however, she reached through the snakes towards the powder. At this, the snakes 'swelled' and attacked her; 'one of them fastened upon her hand and twisted up all about her arm.' Crying out in rage and terror against the spirits of the place and praying earnestly for God's help, she finally wrenched herself free and fled from Ratcliff. So great was her shock that when she stumbled into a nearby public house the patrons, seeing her eyes 'sunk in her head', thought she must be dying.

This harrowing experience proved that some, at least, of the guardians of Ratcliff were evil spirits—a fact confirmed by Ahab, who identified Shashbesh as the chief offender and as the snake that had bitten Mary's hand. Goodwin, therefore, was obliged to exorcize Shashbesh before any progress could be made. This he did one night in Red Lion Fields, where Shashbesh had repaired to guard his Sticestead treasure against Mary. Circling the site three times and repeating the incantation, Goodwin routed Shashbesh from his lair in spite of his clearly audible groans. This exorcism, pronounced good by Ahab, cleared both Ratcliff and Sticestead's of their most potent evil spirit.

It did not, however, end Mary's troubles at the two treasure sites. The subordinate guardians at Sticestead's transferred their allegiance to Cardinal Wolsey and soon proved to be as slippery as their new master. Similarly, the guardians at Ratcliff continued to devise tests for Mary's courage. Once they produced a roomful of monstrous forms—bears, satyrs, and toads—'howling and screeching in the most dreadful manner imaginable'; and twice they 'raised her 8 or 9 feet' in the air and shook her like a leaf. But when Mary remained bold and defiant, the guardians became more cooperative. Their new leader occasionally ordered some treasure delivered into Goodwin's closet, where it was safely locked away; and he introduced Mary to a talented lady alchemist (a mortal lowlander, not a spirit), who supervised the laboratory at Ratcliff. Unfortunately, the lady alchemist developed a lust for Goodwin that completely corroded her character, and God was obliged to end her life.

While Mary was boldly facing the spirits at Ratcliff, Goodwin was demonstrating a different kind of courage. A lesser man might have given way to despair as the glory promised by the Lord proved as elusive as that promised by the angels. Goodwin, remaining stalwart, worked out a theory to account for his frustrations. He had already observed that God does not abrogate the freedom of men or spirits and that freedom makes the prediction of events amazingly complex. Now, in mid-August, he reached another important conclusion. Since his coming triumph involved nothing less than a new dispensation, the events which thwarted him were not mere trials but 'necessary contingencies' in God's ultimate design and, at the same time, 'mighty obstructions framed by Satan' in his frantic effort to avert final defeat.

In late September Goodwin learned that the obstructions of Satan and the pleas of the 'hanging spirits' (devils of a particularly virulent sort) were to prevail for some months longer. Goodwin's complete triumph, a revelation said, would be postponed until Christmas Day, after which it would not be further delayed for all the spirits in the world. Meanwhile, he would continue to receive visions and oral revelations in further preparation for his great calling.

Goodwin's visions and revelations sustained him through the otherwise frustrating weeks of late 1686; they filled his days with profound significance and cast him as the protagonist of a cosmic drama. One of their recurrent themes was the political state of England—a subject that was becoming a national anxiety as the pro-Catholic policies of King James grew more and more threatening. While the King was bringing Catholics into the government and attacking the Anglican Establishment, Goodwin's dreams were correctly predicting the failure of the royal policy. In one particularly impressive vision, Goodwin saw a religous procession of the sort he had seen as a boy in France; as he watched, the priests carrying the host, along with their followers, 'were scattered strangely', losing 'all their things'. The symbolism of the dream was so obvious that he needed no help to interpret it; he simply concluded 'that the papists would fall'.

About Goodwin's own part in political events, his visions of 1686 were puzzling. Once he dreamed that he would be exonerated by Parliament for his notorious speech against King James. Lord Wharton, a vision told him, would appear for him in the House of Lords and John Wildman in the House of Commons. Another vision told him that with the help of his brother Tom he would be returned to Parliament as Knight of the Shire for Bucks. These prophecies, though clear as visions, seemed implausible in the current state of affairs. King James had prorogued his recalcitrant Tory Parliament and showed no sign of convening another; John Wildman was in exile; Lord Wharton seemed unlikely to vindicate Goodwin's speech anywhere, much less in the House of Lords;[6] and Tom appeared more apt to snub Goodwin in public than to help him win an election.[7] Under these circumstances, Goodwin did not expect the prophecies to be fulfilled immediately; he waited instead for drastic changes in English politics.

Though Goodwin's family sometimes appeared in his political dreams, they appeared more vividly and obsessively in dreams that had nothing to do with politics. In one symbolic vision he saved the entire family from a flood that threatened to overwhelm them. More than once he saved Lord Wharton from being executed for treason; several times he brought Tom to repent of his 'mighty crimes'; and once or twice he reclaimed the incorrigible Henry, whose indifference to religion had gravely endangered his soul.

Other dreams about the Whartons were more sombre. One nightmarish vision involving Lord Wharton was especially depressing:

I thought I was in pain [Goodwin wrote later], as if it were made upon me by some artifice, or as if needles were run into my back and farther I thought my father was by me, and seemed as if asleep (but was not), and would not wake to help me.

As the dream went on, Lord Wharton became confused with God, and Goodwin could not be sure whether it was his father or the Lord who refused to relieve his pains. Although Ahab explained that the dream referred to the Lord and that the pain and seeming indifference represented temporary trials, the explanation could not entirely blur the vision of Lord Wharton pretending to sleep while Goodwin suffered.

Even more nightmarish were two visions about Tom. On successive nights, in Goodwin's dreams, Tom attempted to have him killed—once by accomplices who tried to strangle him and once by assassins who waylaid him on the road. Both dreams, Ahab said, were genuine revelations. Tom had indeed planned to murder Goodwin and had once followed him to Hounslow for the purpose. Fortunately, Ahab added, Tom's 'murderous design' was now 'wearing off'. Soon he would undergo a complete change of heart and become 'quite another thing'.

About Henry, Goodwin's dreams were less threatening but ultimately more discouraging. They showed that in spite of Goodwin's brief success in reclaiming him, Henry was headed towards destruction. Having persisted in 'wild' living for many years, he had inevitably relapsed beyond hope. His death, a vision declared, was not very far off; and a later vision specified that he would die violently—a fate which Goodwin thought predictable enough from mere reason, considering Henry's penchant for drunken brawls.

Most vivid of all the Whartons who troubled Goodwin's dreams was his dead sister-in-law Anne Wharton, who first appeared on 30 August. As in life, she looked beautiful—'very fine'—and as always she offered a temptation. Sitting beside him and talking with him about their love affair, she again offered to make love with him, saying in French, as if she took his refusal for granted, 'Vous pouvez et vous ne voulez pas manger.' Goodwin found himself able to resist the temptation. 'It is true,' he said; 'I will not do it.' Thus rebuffed, Anne did not argue. 'Perhaps', she said, 'you have some person of your own.' Goodwin ignored the comment, and Anne then withdrew.

Anne's first appearance troubled Goodwin. The clarity of the vision convinced him that this was no ordinary dream, and he feared that Anne, despite her pious death, had returned to tempt him into sin. On the other hand, it seemed reasonable to hope that Anne had been sent to help him demonstrate his new firmness of mind. This hope was strengthened by the angels, who said that she had come in kindness; and it was made a certainty by later dreams. In late November, Anne reappeared with all the charm possible; and though Goodwin's carnal mind told him she was again offering herself and prompted him to desire her as much as ever, he made himself turn away from her without saying a word—an action which, Uriel said, demonstrated more strength of mind than if he had been awake and Anne had been living.

Unfortunately, Goodwin's sleep was sometimes invaded by spirits or lowlanders a good deal less scrupulous than Anne. During the late summer of 1686, lowland women were particularly troublesome. Besides Queen Ursula, who abused him shamefully, the lady alchemist of Ratcliff and Father Friar's daughter used their magic peas and their sexual artistry to seduce Goodwin and complicate his dreams. On 27 September, Uriel told him he had been more barbarously maltreated than any other uplander in history.

Goodwin was likewise troubled by his own virility. Experience had demonstrated that if he abstained from sex for three or four days he produced 'an unimaginable quantity of seed'. Experience had further shown that neither Mary's routine ministrations nor the stealthy exercises of the lowlanders could entirely remove ordinary mortal women from his thoughts and dreams. In the midst of such perplexities, Goodwin received a clear vision that outlined his sexual duties in blunt unmistakable terms. That it came from the Lord there could be no doubt. The Lord's own voice had instructed him to lie down to receive a vision, and the vision arrived precisely on time. The revelation consisted of five separate sentences, each so memorable and distinct that Goodwin could record them verbatim when he awoke.

'Swear not at all,' a voice within his vision began.

'Fuck every week where you used to do,' the voice continued.

Goodwin was startled at the indelicate word and for a moment he paused in his vision as if he had misunderstood, but the sentence was repeated in identical terms.

'That is,' the voice then explained, 'give her her due.'

The *her*, Goodwin knew at once, referred to Mary. Then as his thoughts suddenly shifted to the problem of controlling the unruly flesh, the voice answered his question before he could formulate it.

'Throw water on yourself,' it said.

The vision faded with the fifth sentence, 'So shall the Lord prosper you,' to which was added a seemingly irrelevant phrase, 'on Thursday'.

As Goodwin recorded the vision, its central meaning was obvious. He was to remain true to Mary and subdue his miscellaneous carnal impulses with cold water. Peripherally it was also obvious that his first reaction to the word *fuck* (which he recorded in capital letters) had been prudish. 'Upon better consideration,' he wrote, 'it is . . . only calling a thing by its true name, . . . and the God of Nature, I hope, may be allowed to speak plainly of all things whatever.' Finally, it was obvious that divines who had disparaged the use of water for combating lust had been wrong.

Infinitely more significant than Goodwin's dreams about women were those that dealt with his divine mission. One impressive vision declared that he would establish God's kingdom on earth, making it 'most glorious and great'. Another vision, almost too precious to record, began near Deptford, where on a creek running into the Thames Goodwin saw a vessel tossing in rough waves. Somehow he understood that Christ was on the vessel, and he was waiting to see Him 'at His forthcoming'.

. . . at last [Goodwin wrote] I perceived Him pass by me, . . . and pass from me so as had I not suddenly seen Him I should have missed Him. I immediately followed Him and left not close following His steps till . . He suddenly turned about to me and gave me occasion to fall down to Him and embrace His knees fast about; a little time after which He stooped down to me as giving me opportunity and leave to kiss Him; but perceiving out of reverence I did not, He said unto me, 'Kiss me.' Whereupon I kissed the Lord's face, and He went, as also my vision, immediately from me.

Interspersed among the dreams of spiritual significance were occasional dreams full of conflict and dread. Twice Goodwin battled with Satan himself, who attacked in the form of a whirlwind. The first assault seemed to paralyze Goodwin, particularly his arms, which remained enervated even after he awoke. The second struck him down with such force that he seemed to feel the life going out of him. Such visions strengthened his perception of an awesome fact: the powers arrayed against him were mighty and indefatigable, and their malevolence accounted for most of his misfortunes.

In late August, while Goodwin waited for the fulfilment of his visions, he learned from Mary and the angels that the beautiful lady he had met at Aix (whom they now identified as Anne Gartwrott, a Spanish princess) would soon come to England in search of him. Princess Anne, Mary said, was knowledgeable about lowlanders and spirits; she commanded, in fact, a spirit of her own, who could make direct contact with Mary. The Princess also possessed a large fortune in her own right and a vast supply of courage. Having fallen in love with Goodwin at Aix, she could not be dissuaded from marrying him. In spite of the disapproval of her powerful relatives, she had decided to slip away from her entourage on the Continent and make her way to England.

Before Princess Anne could shake herself free, Goodwin received the 'sudden news' that his father had returned home, and on 14 September he again found himself explaining to Lord Wharton why he was still unmarried and penniless. In spite of Goodwin's preliminary agonies, the conversation (which took place in Lord Wharton's coach) turned out to be almost painless. Inspired to keep his explanations simple, Goodwin stuck to the basic story he had invented at Emmerich. The mother of his fiancée, he said, had remained alive against all expectations and had continued to oppose the marriage. The young lady, nevertheless, remained resolute; and since she would soon come of age, the marriage itself was perfectly safe. Unusually complacent, Lord Wharton listened patiently to Goodwin's story and merely observed that as long as the marriage was safe, all was 'well enough'; and at the end of the interview Goodwin silently thanked God for having governed his father's heart.

At the time Lord Wharton returned, Goodwin still looked for a quick end to his miseries, but his expectations were crushed two weeks later by the revelations which said that the hanging spirits would prevail until Christmas. These pronouncements effectively postponed all his major projects and left Princess Anne Gartwrott as his only hope for an early rescue. At first, this hope seemed very bright indeed. Evading her relatives and travelling incognito, the Princess arrived safely at Canterbury, where she planned to remain until she could arrange to meet Goodwin. This plan she conveyed to Mary by way of her spirit, and Mary relayed it to Goodwin, who proposed a meeting at Gravesend. Before he could set out for Gravesend, however, he received word that Anne had come down with smallpox. Though Goodwin himself was immune to smallpox (having contracted it at Caen as a boy of ten), he knew only too well the seriousness of the disease; and when he heard of Anne's illness, he saw that all hopes of an early meeting were gone.

While smallpox and hanging spirits were destroying Goodwin's plans, the living conditions at Grafton Street were becoming intolerable. The noise of the place had always been a menace to visions, and in early October the house had become dangerous; creditors were beginning to make enquiries. Under these circumstances, Goodwin was pleased when Mary brought word that two angels had directed her to a safe place in Essex Court.[8] He prayed at once for permission to move, and on 11 October he conveyed his personal belongings and the treasure trunks to the new quarters.

Although the move to Essex Court went smoothly enough, it inadvertently touched off a violent family quarrel. To escape from the landlady at Grafton Street and to rent the new lodgings, Goodwin was obliged to get money from Lord Wharton. This sum, mostly committed in advance, melted away like snow, and within ten days he was again desperately poor. Thus when Princess Anne began recovering from smallpox and invited him to Canterbury, he did not know what to do. He could not afford the trip without help, but he could not bring himself to ask his father again for money.

At last on the morning of 25 October, an oral revelation commanded Goodwin to appeal to Lord Wharton. He was to explain that his fiancée had sent for him and that he had neither money nor suitable clothes for the occasion. As Goodwin was digesting the revelation, a crucial part of it was repeated:

> Hezekiah, my son [the Lord's voice said], once more I tell thee thou
>   must to thy father go.
> Ask him whether he will stick by thee or no;
> For other probability I cannot see
> That will be done for thee.

In obedience to this clear command Goodwin went to Lord Wharton, explained the situation, and asked him whether or not he would 'stand by' his son. The question enraged Lord Wharton. He had poured hundreds of pounds into debts caused by Goodwin's abortive schemes. To be asked now to finance a marriage project that always receded like a mirage and to be accused, by implication, of paternal delinquency if he refused struck him as monstrous. He proceeded to give his son an unforgettable dressing down, declaring that he did not believe anything Goodwin said and (even more memorably) that Goodwin 'had the worst reputation of any man in England'.

When Lord Wharton cooled down and Goodwin, much more humbly, begged for help, the matter was composed. But the blows had struck home. Although Goodwin had God's own sanction for his relationship with Mary, he knew that he was continually dirtied with 'aspersions' and that his own brothers and sisters took a cynical view of the subject (his sister Anne Wharton Carr would soon call Mary 'whore and witch').[9] He had hoped, however, that his father accepted the fiction constructed for his benefit. It was bitter to find that he suspected the worst and that he questioned the whole story of the wealthy fiancée.

The unfairness of the charges also rankled. Goodwin knew that his reputation, however tarnished, was not the worst in England; it was not even the worst in the Wharton family.[10] His brother Tom was adding every day to his notoriety as the country's foremost rake. He had recently taken up with Lady Sophia Bulkeley and produced a scandal that was to be immortalized in Dorset's witty poem, 'A Faithful Catalogue of Our Most Eminent Ninnies'.[11] Henry, meanwhile, was acquiring a reputation for sexual intrigue to go along with his eminence as a brawler.[12] With two such reprobates in the family, Lord Wharton's attack upon Goodwin was proof of blind partiality.

More serious than Goodwin's humiliation, however, was his perception that God had subjected him to cruel and unnecessary punishment. As he retreated to his new quarters in Essex Court, he could not help seeing that he had followed God's orders into a degrading indignity; and two days later, he was assailed by the most potent temptation he had yet experienced—a sudden impulse 'to curse God'. Though he managed, after a short, violent struggle, to fall upon his knees and bless God's name instead, he barely averted a sin that would have ended his hopes forever.

As always, Goodwin profited from near disaster. Perceiving that his evil thoughts had been the work of Satan, he again steeled himself to bear his disappointments, including one that followed shortly. When he received money from Lord Wharton, he was forbidden to go to Canterbury after all. Princess Anne had been discovered by her powerful relatives, and although she stoutly resisted their efforts to take her back to the Continent, she could not elude their constant surveillance. She would remain under siege, Goodwin learned, until after Christmas, when his own rise to power would make all objections ridiculous.

Goodwin's expectation that God would end his troubles on Christmas Day was firmly based on a series of carefully recorded oral revelations transmitted on 30 September. Goodwin must undergo one more trial, the revelations said, but the date of deliverance was unalterably fixed. One passage was especially crucial:

> The day is set, it cannot be denied [the Lord's voice said].
> It is the day, the greatest here, when thou need'st not thyself to hide;
> That is the day, the very day, that I will come to relieve thee,
> So thou art sure in heart and mind to wait for Me,
> The 25th of December next; and that, I say to thee,

It is the last vow that e'er I made, or e'er shall be to thee,
If all the spirits in the world should constant follow Me.

As Goodwin struggled through November and December, the Lord's promise helped him endure the daily vexations he suffered, including several arguments with Mary and frequent disappointments at the hands of Cardinal Wolsey. On Christmas Day, however, instead of deliverance, he received a revelation which spoke of a six-day 'dispute' between himself and the Lord. Six days later he learned that the 'dispute' was a question of whether he would go through another sorrow for the Lord before achieving 'pomp and dignity'. He was free, a revelation said, to refuse and hold the Lord to the original promises; but if he did so, he would certainly lose Mary and her two unborn children, Hezekiah and Susan, and probably his son Peregrine. If, on the other hand, he assented, he would be taken to the wilderness, where he would suffer for forty days and then emerge for his final triumph.

Once Goodwin understood the alternatives, he did not hesitate for a moment. He would never sacrifice Mary or his children for worldly glory and he would cheerfully answer 'Yes, Lord' to whatever trial the Lord imposed. Rejecting Mary's suggestion that he pray to be relieved of the new sorrow, he prayed instead for others. He asked that Mary should be preserved from want while he was away, that his father should be 'better pleased', that Princess Anne should be comforted, and that his creditors should be paid off. Meanwhile he would trust God to transport him to the wilderness and bring him back safely.

In this mood of quiet heroism Goodwin ended the first volume of his autobiography. He had expected to end his narrative, along with his troubles, on Christmas Day, but the sudden reversal of fortune had given him at least one more harrowing episode to record. He would reserve that episode, however, for a new volume and use the last remaining sheet of paper in the original volume for the instruction of his son Peregrine. As he reviewed his tribulations, he saw that God had enabled him to bear them, and he called upon Peregrine to show similar faith and courage. Since his own experience showed 'the imperfections of the best spirits, the deceits of the intermediate ones, and the gross lyings of the evil ones', he cautioned Peregrine to learn correct spiritual judgements. He concluded with a ringing affirmation of the truth of his narrative, which God had pronounced inspired, and with a tribute to Mary, whom Gabriel had once described as 'fit for heaven and not for earth'. This description, Goodwin told Peregrine, was now confirmed by direct revelation; God Himself called Mary 'the best of women'.

12

The Inner Voice

WHEN Goodwin volunteered to suffer in the wilderness, the procedure seemed simple enough. His visions suggested a wilderness in the biblical style, perhaps near Mount Sinai, and he expected God to carry him there, leave him for forty days, and then return him to London. But the procedure of going to the wilderness turned out to be amazingly complex, and through the winter and spring of 1687 Goodwin suffered almost as much anxiety in finding his way into the wilderness as the Israelites did in finding their way out of it. Before he could start, an oral revelation explained, he was required to spend two weeks at Wooburn, and this assignment proved to be only the beginning of a series. Again and again through the months that followed, he was sent back to Wooburn, and the date of his departure for the wilderness was postponed—from January to March, from March until Easter, from Easter to Ascension Day, and from Ascension Day to the indeterminate future.

At Wooburn Goodwin found himself 'greatly tired' before he had completed the first weeks of his sentence. Unaccountably cut off from oral revelations and even significant visions, he began to suspect that Wooburn itself might be the wilderness— the moral equivalent of Mount Sinai—and that when he returned to London after forty days he would find his trials ended; but this hope guttered out in mid-February, when the forty days had passed and a reunion with Mary showed that the projects of the partnership remained in 'miserable suspense'.

To make matters worse, Princess Anne Gartwrott, who had tried to shake off her relatives by moving to Romford, was again surrounded and more heavily beset than ever; and affairs in London were similarly tense. Goodwin's creditors, temporarily thrown off the scent by the move to Essex Court, had picked up the trail, and the new place had become too dangerous to occupy. Goodwin, therefore, spent part of his brief reprieve from Wooburn in moving back to the old quarters on Vere Street—the only place he could afford.

When he returned to Wooburn in early March, he took with him an additional worry. His instructions told him that he must remain there until 24 March, and the angels had told Mary that she would deliver her twins on 10 March. Once more he was separated from her during her hour of danger—during a time, moreover, when visions were sparse and oral revelations had ceased entirely. After 10 March, his anxiety became acute. As the days went by he received no letters from Mary, who had promised to write him if she survived the delivery, and by 16 March he was very near despair.

In this distress Goodwin received a new kind of revelation; he heard what seemed to be an 'outward voice' saying, 'Hezekiah, come to her.' Since the message contradicted his orders to remain at Wooburn he could not be sure the voice was genuine, but the next morning when it told him that Mary was dying, he could wait no longer. Returning to London post-haste, he hurried directly to the house of the midwife Mrs Martin, where he supposed Mary lay dying, and when the lady obstinately denied knowing anything about Mary's delivery, he continued on to the lodgings at Vere Street. There, to his intense relief, he found Mary herself, sufficiently recovered to be 'below stairs' with company. The delivery itself, she later explained, had gone off without trouble. In less than an hour on 10 March she had produced twins, Hezekiah and Susan, whom she had sent, as ordered, to two separate nurses. Later complications, however, including a badly extracted tooth, had almost killed her, and Goodwin's voice had correctly warned him of her great danger. In short, Mary concluded, Goodwin's revelation had been authentic—the voice of the archangel Michael.

Very soon Goodwin would learn that his new outward voice was only a prelude to an 'inner voice' which would transform his life, but for the time being he was preoccupied with present miseries. His journey to the wilderness was continually postponed; he lost his new daughter Susan, whom he never saw, when a careless nurse rolled over in bed and smothered her; and the strange silence of the Lord continued. It was not until 5 April that Goodwin began to receive oral revelations; and these messages spoke of new covenants and new delays.

Under these demoralizing circumstances, it was almost a relief when a clear vision told Goodwin that he was at last to suffer significantly. The very next day he was to go to St. James's Park, where some officers of the King would lie in wait for him. There, perhaps in the Park itself or perhaps in one of 'the dark passages in St. James's House',[1] they would seize him, hurry him into a coach, and inflict whatever tortures 'a revengeful Prince' might command.

The vision was at once vivid and consonant with the facts. A previous vision had told him that he was to suffer great pains before his final ordeal in the wilderness, and common sense told him that his pains might come from King James, who could not have forgotten his incendiary speech in the Exclusion Parliament. The next morning, therefore, Goodwin divested himself of all his magic charms against suffering and strode off to keep his dangerous appointment at St. James's Park.

For several years, Goodwin had pulled his hat down over his eyes to hide his face 'from all men'. Now, as he walked about the Park, he deliberately showed his face to the passers-by, tacitly inviting the King's henchmen to do their worst. After about two hours of pacing up and down, during which no one ventured to attack him, he made himself face what he judged to be the focal point of all danger—the dark passages in the route through St. James's Palace. Disdaining the company of a brother-in-law, whom he met by accident in the Park, and giving his assailants a perfect chance to attack if they dared, he walked 'softly' but resolutely through the critical passages until he came out on the other side, on Pall Mall. Untouched and as far as he could tell unobserved, he then retraced the route through St. James's and came out in the Park, where he walked openly until dark. At last, convinced that he had done his duty and that the Lord would accept his willingness to suffer, he made his way safely home to Vere Street.

Before dawn the next morning, however, he learned in another vision that his quiet resolution had frightened off his enemies, who had indeed lain in wait for him but had concluded, mistakenly, that he intended to fight. He was to return to the Park, the vision said, for another trial—an attack by two hired ruffians. This time, his vision added, he would be allowed to fight; he was not required to submit passively to torture.

For the new encounter, Goodwin armed himself with his best sword, not a 'genteel town-sword', but a weapon with a blade almost 30 inches long; and about eleven in the morning, he began a bold and defiant promenade around the Park. As he walked along, 'with a smiling countenance', he noticed that although he experienced brief tremours of 'aversion' when villainous-looking strangers came near him, he was not really afraid; he was certain that he could beat the two rogues assigned to maim him.

After two or three hours he began to regret having come so heavily armed; his long sword, he realized, was an obvious sign that he was prepared for his enemies. Just how formidable he looked he was able to judge by the behaviour of two men he met during his walk. As they passed him, they stopped and turned around to stare. 'Look there,' one of them said, apparently speaking of Goodwin's sword. 'God's wounds,' the other one said. By mid-afternoon it was clear that the King's hirelings had lost heart. For form's sake, Goodwin waited until the Park was practically deserted and then retired, more disappointed than relieved, to Vere Street.

While Goodwin was reflecting upon his escape from injury, he received an explanation for his continual frustrations. His affairs could never thrive, the Lord said in an oral revelation, and he could never go to the wilderness, until he had become 'frank and free' with his brothers and sisters. This revelation confirmed what Goodwin had often suspected, that his alienation from his family had caused his continual misery. It explained too why he had been sent so often to Wooburn, and it promised a quick ending to the long estrangement; this time, the Lord said, Goodwin's father and brothers would 'make an end of all the trouble'.

Goodwin went to Wooburn prepared to accept the apologies of the Whartons, who assembled there in early May. As the injured party in the old disputes, he never dreamed of making the first move towards reconciliation; he simply waited for others to bring up the subject. But the whole Wharton family remained stonily silent, and on 11 May when Tom prepared to leave without apologizing, the situation became alarming. Tom was a prime source of the troubles, Goodwin knew, and if he left unreconciled, all was lost. Reluctantly, therefore, he confronted Tom and broached the subject of injuries.

Tom, unfortunately, remained unrepentant. Although he had once struck Goodwin and ordered him to stay away from Winchendon, he persisted in acting as if it were he, not Goodwin, who deserved an apology; he would not even concede that Goodwin had been 'a very good friend'.[2] He hoped, he said, that he and Goodwin could live more civilly with each other, but he stubbornly refused to apologize for Goodwin's love affair with Anne. In the end, therefore, Goodwin could achieve nothing better than a truce. Though he promised to return Tom's civilities as they were offered, he knew that he retained the old 'inward distastes' for his brother and that the new agreement was nothing like a true reconciliation.

The failure of the Whartons to become frank and free, as the Lord had promised, put Goodwin in a dangerous and desponding mood. After reading Gilbert Burnet's account of some wicked friars who had denied God in their attempts to produce a fraudulent miracle,[3] he again felt strong compulsions to deny God altogether. And a few days later, after he learned that Mary's projects were stagnant and that Princess Anne had been taken to Rye (where her relatives hoped to get her aboard a ship for France), 'temptations flew thick like hail' into his thoughts, prompting him to abandon everything and 'throw the Covenant out of the window'.

On the verge of despair, Goodwin perceived nevertheless a few gleams of light. One of these was his good fortune with children, both living and dead. Peregrine, still at Shirburn, continued to be treated like a young nobleman, and young Hezekiah had been taken to Windsor, where he was equally well treated. Goodwin had always known that the children who had died in infancy—Charles, Susan, the quintuplets, and the twins delivered while Goodwin was in Holland—were safely lodged in heaven; but in late May he also learned that embryos receive souls as early as nine days after conception and that even Mary's miscarriages had helped to stock heaven with angels.[4]

While such comforts were saving Goodwin from some irretrievable rebellion, a process was growing up, almost unnoticed, which was about to launch him into adventure and high drama. During the summer of 1687 he gradually evolved a new way of communicating with God—a method that rendered him independent of Mary and the angels. This process had begun at Wooburn in mid-March, when he had received two visions that seemed to occur on the 'waking' side of the ill-defined and tenuous boundary between trance and ordinary consciousness. In one, the Lord said, 'I will leave thee master of thine actions'; and in the other, as Goodwin was merely 'ruminating towards a vision', he heard the Lord say 'Amen.'

By late May, 'waking visions', as Goodwin came to call them, began to occur more frequently. Sometimes they began with a surprising and provocative phrase, like one which said 'Zion is sold'; and sometimes they seemed to flow more naturally from waking thoughts, like one which said that Mary had descended from the lineage of the Virgin Mary. In either case they seemed to separate themselves from random musings or consciously contrived chains of deduction.

Though Goodwin was quick to see that 'a waking vision, or inspiration, or revelation' differed from regular visions, he did not immediately perceive the consequences of his new resource. At first he regarded such visions merely as supplements to the visions and versified revelations which guided his life while he was in London. But the discouraging events of the summer changed his point of view; as one disappointment followed another, he became more and more aware of the deficiencies in regular visions and revelations, which were often ambiguous and sometimes led to staggering disappointments.

Goodwin's full illumination on the validity of waking visions came during some of his darkest hours at Wooburn. In late June, before leaving London, he was promised in an oral revelation that at five o'clock on a Sunday afternoon the Lord would meet him in a lower walk of the Wooburn gardens. At the appointed time, he took up his station, ready for the Lord's appearance; but nothing happened. He waited and prayed earnestly, and still he saw nothing. After about an hour he began to hear 'great groans round about', and later that evening as he walked in the fields he again heard 'the same groan'. At the time, he did not connect the groans with the outward voice he had heard in March, but when he returned to London Mary informed him that they had come from the angels, who sympathized with him and who groaned too at her latest miscarriage, which had cost her twelve recent conceptions.

On the next Sunday, back at Wooburn, Goodwin again waited for the Lord to appear and again found the garden empty. This time there were no moans, but after an hour or so he seemed to hear 'as in vision' the sentence, 'It cannot be done today,' and when he asked, 'Shall it be tomorrow,' the voice replied 'Perhaps so.' The next Sunday, 10 July, he was equally unsuccessful in seeing God's face in the garden, but the voice of the vision became clearer. He heard the words 'It cannot be done' as if they were 'whispered' to him. Similarly, on Sunday 24 July, the voice clearly repeated the phrase, 'It cannot be done' and added, when Goodwin asked why, 'Thou thyself art the cause.' By Sunday, 31 July, he was able to hear the voice in the chapel, as well as in the garden, and he had concluded that it was the voice of the Lord.

In early August the voice that had once spoken only in moments of crisis began to speak often, without regard to place and time. The Lord spoke 'softly', Goodwin noted, as if the voice were internal. His statements and commands, however, were nonetheless clear, and Goodwin soon perceived the inestimable value of his new gift. He was no longer isolated at Wooburn, or anywhere else, from knowledge and comfort; he no longer had to depend for information upon well-meaning but ill-informed angels. He was free too from the confining procedures of regular visions and revelations. There remained only the problem of distinguishing between his own thoughts and the internal voice and of making his own thoughts conform with divine truth. This problem was solved on 14 August by the Lord's promise that when he was seriously thinking of spiritual matters his thoughts would be 'all infallible'.

Goodwin's gift of infallible internal revelations arrived just in time to help him deal with James II. The King, who had antagonized Tories and Anglicans by his attacks upon the established order, found himself obliged to seek support from Whigs and Dissenters; and by August 1687 his attempt to woo his former opponents was in full cry. On 4 April, he had issued his famous Declaration of Indulgence, which not only granted toleration to Dissenters but also made them eligible for government appointments. At once an act of arbitrary power and a shrewd political manœuvre, the proclamation nullified several parliamentary laws, including the Test Act, and made nonsense of the concept of limited monarchy. To Dissenters, however, the relief granted by the Declaration was welcome, whatever its legality; an edict which emptied gaols and opened chapels was calculated, rightly, to earn gratitude.[5]

If the bait was tempting, the hook was nevertheless obvious. In return for toleration, the King's new allies were expected to procure him a parliament that would legalize his arbitrary actions, subsidize his army, and look on approvingly while he filled the highest civil and military offices with Catholics. Few wise men were deceived by James's appearance as a champion of religious liberty. Most saw the Declaration, which granted the same rights to Catholics as to Dissenters, as a long stride towards Catholic supremacy.

As the King looked for new friends among his old enemies, he naturally thought of Lord Wharton, whose influence among Dissenters was great. When the Court moved to Windsor for the summer, on 19 May, one of its first official acts was to grant Lord Wharton permission to hold fairs at Shap, Healaugh, and Wooburn;[6] and he was among those invited to the Court. Lord Wharton had long since learned the art of survival during stormy times. It was allowable to be personally friendly with unpopular rulers, but to forward their schemes might later prove fatal; it was permissible to receive favours, but it might be disastrous to earn them. This wise policy, which had enabled Lord Wharton to survive the rise and fall of the Cromwell regime, he now applied to King James. He was perfectly willing to have himself and his sons received at Court; he was only unwilling to support the government.

Goodwin, on the other hand, saw no reason for going near King James. His revelations told him that the papists would fall; the angels and Cardinal Wolsey told him, via Mary, that James was a very bad king, 'going as fast as he can to hell'; and political experience suggested that before receiving him the King would demand an apology for his notorious speech. Goodwin was determined never to apologize, and this decision was firmly backed by his new internal voice. It would look 'very pitiful and mean', the Lord said, if he asked pardon for having followed conscience and duty. The Lord's intervention settled the matter.

Though Lord Wharton more than once 'pressed' Goodwin to kiss the King's hand, Goodwin refused so stoutly that the matter was dropped.

Shortly after his new voice had forbidden Goodwin to curry favour with the King, it began to tell him how to deal with the growing temptations offered by Mistress Letitia Poulett, the grandniece, protégée, and companion of Lady Wharton. Letitia, the daughter of John, third Baron Poulett, and of Essex Popham Poulett,[7] was twenty-one years old in the summer of 1687 when she became a problem to Goodwin. Although perhaps not as beautiful as Queen Ursula, she was nevertheless beautiful, and her disposition, full of modesty, good sense, and warmth, was dangerously attractive.

Counselled by his voice, Goodwin was striving to centre his thoughts upon pure friendship when a surprising incident demoralized him. One evening in mid-August as he passed by the corridor that led to Letitia's chambers, he could see by the light and shadow cast upon the wall opposite her door that the door was open and Letitia was standing just inside it. Even as he looked, the shadow seemed to retreat from the open doorway, as if Letitia were stepping back to allow him to enter her chambers. Though instantaneously convinced that she had been waiting for him and that she was inviting him to bed, he 'stopped not quite', but continued automatically to his own room. There, struggling with his carnal impulses, he registered a complaint. 'Lord,' he said, 'what strange trials dost Thou put upon me.' To this he received a reply more surprising than the temptation itself: 'I give her to thee,' his voice said.

The next day, acting upon the Lord's permission, Goodwin apologized to Letitia for not following her into her room and explained that he was now at her disposal. Contrary to his expectations, however, she seemed offended rather than pleased, turning away from him in what appeared to be disgust. Goodwin could understand her response well enough; she was obviously angry at being rejected—insulted because, in his too-hasty confession, he had admitted seeing her shadow on the wall and ignoring the invitation it implied (something she could not have known if he had not told her). What he could not understand was her continuing resistance. Nothing he could say would persuade her to meet him in the hall that night, and he found when he went by her chambers early in the evening that her door was securely locked.

Shaken by the rebuff and by Letitia's continued coolness, Goodwin suspended operations for several days. When Letitia returned, however, from a brief visit with her brother-in-law Sir William Fermor,[8] Goodwin learned from his voice that he should take up the pursuit once more. Acting on his new orders, he attempted that night to waylay her at her door as she returned to her chambers. This strategy, however, involved the danger of being seen by the family as he lurked about her corridor—a danger which ultimately defeated him. When Letitia arrived, she slipped inside the door so quickly that he did not have time to follow her in, and before he could get her to reopen the door, he heard someone coming and was obliged to hurry away.

Goodwin's next effort was foiled by the security system of Wooburn. Because the house was full of company, he was quartered in a room above the stables, and at night when he tried to re-enter the house he found the 'great gate' locked. By the time he managed to get the gate open, Letitia had locked her door. This annoyance was followed the next evening by a shattering rejection. There was dancing at Wooburn, and Goodwin seized the opportunity during the few moments they became partners to tell Letitia that he would come to her chambers that night 'in spite of hell'. Her answer, in 'a fierce tone', came back immediately, before she danced away. 'I wonder', she said, 'what you take me for, Sir.'[9]

Goodwin did not remain shattered long. Before morning, his voice explained that Letitia had already repented of her anger, which had been caused by some slander invented by Henry, and that he should again proceed to seduce her. The next evening, therefore, Goodwin launched his final assault.

Throughout the day he had noticed that Letitia's countenance registered joy, and he expected that when he arrived at her door he would find it open. When he actually reached the door, however, he found it not only shut but locked—a circumstance which so confused him that instead of waiting for Letitia to come, quietly, and open the door, he twice lifted the latch and then knocked.

Letitia's apartment consisted of three rooms—an antechamber, which opened on the corridor; her own bedroom, which opened on the antechamber; and the bedroom of her serving woman, which lay behind Letitia's. To Goodwin, waiting nervously in the corridor, it seemed inevitable that Letitia, whose room was closest to the door, would answer the knock herself. As the door opened, therefore, he lunged quickly into Letitia's outward room, only to find himself face to face with Mrs Coxe, Letitia's servant. Although momentarily as startled as Goodwin himself, Mrs Coxe quickly took command. She would not open the door to Letitia's bedroom, which she had locked, or carry a message to Letitia. Instead, she ordered Goodwin to leave instantly and threatened to expose him to Lady Wharton. At a hopeless tactical disadvantage, Goodwin was forced to withdraw, discomfited and baffled.

Goodwin's voice soon pointed out that he had been much too hasty and impatient. Letitia, the Lord said, had intended to bring him into her chambers as soon as her woman was safely in bed—an intention defeated by his haste. Accepting the Lord's reproof with proper humility, Goodwin quickly constructed a story to account for his strange behaviour, which was duly reported to Lady Wharton. His visit to Letitia, he alleged, was 'not at all secret'; he had intended to pay a social call and had been met with impertinence. This tale, at least faintly plausible, prevented an outright explosion; but the escape was so narrow that Goodwin asked to be 'dispensed' from pursuing Letitia. Such intrigues, he complained, would 'quite ruin' his reputation. This request the Lord granted; and thereafter, though Goodwin sometimes observed that Letitia still languished for him, even after she was married,[10] he never again attempted to seduce her.

While Goodwin was stalking Letitia, his communications with his internal voice increased so rapidly that he gave up trying to record everything said to him and contented himself with noting only the most significant of the Lord's commands. Of these none seemed more noteworthy than the series that dealt with his stepmother. For years Goodwin had brooded about the wrongs done him by Lady Wharton in revenge for the unfortunate letter he had written in defence of her son Alexander.[11] Now, with his new powers, he could at last learn the whole truth about the original argument and begin to undo the damage. His first revelations on this subject told him an important fact about the letter itself. Alexander, to whom it was addressed, had forged many additions to it before handing it to his mother, and it was precisely those additions which had caused all the trouble. Thus, Goodwin, entirely guiltless, had been convicted without a hearing upon forged evidence. To requite the injustice, his voice told him, he was to touch Lady Wharton with the magic frog bone (which he had brought to Wooburn) and stir up her long-stifled feelings. Once touched, she would fall hopelessly in love with him and eventually die of frustration.

When Goodwin applied the bone to Lady Wharton, on 26 August, he observed that 'it began quickly its operation'; and four days later, as he journeyed to Acton for a brief meeting with Mary, his voice further informed him that Lady Wharton had indeed been in love with him in the days before their quarrel. At Acton, however, a complication was suddenly added to the plot. He could not merely sit passively by and watch his stepmother pine away, the Lord's voice said; he must kiss her to make her 'die the sooner'. As Goodwin was digesting this command, he received a more shocking order: he must 'lie with her', his revelation said, to convince Lord Wharton of her treachery.

Though unused to disputing the Lord's commands, Goodwin protested. 'Lord,' he argued, 'I will do all Thou bid'st me, but how can I do this?'

'It is to accomplish the measure of her iniquity,' the Lord said. 'Thy father doth not touch her; she shall have a son by thee, shall drown it, shall die of grief and love and be damned; and thou shalt not pray for her.'

'Sure, Lord,' Goodwin answered, 'there were never such things.'

'No,' the voice said, 'nor never will be again.'

As Goodwin set about following his orders, he saw that Lady Wharton was already in love with him. Dancing with her at Wooburn, he saw her 'lift up her eyes in a strange sort of ecstasy', and the next day when he asked for a private interview, she embraced the proposal 'with all the passionate words and eyes imaginable'. Yet for all her infatuation, Goodwin found her actions perverse. Instead of receiving him in her chamber, she met him outside the house in an arched walk. And when he brought up their old argument about Alexander, she did not apologize, but merely told him several things about the case which he had never heard before. Nor did she leap at his suggestion that parts of the offending letter had been forged. She merely remarked that his theory was presently unverifiable, since the letter was not at Wooburn. Discouraged by her manner, more like a lawyer's than a lover's, Goodwin gave up the interview and walked away.

Lady Wharton's perversity almost persuaded Goodwin to leave her unseduced; but on the morning of 5 September (the day he was to leave Wooburn), his voice positively ordered him to try once more, and he managed to arrange an interview with Lady Wharton in the 'long gallery'. There, seated among the Vandykes and Lelys, he began by apologizing for his recent coldness. He had been 'out of humour', he said, because of the formal tone of their first meeting and because he feared that she had told his father the servant's version of the Poulett fiasco. Lady Wharton was graciousness itself. She had not meant to offend him at their first meeting, she said; nor had she reported the Poulett episode to Lord Wharton.

At this response, Goodwin kissed Lady Wharton's hand; then, pressing forward from his initial success, he gently taxed her with having treated him unjustly in their early disagreements over Alexander. To this Lady Wharton replied that she had long ago forgotten such unpleasant details. Furthermore, Goodwin then added, she had been unjust 'to one that she knew loved her'. When Lady Wharton seemed to accept this statement, he kissed her hand a second time, noting as he did so that she 'smiled and seemed as well pleased as possible'.

It was at this point that Goodwin's impetuosity (as his voice later explained) again led him into error. Suddenly overconfident, he attempted without further preamble to kiss Lady Wharton on the mouth. Instead of melting in his arms, however, Lady Wharton leaped to her feet and 'flew' from him in what seemed to be 'a very great passion'. As Goodwin rallied from his confusion, he learned from his voice that he had merely been too quick—that for the sake of decorum his stepmother had not wished to yield 'so strangely soon'—but he did not stay at Wooburn to give or receive explanations. He set out at once for

London, leaving the duty of seducing Lady Wharton for some future occasion.

In spite of Goodwin's misadventures at Wooburn, his confidence in his new powers grew steadily and he returned to London a more commanding figure than the one who had left there six weeks earlier. He now knew for certain what he had sometimes suspected, that Mary's usefulness to his career had ended. She had herself complained often that she could not live long, and recently both his sleeping and waking visions had indicated that she was right. Although he wept at such revelations, he saw that his divine voice had made her help unnecessary and that she actually impeded the projects involving women.

On the Lord's advice, Goodwin did not tell Mary about his voice or her own life expectancy, nor explain that oral revelations and dreams had been largely superseded. For the sake of appearances, his voice told him, he would continue to receive rhymed revelations while he was at Vere Street, but he would receive most of his revelations in secret. One of these messages gave him permission to open his trunkful of gifts from Cardinal Wolsey, and he was disturbed at first to find that all the gold had been removed. His voice soon explained, however, that the clever Cardinal, suspecting his intentions, had removed the treasures 'to fret' him. Similarly, his voice continued, he would find it useless to open his other accumulated treasures until after Mary was dead. These facts, of course, Goodwin carefully kept from Mary; and he also concealed the much more important fact that he was preparing to have a glorious love affair with Queen Mary Beatrice, the wife of James II.

Goodwin had known for years that he was destined ultimately to rule England, but his informants had never been clear about how he would attain power. On 30 August at Acton he received a vital hint when the angels told Mary that he would become 'very great' at Court. They did not explain how he could rise at a court ruled by King James, his inveterate enemy; but his internal voice later gave an answer almost dazzling in its beauty and simplicity. His rise, the Lord said, 'should be by the Queen, who should fall in love' with him.

Once his voice had provided the master clue, the subordinate revelations flowed easily. Queen Mary Beatrice had been unfortunate in the matter of children. In the early days of her marriage she had borne five living children, but only one of these, the Princess Isabella, had survived beyond infancy, and even Isabella had died at the age of five. In recent years, the Queen had failed to produce any living children, and it now appeared that she would never bear another.[12] It was precisely this difficulty—a fact of immense political significance—that Goodwin was called upon to remedy; he would lie with the Queen, his voice said, and she would produce a healthy child. As for King James, who was desperately anxious for a male heir to the throne, he would forgive everything when he learned that only Goodwin, with his remarkable potency, was capable of getting the Queen with child. He would willingly 'resign the Queen alone' to her lover.

In the succeeding days, Goodwin learned that he must neglect everyone else, including Princess Anne (still at Rye), and concentrate upon the Queen. As soon as possible, he was to follow Mary Beatrice to Bath, where she had arrived with her Court on 18 August. Meanwhile, since she had not seen him for several years, care would be taken to bring him again to her mind and to prepare her for his coming. Finally, Goodwin learned, the Queen would not be alone in loving him. All the women who ever saw him—especially all the ladies of the Queen's Court—would find him irresistible.

Full of his new plans, Goodwin remained in London only long enough to wind up a few business details and get Mary's permission to go to Bath. Philip Swale, one of his father's stewards, had already lent him £50, and he had little difficulty persuading Mary that he should seek his fortunes at Court. After an oral revelation, in which the Lord promised 'honours' for Goodwin, Mary pronounced herself satisfied with his plans; and on Friday, 9 September, he set out for Bath in a public coach, taking along with him his precious journal so that he could record every detail of his great adventure with the Queen.

13

Mary Beatrice Anne Margaret Isabel of Este

QUEEN MARY BEATRICE[1] arrived at Bath on 18 August 1687, ready to play her part in what a later age would call a public-relations campaign. While the King was conducting a progress through the West, attempting to rally support for his policies and to quiet the increasingly strident voices of alarm and outrage, it was the Queen's duty to charm the residents of Bath and the gentry of the surrounding country—to create goodwill for the monarchy and counteract the sullen English prejudice against foreigners and Catholics. She was to make the provincials forget that she was an Italian from Modena and make them remember that she was the Queen of England, the natural centre of loyalty and love.

Besides charming Western England, a mission for which she was admirably qualified, 'the beautiful Queen' (as Goodwin called her) had another, more vital object in coming to Bath. After many years of failure, she still hoped to produce a male heir to the throne, and it was possible, she thought, that the medicinal waters of Bath might help her to a pregnancy. In this hope she was only mildly encouraged by her cautious medical advisors,[2] who would only agree that the waters of Bath could not hurt her and that if they did nothing to cure sterility, they might at least help her regain her general health, which had been noticeably weakened by the death of her mother, the Duchess of Modena.[3]

During her first weekend in Bath,[4] Mary Beatrice was joined by King James, who received several deputations and touched dozens of his ailing subjects for the scrofula.[5] On 22 August James set out for Gloucester, and the Queen launched her personal campaign to promote the interests of the Crown. Her morning routine usually began at the Cross Bath,[6] the most private and easily policed of the four public baths the town afforded. There, accompanied by her ladies and by Mary Chapman, her official Bath guide, she dutifully drank the waters and bathed in the warm pool. To this ritual the public was invited. While the Queen and her attendants, chastely clad in long canvas dresses, bathed and chatted, spectators were allowed to watch from the gallery.

In the early afternoon the Queen customarily toured the countryside in her coach, showing herself to her subjects in the small hamlets. Later, at the Abbey House,[7] she gave audiences for the families of country gentry and prominent townsmen. Practically anyone with social pretensions, in an area traditionally royalist, had the opportunity of speaking with the Queen and kissing her hand. By the time the King returned, on 6 September, Mary Beatrice had conquered the city for the Crown.

The King himself had not been so lucky. By a monumental blunder at Oxford—an attempt to capture Magdalen College for the Catholics—he had turned a goodwill tour into a national grievance.[8] But if his tour had been politically disastrous, it had been spiritually uplifting. In Gloucestershire, he had visited St. Winifred's Well (a medieval shrine), drunk the waters, and prayed for a male heir to the throne.[9] When he returned to Bath, therefore, he hoped that with the cooperation of the Queen, who had employed the secular treatments offered by the Cross Bath, he might change the succession to the English throne.

As Goodwin travelled towards Bath, he had his own plans for the English throne, and his revelations had already solved the most vital problem—the question of the male heir. That the Queen should invite Goodwin to her bed was natural enough, but that he, Goodwin Wharton, should father a child who would be raised as a papist and continue the King's attack on English institutions was unthinkable. The last thing England needed was a popish heir to the throne, and any man who helped provide one would be a traitor to the nation—on a par with Sunderland, Jeffreys, Dryden, and Peterborough. To this knotty problem, Goodwin's voice provided a simple answer. Once Goodwin had established himself as the Queen's lover, he would convert both Mary Beatrice and James to Protestantism, thus ending for all time the threat of royal subversion.

His internal voice also explained that Goodwin would be introduced to the city of Bath and to the Royal Court in a suitably dramatic way. Soon after his arrival he would be set upon by six men (acting under the mistaken notion that the King still wanted him destroyed). Using nothing more than his dress sword, he would rout the whole crew, wounding four and disarming the rest. To this feat, the King himself would be a witness, arriving just in time to see Goodwin finish the battle.

Goodwin arrived in Bath on the afternoon of Saturday, 10 September, and after he had found a lodging in the house of a young haberdasher and his pretty wife,[10] he walked forth to show himself on the streets of Bath—to let the gang of would-be assassins know that he had arrived. By the time he retired for the night, he knew that he had been recognized and that his dramatic introduction to the city would take place at seven o'clock the next morning. He knew, furthermore, that before he reached Bath the Queen had wept for fear he was not coming. His features, as the Lord had promised, had now returned vividly to her mind and she wondered why she had not fallen in love with him years before.

In the morning, when Goodwin awoke, it was raining, and he was inclined to lie in bed and muse a while before setting out for the area of the King's Bath,[11] where the attack was scheduled to occur. As the clock struck six, however, his voice chided him for lingering and implied that he was fearful. As soon as he could pray, dress, and arm himself, therefore, he hurried through the rain to the Dry Pump Room, where he hoped to stay until his opponents appeared. He found, unfortunately, that the door was locked, and he was obliged to seek shelter under a shed in a nearby street.

At seven, when he returned to his battle station, the whole area seemed as deserted as ever; and as he looked for his attackers, his voice brought him a grim message. Because he had suffered 'an apprehension', the Lord said, the angels had inspired one of the conspirators to discover the whole plot to King James, who had immediately ordered the gang to desist. Goodwin was deeply troubled. The King, he knew, could send for him anyway, fight or no fight; the Lord, in fact, now promised that James would do so. But Goodwin had set his heart on the spectacular public 'quarrel' which the Lord had promised him. Now this prize was to be snatched from him and he was to be charged with cowardice into the bargain. As he brooded, his voice brought comfort. The accusation, it said, was only a trial; he had 'done all well' and the misfortune could not be helped. One of the conspirators had betrayed the plot to King James without any prompting from the angels.

In recompense for the disappointment, the Lord provided another public demonstration of Goodwin's courage by sending him to Bath Abbey, where the Protestant members of the Royal Court were attending the Sunday service. Since most courtiers considered themselves his enemies, his very appearance among them constituted an act of defiance. As he marched boldly into the Abbey, he found that his enemies had indeed assembled, as the Lord had predicted, and that the whole Court was staring at him. To those who ventured to bow to him, he nodded graciously; to those who were afraid to be civil, he gave a stare of contempt. To all he showed a total lack of concern—a demeanour so impressive that as he left the Abbey his voice said that no man in Bath would dare to 'meddle' with him.

Having proven his courage, Goodwin waited for James and Mary Beatrice to invite him to Court and to the royal bedroom. As the day wore on, however, it became clear that James was reluctant to send for him. In spite of the pleas of the Queen and the promptings of his conscience, the King hesitated to take the final, irrevocable step. Luckily, Goodwin now possessed another advocate in Bath besides the Queen—an ally whom James and Mary Beatrice had unwittingly provided for him. For several years, as the Lord explained to Goodwin, the royal couple had consulted a spirit named Phocas, whose services were lent to them by an unsavoury conjuror. Since Phocas had been acquired through the black arts, they naturally supposed that he was diabolical. In fact, however (as the Lord told Goodwin), Phocas was simply a 'terrestrial spirit', like George Whitmore. He reported to the Queen every afternoon at three o'clock, and for the past two weeks had been bringing her information about Goodwin. He was especially helpful after Goodwin's adventures at the Dry Pump and the Abbey. He praised Goodwin's conduct and courage so warmly that the Queen resolved to compass her love affair though it should cost her her life, and King James solemnly promised the Queen that before leaving Bath for Winchester on the following Wednesday, he would invite Goodwin into her bedchamber.

The next morning, while the King and Mary Beatrice went to visit their loyal subjects in Bristol,[12] Goodwin inspected the city of Bath. As he considered using the famous hot baths himself, his voice warned him of a hidden danger. Customarily ladies and gentlemen put on their bathing costumes at their lodgings and had themselves carried to the baths in sedan chairs; but Goodwin, the Lord said, would 'be certainly killed' if he should be caught unarmed in a sedan chair. This warning meant, of course, that he still had secret enemies and that he must wear a sword at all times. As long as he was armed, however, he was perfectly safe; and when he met a friend, Sir Thomas Travell,[13] he did not hestitate to dine with him, even though the company included several officers from the royal guard.

When King James returned from Bristol that evening, as Goodwin's voice explained, he seemed almost ready to do his duty, and the Queen, for her part, refused to sleep with him until he had sent for Goodwin. By morning, however, the King's stubborn, wilful temper had reasserted itself. Remembering his old and 'inveterate' enmity, he 'hardened his heart, like Pharaoh', and absolutely refused to do the lovers justice.

Goodwin was only slightly discouraged by the King's last-minute rebellion against God's will. It was possible, his voice told him, that once the King left Bath he would see his errors and send the Queen permission to consummate her affair. It was also possible that the Queen would have the courage to defy the King and invite Goodwin to her chamber without the King's permission. In any case, it was Goodwin's duty to remain at Bath and pursue his intrigue. By the next day, then, when the King set out for Winchester, Goodwin was fully resolved to persevere; and as he watched the King and the guards pass by under his window on their way out of town, he was filled with contempt. His own powers, he realized, were so far superior to those of James that it was really beneath his dignity to be watching the King ride away.

With James safely removed, Goodwin turned his full attention to Mary Beatrice, who had been placed in a cruel dilemma. It was no small matter to brave the wrath of a king and it was equally difficult to resist the power of a consuming love. Almost before James was out of sight, Goodwin's revelations confirmed these obvious truths. The Queen, the Lord said, was suffering agonies of indecision. During the day of James's departure, she changed her mind several times. About three o'clock, Goodwin learned, she was 'absolutely resolved' to send for him that night, and the only question seemed to be whether he should take her to bed immediately or spend the first evening in conversation. But about seven she cancelled her plan because of company come to Court, and at last she decided not to proceed further until she had made one last attempt to secure the King's consent.

Meanwhile, in between revelations about the Queen, Goodwin received a divine pronouncement of great moment. Mary Parish, his voice suddenly told him, was now dead; she had been 'taken away' only a few minutes before. Goodwin offered a tentative protest; she had died too soon, he said, and the world was now left without her equal. These complaints the Lord silenced at once, declaring that Mary 'had no more left to do' on earth, that Goodwin himself had already assented to her death, and that her equal could still be found.

On the night of Mary's death (Wednesday, 14 September), Goodwin expected momentarily to hear from the Queen, and he could not give Mary the attention she deserved; he merely noted in his journal that she had been born a gentlewoman, 'directly descended from the blessed Virgin Mary'. The next morning, however, he remembered her solemn promise to appear to him as soon as she was dead, and he was constrained to ask the Lord why she had not done so. Mary could not appear immediately, his voice told him, because of her spiritual eminence; at least a fortnight would be required to 'settle her in her seat'. About noon, as Goodwin asked for Mary's prayers, he finally began to shed tears, and he continued to weep until the Lord told him to go and seek his fortune.

Goodwin was not yet prepared to seek his fortune by asking for a private audience with Mary Beatrice. Although he knew the Countess of Peterborough,[14] the Queen's Groom of the Stole, he would not trust her (or any other royal servant) to intervene. While he waited for the King's letter of permission to arrive from Winchester, he could not risk the appearance of an intrigue carried on behind the King's back. He did use the Countess as a source of information about the Queen, but in general he avoided courtiers.

While Mary Beatrice struggled with indecision, the Lord

authorized Goodwin to seduce three young ladies from Bath—Ann Chapman,[15] the younger sister of the Queen's guide; Cecilia Gay,[16] the attractive stepdaughter of Alderman Edward Bushell;[17] and another, less appealing young woman. These three, the Lord explained, were among the few undebauched women in the whole town, and it behoved Goodwin to lie with one of them while he waited for his affair with the Queen to prosper. Prolonged abstinence, his voice said, would spoil him and corrupt his seed.

Before Goodwin could seduce anyone, however, he received astonishing news. On Saturday, 17 September, the mail from London brought him a letter from Mary. It was dated Thursday, 15 September, the day after Mary had died, and it said nothing about her death. For a few moments Goodwin was staggered, his thoughts 'in a very great maze'. This clear contradiction of the Lord's explicit word seemed to cast doubt on his inner voice and his whole method of procedure. Mercifully, the Lord soon intervened. Mary 'was indeed dead' at the time of the crucial revelation, Goodwin's inward voice declared, but she had been restored 'for something she had yet more to do'. Her death, the voice added, was the greatest trial that Goodwin would ever face.

Once the Lord's voice had solved the central mystery, Goodwin's reason supplied the supporting details. Mary's letter, he noted, said that she was very ill. It was not surprising, then, that she had slipped out of mortality and back in again without remembering the transitions. As for the Lord's description of her settlement in heaven, this could be taken as a prophecy of her future state, after her final dissolution. For the moment it was idle to speculate about what Mary's unfinished task might be or why the Lord had said earlier that she had nothing left to do; these matters, no doubt, would be clarified later.[18]

Shortly after this crisis, Goodwin actually saw Mary Beatrice for the first time. One morning when he went to the Cross Bath, he learned that the Queen was expected soon. He rushed out immediately to get himself shaved, and upon returning he found the Queen standing in the gallery[19] with some of her attendants. That he should intrude into the Queen's party was out of the question, of course, just as it was impossible for Mary Beatrice to mark him out for special, incriminating attention. Neverthe-

Goodwin Wharton, *c.*1694

Philip, Lord Wharton, 1632

Thomas Wharton, *c.*1685

Philip, Lord Wharton, Jane Goodwin Wharton, and Henry Wharton, 1657

Bath in 1692

Jersey in 1694

Page from the Autobiography of Goodwin Wharton

Mary II, *c*.1690

less, he stood 'behind her all the time' she stayed in the gallery, and he observed that after seeing him there she looked back 'as much as she well could'. Unfortunately, she could not long endure the pain of being so near him, and she soon left the gallery to go weep by herself.

Though a splendid triumph, Goodwin's first meeting with the Queen added complications to an already complicated situation. Finding herself so powerfully affected, the Queen doubted her ability to dissimulate her passion. For that reason she did not dare invite him openly to Court (although she was once on the verge of sending her Chamberlain, Lord Godolphin,[20] to summon him). Fearing to 'betray herself too much', she did not even venture to come and see him at the bowling green, which was only a few steps across the Abbey Garden from her lodgings.

The first meeting also produced an inadvertent romantic problem. While Goodwin studied the Queen, he was himself being eyed by the celebrated beauty Frances Teresa Stuart, Duchess of Richmond,[21] who thereupon fell in love with him. Goodwin behaved with commendable caution. Although he was justifiably pleased when his voice told him that the Duchess had been given to him, he did not want to begin an intrigue that might tangle his affair with the Queen. On Friday, 23 September, when he arrived at the gallery of the Cross Bath, he saw both ladies standing in the pool talking with each other. When they registered his presence, they tried to disguise their concern, and for the time being they appeared to succeed. The Queen left shortly after Goodwin arrived, and although her countenance was 'full of signs of joy', she did not reveal the cause of her happiness to anyone but Goodwin. The Duchess, for her part, feigned indifference so well that Goodwin suspected her of trying to establish dominance in the affair.

In the end, however, the Queen was not deceived. Reviewing the situation next morning, she recalled the looks that the Duchess had cast upon Goodwin and correctly judged that they signified love. Immediately, 'a world of jealous thoughts' rushed into her head; and later in the day when Goodwin saw her again in the waters of the bath, he noted 'the greatest change in her face imaginable . . . as if it were racked to pieces with tormenting thoughts'.

Goodwin had been patient with the Queen's highly reasonable fears about the King, but he could not be patient with irrational jealousy. Making his own face reflect displeasure and trouble, he deliberately avoided the Queen's eyes for the short time he stayed in the gallery, and then he strode off, leaving her to repent of her folly. Although this manœuvre brought Mary Beatrice to her senses and made her realize that Goodwin could not help being beloved, a certain amount of damage had been done. She had been given another reason for her chronic indecision.

The same evening as a further disciplinary measure, Goodwin took Phocas away from the Queen, but the punishment produced only hysterical weeping. She could not bring herself to send for Goodwin that night, and the next day—25 September, the Queen's twenty-ninth birthday[22]—Goodwin's inner voice declared that she would be 'cast sick' and die almost immediately. Her death, the Lord said, would be better for Goodwin, and he was not to pray against it; he could pray only for her salvation, which would be granted. Goodwin was quick to see the Lord's justice. The Queen could not reasonably complain of going to heaven, and since she had sworn to die if she could not compass her affair with Goodwin, it was only fitting that she should keep her oath. Nevertheless, as Goodwin prayed for the beautiful Queen, he became so deeply touched that if he had not been committed to continue in God's service, he would have given his own life to save hers. And at last his compassion saved her. In the night as he sat alone, his inner voice told him that she would be spared after all. Since he had wished death for her, and she for him, they would soon become the happiest couple in the world—though she would not live long.[23]

While Goodwin managed his tortuous affair with the Queen, he exploited his new freedom and power to achieve a social success he had not enjoyed since his days in Germany. Far from his London creditors he roved freely about the city, watched the bathers and bowlers, frequented the taverns, attended services in the Abbey, renewed his acquaintance with courtiers, and met prominent citizens, including Mayor Benjamin Baber.[24] He observed with satisfaction that he 'found favour in the sight of all men' and that no one saw him without 'a certain unusual esteem, pleasure, and veneration'.

In technical and financial matters, unfortunately, he was less successful. Although by a special prayer he cured the baby of his landlady when the child became ill from the young mother's soured milk, his attempts to use his magic pea and to make a profit from gambling produced strange results. Goodwin had brought the magic pea to Bath at the direction of his inner voice, which promised that when he had reconsecrated it he could at last become invisible. He proceeded with the reconsecration, therefore, according to the approved method—placing the pea upon one edge of a clean napkin and repeating special prayers to make it move across the napkin and fall off on the other side. Throughout the process, which lasted ten days, he kept the napkin covered with paper to conceal the pea from prying eyes, and he himself carefully refrained from peering under the covering to see how the pea was moving.

At the end of the process, when at the command of his voice he removed the paper, he received an odd jolt. The pea remained on the napkin exactly where he had placed it. While he puzzled over this anomaly, unprecedented in his experience with magic peas, his voice explained that the ritual of the moving pea was designed for other people, not for him. Though unmoved, the pea was properly consecrated and ready for use. But when Goodwin put it in his mouth, expecting to disappear, nothing happened. To himself, at least, he remained completely visible. He could not be certain that the pea had actually failed, of course, until he had tried it out in public, and for the definitive test he went forth into the streets of Bath. Several times in several places he slipped the pea into his mouth and watched for any sign that he had become invisible to the passers-by. Each time it was obvious that people could see him very clearly. In the end he was forced to conclude that the pea 'was not effectual at all'.

The failure of the magic pea (soon explained as the result of a curse placed upon it by Queen Penelope) was followed by equally strange frustrations in gambling. Goodwin naturally supposed that with God's omniscient help, he could infallibly win at any game of chance, and at first his voice agreed. After three consecutive days of experimentation, however, during which he lost at cards, lottery,[25] and again at cards (though he played 'exactly by the Lord's directions') Goodwin found himself mistaken. And a few days later, after he had lost heavily in a dice game, he learned the reason for the anomaly. It was simply too much trouble, the Lord said, to 'overrule' cards and dice. It was unreasonable, in other words, to expect the Lord to bother with trifles; and Goodwin was ordered to give up gambling forever.

Goodwin's unsuccess with dice and magic peas did not, of course, affect his romance, which took a dramatic turn for the better after he saved the Queen's life on her birthday. Snatched from the brink of death, Mary Beatrice was not only grateful to her lover but cured of her irrational jealousy. Furthermore, she had received from King James a letter that gave his full and unequivocal consent to the love affair (unlike an earlier, ambiguously-worded letter that had been designed as a trap). On 26 September, therefore, when Goodwin next saw her at the Cross Bath, she showed an appropriate 'submission and modesty', and the looks she turned on him were 'full of all the tenderness imaginable'—a tenderness so obvious that the Duchess of Richmond, standing nearby, almost swooned with jealousy. Again the next day, the Queen gave him so much encouragement that he remained in the gallery of the Cross Bath for almost three quarters of an hour, looking upon her pleasantly as she bathed.

Yet in spite of all favourable signs, the Queen relapsed into her familiar pattern of making resolutions every day and breaking them every night. Once she went so far as to order a servant to summon Goodwin, but she surrendered to panic and recalled the servant. Twice Goodwin was ordered to remain at home and save his strength for love-making—so that he could give her twin boys at the first encounter; but both times his orders were countermanded at the last minute.

Meanwhile, Goodwin's sexual frustrations were becoming desperate. The three young ladies from Bath—particularly Ann Chapman and Cecilia Gay—had proven too socially prominent and too well guarded to be readily seducible. Similarly, the Queen's Maids of Honour,[26] whom the Lord authorized Goodwin to pursue, seemed inaccessible. Though they ogled him shamelessly at church, they were under constant surveillance. Finally, great beauties like Lady Sophia Bulkeley[27] and Hortense Mancini, Duchess of Mazarin,[28] though obviously smitten (fatally smitten, the Lord said), were difficult to approach. For these reasons, Goodwin had taken none of his conquests to bed, and by 29 September he stood in imminent danger of spoiling himself with abstinence. In this emergency, the Lord commanded him to lie with his landlady.

Goodwin was 'strangely surprised' by the revelation, for although he was attracted by his pretty and compliant landlady, he had considered a love affair impossible. Here, if anywhere, he supposed, was a clear-cut case of adultery. The essence of adultery, as Goodwin knew (and God now confirmed) was that it produced a 'mixture of seeds', which in turn produced defective children. For this reason, it was a crime to lie with the wife of a healthy and sexually active husband, where a mixture of seeds was inevitable.

As Goodwin mulled over these considerations, his voice resolved the difficulty. As soon as he had made love to his landlady, the Lord said, her husband would be injured and rendered impotent until after she had delivered Goodwin's child. (In the event, he tore 'his privities with a tenter hook'.) Goodwin had barely reached this conclusion when the young woman herself came upstairs. He had no difficulty in bringing her into his own room and drawing her down upon the bed; but there, for the time being, his progress ended. The landlady, disconcerted by the haste of the encounter and frightened by some noises from below stairs, refused to let him complete the seduction.

This hopeful beginning of a sexual intrigue was followed shortly by a splendid triumph in an affair of honour. On the previous day, his friend Sir Thomas Travell had brought him an account of an insult offered by Lieutenant-Colonel William Legge.[29] In a sneering reference to Goodwin's famous speech, Legge had said (at a Bath coffee-house) that the sight of Goodwin made his 'blood rise' because Goodwin had once called King James a coward. The slur touched Goodwin in a sensitive spot. He knew very well that the speech had damaged his reputation; he knew too that in his present position of eminence he could not afford to bear insults. Finally, he knew that the specific charge was false; he had called King James many things, but 'coward' was not one of them. He saw at once that he could not ignore the incident, and his voice said that he would be a coward himself if he did not call the Colonel to account. Following the Lord's directions, therefore, he wrote Legge a formal letter giving him the option of apologizing or fighting a duel and sent it to the Colonel at his lodgings.

Colonel Legge replied at once, not in writing but in person. He appeared at Goodwin's quarters with what amounted to a denial of the story Travell had heard. He did not believe, he said, that Goodwin had slandered the King and he had not said anything to that effect. He was willing, furthermore, since Goodwin said the story was false, to contradict it if he should hear it and to call the retailers of such gossip rascals and sons of whores. Goodwin suspected that Legge's conciliatory statements were 'extorted', but he could not reasonably ask for any further satisfaction; his own honour had been clearly vindicated.

The next morning Goodwin learned that the episode had produced great effects. Colonel Legge, the Lord said, had told the Queen the whole story and had given her, besides, Goodwin's manly and masterful letter. Mary Beatrice was so highly impressed that when Goodwin saw her bathing in the Cross Bath, she gave him the 'most kind' look she had ever bestowed upon him, and presently he could see that she was telling her ladies about his conduct. It was clear that she was more deeply in love than ever, and it seemed certain that she would send for him presently—certainly before 4 October, when she was scheduled to leave Bath. The Lord said, in fact, that she would summon him on Sunday night, 2 October, and advised him to postpone making love to his landlady, since he would need all his strength for the Queen.

On Saturday morning, further to influence the Queen, Goodwin sent Phocas back to her, thus opening up direct communications once again. Delighted with the gift, Mary Beatrice declared that she would remain faithful to Goodwin as long as she lived; and about four o'clock in the afternoon, as she and her guards passed by under his window, she blushed and smiled in an appropriate display of love and gratitude.

But the Queen did not send for Goodwin on Sunday night. About five o'clock on Sunday afternoon, as she toured the town in her coach, she had seen Goodwin talking with Elizabeth Baber, the Mayor's wife, and had decided, in a fit of foolish pique, to postpone the rendezvous once more. Before morning,

of course, she was reproaching herself for wasting one of her last
nights in Bath and suffering agonies for fear Goodwin would go
away and leave her. For his part, Goodwin rejected all thoughts
of revenge. Although he was commanded to let the Queen suffer
through the night, he would not leave town in the morning as
she feared. To do so, the Lord said, would kill her. He was
to give her one last chance to bring the affair to a happy
conclusion.

Mary Beatrice had publicly announced that on Monday
morning she would make farewell appearances at her favourite
places around the city, including the gallery of the Cross Bath.[30]
Goodwin knew that she would hope to see him at the gallery,
but he also knew that in view of her recent errors it was beneath
his dignity to be there. Early Monday morning, however, his
voice brought further information. The Queen was praying on
her knees that he would come to the Cross Bath; and if he
appeared she would speak to him directly, for the first time, and
invite him to Court. For these reasons, his voice said, he must
see her in the gallery after all.

About eleven o'clock, then, when Mary Beatrice and her
entourage came into the gallery, Goodwin was waiting. It was
not enough, he knew, merely to see the Queen; if she was to
invite him to Court, he must get within easy speaking range.
Ordinarily, the stares of her courtiers might have given him
pause, but there was no longer time for such worries. As soon as
he saw Mary Beatrice he manœuvred his way through the
crowd and took up a position beside her. Then, having given her
a perfect chance for immediate happiness, he waited for her to
take it.

In a few moments of silent drama, Mary Beatrice fumbled her
opportunity. Although Goodwin 'stood close by her', she did
not address a single word to him, nor did she favour him with a
look worth recording. Dissembling perfectly, as if the meeting,
so fateful for both of them, were simply part of a routine
ceremony, she briefly acknowledged the assembled company
and then turned away to lead her party out of the gallery.[31]

Mary Beatrice was scheduled to visit the other baths, and
most of the crowd followed her out, but Goodwin remained
where he was. His voice told him that she had not spoken
'because her heart failed her', and he sensed that the failure was

crucial. After such a clear demonstration of cowardice, there was no use hoping that she would arrange a clandestine meeting or issue a formal invitation to Court. Some other way must be found to raise his fortunes and to bring the love affair to a happy consummation.

What that way might be the Lord outlined a few hours later. King James, Goodwin's voice said, would be pleased to learn that the lovers had not lain together, in spite of the permission they had extorted from him, and that they had avoided scandal. In gratitude, he would give Goodwin a title of honour and raise him at Court, where their union could be brought about in a more natural and honourable way.

Meanwhile, the Lord said, since Goodwin was not to lie with the Queen immediately and since there was no reason to save his strength, he should seduce his landlady at once. Goodwin hastened to comply. Although the first encounter was hurried— it took place while Goodwin and his landlady were 'standing in an entry'—it was highly satisfactory. The Lord said that Goodwin had done well and that the landlady had conceived of a boy who would eventually become 'glorious'. This prosperous beginning was followed early next morning with an equally prosperous sequel. Under more comfortable conditions, Goodwin gave the landlady another boy, and his voice commanded him to postpone his departure from Bath until he could give her still another one.

Though pleased with his success, he did not for a moment forget that his first concern was the Queen, who was preparing to leave the city. With the permission of Sir Richard Bassett,[32] the commander, he treated all the officers of the Queen's guard to their 'morning's draught' of wine—a gesture that earned him 'great notice' and that was duly reported to the Queen. As a final expression of his good will, he told the Queen by way of Phocas that he forgave her caution and that everything had happened for the best. The Queen, of course, was overjoyed at this magnanimity. As she passed by Goodwin on her way out of town, she showed on her countenance 'all the acknowledgement and pleasantness' she dared reveal among so many attendants. She even ventured to bow in his direction.[33]

Goodwin intended to leave Bath himself as soon as he had provided his landlady with a third boy, but when he got her into bed he found himself so 'dried' by his earlier exertions and by the wine he had shared with the guards that he could not get her with child. He was obliged, therefore, to remain in Bath an extra day; and this delay turned out to be providential. At a ball that evening, he was at last introduced to Cecilia Gay, the most eligible of the young ladies the Lord had selected for him. When he danced with Mistress Gay, he found her very much a gentlewoman and completely charming—so charming, indeed, that his voice commanded him to give a ball in her honour with what little remained of his money and to stay in Bath until he had seduced her.

During the next two days, Goodwin learned that the process of seducing Mistress Gay would be a long one. Although his voice first suggested that she had been seduced before[34] and although the young lady herself accepted his invitation to a ball on the evening of 5 October and showed clear signs of being in love with him, yet when he called upon her the next afternoon, it became clear that she was not yet ready to make love and that the seduction would have to be completed in London, where she intended to spend the winter. For this reason, Goodwin contented himself with giving her his London address, and his voice (rescinding the order to seduce her at once) commanded him to leave Bath the next day.

Goodwin had arrived in town as a passenger in the Bath coach; he left, more gallantly, on a saddle-horse the Lord had commanded him to buy. After a residence of almost four weeks, he had many reasons to regret leaving. In Bath, he had been free from his routine worries—the Whartons, the Cardinal, the bailiffs, and the landlords; he had been adored by many women and admired by all men. Nevertheless, he left town 'very cheerfully', confident that he was riding towards an even more exciting future. And as he clopped along the Bath-London road, through Calne, Beckhampton, Marlborough, and Newbury, his voice confirmed his hopes. It told him, among many other things, that King James had already decided to create him Baron of Wooburn and Earl of Hounslow and that Mary Beatrice, humbled by her failures at Bath and released from her marriage vows, would be waiting for him at Windsor Castle.

14

Prelude to a Warming Pan

BEFORE Goodwin reached Wooburn, his voice had revised his general strategy for dealing with women. In Bath he had used his great powers sparingly, charming only those women who seemed worthy of seduction and humanely 'looking off' the rest. Now he was commanded to spare no one, since he could never tell who might be selected for him. His voice also confirmed, what he already suspected, that his two wives, Mary Parish and Princess Anne Gartwrott, were not to figure in his plans. The Princess, weakened by ill health, had returned to France, where she would soon die. Mary, of course, had been saved temporarily to complete some mission or other, but she was not to share his great secrets—particularly his secrets about women.

Similarly, his voice changed his views on the Whartons. Lady Wharton, the Lord said, had forgiven his impulsive attempt to kiss her and had come to consider him the most honest man in the world; while Lord Wharton had not only repented for his past injustices but through several revelations of his own had recognized his son as a true prophet. Even Goodwin's haughty sister Margaret had become worthy of a reward. When Mary Beatrice died, after a glorious love affair with Goodwin, the widowed Margaret would marry King James and become the next Queen of England.

When Goodwin actually arrived at Wooburn, however, he was warned by his voice that his father and stepmother would conceal their new admiration. And so it proved. Disappointingly, Lord Wharton seemed at least as cold as usual, and Lady Wharton seemed colder than ever; she ignored him as if he had ceased to exist. More disappointing still was the news the Lord brought from Windsor, where Goodwin expected to appear the next day (Monday, 11 October). Hitherto, King James had known about Goodwin's famous speech only from hearsay; he had never actually seen a copy. Now, Goodwin's voice said, James had read the speech in its authentic form. Naturally he grew furious at the impolitic truths the speech contained. Revoking an earlier promise to renounce his own rights to the Queen and yield her to Goodwin, he flatly refused to send for his old enemy.

Through the next three days, while the Court moved from Windsor to Whitehall,[1] James meditated a scheme of revenge; and on his birthday, 14 October, he attempted to have Goodwin's speech burned by the hangman. He found, however (as the Lord reported to Goodwin at Wooburn), that the paper would not burn. Three times the hangman threw copies into the fire, and three times the speech lay defiantly on the flames or floated serenely off towards heaven.[2]

These miracles broke the King's spirit. He not only agreed to invite Goodwin to Whitehall as soon as possible but also decided to renounce Catholicism. For various complex reasons the King's formal invitation did not reach Goodwin at Wooburn, but as Goodwin set out for London, on 17 October, this fact seemed trivial; his only serious problem was how to evade a band of popish assassins who (as the Lord revealed) intended to kill him on the Bath Road between Colnbrook and Hounslow. This problem he solved by leaving the Bath Road, striking into the Acton Road, and then tacking southeast on a series of bypaths until he reached Turnham Green and safety. During the process, however, he experienced a subtle and dangerous form of temptation. An internal voice which he recognized as the Devil's suggested that his precautions were foolish; and as he neared Turnham Green, the Devil said, 'I made thee now go two or three miles out of the way.' Goodwin rebuked and silenced the Devil, but the experience was troublesome. Except for the cynical nonsense it talked, the Devil's voice might be mistaken for an internal revelation. For the future, Goodwin realized, he must take great care to distinguish between sly suggestion and divine truth.

When Goodwin arrived at Vere Street, he could devote little attention to Mary, whose negotiations with the Cardinal and the lowlanders during his absence paled before his own achievements. He did take her to bed, where she conceived triplets (as his voice told him); but his serious thoughts were concentrated upon Whitehall. King James, the Lord said, had indeed invited Goodwin to Court, but he had supposed that

Goodwin would not dare to appear there; he had resolved, furthermore, that if Goodwin failed to appear he would challenge him to a secret duel. It was therefore necessary, the Lord said, for Goodwin to show himself in the drawing-room of the palace as soon as possible.

The next morning, Goodwin had got as far as Covent Garden on his way to Whitehall when his voice brought him a fresh bulletin. King James, warned of his coming by Phocas, had suffered a complete loss of nerve; desperately wanting a respite, he begged that Goodwin would stay away from Whitehall for the present. Generously agreeing to save the King's face, Goodwin walked only as far as St. James's Park, where he took a turn or two with Sir Thomas Travell before returning home.

Meantime King James, who had shrunk from meeting Goodwin in public, remained determined to meet him privately in a duel; in the heat of this resolution, he penned a challenge and engaged Colonel Legge to deliver it. To Goodwin the prospect of fighting a duel seemed infinitely less fearful than 'going into the drawing-room to be stared upon', and he calmly awaited the challenge. By the next morning, however, when Legge did not appear, it became obvious that James had again lost heart.

In view of the King's poltroonery, Goodwin issued a challenge himself by way of Phocas. The challenge specified Lamb's Conduit Fields as the place, the next morning at eight as the time, and Colonel Legge and Sir Thomas Travell as the seconds; it suggested, finally, that the King's evasions smelled of cowardice. Stung by the imputations, James accepted the challenge, and his courage remained firm throughout the afternoon. In the evening, therefore, Goodwin engaged Sir Thomas Travell to act as his second.

As Goodwin and Sir Thomas approached Lamb's Conduit Fields[3] the next morning, Goodwin's voice whispered the disconcerting news that neither James nor Colonel Legge would dare show up; 'their hearts failed them,' it said. This news Goodwin could not share with Sir Thomas. Since secrecy was absolutely necessary, he had not told Sir Thomas who his opponent was; he had expected that everything would be clear enough when King James and Colonel Legge appeared. He would now appear ridiculous, he knew, if he suddenly announced that the duel had been cancelled.

For this reason Goodwin continued to act as if his opponent might arrive at any minute; and for almost two hours the two men, armed with rapiers, walked up and down Lamb's Conduit Fields. During this interval Goodwin changed the course of his life. As he paced back and forth with Sir Thomas, he explained that he was waiting for King James, he sketched in enough background to make this fact understandable, and he described a few of his rare powers. With the help of the Lord, who gave Sir Thomas 'faith to believe', he told his story so well that by the time the two men had concluded that they had waited longer than honour required, Goodwin had taken the first steps in securing a partner and patron—a replacement for the exiled John Wildman.

Once Goodwin realized that Sir Thomas had a large fund of faith, he knew that his friend would make a valuable ally. Though only thirty, Sir Thomas was already wealthy in his own right as the heir of a family of rich London merchants.[4] He also possessed a certain amount of social distinction which could be employed to good advantage in the new scheme of things. He had been knighted by Charles II in 1684, and he was welcome at Whitehall, where he could keep an eye on proceedings.

On the crucial morning of 20 October after Sir Thomas and Goodwin left the duelling grounds, Goodwin learned from his voice that King James had sent spies to watch their motions, and when his agents reported them gone, the King showed up at the Fields, along with Colonel Legge, as if he had simply mistaken the time of the duel. Though Goodwin was not deceived for a moment, he pretended to accept the story so that James would invite him to Court. At the Lord's direction he also seized the occasion to strengthen the faith of Sir Thomas, whom he despatched to Whitehall that evening. There Sir Thomas learned that James and Legge had indeed been absent from Court about ten o'clock, when they had made their secret journey to the Fields, and he returned convinced that Goodwin's account was accurate.

Sir Thomas made such rapid progress that within a week the Lord declared him worthy to read the first volume of Goodwin's autobiography, and shortly thereafter he was subsidizing

Goodwin's projects. With the help of the Lord, who kept Goodwin's creditors 'strangely quiet', Sir Thomas enabled Goodwin to emerge from hiding and appear openly on the streets of Westminster. In an otherwise lean season, it was Sir Thomas who financed Goodwin's love affairs and his war of attrition against King James.

Goodwin's new campaign to exploit his power over women had begun on 19 October when he called upon Mistress Cecilia Gay at her London lodgings and made excellent progress. Although she was surrounded by company, Goodwin could tell that she was fully conquered—that he 'wanted nothing but an opportunity'. This opportunity finally occurred on 28 October when he found Mistress Gay alone. Once again, however, as in his advances toward Lady Wharton, he moved too abruptly. When he actually laid hands on her, 'she strove so much' that he was obliged to let her go, and his voice called him 'fool'.

Meanwhile he had begun seeing Mary, Lady Soames,[5] the widow of Sir William Soames, the King's ambassador to Turkey. Goodwin had known Lady Soames very well before her marriage, when as Mary Howe she had been the dear friend of his sister-in-law Anne Wharton[6] and had nursed a great passion for him. Now, eager to make up for his 'long coldness', he called at her home on Pall Mall, where he was received with kindness; and soon he was able to note that the affair was going 'very forward'.

Concurrently, the Lord directed Goodwin to seduce a 'vast rich woman' named Theodosia, Lady Ivy.[7] Goodwin had learned a good deal about Lady Ivy before he met her. From the reports of a mutual acquaintance, a woman named Parcely, he knew that Lady Ivy, now a sixty-year-old widow, owned extensive properties in Shadwell, Wapping, and Stepney, an estate in Wiltshire, and some profitable copper mines; and he knew that the sole heir to all this wealth was a daughter named Frances, the wife of Sir Robert Clarke.

When Goodwin first met Lady Ivy, on 24 October, he found her 'very handsome', surprisingly youthful, and obviously smitten. Within ten days, therefore, he paid her three additional visits, each more encouraging than the last. On the third visit she allowed him to kiss her and on the fourth she seemed to agree that she could be lawfully his without going through a marriage ceremony. The Lord, meanwhile, had explained that Lady Ivy, still fertile in spite of her age, would bear him a child and allow him to command her estate.

Unfortunately, Goodwin met Lady Ivy at a time of great crisis. For several years she had been engaged in a complex legal battle with Thomas Neale[8] over some rich properties in Shadwell, and after a celebrated trial at the King's Bench on 3 June 1684, she had been indicted for the forgery of two leases.[9] Her trial on these charges, finally set for 10 November 1687, diverted her attention from romance and filled her house with lawyers.

To expedite matters, Goodwin intervened at the trial. Using his influence with the Lord, he prejudiced the judges and jury so completely in Lady Ivy's favour that she won an acquittal in spite of strong evidence against her.[10] But the triumph made her difficult instead of grateful. In principle she agreed that she might justifiably lie with him, but in practice she invented womanish excuses. Gradually Goodwin left off his hot pursuit while he attended to some of his other prospects.

Among aristocratic ladies, Goodwin's list included Anne Montague Rich, Dowager Countess of Warwick;[11] Rose O'Neill Mac Donnell, Dowager Marchioness of Antrim;[12] Lady Mary Stuart,[13] daughter of the Earl of Moray; and Lady Mary Tudor Radclyffe,[14] the youngest (illegitimate) daughter of Charles II.[15] Among untitled women, he was most attracted to Mistress Parcely, whom he would have taken to bed if his voice had not warned him at the last minute that she was infected, and if she had not resisted violently.

On 28 October Goodwin took a bold step in forwarding his affair with Queen Mary Beatrice. While waiting for an official invitation to Court, he decided to approach the Queen 'privately' through the discreet and trustworthy Catherine Fraser,[16] the first among the Queen's Maids of Honour. Mistress Fraser, Goodwin knew, occupied an apartment in the royal palace[17] and could easily deliver secret messages to the Queen; she could also arrange a quiet interview, perhaps in her own lodgings.

When Goodwin presented himself to Mistress Fraser, she received him kindly and listened to his request with apparent sympathy. She seemed to find nothing strange in being asked to deliver a private oral message to the Queen, nor did she see anything incriminating in the message itself—that Goodwin would do anything the Queen asked of him. Without argument or cross-examination, she promised to transmit his simple statement to Mary Beatrice. At the end of the interview, Goodwin felt that his mission had been happily accomplished. The Queen, his voice said, 'was overjoyed'.

Before his next visit to Whitehall, scheduled by the Lord for the following Monday, Goodwin heard a bizarre rumour: Mary Beatrice (so the story ran) had become pregnant; she and the King would soon announce their hopes of a male heir to the throne.[18] Goodwin knew, of course, that the story was false; for many weeks his voice had kept him fully informed of the Queen's actions, and it could not have failed to mention a fact of such transcendent importance. Beyond that, the time sequence alleged in the story was clearly impossible. The Queen could not have become pregnant at Bath, since he had himself treated her for a severe menstrual flow after the King had left town, and she could not have conceived later, since she had forsworn the King's bed.

In spite of the unsettling rumour, Goodwin returned on Monday to see Catherine Fraser, who again received him warmly. When he asked her about his message to the Queen, however, he received a surprising answer. She had not delivered the message, she said, because the Queen had been ill.[19] She hoped to see the Queen soon, but meantime she wanted him to put his 'proposition' in writing so that she would make no mistake in transmitting it.

Goodwin suspected a trap. He did not believe for a moment that Catherine Fraser had failed to see Mary Beatrice, nor did he believe that she needed help in remembering his simple message—that he would do anything the Queen asked. And as he argued with Mistress Fraser, he became more suspicious. When she refused to agree that the message was too simple to forget, he concluded that she was acting under the Queen's orders. For some reason, probably bad, Mary Beatrice wanted a paper in his own handwriting—a paper than might be used to 'ensnare' him.

Though full of suspicion, Goodwin wavered. The writing Catherine Fraser insisted upon was, after all, only a few noncommittal words; if these would satisfy the Queen's whim, he would be foolish not to write them. Before asking for pen and paper, however, he consulted his inner voice once more, and his voice reversed itself. Earlier it had said 'Give it her'; now it said 'Be gone.' Goodwin debated the matter no further. Taking a polite leave from Mistress Fraser, he walked away from Whitehall.

At a nearby coffee-house, Goodwin's voice explained that Mary Beatrice 'had done ill'. Ignoring the risks involved, she had imagined that by showing James a note from Goodwin she could bring him together with Goodwin and herself for a final agreement on divorce and remarriage. By way of Phocas, Goodwin immediately reprimanded her for her well-meant but 'foully managed' plot—for supposing that James could be trusted.

A few hours later Goodwin felt obliged to chastise her for another fault, perhaps more grave. She had not contradicted the rumours about her pregnancy; indeed, she seemed willing to have people believe that she was with child. For this fault, he knew, she had a strong motive. Both she and the King were embarrassed by the fact that they no longer slept together, and they wished to use a pretended pregnancy to make their estrangement 'less suspected'. They were aided in their pretence by the Queen's melancholy over Goodwin, which had made her ill and given rise to the story that she was pregnant. Despite the convenience of the fiction, Goodwin could not condone it, and he reprimanded the Queen for suffering it to be spread.

By way of discipline, Goodwin waited three days before returning to see Catherine Fraser. The Queen, his voice said, was expecting him 'with great impatience' and was prepared to meet him that night. Yet Catherine Fraser, still feigning ignorance, again denied that she had seen Mary Beatrice and again asked him to put his messge in writing—to convince the Queen, she said, that the message was genuine. Goodwin agreed to write the message if she insisted, but he pointed out that if the Queen would not believe her word she might also suspect the note. At this answer, Mistress Fraser excused him from writing; she would be 'discredited', she said, if she forced him to act against his will. She then went on to engage him in a pleasant conversation, during which he commended 'the Queen's person'.

The graciousness of Catherine Fraser did not blind Goodwin

to the Queen's bad faith. Mary Beatrice, he knew, had been 'blooded' for her illness and confined to her bed that day,[20] but such treatment should not have prevented her from sending a message. Clearly she had yielded to some whim. From his coffee-house, therefore, he warned her, via Phocas, that her freakish humours might kill her and advised her that he would not return to Whitehall until the following Monday. If he again found himself ill-used, he promised he would never come back.

By Sunday the Queen had resolved to mend her ways and pursue her love affair to the death. Yet as Goodwin made his way toward Whitehall on Monday afternoon, his voice warned him that she would not dare to meet him alone. This prediction was quickly confirmed by Catherine Fraser, who not only denied speaking with the Queen but asked to be released from her promise to do so. She had exceeded her authority, she said, in making such a rash promise; and she advised him, 'as from herself', to ask the Earl of Sunderland to introduce him and his business to Mary Beatrice in accordance with normal court proceedings.

This time as Goodwin left Whitehall, he did not send a message to the Queen. Her cowardice, as demonstrated in her retreat behind a wall of protocol, seemed somehow irreparable. And indeed, his repulse that day—7 November 1687—essentially doomed his plan of meeting the Queen through Catherine Fraser. Although the Queen soon apologized (as his voice reported), she did not change her orders to Mistress Fraser; and when he next visited Whitehall and found Mistress Fraser immovable, he realized that he must concentrate upon disciplining the King, whose sins, both public and private, were the real cause of all the trouble.

To Goodwin the most alarming of the King's errors was his role in the Queen's alleged pregnancy. Every day it became more evident that what had begun as a face-saving story had turned into a royal plot; James obviously intended 'to foist a counterfeit boy upon the nation'. At first Goodwin hoped that Mary Beatrice would refuse to co-operate in the fraud, but on 22 November, when he learned that she had joined with the King in holding 'a solemn thanksgiving' for her pregnancy, it became clear (as his voice said) that she had been bullied into a temporary compliance with the King.

Less threatening to Goodwin but deeply disturbing to the nation in general were other royal sins of the first magnitude. Besides renewing his attack upon Oxford, James launched his long campaign to create a captive parliament—dismissing county officials who would not support his policies and revising municipal franchises in order to assure the return of royal candidates.[21] Finally, in an act that struck his subjects as highly ominous, he appointed Edward Petre, a Jesuit, to the Privy Council.[22]

In punishing James for his sins, Goodwin afflicted him with a rare assortment of torments. On the physical side, the King was racked with bodily pains ranging from headaches to systemic agony, supplemented by a kind of vertigo which made him unable to hunt without falling off his horse. (On 1 December he suffered 'no less than three falls'.)[23] On the psychological side, he was berated by Phocas and harassed by the spirit of Charles II, who kept him from resting and who one day pulled him by the nose fifty times.

As a final refinement of torture, the Lord commanded Goodwin to render James impotent—to 'tie him up from all the whores in which he now abounds'. Goodwin knew Catherine Sedley, Countess of Dorchester,[24] the King's most famous mistress, and Mrs Dorothy Graham,[25] whom Goodwin classed as the King's second choice; and he bore them no ill will. Nevertheless he did his duty without hesitation or remorse, and King James found, 'to his great grief and astonishment', that he could not make love to a new whore he had acquired nor to his regular clientele.

While Goodwin was harrying the King, he began attending concerts and plays, where eligible ladies were most likely to be found. About plays his voice was at first dubious, like his Puritan tutors, but it gave him permission to go; and on Saturday, 19 November, he saw his first play in 'many years'. He did not, however, see anything worth recording in his journal. On Thursday, 24 November, he was somewhat luckier; although the play was not worth mentioning, he saw Mrs Dorothy Graham. Similarly, on 12 December, he saw Mary Tudor Radclyffe and let the play itself (perhaps Aphra Behn's *Emperour of the Moon*) pass by without comment.[26] Meanwhile, at Stationer's Hall on 22 November, he attended the first performance of Dryden's famous 'Song for St. Cecilia's Day', as scored by Giovanni Baptista Draghi.[27] There he saw no mortal worth noting, but as he mused about St. Cecilia, the Lord promised that she would appear to him.

More instructive than plays, Goodwin found, was the drama of training Sir Thomas Travell for his new role. From the first, Sir Thomas proved himself an apt spy upon the moods and movements of the King and Queen. Briefed by Goodwin on what to look for, Sir Thomas easily detected the Queen's melancholy and the anxiety and pain which James concealed from other observers. Sir Thomas showed a similar aptitude in spiritual matters, readily grasping the ways of the angels and spirits, as explained by Goodwin, as well as the true nature of adultery. He showed, nevertheless, one distressing fault. A rapt listener but a slow reader, he was seriously remiss about reading Goodwin's autobiography. This, the Lord told Goodwin, was 'intolerable', and Goodwin was forced to discipline him by twice taking the book away.

Goodwin's decision to let Sir Thomas read his journal led to a significant discovery. In reviewing his first volume before handing it over, he came upon his story of the Second Covenant—how it had first appeared as a plain gold plate, how it had been taken away and returned tightly wrapped, and how he had been forbidden to unwrap it. Now, as he reread his journal, his voice commanded him to 'take the Covenant and open it.'

Obeying his orders, Goodwin saw at once that the Covenant was not engraved at all; it was the same 'plain plate' he had seen 'long since'. Somehow, as if he had always suspected some deception, the sight failed to upset him. The plate, his voice explained quickly, had been given to 'amuse' him—to divert him in a period of despair. Having served its purpose and become useless (his voice added), the Second Covenant could now be sold. When he attempted to sell it, however, he found that the plate which he had taken to be pure gold was in fact nothing but brass.

Since Goodwin no longer needed advice from Mary upon theological matters, he did not consult her about his new discoveries. Ordinarily, in fact, he did not even consult her about pregnancies—a subject on which his voice was always lucid. Mary had miscarried in September, losing all the children she had conceived during the summer (nine in all) and allowing him, upon his return from Bath, to start over with a clean slate; she conceived triplets on his first night home, and thereafter she conceived twins or single children at frequent intervals until by Christmas (according to his careful notes) she had accumulated twenty-six.

Outside the bedroom Mary continued to manage negotiations with the Cardinal, the lowlanders, and her legendary uncle Sir John Tomson, who seemed about to die and leave her a fortune. In December, she also received an offer, through a spirit intermediary, to replace Sir Thomas Williams as Chemical Physician to King James. Through 1687, however, none of her projects thrived; the Cardinal remained evasive, the lowlanders installed a pretender on the throne, Sir John Tomson stayed alive, and King James kept breaking his appointments to discuss with her the position in the royal laboratory.

Almost as annoying as Mary's failures was the recalcitrance of the Wharton family, who persisted in contravening God's will. In late October, only three weeks after the Lord's revelation that Margaret would marry King James, she surprised and disgusted Goodwin by marrying Sir Thomas Seyliard[28]—an act of folly beyond divine control, the Lord said. By mid-November, Lady Wharton had again fallen from grace; when Goodwin saw her at the home of his sister Anne Carr, he observed that she was full of wicked inclinations. And in early December, he found cause to worry about all the Wharton women. While he was sleeping, 'in the morning watches', the Lord told him in a vision that he would be required to lie with all his sisters.

This command Goodwin ventured to question when he awoke. He hoped, he said, that like Abraham he was only being tested. His voice replied that although he might be excused when the time came, he should hold himself ready to obey God's command. This equivocal response left Goodwin uneasy, not only because God might reissue the order, but also because his sisters might not try to resist him. Recently, indeed, he had recalled an episode from his youth when his sister Philadelphia had seemed willing to explore sex with him and when his own strong principles had probably saved her virginity.[29]

Lord Wharton, meanwhile, was causing Goodwin more distress than all the Wharton ladies combined. In trying to find room for guests at St. Giles, he had been obliged, he said, to put servants in the quarters customarily reserved for Goodwin and Henry. Goodwin cared nothing about his seldom-used room, but he cared a great deal about the principle. Suspecting that Lord Wharton was trying to get rid of him, he openly accused his father of turning him out of the house. Outraged by the accusation, Lord Wharton 'flew into a passion' and proceeded to review Goodwin's sins, interrupting his narrative occasionally to call Goodwin 'villain' and to tell him he lied. Goodwin bore the tongue-lashing with more dignity than usual. Sustained by God's approval, he did not attempt to argue; he merely promised that in the future Lord Wharton would not be troubled by his presence.

As Goodwin brooded about the wrongs done him, his voice ordered him to set down a 'retrograde character' of Lord Wharton in his journal. Heretofore he had tried to use restraint in recounting his father's errors, but now, at the Lord's command, he described the most flagrant in detail. More helpfully, the Lord suggested that Thomas Cole,[30] a prominent Dissenting minister, should be called in to mediate the dispute. Years before, Cole had resolved other disputes between Goodwin and Lord Wharton, and he had intervened in the most bitter of all the Wharton family arguments. Lord Wharton had been furious when his daughter Anne insisted upon marrying William Carr, Lady Wharton's brother, thus becoming her father's sister-in-law. He declared her a disobedient child, unworthy to receive church sacraments, and refused to give her a marriage portion.[31] Interposing on Anne's behalf, Cole reproved Lord Wharton for unfatherly and unchristian rigour and assisted in bringing about a reconciliation.[32]

In the present case, Cole moderated with great skill. Under his soothing influence, Lord Wharton apologized for having given the appearance of putting Goodwin out of the house. He also listened patiently to Goodwin's financial grievances, and though he did not agree to settle all Goodwin's debts, he did seem willing to help. Much relieved, Goodwin himself became conciliatory, and as the meeting ended, Lord Wharton invited him 'to be often with him' at St. Giles.

Goodwin was soon to find he had made peace just in time to help his father and stepmother survive a terrible blow—the death of his half-brother William. The disaster began, innocuously enough, in the summer of 1687 when William, who had poetic ambitions, reflected in writing upon the literary pretensions of a minor poet and critic named Robert Wolseley. Wolseley, who fancied himself the literary heir of Rochester, riposted with a satirical sketch of William in a poem entitled 'A Familiar Epistle'; he sneered at William's small stature, his foppishness, and his Puritan family and ended by calling him 'a merry blockhead, treacherous and vain'.[33] William countered with 'A Familiar Answer', which derided Wolseley's bulk, dullness, lechery, and lack of talent. Thereafter, in several more poems, Wolseley and Wharton exchanged insults of increasing venom. Naturally the town wits found the verbal battle highly amusing, and they found it more amusing still when a much better poet (almost certainly Dorset) intervened with a poem called 'The Duel',[34] which dubbed the pair *Bavius* and *Maevius* and gave a mock-heroic account of their 'bloodless rhyming strife'.

Soon after the poetic 'Duel' came an actual duel; William and Wolseley met on 9 December 1687 to settle their differences with rapiers. And at first the encounter appeared to be another episode in the comedy. The diminutive Wharton 'had the better in the action' against his hulking opponent;[35] he also sustained the only injury—a slight, undignified rapier jab in the left buttock.[36] Before any wit could write a commentary, however, William's wound showed itself to be dangerously infected.

Goodwin's voice gave him no inkling of his brother's danger, nor was he worried on other grounds; the wound, he knew, was 'very slight' and until 12 December William had been 'very well'. But at St. Giles on the evening of 13 December, Goodwin sensed that the illness had become critical and as he left his brother's presence, the Lord peremptorily declared that William would die. Surprised, Goodwin expostulated. Recently, his brother had brought him a friendly greeting from Catherine Fraser, and he had begun to hope that William might help him in dealing with the Court. But when Goodwin asked that he should be spared, his voice said, 'No.' William, it declared, would die as a punishment to Lord Wharton. Goodwin could save his brother's soul but not his life.

By seven o'clock the next morning William was dead. Impressed by the summary execution of the Lord's judgement, Goodwin also perceived the pattern of mercy that lay behind the tragedy. William, he learned, had repented on his deathbed for the way he had treated his brother, and it was clear that he would be saved. It was also clear that Lord and Lady Wharton were duly punished for their sins. At St. Giles on the day of William's death, Goodwin saw that his father was indeed afflicted and that Lady Wharton, who had 'doted' on William 'to an excess', was full of woe. Lady Wharton would now transfer all her affection to Goodwin, the Lord said; through Goodwin's prayers, she could yet be saved. To these mercies was added a final act of grace. For Goodwin's sake, the Lord said, William would be made 'a great saint'.

While Goodwin dealt with family troubles, his all-important romance with Queen Mary Beatrice remained suspended. The Queen, to be sure, approved of the punishments that he inflicted upon the King and wept for the delays in their mutual happiness. ('She oftener cries for thee', the Lord once told him, 'than thou dost think of her.') But she continued to behave as if she were pregnant; she could not be persuaded to denounce her pregnancy as a hoax. Goodwin's hopes rose briefly on Christmas Eve when his voice said that the Queen had resolved to drop 'the mask of being with child'. On Christmas Day, however, he learned that King James had issued a proclamation (dated 23 December) 'appointing a time of public thanksgiving and prayer' for the Queen's pregnancy.[37] Goodwin found the news chilling. It seemed impossible that Mary Beatrice would dare to counter the King's public declaration. And so it proved. The Queen, his voice told him, had contended nobly until Christmas morning, but had been at last obliged to yield; now, though 'the most troubled woman alive', she would 'carry on the cheat of the child'.

Goodwin found, nevertheless, consolation in his apparent defeat. Though Mary Beatrice was locked into the royal plot, the plot itself was doomed. Most Englishmen, he knew, already suspected what he himself had learned from revelation, that there was a conspiracy to foist a popish successor upon the nation. The King was wasting his time, therefore, with his proclamations and thanksgivings, designed to persuade his subjects that the Queen's pregnancy was real. The 'providence of God' was working against the plot, inspiring good Englishmen to treat it with contempt.

There is a spirit of incredulity gone out amongst men in this matter [Goodwin wrote], and very few but take the liberty to say, where they dare, they do not believe it to be true; and some have said that as long as there is a beggar boy in London, there is no danger but there will be found a Prince of Wales.

15

The Inglorious Revolution

As Goodwin entered the memorable year 1688, he made one small hedge against misfortune. While waiting for the King and Queen to come to their senses, he decided to re-enter the diving business. Perhaps influenced by the fabulously successful salvage, off Haiti, of the Spanish treasure galleon *Concepción*,[1] he engaged a technician named Osmond Cook to produce an improved diving suit. By mid-January, Cook had made encouraging progress, and it was evident to Goodwin that if his other projects failed he could make a diving expedition during the summer of 1688, perhaps to the Isle of Jersey.

Meanwhile, beginning in early January, Mary was making Goodwin's caution seem unnecessary. No less than seven times she reported interviews with King James at Whitehall. James, who remembered her perfectly from her days as assistant to Sir Thomas Williams, seemed anxious to have her replace Sir Thomas as Chemical Physician, and he was obviously eager to be reconciled with Goodwin. Equally exciting were Mary's negotiations with Cardinal Wolsey, who promised to steal the lowlanders' most valuable treasure and had actually removed a trunkful or two before the lowlanders knew what was happening.

In early February both projects came to a halt. The King, who did not dismiss Sir Thomas Williams, again fell into his pattern of breaking appointments with Mary; and the lowlanders, though unable to see the invisible Cardinal and his henchmen, took such effective counter-measures that nothing could be accomplished.

The new flurry of activity did not change Goodwin's perception of Mary's fate. For all her endeavours, her days with the partnership were drawing to an end. Ever since 2 January, when she had conceived for the twenty-eighth time, Goodwin had been informed that each conception might be her last; he was certain by the time she conceived number thirty-seven, on 13 February, that she would not conceive many more. She would be lucky, he thought, if she lived to see the happy conclusion of their troubles.

As long as Mary lived, of course, she was a threat to his adventures with women. And these, unfortunately, failed to thrive, even without her opposition. Queen Mary Beatrice once planned to meet him at a masquerade ball, but her plan was foiled when the affair was changed to an ordinary ball. And when the Queen moved into her splendid new apartments, directly below the lodgings of Catherine Fraser,[2] she considered coming up to Catherine's apartment while Goodwin was there. But before she could muster enough resolution, Goodwin began having trouble finding Catherine at home, and after two or three fruitless visits he let the matter rest.

Cecilia Gay also remained unseduced. After his first bungled attempt to lie with her, he had neglected her for a time, and when he saw her again, he felt obliged to use restraint, like the serious wooer of a young gentlewoman. In mid-February she began talking of a match that had been proposed for her, and Goodwin, though careful to promise nothing, feared that she expected him to propose marriage himself.

On 18 February, Goodwin's romantic skirmishing halted abruptly. On that date Mary noticed that a spot had broken out on her shoulder—a sign, she concluded, of the pox. In 'a violent passion' she accused Goodwin of having lain with another woman and of bringing home an infection. Though Goodwin had observed no symptoms himself, he knew that he had indeed lain with another woman in recent months—the landlady in Bath—and that if Mary cross-examined the angels she could easily find out the truth. Reluctantly, therefore, he admitted the affair at Bath, but he stoutly denied the consequences; he was not poxed, he said, and he had done no wrong. He had received the Lord's permission to lie with the woman.

Mary remained violently unconvinced. The Lord, she said (after consulting the angels), had suffered him to be misled because he had conceived a sinful desire for his landlady. This allegation was absurd, of course, since it impugned the infallibility of his voice; but Goodwin found her 'positiveness' disquieting. He also found himself obliged to reveal more than he cared to about his internal revelations. But he conceded nothing, and after a time his voice explained Mary's (and the angels') mistake. The strange episode, the Lord said, had been designed to bring about the final break between him and Mary and to make her miscarry of her too-numerous children.

Fortunately, Mary did not challenge the general validity of his internal revelations; she merely accused him of misinterpreting one of them. In fact, as her wrath cooled, she claimed credit for his inward voice, which had been granted, she said, through her prayers. In the present doubtful case, she added, she was ready to go to church and pray that God would reveal himself to Goodwin 'by the outward ear and visible form'—thus ending all ambiguity and argument. This offer Goodwin accepted, and when Mary returned from church, she reported that her prayer had been granted.

While Goodwin waited for the definitive revelation, he regained his confidence. His voice repeated what it had told him before—that 'this business' was to make Mary miscarry and induce her to leave him. As his assurance grew, he gradually 'told her a great deal of the design', including the fact that she might not live much longer; he even ventured to hint that he might be permitted to have several women. And after lying with her on 22 February, he frankly informed her that the resulting conception (her thirty-ninth) would be her last.

Three nights later, Mary countered with pronouncements of her own. She did not believe, she said, that Goodwin had been authorized to lie with his landlady or that she herself was soon to die; the angels had pronounced him guilty and promised that 'she should live yet many years.' Since, however, he seemed to insist upon having other women, she had resolved never to go to bed with him again and had 'farther resolved to marry another man who now wooed her'.

Shocked at first and inclined to argue, Goodwin gradually realized that Mary had offered an ideal solution to his problems. And when his voice agreed that her plan would 'do well'—that she should leave him and marry a 'sober old rich man'—Goodwin accepted the new arrangement. He gave Mary complete freedom, promised to stay away from her bed unless specifically invited, and admonished her not to trouble herself about his love affairs. Feeling at once liberated and magnanimous, he expected to begin a life vastly different from the one he had led for the past five years.

Before he was 'well awake' the next morning, Goodwin heard the Lord's voice, 'articulately' from beyond the door, as he had done in the days before his inward voice had superseded oral revelations. At first he could not understand a word it said; but it soon began again, delivering three or four lines of verse from which he gleaned the astonishing gist: his affair at Bath had been 'a sin' and 'Satan's temptation'. Then as he lay in his bed, 'extremely troubled', the Lord's voice spoke for the third time. Again the message was garbled, but one thing Goodwin understood clearly enough: he was not to part from Mary. 'She is thy wife,' the Lord said; 'keep her still.'

Shocked and confused, Goodwin first thought of asking Ahab for a complete reading of the Lord's half-intelligible revelations; but as he revolved the matter, he saw that he was beyond rescue by textual niceties and that he must face a staggering uncertainty about the counsels of his inward voice—particularly as they dealt with women. He also saw, as he wrote in his journal, that the Bath episode was crucial.

For to have that which I took to be the Lord's wonderful orders and providence to me (of which I saw all the foregoing reasons as well as all the consequent circumstances exactly agree, as I had done in all other matters, and had in my integrity accordingly acted myself)—that this should be called in question, and by the Lord in another manner called a sin, puts me into a strange pause.

While Goodwin strove to understand the mistake and assess the permanent damage, he performed the one task immediately commanded by the Lord's voice; he made up his differences with Mary, whose heart, he found, had changed from its recent unkindness. He also adopted a tentative policy for dealing with his inward voice. If its counsel seemed to conflict with the Gospel, he would delay action until he had received some unambiguous sign that he was not being deceived by the Tempter.

On Sunday, 4 March, Goodwin's burdens were lightened by an oral revelation which defined more precisely the nature of his error at Bath.

Hezekiah, my son [the Lord said], I wonder thou dost lay to me
The giving of that woman to thee,
So often as I did say to the contrary.

I never did give a harlot to thee. [Here the Lord paused.]
I never did give one to thee
But what is of thy degree.

Goodwin grasped the fundamental point at once. Harlots, obviously, were forbidden, and not suspecting his landlady to be a common prostitute, he had ignorantly considered himself free to lie with her. Now enlightened, he asked the Lord to pardon him, and his inward voice replied that he was forgiven. For the future, he reasoned, it only remained to avoid harlots and to select women of his own degree—though he had no clear idea of the kind of women who might have attained proper status.

While Goodwin was striving to regain his shaken confidence, he was assailed by troubles from other directions. One of these was the treachery of Osmond Cook, his inventive assistant in the deep-sea-diving business. In late January, Cook defected from Goodwin's service, taking with him the designs he had made for improved equipment; and in early March Goodwin learned that the man had leagued himself with Mistress Parcely in a plan to cut Goodwin out of all future operations. Parcely had introduced Cook to Lady Ivy and helped him obtain Lady Ivy's backing in his attempt to patent the equipment himself[3] and organize his own diving expedition. It appeared, when Goodwin first heard of the conspiracy, that the plan was on the verge of success. Cook and his allies were already applying to King James for permission to retrieve the treasure sunk at Jersey.

Goodwin realized at once that the key to the problem lay with the King, who had the ultimate power to grant patents and permissions. He also realized that James remained prejudiced against him and that he could not present his own case—that he must find an emissary capable of persuading James to block the schemes of the conspirators and to recognize his rights to the patents he had financed. To this basic plan his oral revelations suggested an addition that he hardly dared think of for himself. Besides getting a powerful advocate, Goodwin was to begin putting himself in the King's way, where without the risk of a formal audience he could force James to notice him and perhaps recognize his claims.

Unfortunately, Goodwin's first attempts to find emissaries failed. His friend Thomas Herbert, Earl of Pembroke,[4] who shared his interests in alchemy, professed to find advocates unnecessary and advised him to go directly to the King. Lord Wharton (Goodwin's next choice) not only declined to speak with the King but opposed the whole venture. And at Whitehall, the Countess of Peterborough could only advise Goodwin to go through regular court channels—to see Sunderland, Churchill, Petre, or the Earl of Arran.

After some hesitation, Goodwin chose Arran (whom he knew only by reputation) as the least obnoxious of the King's henchmen; but in the interview that followed, Arran seemed bad enough. Aware of Goodwin's famous speech, he put Goodwin through 'a long, sifting discourse' and then asked for a pound of his flesh. He would speak for Goodwin, he said, if he could tell James that Goodwin had apologized for his earlier opposition and was now willing to support the Crown in abolishing the Test Act. To these odious terms Goodwin's internal voice said, 'No, no, no'; and Goodwin brushed off the proposal and withdrew. As he retreated from the palace, brooding about Arran's attempt to corrupt him, his voice said that Sunderland would be worse.

After the defeat at Whitehall Goodwin temporarily suspended his search for an advocate and concentrated upon his other line of attack—his strategy of appearing in King James's presence. Since the King frequently walked in St. James's Park and sometimes attended plays, the physical problem of seeing him was simple. But when Goodwin was commanded by revelation to walk where he could see the King, he found the mental problem formidable. To meet James face to face after all that had passed between them required extraordinary courage. As a result, Goodwin fumbled his first two assignments at St. James's Park. He saw the King and his entourage from a distance—from the west end of the Mall—but they had retired to Whitehall before he could nerve himself to confront them.

On the morning of 4 April, as King James came walking along the Mall, Goodwin braced himself to meet his old enemy 'full butt'. He was pleased to notice that his fear evaporated as the King approached; his spirits, indeed, became so calm that he even tried to 'fix' James with his eyes. Unfortunately (as Goodwin's voice later explained), the King was more nervous than Goodwin, and having seen Goodwin at a distance, he contrived to be looking away from him as they met. In revenge for this cowardly manœuvre, Goodwin gave the slightest bow possible.

Goodwin found his next assignments on the Mall easier. On 23 April, he was only prevented from confronting the King by the huge crowd of attendants; and two days later he forced his way through the 'great company' and approached so near that James was compelled to look 'full upon' him. The King did not speak, however, or acknowledge Goodwin's 'decent' bow. Awestruck (as the angels later explained) by a halo that appeared over Goodwin's head, he simply passed by automatically 'without stirring his hat'.

On the same afternoon, Goodwin shifted his campaign from the Park to the Theatre Royal, where James attended a performance of John Crowne's *Darius, King of Persia*.[5] Sitting where he could face the King, Goodwin studied James throughout the play, observing no sign of enmity. Once, indeed, when Sir Thomas Travell came in and sat behind Goodwin, James seemed to blush and momentarily hide his face, but in general his demeanour seemed softened. When his gaze met Goodwin's, as it frequently did, he let it pause briefly and then looked gently away.

Goodwin next saw the King on 14 May at a performance of Thomas Shadwell's *The Squire of Alsatia*.[6] On this occasion, sitting directly in front of the royal party (which included the Prince and Princess of Denmark and the Earl of Arran), Goodwin treated King James to a study in nonchalance. In the intervals between the acts, he stood up 'just before' James's face where the King was obliged to see him; and during the play itself he seldom gave the King so much as a glance. Goodwin did, however, exchange one significant look with Princess Anne (later Queen Anne), who gave the first sign of what turned out to be a lifelong passion for him.

Before Goodwin saw King James again, a new development in his affairs altered his strategy. In late April, Lady Ivy had experienced a change of heart and began to undo the damage that her treachery had caused; and by mid-May she had herself taken over the task of finding an advocate for Goodwin. As Goodwin understood the transformation, Lady Ivy had become disillusioned with Cook and Parcely and with the endless contests over patent rights. On 17 April she wrote Goodwin a conciliatory letter suggesting that they should make up any differences and pool their resources for a joint venture in the diving business. She had been unaware, she said, that Cook had carried off Goodwin's equipment or that he had been pledged to Goodwin's service. She would make amends by persuading the talented Cook to return to Goodwin under bond and by helping Goodwin to secure the King's permission for the Jersey expedition.

By 1 May, affairs had moved so briskly that Cook was under a bond of £10,000 not to desert Goodwin again,[7] and the angels were advising Mary that Goodwin should actually marry Lady Ivy—though not at once—and that for the present he should see her often and pretend all possible love. Obediently, Goodwin visited Lady Ivy every day and even offered to share his diving patents with her—an offer she took very kindly. For her own part, Lady Ivy found among her powerful acquaintances an intermediary who could influence the King; on 19 May, she sent Goodwin to see William Penn, 'the great Quaker'.

With the possible exception of Sunderland, Goodwin could not have found a more effective advocate than the man he called 'Will Penn'. Though not an official member of the King's government, Penn had long been James's personal friend; and in recent months he had helped construct the celebrated Declaration of Indulgence, publicly defended the King's new policies, and served in effect as the King's ambassador to the Nonconformists.[8]

Goodwin found Penn helpful. After listening to Goodwin's explanation of the case, he agreed to present it to the King. Unlike Arran, he did not try to extract any promise from Goodwin, and if he was at all worried about Goodwin's reputation as a political dissident, he did not say so. A week later, on 26 May, he took Goodwin to Whitehall, where he planned to present him to James 'if opportunity served'. On this occasion, Penn applied a modest amount of political pressure. He hoped, he said, that he could present Goodwin as one who approved of the King's 'designs as to the public'. But when Goodwin made it clear that he did not approve of the King's designs and that he would not be introduced under false pretences, Penn did not insist.

As matters turned out, Penn could not get an interview with the King that day, and for a month thereafter he was too busy with affairs of State to present Goodwin's case. During this interval,

James was committing the series of blunders that would cost him his crown, and Goodwin was making the most dramatic mistake of his life. James, under the delusion that he was bringing the Church of England to heel, was instituting the prosecution of seven Anglican bishops; and Goodwin, in the mistaken belief that he had God's approval, was making love to Mistress Cecilia Gay.

Goodwin's mistake arose from his uncertainty about the meaning of the word *degree* and from Mary's advice, relayed from the Lord and the angels, that he should marry Lady Ivy. Ever since the shocking reversals of late February, he had been cautious about all women. Though God's oral revelations, carefully written down, apparently allowed women of his own degree, he did not want to make another mistake. Through March and April, he remained so wary that he refrained from making serious advances towards Mistress Mary Howard, the beautiful daughter of Lord Howard of Escrick; and by inventing little quarrels he strove to keep the obviously genteel Cecilia Gay at an unincriminating distance.

Then, in early May, Mary brought home the Lord's message about Lady Ivy—a message which cast a new light on the classification of women. Since the Lord advised him to marry Lady Ivy, Goodwin reasoned, it followed that Lady Ivy was of his degree; and if Lady Ivy, with her bourgeois birth and her slippery character, qualified as his equal, it followed that almost any gentlewoman could meet the test. Certainly Mistress Gay was as much his equal as Lady Ivy.

As Goodwin's logic was sapping his fears, he met a formidable temptation. On the night of 27 May Mistress Gay seemed especially attractive and vulnerable. Obviously distressed by the 'long squabbling' that had arisen between them, she was willing to take the blame upon herself. Goodwin, touched by the 'fresh kindness', was suddenly inclined to think that he might seduce her. In his final moments of wavering, he prayed for guidance, asking the Lord to 'order the event as He liked best'; but he did not wait long for an answer, and when neither his inward voice nor Mistress Gay tried to stop him, he proceeded to make love to her.

For several days Goodwin received no sign of disapproval. His numerous oral revelations said nothing at all about sex; they dealt almost exclusively with the diving business—advising him to trust Penn and get ready to go to sea. The love affair itself Goodwin found gratifying. The first encounter seemed to prove what Cecilia had told him, that she was a virgin. And although she seemed startled when in obedience to his inner voice he told her that she was pregnant, she did not ask for a promise of marriage. As a token of her truth and affection, she gave him a heart-shaped diamond locket containing a lock of her hair, and he gave her a similar locket in return. Feeling more secure every day, he continued to make love to her through the first two weeks of June.

The first portents of trouble appeared on the night of 14 June. Returning from Mistress Gay's, Goodwin found Mary full of suspicion and jealousy. She had been told by one of her friends that Goodwin was seeing a woman. She had also noticed his recent custom of coming home late, and she had observed the condition of his clothes. One of his shirts which had suffered much from a love encounter seemed particularly damning. Mary's suspicions were confirmed next morning at church, where the angels told her that Goodwin had been deceived by the Devil and that God was ready to cut him off—a message she repeated, 'in great rage and furies', to Goodwin.

Although severely shaken, Goodwin still retained a faint glimmering of hope, since he had not yet heard from the Lord himself in oral revelation. He tried to remain calm therefore as he explained to Mary his crucial revelations about degree and the principles upon which he had acted. On the morning of 18 June, however, his hope was shattered by three successive oral revelations. The first called his liaison a sin and declared that if he married Mistress Gay he would die a beggar and a cuckold. The second reminded him that Mary had proved 'young and faithful' to him and had borne him many fine children. The third declared that there had never been such a woman as Mary; it was amazing, the Lord said, that Goodwin could treat her so shabbily.

Though too demoralized to grasp all the implications of the Lord's pronouncements, Goodwin saw one thing clearly. He had been misled by Satan in the matter of women. They were not 'allowable', as he had supposed from the ambiguous promptings of his internal voice. He also saw that he had grievously wronged Mary and that his errors had begun when he had started acting without her knowledge. Hereafter, he resolved, he would 'do all things plainly and above-board';

certainly, he would meddle with no more women during her lifetime without her explicit consent.

As Goodwin faced the horror of losing God's favour, he was made to realize the enormity of his mistake about Mistress Gay. Mary brought word from the archangel Gabriel that the young lady 'had been lain with by above twenty men', and the Lord revealed by articulate voice that only a half hour before she had made love to Goodwin for the first time, she had lain with another man. Goodwin was shocked at such depravity and at 'the abomination of women in general'. That a young lady not yet twenty could sin so copiously and lie so glibly was astounding. She had been utterly convincing when she told him that she had resisted the only gentleman who had ever tried to seduce her, and she had feigned virginity so well that she seemed to lose her maidenhead during their first encounter. Resolutely, therefore, Goodwin broke off the connection. On 20 June, he cut the string of the locket she had given him and sent it back to her, without explanation, by way of a porter. She returned a note asking to speak with him, but he refused to be tempted. He did not see her again.

Fortunately for Goodwin, Mary recognized the true depth of his despair. Magnanimously ignoring her own injuries and surprising the angels themselves at her ability to forgive his crimes, she went to church three times a day to plead for his reinstatement. Meanwhile, she patiently defined their relationship and the correct doctrine of marriage. She did not intend to monopolize him, she said. Though their marriage had been sanctioned by the Lord, she considered herself his wife only 'by the way'; she would never stand in the way of a rich, legal marriage. But God would never approve of harlots or adultery; Goodwin was not to lie with any woman outside wedlock or marry anyone during Mary's lifetime unless he was told to do so 'articulately' in an oral revelation.

In the end, Mary's prayers turned the balance. After revelations had warned him that he must never again blame his sins on the Lord, Goodwin was at last restored to favour—chosen once more to be God's son. Rescued by Mary's faith and magnanimity, he gratefully echoed the Lord's praise of her virtues, including her youthful sexual prowess, which he had found 'at no time elsewhere overbalanced or indeed equalled'.

Yet as Goodwin recovered from his close brush with damnation, he sensed that his losses had been frightful. His inward voice returned now and then, but it had been reduced to something like a vestigial remnant, and its past revelations had become problematical. Goodwin's gift for receiving visions had also been damaged. Visions had been unnecessary when he had spoken constantly with God, and they now came on rare occasions and on trivial subjects. Essentially, Goodwin found, he had been stripped of his great independent powers and forced to rely once more upon spirits, angels, and occasional verse revelations.

While the world of the partners was being revolutionized, Goodwin continued to pursue his one untarnished hope; he prepared to go to sea whenever William Penn could get the King's authorization. In late May and early June he had received some help from the angels in designing diving apparatus; and on 8 June, with the financial aid of Lady Ivy and Sir Thomas Travell, he had bought a ship. Throughout mid-June he visited William Penn as often as he decently could without seeming importunate. Though impatient, he recognized the validity of Penn's excuses for not pressing the case before the King: King James had created a crisis of his own—a crisis that would change English politics forever.

James had begun his suicidal blunders on 27 April, when he reissued his Declaration of Indulgence.[9] To the original text, which suspended the laws designed to protect the Church of England, he added an ominous commentary explaining that he had purged the government and armed forces of all his political opponents and reminding his subjects, not too subtly, that his army was strong enough to make resistance impossible.

Having rattled England's chains, he next proceeded to humiliate the Anglican clergy. He directed that on 20 May his Declaration should be read in all churches and that the bishops should distribute the Declaration in their dioceses.[10] To the Anglican clergy, who saw the Declaration as arbitrary and illegal, as well as an attack upon the Church of England, the King's order meant that they were to become accomplices in wounding the church and subverting constitutional government.

After much agonizing, the bishops elected to disobey the King. Seven of them, including Archbishop Sancroft, drew up a

petition instead—a petition which began with protests of loyalty
to the King but ended by denying the legality of the dispensing
power. The bishops declared that they could not 'in prudence,
conscience, or honour' distribute a declaration which contravened the laws of Parliament.[11]

Naturally, James was enraged by the petition, which called his
prerogative into question and struck at the heart of his policy.
And he soon received a demonstration of the bishops' power.
On Sunday morning, 20 May, only four or five among the
dozens of Anglican divines in the London area read the
Declaration. The bishops, solidly backed by their clergy and
enthusiastically supported by the London populace, had dealt
the King a shocking defeat.

This defeat James turned into disaster. The bishops were
summoned before the King and his Council, charged with
'seditious libel',[12] and ordered to appear for trial before the
King's Bench, where (James and Jeffreys supposed) hand-picked
judges would direct a verdict for the Crown. But the bishops,
claiming their rights as peers of Parliament, refused to give bail;
and James found himself with the choice of dropping the
charges or imprisoning the bishops. Fatefully, he issued a
warrant committing the bishops to the Tower. And as the royal
barge with its distinguished prisoners made its way down the
Thames, the multitudes who watched it saw an unforgettable
symbol of tyranny. James had created seven Anglican martyrs.

While the King was goading his subjects towards revolution,
the Queen was preparing to deliver a child. In late May she
announced that she would lie in at St. James's Palace,[13] and on
Saturday, 9 June, she was carried in a sedan chair from
Whitehall to St. James's.[14] As it happened, Goodwin was
walking through the Park as the Queen's chair came by, and he
quickly improved the opportunity. He had not seen Mary
Beatrice close up since she had stood elbow to elbow with him at
the Cross Bath and pretended to ignore him. Now he gave her
another chance to show some sign of the understanding between
them. Twice he went up close to her chair and gazed upon her
intently, and both times the Queen missed her opportunity. If
she saw him at all—and he could not be sure that she looked at
him—she concealed all traces of recognition. Goodwin could
understand that 'her head might well be full of business', since

she was about to help perpetrate an elaborate and dangerous fraud. He was displeased, nevertheless, with her conduct. He knew already that her hoax would not thrive; now it seemed doubtful that her love affair would thrive either.

The next morning, shortly after ten, came the announcement that Mary Beatrice had produced a son. The Queen—so the official proclamation ran—'was safely delivered of a prince at St. James's'.[15] It was an announcement that Englishmen were fully prepared to disbelieve. For months they had insulated themselves against the odious possibility of a popish successor, and for weeks they had canvassed every suspicious detail of the Queen's behaviour. The question for debate had become not whether the pregnancy was genuine but how the hoax would be carried out. The most popular theory was the warming-pan story, already confected when the Tower cannon spread the news of the alleged birth. An infant male child had been procured by Jesuits and smuggled into the Queen's bed in a warming pan while the Queen pretended to go through labour. Now the child was being passed off as the Prince of Wales in order to fasten popery and slavery upon England forever.

In the tense interval between the birth of the Prince and the trial of the seven bishops, William Penn finally approached King James on the subject of Goodwin Wharton. Penn was rebuffed when he suggested an audience for Goodwin; the King, who remembered very well that Goodwin had not 'used him like a gentleman' in the House of Commons, would not see him or hear him present his own case. But when Penn pleaded the cause himself, James gave permission for Goodwin and his partners to salvage sunken treasure in Jersey; and on 29 June (the day of the bishop's trial), Penn reported his success to Goodwin.

At Westminster Hall, meanwhile, in the most dramatic and heavily attended trial in English history,[16] the King's alleged right to suspend statutes of the realm was being shredded by the counsel for the bishops. The judges themselves—perhaps over-awed by the hostile multitude—did not venture to defend the dispensing power; and one of them, Sir John Powell, denounced it in resounding terms. The King had no such power, he said, and a protest against a 'pretended power' could not be illegal.

About ten the next morning the jury brought in its verdict, declaring the bishops not guilty. Spontaneous shouts of joy arose in Westminster Hall, and the cheers were soon echoing throughout London; they were even taken up by the royal army at Hounslow. King James himself was too dull to realize how deeply his power had been shaken, but canny politicians were not. For the past few months some of his influential subjects had been planning resistance and concerting measures with the Prince of Orange. On the night of 30 June, they decided that the nation had had enough of King James and that the time to destroy his power would never be better. Seven of them—Sidney, Shrewsbury, Devonshire, Compton, Danby, Lumley, and Russell —signed a letter to the Prince of Orange, inviting him to come over from Holland with his army and save England from King James.

Though unaware of the conspiracy, Goodwin had private reasons for knowing that the King was in desperate trouble. After his first joy over Penn's message, he began to brood about the King's ungracious refusal to see him. Such behaviour was monstrous, he knew; and his view was confirmed in an oral revelation: the King had been 'very strange', the Lord said, and would assuredly be made to suffer. James's humiliating defeat at Westminster was obviously the first instalment on his suffering, Goodwin saw, and there was no doubt much worse punishment in store.

16

Lilliburlero

FREE to conduct a diving expedition to the Isle of Jersey, Goodwin concluded his preparations with all possible dispatch. Even while the delicate negotiations with the King had been stalled, he had acquired a ship, selected his diving crew, appointed Sir Thomas Travell his second-in-command, and secured enough money for the voyage. Only two problems remained to be solved before he would be ready to begin what the Lord promised would be a prosperous journey.

One of the problems was the treacherous Osmond Cook. A native of Jersey, Cook was valuable for his knowledge of the area as well as his mechanical skills; but as the time for sailing drew near, Goodwin became convinced from the difficulties Cook raised over the terms of their agreement that the man was more troublesome than useful. When Cook resigned, after a bitter argument, Goodwin felt as if he had been delivered from an enemy and a spy.

The second problem was technical. Like his contemporaries, Goodwin knew that the critical weakness in diving operations lay in the crude methods available for delivering air to submerged divers. The combination of hand-operated bellows, semi-rigid air hoses (usually metal 'pipes'), and clumsy headgear made breathing difficult and manœuvring dangerous. What was necessary, Goodwin saw, was some device for freeing the diver from reliance on surface paraphernalia—something a later age would call self-contained underwater breathing apparatus.[1]

As Goodwin studied the problem, he concluded that the solution lay in the fact that water is full of air. If he could find a fabric impervious to water but permeable by air, he could build a filter, or strainer, that would permit a diver to draw air from the surrounding water. When Mary consulted the angels, they agreed that such a device was possible, and after giving her a paper 'model' of the apparatus, they delivered some of the crucial filter material. Goodwin saw at once that the fabric was not rare or difficult to obtain—though no one except the angels had ever thought of using it for an air strainer. He also saw that it was too thick to be used next to the face and that it would need to be mounted in a frame, or face-piece. The angels promised to complete the device themselves and deliver it, with filter installed, before his ship sailed.

And the angels promised something even better. They would produce a thinner fabric—a material unknown to mortals—that could be used 'close by in the mouth'. From this they would construct a device less complicated than the first filtering system—a mouthpiece that would not require face masks or headpieces. Naturally, such an invention could not be produced at once; it would be ready, however, before Goodwin arrived at the diving site, and it would be delivered to him on shipboard.

Although the angels had theoretically solved Goodwin's technical problems, they did not deliver the completed headgear before he boarded ship on 11 July, and they did nothing about the winds. A strong east wind kept the vessel in the port of London for three days; and after the Captain at last manœuvred the ship past Deal and turned it southwest, the wind became 'two or three perfect hurricanes', which tore the mainsail, almost broke the mainmast, and threatened to overturn the ship. Then as the storm subsided to a mere gale, the wind shifted from east to west and blew 'so flat' in the ship's 'teeth' that the Captain turned back into the Downs for shelter and at last anchored at Deal.

Unable to communicate with God or the angels, who had obviously failed to complete their work, Goodwin decided to help himself. He constructed three face-pieces of his own and mounted in them the fabric Mary had received from the angels. Then, on the morning of 21 July, he tried out his new devices in water. To his great amazement, water passed easily through the fabric along with the air; the filtering system did not work at all. This stunning failure convinced Goodwin that he must return to London for explanations and instructions. That afternoon he ordered the Captain to beat his way to the Isle of Wight and wait for him there; then he set off with Sir Thomas Travell, who had been desperately seasick and was happy for the reprieve.

In London, he soon learned from Mary the cause of the

troubles. Osmond Cook's wife, 'a furious devil', had not only conjured up a storm but wrought a curse upon the treasure site in Jersey. Until the spell was lifted, it would not be safe to proceed. As for the air filter, Mary said, the angels themselves had not yet discovered the flaw in their invention. They concurred, however, when Goodwin produced a diagnosis of his own. The fabric, he concluded, had been overstretched and rendered porous; in the future it would be necessary to exercise greater care in mounting the material in its frames.

Using her influence with the angels, Mary quickly countered the Jersey spell, and within two days she had procured a new supply of filter fabric. She was also promised that after delivering her children she could join the expedition at Jersey and supervise the recovery of the treasure. Goodwin himself was promised, in audible revelations, that the Lord would come to him at sea and deliver the magic mouthpiece in person. By 30 July, when Goodwin left to rejoin his ship, his confidence was fully restored.

London as he left it seemed quiet. Except for active conspirators, the town confined itself to gossiping about the alleged Prince and watching the manœuvres of the King, who had obviously learned nothing from his errors. He dismissed Sir John Powell and Sir Richard Holloway from the King's Bench for opposing the Crown;[2] he convoked his Ecclesiastical Commission, which threatened punishment for those who had failed to read the royal Declaration;[3] and he continued to remodel corporations in preparation for the coming elections.

Across the sea in Holland, meanwhile, William of Orange had begun preparing for a descent upon England—a task involving several delicate steps.[4] In the face of French power, which menaced the Rhineland and which might move against the Netherlands, William was obliged to put together a coalition capable of holding off the French while he himself, with a Dutch army, was invading England. He also had to persuade the States-General to risk an army and the safety of the Republic upon the success of an English revolution. Finally, he was obliged to assemble the invasion army and provide it with a covering fleet strong enough to hold off the English navy. And he was obliged to make all these moves without giving away his ultimate intentions. During July, while Goodwin was coping with adverse winds and faulty equipment, William was moving forward on all his projects and masking his preparations so carefully that James and his ministers remained comfortably deceived—hardly better informed than Goodwin, who was about to sail for Jersey.

Goodwin and Sir Thomas arrived in Jersey on 7 August, after a prosperous crossing from the Isle of Wight. The reception at St. Hélier was also prosperous. 'Having acquaintance' in Jersey, they were soon introduced to all the notables on the island, who treated them with great civility and convinced Goodwin that he was 'very much beloved and respected' in that country. At the diving site, however, prospects were less cheering. The place where the treasure lay was surrounded by 'dreadful rocks', and it would be 'mighty dangerous', Goodwin saw, to begin salvage operations before the lowest possible tide—before the next full moon, on 29 August.

Meanwhile, there was still the matter of the face masks and the magic mouthpiece. The angels had delivered more filter fabric but they had not provided frames; they had left Goodwin to use his own face-pieces and to install the filters himself. But when he tested his carefully constructed devices, water continued to pass through the filters as if they were sieves. As for the often-promised mouthpiece, it simply failed to arrive. In spite of Goodwin's prayers, God neither spoke nor delivered the mouthpiece. (Goodwin later learned that the angels had taken the device to London by mistake.) And when the diving-suit designed by Cook proved too small to fit any of the divers, Goodwin found himself compelled to conduct operations with his own conventional equipment.

While waiting in St. Hélier for the full moon, Goodwin clung to the hope that Mary would join him, but Mary too failed to appear. The only ship that arrived from England during the waiting period brought his old enemy Osmond Cook, who had 'deceived some gentlemen and merchants with his great brags' and organized a diving expedition of his own. On 13 August, he arrived in St. Hélier, with some of his backers, bringing with him the written permission of Lord Jermyn, Governor of Jersey, to salvage the wreck that Goodwin had staked out for himself. He now tried 'to ruin and frustrate' Goodwin 'in all things'.

Luckily, Goodwin's legal position was unassailable. His

permission to proceed came from the King rather than a mere governor, and he had, besides, Cook's earlier promise under oath not to desert him or help anyone else. He brought suit at once in the Royal Court at St. Hélier, and the merits of his case were so apparent that on 24 August the Court ratified his rights. Ultimately, Cook was ordered to ask pardon on his knees for his offences against God, the Court itself, Goodwin, and the people he had deceived; and he would have been ordered to stand in the pillory if Goodwin had not requested clemency.[5] In spite of this complicated interruption, then, Goodwin was ready to proceed by the time of the full moon.

The morning of 29 August brought 'foul weather', but Goodwin, on the advice of his now faint inward voice, ordered the Captain to get the ship under way, and on the voyage towards the treasure site the weather became 'fairer', confirming God's internal message and proving that Goodwin had not been abandoned. The condition of the treasure site gave further encouragement. With the tide at a remarkably low ebb, the place resembled a pond—surrounded by rocks, to be sure, but easily accessible—and the water was so shallow that 'there was no occasion for diving'. But a search of the area yielded nothing but frustration. Goodwin and his crew could find no trace of the wreck and its treasure. After an hour of hunting and probing, they had not discovered 'the least thing whatever'. Goodwin later learned from Mary that the treasure had been silted up and that he had once been within a foot of it, but for the present all the time and money spent upon trying to salvage it had been wasted.

Back at St. Hélier, Goodwin decided to recoup his losses by exploring an alternate site suggested by a gentleman named Humphrey Trafford, who proposed that Goodwin should salvage the *Pembroke*, a vessel sunk near Portland.[6] Goodwin wrote Mary for advice and asked her to join him at Southampton; then, after settling his affairs in Jersey, he sailed for the mainland, arriving at Southampton on 14 September.

Although Mary herself could not join the expedition until 25 September, at Portsmouth, her messages were encouraging. The angels, she said, had given tentative approval to the *Pembroke* project, which would realize £20,000. More significantly, they had delivered to her the magic mouthpiece, which would make all diving projects simple. This device (constructed, she said, of material thin as cambric) she wrapped and sealed and sent along to Goodwin with instructions that it was to remain sealed until salvage operations began.

While Goodwin was waiting for Mary and pacifying his sailors, who feared to undertake another expedition so late in the season, King James and his ministers woke to the deadly danger that threatened them from Holland. The army that William was assembling, they finally learned, was not to be launched against France but against England. They realized too that they could get no help from Louis XIV, who had committed his armies to the upper and middle Rhineland, relieving the immediate pressure upon the Dutch and leaving William free to invade England. Finally, they saw that they had alienated the King's subjects, perhaps beyond recall, and that the loyalty of their own troops was suspect. With a haste bordering upon panic, they began enlarging their forces, strengthening their garrisons, and tightening the security around naval bases like Portsmouth, while they strove on the political front 'to sweeten up the nation' by reversing the policies that had brought them into peril.

On 25 September when Mary arrived in Portsmouth, the town was buzzing with political rumours, but Mary confined her attention to the affairs of the partnership. During Goodwin's absence, she revealed, she had been delivered of twin daughters, whom she had named Susan and Sarah. Goodwin was puzzled at the 38-child discrepancy between the forty children promised by his inner voice and the two children actually produced, but he did not comment. (Mary later explained that her jealousy and grief had caused multiple miscarriages.) As for the diving business, Mary said, the attempt on the *Pembroke* would not be feasible after all. This view was confirmed on 26 September by the angels, who declared that the season was too far advanced, and a few days later by the Lord himself, who told Goodwin in an oral revelation that he must suspend all diving activities until the following spring. Goodwin would be happy, the Lord said, 'in one-half year and a month'.

As he waited for his final revelation, Goodwin was being watched by the officers of the Portsmouth garrison, who suspected from his reputation as a virulent Whig that he had come to spy on their defences. This fact he learned on the evening of 28 September from Colonel Henry Slingsby,[7] the commandant, who said that he had been ordered by the Duke of Berwick,[8] Governor of Portsmouth, to find out what Goodwin was doing. Goodwin was insulted. Innocence itself, he concluded that the young Duke, whom he had met socially in Southampton, had been turned against him by the spite of some popish officers, particularly Captain Samuel Bridges.[9] All this Goodwin explained to Colonel Slingsby, who professed himself satisfied. But the next morning Slingsby went hunting; and while Goodwin was walking on the Saluting Platform, he was accosted by Slingsby's second-in-command Colonel Robert Ramsey,[10] who ordered him to get off the platform[11] and out of the garrison before he was laid by the heels.

Unwittingly Colonel Ramsey had done Goodwin a favour by chasing him out of Portsmouth. A warrant for Goodwin's arrest, issued on 28 September,[12] was already on its way from Westminster, and when he sailed away he evaded capture. Unaware that he was a fugitive, Goodwin returned to Southampton and remained there unmolested while he laid up his ship and paid off his men. He even had time, before Mary left for London, to view with her 'an old forsaken gate of the town', where a great treasure had been hidden during an invasion in the distant past—a treasure which the attendant spirits promised to deliver after the next New Year's Day. It was not until 5 October that he received the shocking news that he was being pursued by a royal warrant.

Unwilling to be taken prisoner, Goodwin left Southampton before one o'clock the next morning and by riding a series of post-horses made the 78-mile journey to London in a single day.[13] On the following morning he hurried to Whitehall, intending to vindicate himself before King James in person, but before he could see the King, Sunderland learned of his presence and dispatched William Bridgeman, a clerk of the King's Council,[14] to put Goodwin under arrest. Bridgeman was polite enough. He agreed that Goodwin had appeared voluntarily, but he insisted upon placing him in the custody of an officer. And after waiting all day, Goodwin learned that he would not be brought before the King or released on his own recognizance; he was to remain in the hands of the King's messenger.

With the nation threatening to fall about their ears, James and his ministers would have been content to hold Goodwin indefinitely and keep at least one suspect off the streets; but the day after his arrest Goodwin received help from his brother Henry, who volunteered, in an uncharacteristic display of 'sincere affection', to go to the King and Sunderland and get Goodwin an immediate hearing. Henry was rebuffed by James, who said somewhat angrily that there would be time enough for a hearing after the charges had been investigated; but Sunderland conceded that it was unjust to hold Goodwin without a hearing and promised that he would be admitted to bail.

On the morning of 11 October, then, after four days in custody and after posting a bond of £1,000 (which he had great difficulty raising), Goodwin found himself free once more— though obliged to stand on his good behaviour and to appear at the King's Bench on 23 October.

Naturally the arrest caused excitement about town. For a time it appeared that the government had captured a genuine agent for the rebels.[15] Goodwin's release on bail, which suggested that he might not be a spy after all, came as an anti-climax; and his appearances before the King's Bench were more anti-climactic still.[16] On 23 October, the Court continued the case when Sir Thomas Powis, the Attorney General, admitted that he had prepared no charges; and on 29 October, when Powis still had 'nothing to say', the Court freed Goodwin and discharged him from bail.

The King's ministers would eventually learn, too late, that they had arrested the wrong Wharton. For months Tom and Henry, as leading spirits in the so-called Rose Tavern group, had been conspiring against the government. At the time of Goodwin's arrest, both men were plotting to subvert the King's army, and Tom was concerting measures with Danby for a rising in the North. Tom would soon have the honour, along with Lord Colchester, of being one of the first two aristocrats to join the Prince of Orange after the landing at Torbay,[17] and Henry would help demoralize the King's army by deserting it at a crucial time.[18]

Meanwhile Tom had already made a contribution to the Revolution more important than conspiracy. He had written the satirical ballad *Lilliburlero*.[19] Composed originally in 1687 to satirize the Earl of Tyrconnel, Lord Deputy of Ireland, the song took on a new relevance as England waited for William's armada to put to sea and James reinforced his army with Irish troops. Besides expressing the nation's contempt for Irishmen and Catholics, *Lilliburlero* furnished the phrase 'Protestant wind', which seemed to describe the very wind that William was waiting for. And in November, after William had actually landed, the song swept through the country. Gilbert Burnet, who came to England with the Prince, was amazed. 'The whole army,' he wrote, 'and at last all people both in city and country, were singing it perpetually. And perhaps never had so slight a thing so great an effect.'[20] Tom himself was later able to boast that he had sung King James out of three kingdoms.

In late October, of course, such triumphs in plotting and propaganda lay in the future; and Tom and Henry, like good conspirators, kept their activities secret from Goodwin—a precaution made easier by the fact that for months they had barely spoken to him on any subject. Although Goodwin could observe for himself that the King had been frightened into making many political concessions and that the papists in general 'looked like dead men', he had no inside knowledge of the invasion plans. After being released from custody, and after forcing an apology from Captain Samuel Bridges (who denied having brought the original complaint against him at Portsmouth),[21] he sought more and more earnestly to learn from God and the angels what William and James would do and how he should comport himself during the Revolution.

The angels' first revelations about the Revolution, given several weeks before the actual invasion, had been mistaken; Mary was informed several times that William of Orange would not reach England until the following spring. It was not until William's troops were loaded in their transports, waiting for a Protestant wind, that the angels corrected their original error— occasioned, they said, by William's last-minute change of mind. By 15 October, they were sure that the invasion would occur but not yet sure of Goodwin's role; they could only suggest, tentatively, that he should go and proffer his services to King James.

From one point of view the angels' suggestion made excellent sense. For more than a year Goodwin's revelations had promised that James would raise him to power, and now events seemed to be forcing the King to take action. That James desperately needed help was clear enough. He was about to be assailed by a powerful enemy, and he was having no luck wooing his subjects, who looked upon his eleventh-hour concessions as extorted. The angels could not yet be sure, however, that he was ready to accept help from Goodwin, and through the last days of October Goodwin was obliged to wait for positive instructions. Meanwhile he maintained a cool, aloof attitude towards the King. On 20 October, when he saw James in the Strand, he did not bow until the King had 'pulled off his hat' to him. And he did nothing to prevent James from making another gross tactical error. He only sneered when James, going 'on the weakest design imaginable', brought together a crowd of witnesses to swear that there was no fraud involved in the birth of the young Prince. The 'circumstances lay so ill together', Goodwin observed, 'that it made the thing worse.'[22]

While Goodwin was waiting for instructions from the angels, the Prince of Orange, with 14,000 men, landed at Torbay. Goodwin expected, of course, that the invasion would force King James to send for him; but although his revelations assured him that he would benefit from the upheaval, they still counselled delay. The King's moods fluctuated so wildly between despair and false confidence that the Lord himself could not predict them; and on 11 November, six days after the landing, Goodwin was commanded to 'stand neuter' until James was properly humbled.

This command caused Goodwin acute anxiety. In offering to serve the King, he had never intended to support the King's policies, much less fight for him. He visualized himself as a divinely-guided minister who could bring peace between the parties, reduce the King's power, and convert James to Protestantism. But if the King refused to employ him, he would not only lose all chance of influencing events but look like a coward and a traitor to England. His 'principles and inclinations', as well as 'all human prudence', told him that he should join the Prince of Orange, and he suspected that people were already sneering behind his back; 'the standing thus long by', he complained, 'brings a blast upon my courage.' Obliged to choose between mere human prudence and divine revelation, he naturally chose revelation; but while he waited for God's promises to be fulfilled, he suffered.

On 13 November, Goodwin's political worries were interrupted by a dramatic change in his personal affairs. For the first time in four and a half years of fatherhood, he was allowed to see—and hold—one of his sons, young Hezekiah. This happy event had been preceded by two weeks of discussion with Mary and several revelations. Mary explained that Hezekiah's nurse had allowed the child to fall and 'bruise itself much' and that a more competent nurse must be found. She also explained that Hezekiah had been living under the surname *Knowles* in order to conceal his true identity as Goodwin's son. By 12 November, Mary had made arrangements for a new nurse, and the next day Goodwin went with her to remove Hezekiah from the care of the unsatisfactory nurse. The meeting proved to be an instant success. 'And as soon as the child saw me,' Goodwin wrote, 'he flew to me, and with all the fondness imaginable would never be out of my arms till I was obliged to get away that he might be carried home.' It was clear that the little boy, then twenty months old according to Mary's calculations, had a natural affinity for the father whom he had never seen before. His behaviour, as Goodwin noted proudly, was 'strangely kind'.

With Hezekiah resettled, Goodwin returned to the process of humbling King James. Part of the problem, he learned, was black magic. Ever since James had known of the invasion plot, he had employed six priests to work diabolical spells against William. They had conjured up the adverse winds that had kept William in Holland, and he had only escaped because they had neglected their rituals one day. Now they were continuing their conjurations, filling the King with false hopes. The other, more public, reason for the King's fits of optimism was that his army remained intact and there seemed to be no great rush to the Prince's standard.

While Goodwin waited for news that the Prince's friends were joining him and that the King's army was disintegrating, he was twice commanded to see the King in person—not to proffer his services but to remind the King by his presence that he was available. The first time, at Whitehall on the evening of 12 November, he got so close to James, who was coming from a Council meeting, and looked 'so earnestly in his face' that James could not avoid seeing him, though obliged to hurry away. Goodwin's appearance, he later learned, was much noticed and 'taken mighty kindly' by the Court.[23] The second meeting took place on Pall Mall on the morning of 15 November. Staying resolutely within the street, Goodwin met the King 'full'—at such close range that James could not help recognizing him. It was immediately clear, however, that James was not yet ready to speak; 'showing shame and want of resolution', he turned his eyes away from Goodwin and passed by without saying a word.

As it happened, Goodwin saw the King in one of James's last hours of confidence. About noon the same day word came from Salisbury that Lord Cornbury and Lieutenant-Colonel Thomas Langston had defected to the Prince with large contingents from three cavalry regiments. And after this defection, which seemed to pull up the King's 'hopes and expectations by the roots',[24] James seldom received anything but bad news. In the West, after the first trickle of volunteers led by Tom Wharton and Lord Colchester, throngs of gentlemen, including Tory magnates, joined the Prince at Exeter; Plymouth and Bristol surrendered peaceably, leaving William in complete possession of south-western England. In the North, successive risings, led by prominent noblemen, captured Manchester, Nottingham, and York from the King's adherents.[25] And when James took over personal command of his army at Salisbury, it began to dissolve virtually under his eyes. Lord Churchill, Prince George of Denmark, the Duke of Grafton, the Duke of Ormond, and several other officers, including Henry Wharton, left the royal camp and went over to William. James even found himself deserted by his daughter Princess Anne, who fled from Whitehall, along with Sarah Churchill, and put herself under the protection of the rebel lords at Nottingham.[26] The King's losses were so grievous that Goodwin, who had a vested interest in them, barely restrained himself from writing 'poor King' in his journal.

Goodwin took advantage of the King's absence from London to make one final attempt to meet Queen Mary Beatrice. On the afternoon of 17 November, shortly after James had left town, he presented himself at Catherine Fraser's lodgings at Whitehall, hoping that Mistress Fraser would at last arrange a meeting, or at least deliver a message. The Queen, he knew, was much upset by recent developments and desperately in need of his help.

Earlier in the day she had sent her child to Portsmouth for safe keeping, and there were rumours that she intended to leave town herself. But Goodwin found himself unable to get past Catherine Fraser's servant, who 'denied' her mistress in the most irritating and persistent court manner. He was obliged to communicate with the Queen by way of Phocas, whom he had not employed for several months and who remained invisible as always. To Goodwin's message of sympathy, Mary Beatrice replied 'that she was almost mad' with worry and that she wanted him to pity her. Goodwin found it easy to pity the Queen and to forgive her for her broken promises. There was something decisive, nevertheless, in his failure to see her, as if her troubles had forced her out of his orbit. Although the Queen actually remained in town until 9 December, Goodwin never tried to speak with her again.

During the King's absence, Goodwin was told by the Lord that the times would 'make well' for him, and for a few days after James returned, demoralized and apparently humble, the Lord's prediction and advice seemed very good indeed. But during the last few days of November, James did not send for Goodwin; he summoned instead a group of bishops and peers, who advised him to call a free parliament, and he appointed Halifax, Nottingham, and Godolphin as his commissioners to treat with the Prince of Orange. On 4 December, the angels themselves conceded that James might never send for Goodwin. They would keep trying, of course, to bend the King's stubborn spirit, but they could only promise that if James had not summoned Goodwin by 10 December, 'he should be cast down within three months from being a king forever.' Meantime, Goodwin must continue to wait.

On 8 December, Goodwin's endurance finally wilted, and he begged for a change of orders. Except for himself, he complained, all the world was in action; his continued presence in London was bringing overt sneers; and the angels in their most recent report had declared that the King would rather hang himself than be rescued by Goodwin. Why, Goodwin argued, should he stay in town to be traduced, if God and the angels could not bend the King? Why should he not join the Prince of Orange, now at Hungerford?

These complaints brought quick results. In three successive

oral revelations over the next two days, the Lord not only gave Goodwin permission to leave town but urged him to make haste. And on the night of 10 December (the night after the Queen, with the aid of Count Lauzun, secretly left Whitehall and sailed for France), Goodwin took horse with Sir Thomas Travell and another gentleman, evaded the cavalry patrols of the King's army, and at last reached a town safely beyond the royal outposts where he and his companions could rest before pushing on to join the Prince.

But the new revelations had come too late. In the night, while Goodwin and his friends were making their way through the royal lines, King James was fleeing from Whitehall and riding towards Sheppey, where a boat was waiting, as he supposed, to take him to France. The King's flight, naturally enough, transformed the whole political scene; when it was discovered, after daylight next morning, it threw London into a turmoil of celebrations and riots, ended all royalist resistance to the Prince of Orange, and sent messengers scurrying in all directions. It also frustrated Goodwin and rendered his exploits useless. When he arrived with his companions at Henley, an outpost of the Prince's army, he learned that the war was over.

The unfortunate timing of the King's departure meant that Goodwin met the Prince of Orange under a handicap. When the Prince came to Henley[27] the next day (13 December) and Goodwin was introduced by his brother Tom, it was clear that the Prince was not impressed. 'I could easily perceive' (Goodwin wrote a few days later) 'that [with] the news of the King's being gone, and my coming being so late, I was looked upon but as indifferently as many that now flocked into him apace.'

Goodwin's uneasy feeling that he had missed the political future—now in the hands of a cool, competent, unimpressionable soldier—was temporarily lightened by strange news from Faversham. King James, attempting to escape in disguise, had been pulled off his boat by some fishermen, finally identified, and sent back to Whitehall. To Goodwin the news brought one last flicker of hope that James, who was still the legal King of England, might call for his help. But when Goodwin summoned Mary to Hounslow on 15 December, she could promise nothing; the angels had given no hint that James had changed his mind. There was nothing for Goodwin to do but remain with the Prince's forces until the Lord's purposes became clear.

Goodwin returned to London on the afternoon of 18 December—one of the most dramatic days in English history. About eleven in the morning King James was sent back down the Thames to Rochester, accompanied by several boatloads of Dutch guards. Shortly afterwards, the main body of William's army, headed by its English contingents, came marching into Westminster; and at two o'clock, William himself, in a coach with Marshal Schomberg, drew up at St. James's Palace. From everywhere Londoners came out to welcome their deliverers. Commoners thronged the Park and the streets, straining to get a look at the Prince; and aristocrats, eager for introductions, crowded their way into the Palace itself.[28]

On that afternoon of orange ribbons, church-bells, and *Lilliburlero*, there was one young aristocrat who did not try to elbow his way into St. James's. Goodwin, returning undistinguished in the civilian crowd that followed the Prince, had a great deal to think about. Although he did not yet know that King James would be permitted (if not helped) to escape from Rochester, he could sense easily enough that James, like Mary Beatrice, had moved out of his life forever. As for the new order, it was hard to be optimistic, even though the Lord had promised prosperity by late April. If prosperity depended upon the Prince's favour, the way seemed long and tortuous. For a late-comer to impress William and vault over the horde of gentlemen bidding for his attention would require a miracle indeed—a miracle that had never quite happened during the reign of James II.

17

The Second-Best World

To all the Wharton men except Goodwin the triumph of the Prince of Orange brought prestige and appointments. Henry became Colonel of his regiment;[1] Lord Wharton became a privy councillor;[2] Tom became a privy councillor, Comptroller of the Household, Commissioner of the Army, and one of the negotiators of the military alliance between England and the United Provinces.[3] Even Goodwin's brother-in-law William Carr gained a prize; through Tom's influence he was appointed Cursitor Baron of the Court of Exchequer.[4]

In promoting the Whartons, William not only rewarded Tom and Henry for their early support of the Revolution but also recognized a fact of political life. The Wharton family was gaining control of a number of seats in Parliament, and the Wharton influence was becoming a force in Revolution politics. In late December 1688, during the election for the Convention Parliament, and in early 1689, when the form of the new government was being decided, the support of thoroughgoing Whigs like the Whartons was particularly vital to William. Although James II had just made the doctrines of non-resistance and divine right ridiculous, it was difficult for good Tories, who had espoused such theories for years, to dethrone a hereditary king. In general, they wished to save appearances by adopting a regency plan.

Good Whigs, on the other hand, suffered from no such scruples. Having tried to exclude James from the throne on the grounds that he was a threat to the English Constitution, they felt no compunction about deposing him after he had proved them right. In the Convention Parliament they cheerfully voted that the throne had become vacant, and then, having carried their point, they went on to nominate William and Mary to fill the vacancy. William, who needed both the title and power of a king if he was to beat back the French and establish order in the British Isles, owed his crown to his Whig friends, and he had particular reason to be grateful to Tom Wharton, who supported him with three effective speeches in the debates on the form of the monarchy.[5]

During the crucial last days of 1688 when the new order was beginning to take shape, Goodwin's merit went unrecognized. Although it was for his sake that the Lord had cast King James down from power, Goodwin could not explain this fact to the Prince of Orange. For the present, Goodwin saw (and the Lord agreed), his only chance for political prestige was to win a seat in the Convention Parliament, and for this purpose he needed the support of his family. His merits, unfortunately, were almost as invisible to his father and brothers as they were to the Prince of Orange. Though the Whartons gave him fair words about seeking a place, they gave him no help in finding one. Tom and Henry concentrated instead upon securing seats for themselves and their political allies. Tom was re-elected Knight of the Shire in Bucks. Henry won two elections, one for the County of Westmorland and one for Malmesbury (where he stood by way of insurance).[6] Tom's friend Charles Godfrey gained the other seat at Malmesbury, and his friend William Jephson was elected at High Wycombe. Left essentially to his own devices, Goodwin suffered disappointments in four or five places; and when he was unable to secure support from Lord Lovelace and Sir John Borlase, who controlled the other seat at Wycombe, he was obliged to give up.

Meanwhile, on 26 December, along with the other surviving members of the parliaments of Charles II, he was summoned to advise the Prince of Orange on measures for establishing a new government. He hoped briefly that the Lord might provide some divine political expedient, but his revelations merely told him to be discreet, and he soon discovered that the veteran MPs did not need any help to produce sensible recommendations. An assemblage of peers had advised William to call a parliamentary convention and asked him to conduct the government until elections could be held. This advice, made inevitable by the second and final flight of James, was endorsed by Goodwin's colleagues on 28 December—after three sessions during which Goodwin did not say a word.[7]

On 31 December, Goodwin received some excellent political advice from the Lord. Although he was presently ignored by the

Prince of Orange (the Lord said) and although he would not be
elected to the Convention Parliament, he must not seem
disaffected; he must appear, on the contrary, as a supporter of
the new regime, and he must go often among the company at
Court. In time, the Lord implied, William would be inspired to
recognize his merits. This advice was to dictate Goodwin's
political strategy for many years and would eventually lead to
substantial rewards. Even in the frustrating present, it produced
an obvious advantage. As a friend of the new regime Goodwin
was welcome at Court, where he could speak with the King and
Queen in person. While he waited for the Lord to enlighten
William of Orange, he could be active on his own behalf.

In the midst of the political confusion, Goodwin strengthened
his social position. On 1 January 1689, he left his lodgings on Vere
Street and moved in with Sir Thomas Travell, who had just
leased a new house in Soho Square, then one of the newest and
most fashionable neighbourhoods on the west side of town. The
house, Number 4, Soho Square, was a handsome three-storey
structure set in a row of similar houses on the west side of the
Square near the northwest corner.[8] Goodwin's apartment on the
second floor overlooked the Square and allowed him to keep an
eye on the other residents, mostly Whig aristocrats.[9] When he
moved in, along with Mary and their collection of treasure
trunks, he became socially visible again after years of obscurity.

The new living arrangements necessarily raised the status of
Sir Thomas Travell, who became something like a full partner.
In the ensuing months, besides consulting Mary about the spirit
of his dead wife, he was assigned a share in all new treasures and
put under the special care of a guardian angel, who spoke to him
audibly (though invisibly) several times. Through obedience and
financial aid, Sir Thomas had become a more than adequate
replacement for John Wildman, who had been dropped from
Goodwin's plans, though he had returned to England with the
Prince and was about to become Postmaster General, an
alderman of London, an MP, and a knight.[10]

On 31 January, as a reward for his fidelity, Sir Thomas was
allowed to accompany Goodwin and Mary to Southampton,
where Mary had discovered a rich treasure concealed in the
abandoned Castle Gate (once the entry to the grounds of the
medieval castle of Southampton).[11] At first Goodwin feared that

digging gold and jewels out of a gate in the middle of the town might be a matter of some delicacy—especially since his only excuse for being in the area was to look after his ship, which lay at a quay outside the city walls. He was relieved, therefore, when Mary, always fertile in resource, arranged to have the spirit guardians bring the treasure to the partners' inn.

Except for some 'very fine' diamonds, which were laid before Goodwin while he and Mary were dining, the spirits delivered their treasure, securely tied up in bags, during the night. The total, as the partners judged by the weight, ran to about £3,000 in gold and perhaps £5,000 in jewels. And there was more to come. A good deal of treasure still remained in the gate, and the partners were promised that if they returned to Southampton on 2 April, after the ship was mended, they would receive the balance. On 25 March they would be allowed to use the gold and jewels they had already collected.

When Goodwin returned to Soho Square his most immediate problem was Lady Ivy. For months, Mary, the angels, and even the Lord had seemed to vacillate on the question of how much kindness the lady should be shown. The angels had not repeated their earlier suggestion that Goodwin should marry her; but they seemed to feel that some drastic step was necessary to secure her attachment, and they sometimes seemed to suggest (though never explicitly) that Goodwin should lie with her. Mary herself, in 'a strange instance of her kind temper' had once told him that he would be wise to seduce Lady Ivy, who would bear him a child and give him control of all her wealth.

Goodwin remained wary. Knowing Mary's passionate temperament, he was not at all sure that she meant what she was saying; and remembering God's lectures on whores and adultery, he was unwilling, in any case, to undertake a seduction without divine approval. In January Lady Ivy had been rendered more vulnerable by the Revolution. Her daughter Frances and her son-in-law Sir Robert Clarke (a Catholic and a clerk of the Crown under James) had been obliged to flee the country,[12] and Lady Ivy herself had 'absconded from her house' during the troublesome times. When she called on Goodwin she was still unsettled, and the Lord commanded Goodwin, in oral revelations, to 'make much' of her. God did not explain, however, what the phrase meant; and when Mary asked the angels whether or not Goodwin should lie with Lady Ivy, she could get no answer.

Shortly after his return from Southampton, Goodwin found himself alone with Lady Ivy, who seemed to give him 'all the encouragement that modestly she could'. Still uninstructed but unwilling to appear reluctant, Goodwin responded by going 'so far as might be without doing the act'. Then he very prudently went to Mary and pressed her to find out once and for all what he should do. Again Mary could learn nothing from the angels. As for herself, she said, she hoped she could endure an action so obviously for Goodwin's financial profit, though she might never be able to lie with him again. Goodwin objected vigorously. Unless Mary would 'continue the same person' she had always been, he would give up the Ivy affair. At last Mary promised that she would remain unchanged, and Goodwin went forth, hesitantly, to conquer Lady Ivy.

But the seduction turned out to be more complicated than he had imagined. Handicapped by the silence of the Lord and by a certain amount of doubt, he found it difficult to work up much enthusiasm for the project. That evening, when he saw Lady Ivy, he did everything his 'opportunity and place would allow', but he again stopped short of completing the final act—not only because the circumstances were not quite right, but also because he found himself virtually impotent. He found too that he had perhaps overestimated Lady Ivy's eagerness to be seduced, for after he concluded the unsatisfactory struggle she began to weep. In these puzzling circumstances Goodwin decided to wait for further orders and he promised Lady Ivy meantime that he would do nothing to afflict her.

Goodwin's failure to overwhelm Lady Ivy soon turned out to be providential. Mary declared that she could not reconcile herself to an affair after all; and during the succeeding months Lady Ivy's business and legal affairs became so thoroughly entangled that in spite of her vast property holdings she was, temporarily, a financial liability. In this situation, at once rich and harassed by debts,[13] Lady Ivy took a house next to Goodwin's on Soho Square, intending to wait more or less under Goodwin's protection until the political and legal storms blew over and suggesting meanwhile that Goodwin should marry her when her affairs returned to normal. But on 24 May a team of bailiffs arrived at Soho Square, and the alliance collapsed. The officers would have seized Lady Ivy herself and carried her off to debtors prison if she had not escaped through a connecting door between her house and Goodwin's and if Goodwin, who was home at the time, had not held them off 'by force'. As it was, they carried away all of her goods, treating the neighbourhood to a spectacle that reflected, Goodwin felt, 'most shamefully and disgracefully' upon her and upon himself.

The next day, as Goodwin mulled over the episode, Mary brought him a pronouncement from the angels: if Lady Ivy could not unsnarl her affairs Goodwin would be allowed to abandon her. Since Lady Ivy could not settle her business quickly, Goodwin wrote her off as a loss—another of his unsuccessful projects—and turned his attention to more vital schemes. In the early months of 1689, these included a campaign to win offices and honours from King William and Queen Mary.

Goodwin first brought himself to William's attention on 18 January 1689, three and a half weeks before William and Mary acceded to the Crown. Acting as spokesman for some gentlemen from Jersey, he appeared before William with a memorial on the dangers that beset the Island from the French and from the Tory appointees of James II. As the audience proceeded, Goodwin stressed the perils strongly, perhaps too strongly for his own good, for as he lectured on the crisis, he sensed that the Prince was somewhat nettled. And although William took the memorial and parted with him civilly, he felt in retrospect that he had mismanaged the conversation.[14]

After his initial failure, Goodwin felt reluctant to put himself in William's way. He was not among the crowd at the Banqueting House on 13 February when William and Mary accepted the Crown; it was not until the next morning, when the Lord specifically ordered him to kiss the hands of the new King and Queen, that he presented himself at Whitehall. Fortunately, he found Mary as charming as William was serious and silent; she took 'particular notice' of him at their very first meeting, and during the ensuing months her attentions almost made up for William's neglect.

On the subject of William's neglect, the angels took a consistent line. God had turned out King James, they said in late February, for neglecting Goodwin, and King William would be turned out too if he made the same mistake. Indeed, if William 'mended not', they added later, he would very likely die. The angels were less helpful, however, in selecting a government office for Goodwin; they left him to make his own choice. During the spring of 1689, he sought to become Governor of Jersey and a colonel in the army.

Since Thomas, Lord Jermyn, the Governor of Jersey, was a Tory—appointed by Charles II[15] and continued in office by James—it seemed to Goodwin that he should be removed on political grounds. Furthermore, Goodwin thought, Jermyn was not bold enough to defend the Island against the French. In his plan to replace Jermyn, Goodwin had trouble finding advocates; neither his father nor the Earl of Macclesfield[16] (who had several times expressed 'a particular kindness' for him) seemed anxious to solicit the King. Eventually, Goodwin found an opportunity to present his own case. Informed by a letter from Jersey that a French invasion was imminent, he rode to Hampton Court on 18 April, showed William the letter, and volunteered to defend the Island if he could be made Governor. To Goodwin's disgust, William seemed unperturbed by the news and not in the least inclined to remove Jermyn. As if it were unthinkable to replace a duly appointed official, Whig or Tory, who had not shown himself unredeemably treacherous, he simply pointed out that Lord Jermyn had a patent for the governorship. And Goodwin, unable to argue, found himself baffled once more by William's calm intransigence.

After this disappointment, Goodwin concentrated upon his alternative scheme. On 8 May, with the Lord's approval, he went to William at Whitehall and volunteered to raise a regiment of cavalry for service in Ireland. To Goodwin it seemed evident that William, waging wars in Flanders, Scotland, and Ireland, desperately needed regiments and would welcome an addition to the expeditionary force being prepared by the Duke of Schomberg. William, however, demurred. He would accept Goodwin's offer 'when he had occasion', he said politely, but not at the present moment.

William's soft answer (and the Lord's promise that Goodwin's suit would prove 'most prosperous') encouraged Goodwin. His hopes were reinforced when William again seemed to promise him a colonelcy sometime in the future, and later when William seemed very thankful for his renewed offer to raise a regiment. But during June William developed an 'untowardness' to talk with Goodwin, and by early July, when Schomberg's army began to rendezvous at Chester, it became clear that no commission would be forthcoming. It also became clear that King William, at least as purblind as James, was 'infatuated with evil counsels' and ripe for the destruction that the Lord predicted for him. For the time being, then, Goodwin abandoned him and concentrated upon Queen Mary.

From Goodwin's first meeting with the Queen he was struck by her charm, and on 1 March she appeared in one of his visions. He was sitting at a table with her and William, he thought, amid 'great rejoicing', and she was showing him 'great favours'. Although the vision was a trifle vague, its general purport was clear: he would probably rise to power through Mary rather than William. This view was endorsed by the angels about the end of April. Since the King was proud and stubborn, they said, he would soon die, leaving all power to the Queen, who would then 'take an affection' for Goodwin and raise him to eminence.

The Queen's affection for him, Goodwin observed, had already begun, and it continued to grow during the ensuing weeks. At Whitehall one day in mid-May, Goodwin 'plainly perceived the love she would seem to stifle', and the next day he observed that she had been weeping. He also observed that she was very lovely. And on 23 May the Lord promised to give Goodwin a beauty and glory that would dazzle her. It behoved him, the Lord added, to go to Court at every opportunity.

In the summer of 1689, this advice meant many journeys to Hampton Court, which Sir Christopher Wren was reconstructing for William and Mary. There on 29 June Goodwin received some flattering attention from the Queen. Mary not only invited him to walk with her 'in a gallery she [had] made for dancing' but also consulted him on a project of permanent value. During the reign of Charles II, Sir Peter Lely had painted a series of pictures of the women at the King's Court—the famous 'Beauties' portraits, then hung in Windsor Castle.[17] Now Mary wished to commission a similar series for Hampton Court; she planned, she told Goodwin, to acquire pictures of the sixteen most beautiful ladies in England and Holland. Goodwin, who had been raised among elegant portraits, heartily approved the general plan (soon to be executed by Kneller), but he suggested that the beautiful women should all be English 'for the credit of the nation'. Mary agreed at once and asked Goodwin to make the preliminary selection of candidates; 'You shall bring in the list of them,' she said, 'and I will pitch upon those I like best.'

The Queen's request, uttered before her entourage, and her manner, 'remarkably civil and kind', drew comments throughout the Court. And at the next interview, on the evening of 6 July, Goodwin found her behaviour even more flattering. As soon as she saw him, she asked him, 'merrily', about his list of beautiful women, and when he told her that he had prepared one, she began 'some pleasant discourse about it'. She would not embarrass him, she said, by showing his list to her ladies, but she 'would fain know' which of the women on his list he loved best himself.

Goodwin evaded the question. He would name the two finest ladies in England, he told Mary, and let her guess which of the two he loved best. But Mary continued to tease him for the name of his favourite, and Goodwin forestalled further questioning by simply handing over his paper.[18] As he watched her read through it and then, 'laughing', put it in her pocket, he was sure that she had seen her own name heading the list and that she understood his meaning. He was also sure that she merited the ranking he had given her:

> And in this list [he wrote] I might call her the handsomest, since she is esteemed the finest woman in England, by a great many; and indeed she is full of the greatest easiness, goodness, and greatness of mind that ever I perceived [in] any person in my life, and deserves her character.

In view of Mary's continuing graciousness, Goodwin later prepared a surprise entertainment for her. On 27 August he went to Hampton Court 'with voices and music' and presented her with a song composed especially in her honour. The performance, Goodwin noted with satisfaction, delighted Mary and the whole Court; even King William put on a 'pleased countenance'. And at dinner Mary gave him 'one or two [of] the kindest looks in the world'. It was clear to Goodwin that if William would only die, in accordance with revelation, his own future would be splendid indeed.

But in spite of bad health (and later in spite of battles) William persisted in living, as if determined to defy the divine order. And William was not the only one who ruined prophecies; in 1689, he was joined by numerous spirits and lowlanders—among them the spirits who kept the treasure at the Castle Gate.

Goodwin and Sir Thomas Travell were frustrated when they returned to Southampton, without Mary, to pick up the balance of the treasure there. Although they waited at their inn on the night of 2 April, as prescribed, they saw no trace of spirits or treasure. More concerned about Sir Thomas's disappointment than his own, Goodwin twice went to the Castle Gate and expostulated with the spirit guardians, but they remained silent, invisible, and immovable. In the end, he was compelled to return to London defeated—consoled only by the fact that Sir Thomas took the repulse in his stride, and perhaps by the reflection that no one had seen him conversing with a crumbling medieval gate.

The third Southampton expedition, managed this time by Mary, went much more smoothly. When the partners arrived, on 20 June, Goodwin's ship was repaired, loaded with grain, and standing out in the deep water a furlong or so from shore. Mary arranged to have the spirit guardians deliver their treasure—worth more than £15,000—directly to the ship, where they concealed it so cleverly in the grain that it remained undiscovered by the crew and the customs inspectors. Mary also arranged to have the treasure unloaded by spirits when the ship reached the London docks. A contingent of Castle-Gate guardians carried the gold and silver to Soho Square and placed it in Goodwin's closet, where it was locked up with the rest of the Southampton hoard—including the jewels that Goodwin had been allowed to carry home in February. There, unfortunately, it became a source of chronic frustration. Though the Lord declared that Sir Thomas was entitled to a quarter of the treasure and though oral revelations frequently set dates for opening the closet, the dates were continually postponed.

Goodwin's problems with the Southampton treasure were repeated, with variations, at Hounslow. In early 1689, he had supposed that his troubles were virtually over. Besides the Portsmouth revelation of 28 September 1688 which had promised him prosperity in seven months, there was a revelation of 8 March 1689 which promised that by May Day he would be happy and great. There was also a significant change at the four trees, where the recovery of treasure was no longer tied to the phases of the moon and where the good spirits were finally able to deliver treasure like other spirits. The guardians first demonstrated their new power in mid-February by throwing a small purse full of gold into Goodwin's coach as Goodwin and Mary neared the four trees. This purse, which the partners were forbidden to open, was followed a month later by a bag containing about £1,900 in gold—a burden the spirits had carried some forty or fifty yards. In subsequent days two more bags were thrown into the partners' coach, after which the spirits delivered the rest of their treasure at the partners' inn.

But as the weeks went by, the new modes of delivery proved to be another, more complicated form of delay, since the partners were never allowed to see or use any of the gold; and as critical dates, like Easter (31 March), 28 April, and May Day, passed without permission to use any of the treasure and without any change in Goodwin's greatness, Goodwin began to lose his enthusiasm for the project. He became so dubious of the spirits' intentions, in fact, that in mid-July the Lord rebuked him for what seemed dangerous cynicism. Goodwin could not argue with the Lord, but as the autumn of 1689 passed in a series of postponements, he was nudged toward the conclusion that he had been right all along.

Meanwhile, he was experiencing a parallel series of reverses at the hands of the lowlanders—defeats made all the more frustrating because conditions at Hounslow were now favourable for the first time in years. The flight of King James meant that the royal army did not clutter the town and the heath. Once more the partners occupied their favourite inn for extended periods of time. Goodwin was even able to lease Nicholson's house again, and prospects seemed lively for mopping up all the Hounslow projects.

The operations of 1689 began in late March when a lowland duchess came to Mary with a plan for getting Goodwin into his kingdom. Ten or twelve bold men, heavily armed and provided with 'wild fire', the Duchess explained, could be introduced by stealth into the lowlands, where they could seize the lowland usurper and frighten his henchmen into obedience. This bold plan ran into unexpected snags, however, and Goodwin soon became disillusioned with his new ally the Duchess, who proved as difficult to see as Queen Penelope When she began postponing meetings because of menstrual periods or un-expected company, he saw that things were happening 'after the old rate'. And though the usurper died on 25 July in accordance with a divine promise, Goodwin was only half surprised to find that there were still reasons why he could not enter his lowland kingdom: a period of mourning to be observed, an assassination plot to unravel, an objection to his religion, or the vast preparations that the lowlanders insisted upon making. Some-times he managed to revive his early enthusiasm, and he once promised to take Sir Thomas into the lowlands with him, but the constant disappointments made optimism difficult.

The delays were also hard to justify. In the old days, predictions about the lowlanders had been made by simple spirits like George or by angels like Ahab. Under the new order, the promises often came from the Lord himself in oral revelations; and it was sometimes hard for Goodwin to remember why the Lord could not predict, much less control, the behaviour of the whimsical lowlanders. And even when he reminded himself that God does not coerce anyone, uplander or lowlander, it was difficult to see why the Lord bothered to make promises that turned out to be as contingent as those once made by Uriel.

In general Goodwin suppressed worries on this score very effectively, but occasionally he found himself nagged by doubts. In the autumn of 1689 he was once troubled by the notion that the voice which for years had spoken to him from outside his bedroom door might be Mary's, not the Lord's. That the distrust was foolish and instigated by the Devil he knew very well; he had sometimes received oral revelations when Mary, as far as he could tell, was nowhere about. It was not, therefore, a suspicion to be investigated seriously but a delusion to be systematically banished. By the end of November he had his doubts so well in hand that he asked God to leave distrust off the list of his sins; he hoped, he said, that he would not be charged 'with so silly a fault'.[19]

While Goodwin's faith was being tried by spirits and

lowlanders, his long-range future was being changed by misfortunes within the Wharton family. The first of these, in very late 1688, was the death of Sir John Bawdon,[20] the husband of Goodwin's stepsister Letitia, who was left a widow with two teenaged daughters, Anne[21] and Letitia. The second loss occurred on 31 March 1689, when Goodwin's brother-in-law Sir George Lockhart, a distinguished judge in Edinburgh, was shot and killed by a demented litigant.[22] Sir George was married to Goodwin's youngest sister Philadelphia, and his death left her with a young daughter and two young sons, both of whom would grow up (without the guidance of their Whig father) to be zealous Jacobites.[23] On 26 May came the death of Anne Wharton Carr, Goodwin's oldest sister. Many years before, after their mother died, Anne had felt responsible for her young brothers, and while Goodwin and Tom were in France she had defended their interests at home.[24] Later, when she had married William Carr against the wishes of Lord Wharton, Goodwin had interceded for her. In recent years, however, the brother and sister had drifted apart because of family quarrels and Anne's distrust of Mary Parish. Anne's death was followed shortly, on 17 June, by that of her husband William Carr, recently appointed Baron of the Exchequer. The two were buried at Wooburn, less than a month apart.[25]

The tragedies in the Wharton family did not end with Anne and William. In early October alarming reports began arriving from Dundalk, Ireland, where Schomberg's army, including Henry Wharton's regiment,[26] had taken up positions. Heavy rains turned the English camp into a bog, and typhus broke out among the troops. Untreatable by the medicines of the time and extremely deadly, the disease quickly became an epidemic.[27] On 6 October Henry wrote his brother Tom to say that although he was devoted to 'the subduing of Ireland' he would be happy to return home for the coming session of Parliament, and his friend Sir Edward Dering added a postscript asking if he too might be recalled to England on some pretext or other.[28]

The fever proved impervious to Irish whiskey and indifferent to rank. Though Henry and his fellow colonels Sir Thomas Gower and Sir Edward Dering drank large quantities of usquebaugh, they could not save themselves.[29] Sir Edward died on 15 October; Sir Thomas died on the evening of 28 October; and Henry died at ten o'clock on the morning of 29 October, after being insensible for three days.[30]

To his brother Goodwin, Henry had always been a trial. Careless of his immortal soul, he had roistered, drunk, sworn, duelled, and drabbed; and except for the occasion when he had intervened with James II and Sunderland, he had generally ignored Goodwin. To his soldiers and his fellow officers, however, he seemed the model of an English colonel, and his escapades, whether drunk or sober, simply showed his high spirits and intrepid nature.[31] In the army, therefore, the loss of the 'Good Colonel'[32] was sincerely mourned. 'Sir, believe me,' Lieutenant-Colonel John Berners wrote to Tom Wharton, 'there's never a friend or relation I had in the world that . . . I could be more concerned for, nor I never knew anyone so generally lamented.'[33]

The news of Henry's death was devastating to Tom, whom Henry had idolized, and to Lord Wharton,[34] who had outlived still another of his children. Even Goodwin found himself full of 'sorrow and misery'. Though his dreams and internal revelations had foretold an early death for Henry and although Henry's behaviour towards him had often been base, Goodwin mourned for him sincerely, in a manner befitting a brother.

Goodwin felt the political effects of Henry's death immediately. Henry had sat for Westmorland in Parliament, and the Whartons were obliged to find a successor for him unless they wanted the position to slip out of their hands. In haste, therefore, they nominated Goodwin; and by 16 November (three days before the House of Commons officially ordered a new election) they had secured the support of Sir John Lowther, the other Knight of the Shire for Westmorland.[35] In December Goodwin was elected to the post, and on 2 January 1690, he took his seat in the House of Commons.

To Goodwin, who had talked with God and who still hoped to be king of the lowlanders, a place in the Convention Parliament was no great honour—especially since he appeared to his colleagues as a mere back-bench MP. Nevertheless, he had a powerful resource at his disposal—a way of obtaining instant fame. In a series of oral revelations, he learned that the Lord would come to the Commons and inspire him with an oration that would awe the House and impell William to give him a post in the government.

Goodwin's party, meanwhile, was badly in need of divine guidance. In its eagerness to punish the abettors of arbitrary government, the Whig majority was becoming violent and vindictive. Not content with bringing in a bill for re-remodelling the town corporations—and undoing the damage done by Charles and James—the Whigs added a proviso (the Sacheverell Clause) which would have barred from political office anyone who had supported the attacks on the town charters. This provision, designed to drive many Tories out of public life, came dangerously close to passing. Defeated after a bitter struggle, it aroused a Tory reaction throughout the country and disgusted King William.

During these manœuvres, Goodwin received no help from the Lord, and he was still waiting for revelations on 27 January when King William, 'unexpectedly to all men', prorogued Parliament. A few days later the Parliament was officially dissolved, new elections were called, and Goodwin found himself standing again after less than a month in the Commons.

In the elections, generally favourable to the Tories, Goodwin did not venture to contest Westmorland; he chose instead to stand for the boroughs of Cockermouth and Malmesbury. As it turned out, the precaution of entering two elections was well advised. At Cockermouth Goodwin was defeated by the illegal practices (as an election petition alleged) of Sir Wilfred Lawson,[36] and if he had not been returned for Malmesbury, he would have been excluded from the House. As it was, he was safely seated in a parliament that lasted from 20 March 1690 until 11 October 1695.

When the new House was organized, Goodwin was placed upon three committees[37]—including the Committee of Privileges and Elections, a large standing committee that dealt with election petitions and other matters of House business. Compared with Goodwin's secret merits, these assignments were absurdly inadequate, but from another point of view they were not to be despised. At a time when divine and angelic promises were failing almost every day, Goodwin found it comforting to hold a firm, if undistinguished, place in the tawdry, second-best world governed by Crown and Parliament. He began, therefore, to attend committee meetings and to earn himself a reputation as a working MP. While he waited for miracles (including speeches dictated by the Lord), he did his prosaic duty. To be a committeeman and a member for Malmesbury was not much, but it was at least something.

18

Tobermory and the Counter-Revelation

INEVITABLY, Goodwin's election to the House of Commons brought a reconciliation with his powerful brother Tom, who managed elections and helped direct Whig strategy—and who had earlier declared himself convinced of Goodwin's innocence in the affair with Anne. The election also meant more help from Lord Wharton. Having entrusted Goodwin with a vote on such issues as the Abjuration Bill and the Regency Bill, Lord Wharton could not ignore him or allow him to be hounded by creditors. Some time after the death of his son William, Lord Wharton had paid off some of Goodwin's largest debts; now, after the death of Henry, he raised Goodwin to respectability.[1]

In dealing with King William, Goodwin was less fortunate. On 27 January William announced that he would take over personal command of his armies in Ireland; and on 12 February, as advised by the Lord, Goodwin went to Whitehall to volunteer for the summer campaign. He wanted to venture his life, he told William, in whatever post the King thought fit. William was obviously pleased by the brave offer, but he could promise nothing. He would have need of friends in England, he said, as well as friends in Ireland.

Lost in the throng of gentlemen volunteers, Goodwin dallied with the idea of explaining his secret powers to King William, and upon one occasion the Lord, in oral revelation, actually ordered him to go to Whitehall and enlighten the King. Providentially (as he later learned), William happened to be engaged, and after waiting all afternoon Goodwin was excused from his 'ticklish task'. Eventually, the Lord formally cancelled the plan; Mary learned that Goodwin was not to waste arcane knowledge on the cool, uninspired King, who 'would not mind it'.

A more hopeful scheme presented itself when the new

Parliament assembled. If William could not understand spirits, Goodwin reasoned, he could at least understand money; and an MP who could introduce a divinely inspired finance bill would certainly merit preferment. Accordingly, Goodwin prayed that God would dictate a money bill, and on 20 March, he was promised by oral revelation that within two days he would be told what to say. The promise was not kept, however, and as Goodwin waited day after day in the House, the message did not come. Once, at Soho Square, a revelation said that he had done some good thinking on his own account, but without specific instructions he could not present a bill in the Commons. He was obliged to remain silent while the weeks of the short session slipped away and his chance of impressing William disappeared.

On 26 May Goodwin's hopes for Ireland received their final blow. When he asked, in the Lord's formula, whether the King had 'any service to command' him, William replied, civilly but definitely, that he had not. Nor was Goodwin luckier a week later when he asked whether he might have a post in England. All the posts were filled, William said; the only thing he needed from Goodwin was the continuance of his friendship.

During the Irish campaign King William paid a price for his imperception. Although he scored a smashing triumph over King James at the Battle of the Boyne, he was frustrated at Limerick, where heavy rains and a stubborn defence compelled him to raise the siege. When news of these events reached London, Goodwin felt completely vindicated. William had been unable to complete the conquest of Ireland without him; and King James, showing himself even weaker than Goodwin had alleged in his famous speech, had fled from his army and Ireland in 'panic fear'. Goodwin, meanwhile, was giving aid and comfort to Queen Mary, who had been appointed Regent during William's absence.[2]

Goodwin got a chance to speak with Queen Mary on 9 June, when he was given a formal audience to present some information 'of moment' about affairs in Cornwall.[3] In spite of the constraint caused by Mary's official position, the interview was pleasant enough; Mary listened with such 'complaisance' that after delivering his report Goodwin went on to warn her against arbitrary councils, exhorting her in particular to dismiss her Tory Secretary of State, the Earl of Nottingham. She would have been glad to continue the conversation, he observed, 'but fearing the interview might be censured as too long', she thanked him and withdrew.

Goodwin's conversation with Queen Mary came on the brink of a great crisis—an attempt by the Jacobites and the French to stage an insurrection and an invasion. From many parts of the country came reports of Jacobite plots, and on 22 June the Queen learned that a huge French fleet—the combined squadrons from Brest and Toulon—had entered the Channel and was headed eastward, apparently aiming to destroy the Channel fleet.

In the midst of the wild excitement, Goodwin had a frustrating vision which clearly predicted that a group of bold Jacobites would try to subvert the Queen herself but which failed to specify who the conspirators were. Days went by before God and the angels would reveal the identity of the chief plotters,[4] and even then Goodwin was warned that he must not go to the Queen with the information, since the plotters might change their minds. This precaution saved Goodwin from warning the Queen against an event that never happened. Four days later he learned from a revelation that the conspirators, frightened by the arrest of several leading Jacobites,[5] would not venture to approach Queen Mary.

Thwarted in his attempt to uncover a Jacobite plot, Goodwin likewise failed to destroy the French fleet. The Battle of Beachy Head, fought on 1 July, ended in a humiliating defeat for the English navy and left the South Coast open to invasion. Under these desperate circumstances, Goodwin asked the angels to complete their diving apparatus so that he could disable the rudders of the French ships; he asked his lowland subjects to steal aboard the enemy vessels and pour water on the gunpowder; and he asked for help in designing a mortar which could throw fire-balls into enemy ships. But the underwater equipment failed to arrive, the lowlanders remained recalcitrant as ever, and the mortar took a great deal of time. Although he began immediately, along with a man named Milford, to design a device for launching 'great stars and darts of fire', he was still trying, months later, to construct an effective spring for the trigger, and the angels gave him no help at all.

Meanwhile the crisis of July passed without serious damage to

England. Heartened by the news of William's victory at the Boyne and roused by the danger of a French invasion, the nation rallied behind Queen Mary,[6] frightening the Jacobites out of their insurrection schemes and stripping the French forces of their allies. Admiral Tourville, the French commander, bombarded Teignmouth and landed a few men, but when he found his troops unsupported by English sympathizers and opposed by increasing hordes of militiamen, he re-embarked his landing party and sailed for Brest.

In the waning days of the crisis, Goodwin saw Queen Mary several times at court functions, and on 25 July she invited him to accompany her on one of her walks around Whitehall. He suddenly found himself with the opportunity to give her some notion of his extraordinary powers and of the secret methods by which God had deposed her father and brought her to the throne. Mary seemed startled when Goodwin volunteered to tell her how she became Queen, as if she feared to hear 'reflections' upon herself and William; but when she understood that Goodwin saw the Revolution as an abstruse act of Providence, she listened very patiently. Goodwin could not, of course, tell about his love affair with Mary Beatrice, but he could explain King James's perfidy, his attempt to cheat the nation with a fraudulent child, and even his dabbling in black magic. Before he broke off the narrative, Goodwin got as far as the story of the wind-conjuring priests—to the very brink of the invasion of England.

As events worked out, Goodwin never finished telling his story to the Queen. At their next walk together, on 28 July, the time seemed unpropitious. Though Mary led him on a tour of the roofs of Whitehall, he did not get the opportunity he needed; and many obligations, including a stay at Wooburn, intervened before he could get another semi-private interview. Eventually he committed some of his secrets to paper and entrusted the Queen with a copy; for the present he contented himself with the glimpses he had given her of his strange knowledge.

At Wooburn, in August, Goodwin found that he retained all his God-given power over women. Lady Wharton, he observed, continued her base lust while pretending to hate him, and Letitia Poulett Monson did all she could to tempt him. This knowledge raised the hope that the Lord might relax the rules against mistresses—especially since Mary Parish, his wife in the sight of God, had recently found sex 'uneasy' and had seldom shared his bed. Upon returning to Soho Square, however, he learned from the angels that the laws remained unchanged; paramours were strictly prohibited. The only thing that had changed was Mary's rate of conception. After multiple miscarriages in December 1688 and July 1690, she conceived at a more normal frequency; she was never again pregnant with more than two children at a time.

In September while the angels were restating the laws of sexual behaviour, Goodwin was revising his political strategy. He perceived when the King returned from Ireland that William remained jealous and that there was no use asking him for a place. He also saw that although the Queen's love had visibly increased, her power had declined. He gave Queen Mary some verses he had composed in her honour, but he expected no political return from them. His real hope of advancement lay once more in Parliament.

During the new session, which opened on 2 October, Goodwin entered another stage in his career. After many days of waiting for the Lord to send him a speech—this time by way of the Archangel Michael—Goodwin finally began to construct and deliver speeches on his own account, without help from revelation.[7] Warned by the reaction to his incendiary speech against King James, he was careful to be temperate, even when he was obliged to castigate William's Tory ministers. By the time the session ended, on 5 January 1691, he saw that he was acquiring influence with his colleagues, and a vision told him that the government would find him a place.

During these political manœuvres Goodwin renewed his attempts to get into his lowland kingdom through the aid of the late Queen Ursula, whose spirit returned from Italy to help him. She would not only install him on the throne, she told Mary, but actually appear to him—something that no spirit or angel had ever done. Then came the all-too-familiar pattern of delays. Although Ursula came to Soho Square and sometimes made herself audible (in a shrill voice), she could not make herself visible. After failures throughout late October and early November, including an effort so strong that Goodwin could hear the 'grinsing' of her teeth, she gradually gave up trying, and Goodwin's plan for entering the lowlands collapsed.

In principle Queen Ursula's failure merely proved that through some mystery Goodwin remained unable to see spirits. And yet, coming at a time when Michael kept failing to appear in the House of Commons and when all Goodwin's other projects seemed stagnant, it became significant by its very predictability. Almost imperceptibly, a note of wistfulness began to creep into Goodwin's journal. It had become hardly worthwhile to record the stages by which a heavenly promise became a disappointment. Now, after a brief notation of a promise, say, that he would see an angel or open a treasure trunk, Goodwin was apt to add a melancholy summary: 'but nothing was.'

Occasionally, Goodwin's failures were counterbalanced by an unexpected triumph. One of these occurred during the 1689–90 campaign when Goodwin made another convert—the eminent Whig MP William Sacheverell, framer of the first Exclusion Bill, author of the Sacheverell Clause, and veteran of dozens of stirring debates in the Commons.[8] By October 1689, Sacheverell had been allowed to read the first volume of Goodwin's journal, and by 5 November he was asking to accompany Goodwin into the lowlands—a request that Goodwin would have granted if his then-current plans had not disintegrated. Through the disappointments of 1690 Sacheverell remained 'very faithful', like the honest gentleman he was; and he might have been made a partner if Goodwin's affairs had prospered. As it was, he died on 9 October 1691, before he could be rewarded for his fidelity.

After his success with Sacheverell and Sir Thomas, Goodwin was instructed by a vision of late 1690 to vouchsafe some notion of his secret powers to a few other people; he was to write down and circulate a portion of his priceless knowledge. He had already composed some verses and a general tract on the nature of spirits. To these documents he added 'a sharp letter' about King James, a criticism of Catherine Fraser, and tracts upon the lowlanders and upon fulfilment of prophecy. During the next few months he showed his compositions to several friends, and the following summer he gave Queen Mary copies of his essays on spirits and prophecies.[9] Though Goodwin delivered the papers 'sealed up', Mary received them kindly and later gave him the impression that she was 'really touched and convinced by them'.

In early 1691, however, Goodwin learned once more that it is easier to write about supernatural powers than to get help from them. They could not protect his ship, which was wrecked and plundered on the coast of Cornwall after a voyage to Seville; and during the siege of Mons they led him into the most faith-shattering reverse of his entire life.

King Louis set the stage for Goodwin's severest trial by invading the Spanish Netherlands and attacking Mons in early March before the allied field armies had assembled for the summer campaign. While King William collected his forces, the French took up their siege positions and posted a covering army where it could parry any attempt to relieve the city. Naturally, the attack upon the huge frontier fortress caused much excitement, and in London, according to the custom of the age, it also caused much wagering on the ultimate success of the siege.[10] This fact, in turn, provided Goodwin with a financial opportunity. Although he had been forbidden to gamble on cards and dice, he had not been forbidden to exploit prophetic knowledge of public events. He asked the angels, therefore, through Mary, to provide him with 'true information' on the fate of Mons, and the angels agreed to help him as soon as they had truly considered the matter.

During late March while the angels pondered their answer, the odds against King William and his allies lengthened, and by the time Goodwin received the information he needed, 'all mankind', he observed, was conceding Mons to King Louis. The angels, however, judged otherwise. When they reported to Mary, about 2 April, they said that the town 'would certainly not be taken', that King William 'was as good as in it', and that Goodwin could wager any sums he chose. Thus advised, Goodwin placed bets totalling almost £100 on the success of the defenders.

Then, on Sunday, 5 April, came shocking news. Letters arriving from the Continent, after several days of contrary winds, alleged that Mons had surrendered to the French. This news, unconfirmed by supporting details, was contradicted the next day by the Lord, who promised Goodwin in oral revelation that he should 'get a great deal by the town', and later a brief bulletin in the *London Gazette*[11] was contradicted by the angels, who 'valued not what the *Gazette* said'. Reassured by the heavenly powers and perfectly aware that dispatches from overseas were often wrong, Goodwin shook off his melancholy and placed more bets upon the allied defence.

Two days later came the official, undeniable account of the capitulation,[12] and with it came a hideous fact: Mons had actually surrendered on 29 March—three days before the angels had first promised Goodwin that it would be relieved and more than a week before God had told him that he would 'get a great deal' from it. Goodwin had been misinformed about an event that had already happened—a 'point of fact past'. Now he faced the demoralizing possibility that the divine powers were grossly ignorant of human affairs or that they had deliberately lied to him. The enormity of the problem stunned him; neither he nor Mary knew 'what to say or do'.

For previous errors there had been explanations, usually revealed to Mary by the angels; for this one, however, there was no explanation at all. Mary could get no information, and Goodwin's oral revelations ignored the subject as if nothing had happened. Left to his own spiritual resources, Goodwin first theorized, tentatively, that the Lord intended to teach him not to originate projects of his own. From this unsatisfactory hypothesis he retreated to higher and firmer ground. He had often affirmed the superiority of faith over mere human experience and he had been subjected to many harrowing tests. Now in the greatest crisis of all—the most severe challenge to faith—he recovered from his initial 'staggers' and reasserted his heroic fidelity. Such trials, he wrote in a paraphrase of Job, 'shall not destroy my confidence in God, which shall not fail though He shall kill me'.

Goodwin's recovery was made easier by a splendid coup in the diving business. On 18 March, after beating out several 'devilish' rivals, Goodwin contracted with Archibald Campbell, tenth Earl of Argyll, to salvage the Spanish galleon sunk at Tobermory Bay; and during April and May, with Argyll's help, he was successfully solving the military, financial, and technical problems involved.

In 1691 parts of the Isle of Mull (then as now the home of the Macleans) were still held by the Jacobites. During October and November of 1690, Argyll himself, with thirteen companies of infantry, had captured most of the island, including the Tobermory area; but the Macleans and Macdonalds still held

Duart Castle, on the strategic point where the Firth of Lorn meets the Sound of Mull, and a few strongholds in the West.[13] Since Mull was only partially subdued and since the surrounding waters were sometimes infested by French privateers, the diving expedition required the protection of troops and naval vessels. Argyll, with a regiment at his disposal, provided a hundred 'highlanders' for the covering force; and the government, who wished to combine a naval sweep of the area with the recovery of a rich treasure,[14] assigned three warships to the enterprise: the *Pembroke* and the *Conception* (both fifth-rates, with complements of 32 guns and 125 men) and the *Eaglet* (a lightly armed ketch suitable for action in narrow and shallow waters).[15]

Goodwin's arrangements with Argyll and the government proved very attractive to investors, and by 15 May Goodwin had raised enough money for a splendid venture. This time he could afford two ships instead of one—the first a small 'bark', the *Seventh Son*, with a crew of 12 and an armament of 4 guns; and the second a 130-ton ship called the *Katherine Ketch*, with a complement of 40 men and 14 guns. As commander of the *Katherine Ketch*, Goodwin received letters of marque or reprisal, authorizing him to capture French and Jacobite vessels and making him in effect an auxiliary member of the English navy.[16]

More intricate than Goodwin's financial manœuvres were his technical preparations for diving. His first problem, of course, was to get the magic mouthpiece. This the angels had once delivered in 1688, but they had later taken it away again for further improvement. Now, after Goodwin's agreement with Argyll, they promised to return it completely perfected, along with three diving suits which would protect wearers from cold and accident. Pending the arrival of the magic mouthpiece, Goodwin provided himself with conventional back-up equipment; he constructed two sets of 'long wire [metal] pipes' (the most advanced air hoses then available) and one set of leather hoses. In addition, he designed a set of bellows that the angels themselves envied.

Mary, who conducted negotiations with the angels, was compelled to interrupt proceedings while she delivered a child (conceived the previous July) and arranged for the burial of Susanna, one of the twin daughters born while Goodwin was in

Jersey. (Sarah, the other twin, had died in late 1688; like Susanna she was never seen by her father.) This interruption and several other untoward events prevented the angels from delivering the magic mouthpiece before Goodwin and Sir Thomas set off for Liverpool to join their ships. Goodwin was promised, however, that an angel would come to Tobermory with the mouthpiece and that an experienced lowland diver named Jeffrey would join the expedition.

Goodwin with his ships the *Katherine Ketch* and the *Seventh Son* arrived off Mull on 1 July. There, a few miles south of Duart Castle, he met Argyll with his highland troops and four small boats; and shortly afterwards the combined force met the *Pembroke* and the *Conception*.[17] (The *Eaglet*, which ran into problems of supply and repair *en route* from southern England, never got to Mull.)

Before proceeding to Tobermory, the expedition stopped to harass the 'Macdonalds and the Macleans' at Duart Castle. In the evening the warships trapped a small vessel in a nearby loch, forcing the Jacobites to beach and burn it; and the next morning they bombarded the Castle. This attack, led by the *Pembroke* and supported by Argyll's highlanders, who exchanged 'small shot' with the defenders, proceeded handsomely until the Macleans managed to bring a 'great gun' into action. When one of its blasts killed a sailor on the *Pembroke*, Captain John Every decided to break off the engagement and avoid further risk to his ship.[18] The *Conception*, under Captain Robert Fairfax, took over the *Pembroke*'s position long enough to deliver one final broadside against the Castle; then the whole expedition 'steered away' for Tobermory.[19]

While Goodwin was setting up his diving equipment at Tobermory Bay,[20] his naval escorts and one of his own ships swept the lochs and islets of Western Mull. In the process, they captured a Jacobite vessel—a sea-going pink—which they handed over to Goodwin as a prize,[21] giving him a minor victory before he was ready to begin operations. This good fortune, however, was the last he was to enjoy for several weeks.

Neither Jeffrey, the diving lowlander, nor the angel bearing the magic mouthpiece appeared at Tobermory, and it was soon obvious that Goodwin would be forced to rely upon conventional apparatus. More alarmingly, it was also obvious that all his conventional gear needed repair. The first tests showed that both sets of metal pipes were leaky and that the leather hoses (once guaranteed by the angels) would not hold out water and deliver air for more than a minute. He was forced to suspend diving, therefore, while he mended his equipment.

Goodwin was equally unlucky with the weather. Though he and Sir Thomas saw many propitious signs, including spectacular rainbows and 'little pillars of fire', Tobermory Bay was rocked with storms for two consecutive weeks. It was not until the end of July that the weather permitted Goodwin to resume testing his now-repaired apparatus.

Since Goodwin's divers (perhaps made wary by the early problems) were nervous about the equipment, Goodwin made the first experiments himself—only to discover additional problems. His primary set of metal pipes had been 'maliciously bored with holes'; and when he tried his alternate set, he found after descending a few feet that the supply of air was inadequate. In a second descent after further repairs, he learned that there was still a flaw in the circulation system. In his third descent, after he had diagnosed and corrected the defect, he encountered one last complication. The frigid waters of Tobermory Bay not only benumbed him but also chilled the air that reached him through the pipes.[22] After about two minutes below the surface, he found his lungs 'so weakened' that 'breath grew useless'.

Goodwin solved his last problem with the help of his long-dormant inner voice, which told him to heat the air—a feat he accomplished by burning brandy in the box that contained the bellows and the head of the air pipes. Some of his men tried out the new method in shallow water with good results, but before he could persuade anyone to brave a descent into the ten or twelve fathoms where the galleon lay,[23] the weather again turned tempestuous. Reluctantly, Goodwin decided to leave the sunken galleon, a difficult project in the best of weather, and to concentrate instead upon an easier undertaking—the salvage of the naval frigate *Dartmouth*, which lay wrecked in the Sound of Mull, a few miles southeast of Tobermory.[24]

The *Dartmouth*, famous for its part in the relief of London-derry, had been caught in a violent storm on 9 October 1690 during Argyll's operations against Mull. Swept from its anchors and shattered against a rock, it was sunk with the loss of

Captain Edward Pottinger and all but four or five of its 130-man crew.[25] Fortunately for Goodwin, the ship lay in relatively shallow water, and in about a week of labour—sometimes in 'very foul' weather—his crew retrieved fourteen of the vessel's thirty-two cannon and a good deal of other gear. This valuable haul transformed the diving expedition from a failure to a success. It enabled Goodwin to see the hand of God in the proceedings, in spite of many broken promises, and it made Goodwin himself into something of a celebrity. When he returned to Liverpool, on 13 September, he announced that he was presenting the cannon to King William and Queen Mary—a gift that impressed many people, including his father. And when he returned to London, the Lord confirmed in oral revelation what he had observed for himself—that he had 'overcome and got the victory'.

After such stirring adventures, Goodwin's business at Soho Square and the House of Commons seemed anticlimatic. For the immediate future, his expectations from the spiritual powers were reduced to practically nothing.[26] God told him that he could not open the treasures in his closet or enter his lowland kingdom for at least a year, and the projects suggested by the spirits were trivial. God, to be sure, promised several times to meet Goodwin in the Commons or in the Old Palace Yard and dictate a finance bill, but these promises were never kept. Goodwin was left to build a parliamentary reputation on his own uninspired efforts.

In the new session, Goodwin's growing expertise was recognized by his appointment to two committees on naval affairs,[27] a committee for dealing with the forfeited estates in Ireland, and three or four minor committees on special problems.[28] He also served, for the first time, as teller during a vote of the House—a function he would often perform in later sessions.[29] Significantly too, he began to emerge as a frequent and effective speaker on important issues.

Though the Lord did not provide a finance bill, mere reason told Goodwin (as it told several other speakers) that government estimates of military expenditures should be reviewed by a special committee before being referred to the committee of the whole House.[30] In the debates over government bribery of MPs, Goodwin suggested that the Secret Service accounts should be brought in and examined as they had been in the days of Charles II;[31] and in a case of election bribery, he recommended that both candidates, equally guilty of corrupting electors, should be barred from serving in the existing Parliament.[32] In the debates on the treason bill, Goodwin followed Sir John Somers in attacking a clause that would have circumscribed the powers of the Commons to bring impeachments.[33]

Perhaps Goodwin's most impressive speech came during the final debate on the land-tax bill when he offered a rider specifying that navy and ordnance obligations should be paid in the order accrued. This clause, probably derived from Goodwin's work on the committee for investigating naval transport, was read three times, approved without a division, and added to the bill.[34] To Goodwin himself, however, his greatest oratorical triumph came on 15 February 1692 during a hot debate over whether a clause providing for Commissioners of Accounts (parliamentary watchdogs) should be added to the poll-tax bill. Towards the end of the contest, which involved twenty-four speakers, Goodwin made what he later described as the decisive speech in support of the clause—the argument which 'carried the House', by a vote of 145–104.[35] Goodwin had reason to be pleased. In December he had modestly recorded the fact that he had sometimes spoken in Parliament and that he 'was not ill esteemed with the Country Party'; now after his victory in the House, he could see that his influence in the Commons 'was superior to anybody's'.

In early 1692 Goodwin's political triumphs were overshadowed by a family crisis. His brother Tom, a widower since 1685, announced his intention of marrying Lucy Loftus, daughter of the late Lord Lisburne.[36] To Goodwin the marriage constituted a long-range threat. As long as Tom remained without a male heir, Goodwin was second in line to inherit their father's title and estates. The announcement, however, obviously meant that Tom planned to marry and produce an heir, and Goodwin believed that he was acting out of spite.

In January the Lord began making threats against Tom's life, and on 19 February a revelation flatly declared that if Tom did not give up his marriage plans at once, he would die within a few days. But Tom lived on through February and March, and his stubborn survival had an important side-effect. His plans for remarriage and his attempt to improve upon his original marriage settlement reminded Lord Wharton that as yet there were no male grandchildren bearing the Wharton name and that Goodwin, now thirty-nine, remained single. During the negotiations, therefore, Lord Wharton pressed Goodwin strongly on the subject of marriage, and Goodwin was inspired to tell him part of the truth: he was already married, he said, and the father of two legitimate sons. Goodwin did not reveal the name of his wife, of course, or explain that he had never seen his older son, and Lord Wharton, who asked 'little hammering questions', remained puzzled about the details. Nevertheless, he seemed 'much satisfied' with Goodwin's confession. Goodwin himself was pleased at his father's response and also at Lord Wharton's refusal to settle more property upon Tom. As time went on, the only thing that disgusted Goodwin was Tom's ultimate defiance of God's threats and promises. In July, though the death sentence was never rescinded, Tom married Lucy Loftus as he had planned—an event, as Goodwin wrote sourly, that 'would have been hardly expected'.

Goodwin was helped to rise above his resentment by an inestimable blessing he had received a few weeks earlier. On 12 April 1692, in a clear and crucial revelation, the Lord revoked His strict rulings on sexual behaviour—the edicts responsible for the ignominious reversals of 1688—and granted Goodwin a generous measure of liberty. This dispensation Goodwin had earned by resisting numerous temptations. Ever since his return to Court and aristocratic society, he had found himself 'more and more beloved by all'—from Queen Mary and Princess Anne to one Mistress Cooke, who appeared to be on the verge of dying for love. He had been forced to frustrate himself and antagonize several women by rejecting their sexual advances.

Harassed by opportunities and doubts, Goodwin recalled his earlier theories on adultery and sexual freedom; he recalled that Mary Parish herself had been given him by a special dispensation; and he thought it possible that if he avoided harlots he might be allowed to take a mistress. He was willing, at any rate, to risk a violent argument by mentioning the topic to Mary. And at first Mary's reaction was more violent than he had feared. When he persisted in asserting his right to a mistress, she concluded that he had already taken one. Declaring in a fit of rage that she would leave him forever, she stormed off to church to discuss the affair with the angels.

Mary returned from church much calmer, willing in fact to hear Goodwin's further explanations. He was not seeing another woman, he assured her; he had, on the contrary, turned down several women, including some wealthy ones. Nor was she in any danger of being displaced; he had already told his father about her two sons (though obliged to conceal her name), and he fully intended to do her justice. Apparently impressed by Goodwin's sincerity, though not by his arguments, Mary quit impugning his motives, and there the matter rested until the glorious revelation that changed everything.

On the morning of 12 April, God spoke from behind Goodwin's door in a clear and distinct voice. Goodwin was 'growing weary' of Mary because of her age, the Lord declared, and he would be allowed to have a mistress. He must not expect Mary to consent formally, however, and he must not tell her about the woman or women he chose. As long as he did not mention an outside affair, 'she should not think of it.'

As always after a vital revelation, Goodwin asked Mary to have Ahab provide her with a verbatim reprise of the Lord's message. Ahab, however, refused; and from this fact Goodwin deduced that he himself must not tell her what the Lord had said—what liberties the Lord had allowed him. Later that day, in a tavern, he did discuss with her the subject of freedom, and Mary volunteered a generous statement: 'as she hoped for heaven', she said, she would allow him any liberty he wished— though she might be compelled finally to leave him. And that night in bed, in spite of being within a few weeks of her sixty-second birthday, she excelled herself as a lover. 'Never', Goodwin wrote, had the two of them achieved 'greater satisfaction'.

Goodwin's first response to his new freedom, attained with such dramatic suddenness, was a becoming gratitude. 'I cannot . . . but take notice of the goodness and kindness of the Lord to me,' he wrote, 'thus to give my mind ease in this particular, which had been so long . . . a greater trouble than is almost to be imagined.' It would be some time, for all his importunity, before Goodwin would be ready to exercise his liberty to take a mistress, but the relief was immediate. After years of subjection, he had been released from bondage.

19

The Colonel and the Queen

A FEW weeks after Goodwin's sexual liberation, Admiral Edward Russell with a huge Anglo-Dutch fleet changed the course of the war. At the four-day battle called La Hogue, he destroyed a significant portion of the French navy, foiled a French-Jacobite plan for the invasion of England, decisively altered the balance of naval power, and laid the coastal cities of northern France open to English reprisal. After a period of frightful crisis, he not only relieved England from all danger but also gave Queen Mary and her Council (ruling during William's campaign on the Continent) a chance to organize a counter-invasion of their own.

Several months later, Russell's victory would furnish Goodwin with speeches in the Commons, but immediately the crisis caused him nothing but frustration. In the tense days before the battle, God revealed that a team of Jacobite engineers was designing an explosive device for destroying the Queen and setting fire to Whitehall. When the 'engine' was finished, the Lord promised, Goodwin would be allowed to seize the conspirators, save the Queen, and uncover the powerful sponsors of the diabolical plot. But the demolition team proved less skilful than either its members or the Lord had supposed. Although they frequently got drunk to celebrate their success, their device was always one crucial piece short of perfection. Long after 23 May, when the final victory at La Hogue defused the crisis, they were still trying and failing to complete their 'villainous design' and still robbing Goodwin of a chance to save the Queen. At last, they gave up the project completely.

Goodwin's frustration once provoked him into grumbling aloud to Mary Parish about the unreliability of God's promises, and his complaints brought him sharp reproof in an oral revelation. Reminded once again that God cannot be blamed for 'the necessity of causes, the obstinacy and corruption of men's wills', or the malice of Satan, he was quickly convinced of his folly. He could not help wishing, nevertheless, that divine promises were more reliable or wondering whether Satan had put the explosion plot 'forward or backward'.

Goodwin was similarly unlucky with the lowlanders. Though he learned that near Tyburn there was an old forsaken entrance to the lowland tunnel system and that there was a lowland base at Brompton, his efforts to meet Jeffrey and the other lowlanders were consistently thwarted. In September, when according to a promise made the previous year he was to enter into his lowland kingdom, his subjects found many excuses to keep him away. It was not even worthwhile, he found, to make the journey to Hounslow.

Early in the year the Lord had directed Goodwin to organize another diving expedition to Tobermory, but He later ordered the operation postponed until 1693 as a favour to the watery spirits who guarded the wrecked galleon. Goodwin was happy for the delay, which not only gave him more time to build equipment and raise the £7,000 that the venture finally cost[1] but also produced military benefits. In early August Sir John Maclean surrendered Duart Castle and Cairn a'Burgh to the government.[2] With Mull in friendly hands, Goodwin no longer needed infantry to protect his diving parties; a naval guard against privateers would suffice.

Amid the aborted projects of 1692, Goodwin was able to achieve one clear success. He brought suit against the rascally Cornishmen who had pillaged his wrecked ship during the winter of 1691, and at the trial, held in Salisbury on 9 July 1692, he gained the verdict. With the help of the Lord, he not only defeated his opponents but inspired great respect among the townspeople. In a summer when victories were rare, he savoured the triumph.

But the most important event in Goodwin's life had nothing to do with trials or diving expeditions; it was the death, on 13 August, of his stepmother, Lady Wharton. For some time, as Goodwin noted, Lady Wharton had been wasting away, suffering from 'a tedious long grief' and an incurable physical affliction which broke her 'to the last degree'. Goodwin was convinced, nevertheless, that she had retained her love for him. Only a short time before she left St. Giles for the country, where she spent her last few days, he saw that 'she fell not from her affection in the least'; and in the final stages of her illness, she spoke to Lord Wharton on Goodwin's behalf (as he learned by revelation), exonerating him from all blame. By this behaviour, Lady Wharton induced Goodwin to forgive her for her injustices and her illicit passion. Her death, he observed at last, ended one of the strangest adventures of his life.

At Lady Wharton's death, Goodwin volunteered in a spirit of self-sacrifice to take up residence with his father at St. Giles, but he withdrew the offer when Lord Wharton, obviously unenthusiastic, insisted that he should bring along his wife and children. Back at Soho Square, meanwhile, the alliance between Goodwin and Sir Thomas Travell was showing signs of strain. During the Tobermory expedition Sir Thomas had proved insubordinate and quarrelsome; and after the return from Mull, where he had seen spirits hovering above the wrecked galleon, he had developed pretensions to spiritual knowledge. There was also the matter of the never-opened closet. Sir Thomas complained occasionally about delays, and at times he seemed to suspect Mary and Goodwin of removing treasure without his knowledge.

Goodwin, though annoyed, was not yet ready to break up the alliance, which now offered political as well as financial advantages. In the election of 1690 Sir Thomas had been returned from Milborne Port. Thereafter he served with Goodwin in the Commons, and their house became a bastion of Whig politics. It was difficult to break with a man, Goodwin saw, who was at once a political protégé and an investor in expensive projects.

When Parliament opened in the fall of 1692 Goodwin, who had already established himself as a debater, found many topics for debate. In Flanders, the military campaign had gone badly. King William had been unable to prevent the French from taking the fortress town of Namur, and when he had launched a surprise attack at Steinkirk, his English and Scots assault regiments, inadequately supported, were finally driven off with heavy losses—a defeat attributed by many to Count Solms and other Dutch generals. At home, the proposed descent on France after the victory at La Hogue had degenerated into an expensive fiasco. In late July an expeditionary force was loaded into transports, where it remained while Admiral Russell wrangled with the Queen's Council and the Admiralty over where or whether a descent should be launched. In the end, the troops were disembarked without having set foot in France.

Privately, Goodwin knew that King William, by neglecting him, had deserved military misfortunes. In Parliament, however, he supported William on the issues most vital for the conduct of the war.[3] He agreed, first of all, that the English army should be committed to the campaigns in the Spanish Netherlands. Against Tory isolationists, who were beginning to argue that England should rule the seas and leave the war on the Continent to their allies, Goodwin countered that control of the seas depended upon control of the Low Countries and of the Dutch navy.[4] Goodwin also agreed that William should continue to command the allied armies in the field. The alliance, Goodwin said, would collapse if the confederates once doubted William's personal involvement. Finally, Goodwin agreed that the land forces should be raised to a total of 54,000 men.[5]

But Goodwin's support for the King's strategy did not imply support for the officers who were conducting the war and the government. During the session of 1692–93, Goodwin found occasion to attack the Dutch generals, the Admiralty, the Secretary of State, the Queen's Council, and the King's 'Cabinet Council', as well as a number of lesser incompetents.

In attacking the foreign generals, Goodwin was reflecting the view of the English officers that they had been badly served at Steinkirk. Three times during the debates on 23 November he spoke in support of a resolution (finally adopted by the House and ignored by William) which advised the King to fill future vacancies in the command of English armies with Englishmen and to remove Count Solms at once from command of the English infantry.[6] In attacking the Admiralty and the great officers of State, Goodwin was speaking for his party. During the enquiry over the fiasco that followed La Hogue, he supported Russell, the Whig Admiral, against the Tory-dominated Council and Admiralty Board; it was Goodwin, in fact, who made the motion that Russell should have the thanks of the House 'for his great courage and conduct' during the summer campaign.[7]

The basic problem, Goodwin argued in several speeches, was not treachery but incompetence. The Lords of the Admiralty meant well enough, no doubt, but they were amateurs. Similarly, the Secretary of State, Nottingham, was probably loyal in spite of his Tory principles, but he was unfit by temperament and training to conduct a bold, aggressive policy.[8] Furthermore, Goodwin complained, there was a problem of secrecy. The King's Cabinet Council—as distinct from the Privy Council—was a small privileged body unknown to the law, and its members were not obliged 'to set their hands' to the advice they gave. It was difficult, therefore, to assign responsibility for bad measures. The Cabinet Council, Goodwin argued, should either be abolished or made responsible.[9]

By the end of November Goodwin had spoken more than a dozen times during the debates on the conduct of the war and established himself as one of the voices of the Whig party in the Commons—not a 'manager' like his brother Tom or Sir John Somers but a significant voice nevertheless. And in early December his support of the war earned him a personal interview with King William, who had discovered an 'esteem' for him and who encouraged him to speak freely on the current posture of affairs. With becoming frankness, Goodwin warned the King against supporting the Tory faction and employing men like Nottingham who did not admit the legality of his title. He further advised William, as he had advised the Commons, that the Cabinet Council should be abolished or restructured. Finally, he recommended that the judicial murders perpetrated by the agents of Charles II and James II should be avenged. The blood of the Whig martyrs still cried unheeded, and the nation still needed to be cleansed by some act of public justice.

Unmoved by the proposal which unforgiving Whigs had been urging upon him since 1689, William merely said that if there were to be punishments they must proceed from parliamentary action. And when Goodwin pointed out that the faction-ridden Parliament could never agree on retributive measures, William seemed to consider the matter closed. At the time, Goodwin was pleased with the interview and not particularly bothered by William's refusal to proceed against Tory malefactors. Two years later, however, after a great tragedy, he perceived that by refusing to vindicate justice William had brought sorrow upon the nation and great personal suffering upon himself.

About the time Goodwin was offering advice to King

William, he received his long-delayed revelation on the subject of government finance. Money should be raised, the Lord told him orally, by a tax upon clergymen and lawyers. Unfortunately, the Lord did not explain, either then or later, precisely what sort of taxes He had in mind or how they were to be levied, and without such details, Goodwin could not bring a proposal before the House. Again he could contribute nothing extraordinary to the debates on supply, and again he missed a chance to earn a peerage.

After his interview at Whitehall, Goodwin returned vigorously to the parliamentary wars. During the balance of the 1692–93 session, he spoke more than twenty times,[10] served on four or five important committees, acted as teller on several divisions, and represented the House of Commons as a conference manager during a dispute with the House of Lords.[11] Some of his speeches were strictly partisan—attacks upon the Tories. He supported a new abjuration bill (which was defeated like its 1690 predecessor);[12] he favoured a resolution asking the King to employ only men who supported him in principle (Whigs);[13] he backed a motion blaming Nottingham and the Queen's Council for the aborted descent upon France;[14] and after trying vainly to save Bishop Burnet, a redoubtable Whig, from having his *Pastoral Letter* burned by the hangman, he moved that Bishop William Lloyd's Tory *Discourse* should be burned too.[15]

On less partisan issues, Goodwin argued that new rules of evidence in treason trials should not come into effect until after the war;[16] he spoke in favour of continuing to employ commissioners of accounts;[17] he led off the debate on the condition of Ireland;[18] he suggested ways of encouraging English privateers and preventing naval supplies from reaching France;[19] he called for an investigation of the East India Company;[20] and he made speeches on parliamentary privileges and procedures.[21] Perhaps most significantly, he became one of the leading advocates of the Triennial Bill, which prescribed general elections every three years and rendered the Commons more independent of the Crown.[22] This measure, passed by both Houses but vetoed by William, was reintroduced in later sessions and finally made law in December 1694.

When the session ended, the King set out for the Continent, leaving Goodwin unrewarded for his parliamentary finesse and leaving Queen Mary as Regent. Almost routinely, the Lord promised that William would die within a few weeks and that in the meantime Mary would appoint Goodwin to an office. Both predictions failed. On 19 July, at Landen, William fought and lost the bloodiest battle of the seventeenth century, but he remained incorrigibly alive. Queen Mary, as if defying revelations, found no post for Goodwin. She did, however, demonstrate her affection in a useful, material way; she ordered the frigate *Dolphin*, commanded by Captain Thomas Kircher, to leave off cruising in the Irish Sea and accompany Goodwin on another diving expedition to Tobermory.[23]

Goodwin's preparations for his second attempt at Mull were less elaborate than those of his earlier voyage. This time he took only one salvage vessel and one escort warship. He also spent less time negotiating with Jeffrey, the diving lowlander, who had missed so many appointments over the intervening two years that his promise to join the expedition seemed frivolous. Goodwin relied instead upon a man named Harrington and another ordinary upland diver.

On the spiritual side, Goodwin was rather better prepared than he had been in 1691. The Lord not only promised him millions from the wreck but also that He would appear to him. Gabriel agreed to accompany the expedition and to guide it, on the return voyage, to another wreck almost as rich as the Tobermory galleon and much easier to salvage. In addition, Goodwin received something more tangible than promises. On the eve before his departure for Liverpool he found, 'wrapped and sealed up' on his table, the long-sought magic 'habit'—the lightweight diving suit with the headgear capable of straining air out of water. A revelation warned him that he was not to open the package until Gabriel, at Mull, ordered him to do so, but the habit itself was finally in his possession.

Goodwin met his salvage vessel and the *Dolphin* at Liverpool; and on 6 June, the two ships set sail on an eventful voyage, which included a brush with French privateers and a storm so violent that Goodwin saw it as a visitation for 'an old crime'—the occasion long ago when he had ventured near the brink of incest with his sister Philadelphia. As the ships neared Mull, Goodwin saw a strange 'white meteor' which flamed a long time in the eastern sky while the sun shone brightly in the west. He did not see or hear Gabriel, however, and when he reached Tobermory, on 17 June, he remained without permission to use his magic gear and was once again forced to rely upon conventional diving equipment.

Almost immediately he ran into unexpected problems. At the first descent, his chief diver Harrington reached the depth of three fathoms and stopped, alleging that he could 'go no lower'. Cowardly in spite of his 'great pretensions', he managed to infect his companion with his fear, and Goodwin was obliged to suspend operations while he recruited and trained volunteers from the crew of the *Dolphin*—a process interrupted by a week of foul weather.

During the lull, Goodwin experienced a surge of hope. On the morning of 6 July, he heard a voice that sounded like Gabriel's. Although he could not make out the words, which were not repeated, he reasoned that if Gabriel was at last speaking, he was bringing permission to open and use the diving habit. Unwilling to act rashly but also unwilling to ignore an order that might make him wealthy, he waited four days before at last opening the package—only to find, to his shock and discomfiture, that the parcel contained 'nothing but four sheets of white paper wrapped in a thin gauze'.

Schooled by years of bizarre disappointments, Goodwin rallied bravely. Eventually he would learn that malignant spirits had removed the magic habit and substituted paper; now, after some initial wavering, he merely prayed for help and returned to the formidable problems posed by the wreck. When the weather allowed his makeshift crew to resume operations, the divers found themselves combating tightly-impacted mud and silt as well as the heavy timbers of the ship's stern. On 18 July, a spear driven through the muck seemed to strike metal ('gold and silver plainly', Goodwin thought); and a week later one of the amateur divers brought up some timbers. But although these feats shamed Harrington and his confederate into trying descents, no one could penetrate to the treasure.

In early August after the *Dolphin* left,[24] Goodwin managed to explode a shell within the wreckage, and this tricky technical manœuvre tore loose a few large timbers. He then jury-rigged a heavy grappling device (consisting principally of two anchors) and pulled away the timbers from the top of the wreck, laying the crucial area bare. He discovered, however, that the compacted mud beneath was too hard to be entered, and this defeat proved final. Convinced at last that with the equipment at his disposal he could not salvage the galleon, he decided to leave; and on 20 August he sailed away down the Sound of Mull.

On his return voyage, Goodwin remembered Gabriel's promise to show him a rich and easy wreck; and when a strong east wind forced the ship to take shelter in northern Ireland and to keep for a while to the Irish shore, he allowed himself to hope that he might yet realize the millions the Lord had promised.[25] But this hope soon proved as empty as the rest; he 'neither saw nor heard the least [thing] about the wreck to be discovered'.

When Goodwin left his ship at Liverpool and returned to London, he left the diving business forever. Although the Lord brought him home safely and although the puzzle of the diving habit was fully explained, the second Tobermory expedition was undeniably a failure, only partially redeemed by meteors and other spiritual portents. Before the next summer, Goodwin's political success further diverted him from diving projects, and in the end the combination of political eminence and technical reverses finished his career as an inventor-projector.

At Soho Square Goodwin found affairs much as he had left them. The lowlanders, as usual, had broken all their promises. They had not brought Mary the keys to any of their establishments or made arrangements for Goodwin to enter his kingdom. Nor had the angels provided an alternative project to balance the failure at Tobermory. They succeeded, to be sure, in forcing the reluctant spirits to transfer an appropriate share of treasure from Goodwin's closet to Sir Thomas Travell's closet, but after the transfer they could not get permission for the partners to open either closet. Even Goodwin's romantic affairs remained stagnant. Though free to find some worthy mistress, he continued to have difficulties in selecting one. The lovely Mistress Cooke was married and hence ineligible on the grounds of adultery; and a certain Mistress Finch proved insufficiently virtuous. Goodwin's understandable caution about whores and adultery, along with his determination to be 'very nice' in his choice of women, meant that after a year and a half of freedom he was still looking for the right lady.

Fortunately Goodwin's frustrations in love and business were alleviated by new opportunities in politics, where King William's defeat at Landen and the French naval ambush of the Smyrna Fleet, a vast merchant convoy, had proved decisively favourable to the Whigs. The King's defeat, caused at least in part by the superior numbers of the French army, had demonstrated the need for more English regiments. These the Whigs were willing to authorize and finance, though the costs would entail new taxes and new financial expedients, including the founding of the Bank of England. The cruel losses suffered by the Smyrna Fleet had been directly attributable to two Tory Admirals, Henry Killigrew and Sir Ralph Delavall, who served as Sea Lords and joint commanders of English naval forces; and there was plenty of odium left over to distribute among other decision makers, including the Whigs' favourite target Nottingham.

The Whig attack, led in the Commons by Tom Wharton and Charles Montague and enthusiastically joined by Goodwin,[26] helped force the removal of the Tory Admirals and the reorganization of the Admiralty. The Whig Russell reassumed command of the fleet and became first Sea Lord, while the Tory Nottingham was removed as Secretary of State and eventually replaced by the Whig Shrewsbury. The new appointments, together with Somers' promotion to Lord Keeper, brought Goodwin's party a notable increase in power. By the summer of 1694, the Whigs held most of the offices in William's government.

Meanwhile Goodwin and his friends had been earning William's favour by their steady support of his military budget. On 20 December, the House voted to finance a land force of 83,000 men[27]—an increase of 25 regiments and almost 30,000 men. The new contingents provided the government with dozens of commissions to distribute among deserving gentlemen. One of the deserving gentlemen was Goodwin, who on 16 February 1694 was made a lieutenant-colonel in the Earl of Macclesfield's new cavalry regiment.[28] Only slightly less deserving was Sir Thomas Travell, who became a captain in the same organization.

Goodwin's commission as lieutenant-colonel, his first office under William's government, meant a significant addition to his social prestige as well as his income. In a title-conscious society, he had become 'Colonel Wharton', not simply 'Mr Wharton';

he had moved out of the shadow of his brother Tom; and he would soon feel impelled to pose in body armour for a portrait. Immediately, however, he was more concerned with military planning than with social esteem. He was engaged, along with the Earl of Macclesfield and several others, in advocating an attack on Brest, the great French naval base—an operation finally scheduled for early May.

While Goodwin waited for the military campaign to start, he continued to do his duty in the Commons. In the latter part of the session (after his attacks on the Admirals), he served on several committees,[29] acted as teller half a dozen times,[30] spoke in favour of the Triennial Bill (defeated this time), defended William's veto powers,[31] and supported the Naturalization Bill, a number of routine supply bills, and the measure which established the Bank of England. During one debate he argued so hotly with the Tory Francis Scobell that the House, fearing a duel, made both men promise to pursue the matter no further.[32]

Almost unnoticed, meanwhile, a significant change was taking place in Goodwin's revelations. Early in the session, the Lord twice promised to reveal the details of His plan for taxing clergymen and lawyers; then He tacitly gave up trying to advise Goodwin on legislation, and Goodwin, without protest or comment, quit asking for help. By this silent change of policy, Goodwin lost forever the once-bright hope of a divinely inspired speech, but he also lost a chronic frustration that had lasted since January 1690.

On military matters, however, the Lord was free with advice and promises. In late April as the time for the attack on Brest drew near, Goodwin was assured by revelation that within nine months he would become a colonel and a general; and on 1 May, shortly before he left for Portsmouth, the Lord promised to be his 'stay and refuge' and cause him to 'overcome the enemy'. He had only to 'go on valiantly' in the Lord's name.

When Goodwin reached Portsmouth his chances of overcoming the enemy seemed very good. The French Atlantic Fleet, under Chateaurenault, had sailed for the Mediterranean, leaving Brest virtually undefended by naval forces. The English had only to secure passage for their ships through the narrow Gullet to the inner bay of Brest and they could destroy the naval installations at will. This strategy depended upon seizing

Roscanvel Peninsula, which commands the Gullet—a manœuvre which required in turn an amphibious attack on the southeast shores of Camaret Bay. The celebrated French engineer and general Vauban[33] had constructed a tower-fortress to defend the southern part of the Bay, but the English expected to neutralize this stronghold with naval gunfire while they were overrunning the Peninsula.

Assigned to lead the attack at Camaret Bay was the intrepid Thomas Talmash, highest ranking English officer in the King's service.[34] Serving under him as Brigadier was John, Lord Cutts, already famous as a leader of assault troops and soon to be dubbed the *Salamander* for his immunity to French fire.[35] Joined with these two men was Goodwin's friend Macclesfield, who was appointed Major-General and Second in Command. The striking force assembled for Talmash included ten regiments of ground troops and a naval contingent of more than forty warships, English and Dutch, under the command of John, Lord Berkeley.[36] Berkeley, a young man but a veteran officer, was assisted by the Dutch Admiral Philips van Almonde[37] and by Peregrine Osborne, Marquis of Carmarthen,[38] the seagoing equivalent of Lord Cutts.

Goodwin and the English army, unfortunately, were delayed for a month by a fateful combination of maladministration and bad weather; and the French War Office, making good use of the time, discovered and countered the English plans.[39] Vauban was sent, along with heavy reinforcements and a vast number of cannon and mortars, to make the Camaret Bay area impregnable and to command the French forces.[40] By the time the English finally arrived, on 7 June, Vauban's batteries were strategically planted and his infantry carefully entrenched. Although Goodwin, sailing towards the French guns, had received a vision which showed Brest in flames, his chances of overcoming the enemy had practically vanished and his chances of being killed had dramatically increased.[41]

Shortly after the English fleet came to anchor, a mile or two outside Camaret Bay, Goodwin (seizing his first chance to 'go on valiantly') volunteered to accompany Lord Carmarthen and Lord Cutts upon a close reconnaissance of the Bay in Carmarthen's yacht. Penetrating deeply towards the south shore, the yacht came under the guns of Vauban's fortress and for a time was in danger of being blown out of the water—an episode which impressed Goodwin and helped change Carmarthen's strategy. Convinced by the fury of the French response that the defence was stronger than anticipated, Carmarthen, who was to command the covering force for the landing, committed eight warships to the task of engaging Vauban's batteries instead of the two originally assigned.

The battle began next day (8 June) as soon as Carmarthen's warships, temporarily becalmed, could be 'rowed and towed' under vicious fire to their battle stations around the Bay.[42] When the roll of the broadsides and the concussions of the shore batteries told everyone the ships were engaged, the landing-craft headed toward the beach. Goodwin, meanwhile, had made another brave decision. As usual, Lord Cutts was to lead the first wave of grenadiers, about six hundred men, who were to be followed, if they made a lodgement, by the regular infantry. Goodwin, determined to heed his revelations, put himself into Lord Cutts's boat and went resolutely forward with the assault echelon.

As the landing boats rowed into closer gun-range, like floating targets in a shooting gallery, General Talmash made a bold decision of his own. Although the volume of cannon fire bespoke extraordinary preparations and although a warning from Carmarthen[43] indicated that the enemy was strongly entrenched in the landing area, he was reluctant to abort the attack. If the troops in the entrenchments and the cavalry that had been seen in the area turned out to be militia, not regulars, he could chase the whole assortment off the Peninsula, and he would be disgraced forever if he broke off the engagement. Reasonably but wrongly, he decided to proceed.

As the boats neared the beach Talmash made another crucial decision. Ignorant of God's battle plan, he did not understand that the first order of tactics was to put Goodwin ashore where he could overcome the enemy. Talmash did realize, however, that Cutts's plan of attack was unworkable. On paper and sometimes on land, grenadiers arrived in neat rows and delivered textbook attacks, but in Camaret Bay they arrived in disorderly batches, and if the operation were delayed while they assembled and launched a probing assault against entrenched enemy forces, failure was virtually certain. The chance for victory lay in landing as many men as possible as quickly as possible and hitting the enemy with a full-scale attack. At the last minute, then, Talmash decided to commit his troops as they arrived and to lead the attack himself; and he ordered Cutts to go back to 'the boats behind' and send along reinforcements.

Suddenly removed as a leader of assault forces, Goodwin found himself a highly endangered spectator at a bloody battle. All round the Bay, French cannon and mortars poured shot into covering ships and landing boats, inflicting grievous casualties. And on shore the scene was bloodier still. Talmash put himself at the head of the first troops ashore, a miscellaneous group of grenadiers and regulars, but before he could mount a charge most of his men were swept away by fire from three lines of entrenchments, two or three flanking batteries of cannon, and a special contingent of musketeers. Talmash himself was shot in the thigh and his assistant Colonel de la Motte was killed outright. In spite of his wound, Talmash tried to launch an attack with the next wave of soldiers who came ashore, but these too were cut down.[44]

As Goodwin watched his redcoated friends on shore falling left and right under a rain of 'small shot', he could not help feeling glad that he was not among them. The Lord had promised him victory, but he 'was not ill pleased' to be off shore beyond the range of musket balls. He was further relieved when Cutts and Macclesfield, judging the assault hopeless, did not land themselves or commit the remaining troops. As the wounded Talmash was brought back, protesting, to the boats, his two subordinates ordered the retreat sounded, and the English busied themselves with saving the remnants of the shattered attack.[45]

Safely back aboard the *Dreadnought* for a council of war, Goodwin had a good deal to think about. It was clear that his revelations had failed once more, but this time he suspected that God's promises had been contingent upon his courage and that his relief at being out of the fight on shore had caused the disaster. Others might blame General Talmash for attacking against heavy odds, but Goodwin was inclined to blame himself. Goodwin's spirits revived momentarily when the wounded Talmash advocated forcing a passage through the Gullet and bombarding Brest;[46] but this plan (which might have produced the promised victory) was rejected by the senior officers as too hazardous. Goodwin was compelled, therefore, to leave Brest undestroyed and sail for England with his guilts, which were not lightened when the gallant Talmash died of gangrene.

In London, fortunately, the angels absolved him of cowardice and blamed the defeat upon the change of plan that had kept him off the beach.[47] Had he gone forward, Mary reported, the French would have been beaten in accordance with revelation. If on the other hand he had retreated to the ships, he would have been killed. Much relieved, Goodwin rejoined the fleet to help Admiral Berkeley conduct strikes against Norman seaports—a strategy that he had recommended himself.[48] He had asked the angels to select targets, but the angels, like the government, left the problem to a council of war, which chose Dieppe and Le Havre. The angels did, however, assist in the destruction of Dieppe, which burned 'like Babylon'—much more fiercely than it could have done from an unaided bombardment. For his own part, Goodwin suggested that French towns should be allowed to buy immunity from attack by paying 'contributions', and his suggestion was accepted by the Queen's Council (though no contributions were offered).[49] At last, during the shelling of Le Havre, he was sent with Berkeley's dispatches to Whitehall,[50] where he had an official audience with Queen Mary, who declared herself 'very well satisfied' with Channel operations.[51]

When Goodwin was not sent back to the fleet by the Council, he busied himself with some very important personal affairs. Deciding after more than five years at Soho Square that he could no longer endure Sir Thomas Travell's 'ill carriage', he took a house of his own in Westminster, on or near the west end of Tothill Street. During the autumn of 1694, as the angels permitted, he moved the treasure trunks that had accumulated in his closet over the years, and by 19 November, when Parliament reconvened, he and Mary were firmly re-established.

In the new session, Goodwin was pleased with the revised administration, now largely Whig, and during the first month the House again passed the Triennial Bill, which was finally approved by King William. Then came what Goodwin called 'a surprising providence'. Queen Mary contracted smallpox—a disease only slightly less formidable than the plague. When the diagnosis was confirmed by the Kensington physicians, Goodwin was deeply troubled, not merely because he adored the Queen but also because he distrusted her doctors, who seemed demoralized by her danger and frightened into trying everything, from bleeding and scarifying to 'intolerable' doses of 'slops'. He tried to take comfort from the fact that Mary could not die without contravening many oral revelations, which had declared that she would outlive William and raise Goodwin to the throne; but he recalled uneasily that God's promises were often contingent when they sounded absolute. Though infallible in principle, they were sometimes wrong in fact.

By the evening of 27 December Queen Mary was obviously sinking, and Goodwin made a final attempt to save her life. Professing himself amazed that she could be dying in defiance of revelation, he called upon the angels for help. Their replies, however, seemed uncertain and evasive. As late as eleven o'clock that night, Gabriel sent word that he still retained 'great hopes' that God would spare the Queen, but he did not send a categorical promise. Less than three hours later, before one o'clock on the morning of 28 December, Queen Mary was dead.

Goodwin was grief stricken at the loss and stunned by the failure of God's promises on 'so great a point'. Before the bells of Westminister had finished tolling, he sent the spirit George Whitmore to ask the spirit of Queen Mary 'how she came to die'. The immediate cause of death, the Queen explained (and George reported via Mary Parish), was the hopeless incompetence of her physicians, whose continual hurry and nauseous potions had 'made her quite weary of her life'; but the ultimate cause was William's failure to avenge the Whig martyrs. Since William had refused to do justice and had left innocent blood crying for atonement, the Lord now cut off the innocent person nearest and dearest to him. By not heeding Goodwin's advice, William had condemned Mary to martyrdom and given himself 'lifelong cause to bewail'.

Although these answers did not quite explain why the Lord had made so many empty promises, Goodwin accepted them and bowed once more to 'the inscrutable wisdom and providence' of God. And soon after the Queen's death, he gave public expression to his love and grief. Appointed to a select committee of the House[52] to draw up an address of sympathy and support for the King, he was able to contribute to the address a treasured phrase from a vision of 3 January 1687. Speaking of Mary Parish, God had formally and impressively pronounced her 'the best of women'. Now, amid the universal mourning, Goodwin quietly transferred Mary's title to the dead Queen; and the committee's condolence to King William (still extant in the House *Journal*) describes Queen Mary as 'that most excellent Princess, the best of women'.[53]

20

The Ruler of the King's Navy

FOR two or three months after Queen Mary's death, Goodwin believed that King William, who had been prostrate with grief, had come to value him. In February 1695, as William gradually resumed public duties, he treated Goodwin with great civility, and in early March, Goodwin was told by the Earl of Sunderland that William had spoken of him 'very kindly'. Some of the new consideration could be attributed to the tragedy, which seemed to soften William; some, again, could be attributed to Goodwin's growing prestige in the House of Commons; but most of it, Goodwin thought, came from the secret papers that William had inherited from Mary—Goodwin's tracts upon lowlanders, spirits, and prophecy. The angels told Mary Parish, in fact, that William had sent for Bishop Burnet in order to 'discourse' about the strange revelations.

Goodwin's private life also took a turn for the better when he at last found a mistress of the highest 'degree'—Lady Elizabeth Gerard, daughter of the first Earl of Macclesfield and widow of Digby Gerard, fifth Baron Gerard of Bromley (her distant cousin).[1] Lady Gerard, who was about thirty-five when she began her intrigue with Goodwin, had not reached him with a spotless reputation. After the death of her husband in 1684, scandal had linked her with Henry Herbert and Robert Wolseley; she had provoked a volley of obscene lines from Dorset, who had called her a 'decayed, incestuous punk'.[2] Goodwin learned in a clear vision, however, that she had been given to him and that she was perfectly eligible to be his mistress. Whatever Lady Gerard's past sins, her liaison with Goodwin continued happily for five years and ended only with her death. It continued, moreover, without disturbing Mary Parish, who could afford to ignore a mere intrigue which did not threaten her status as Goodwin's wife and which left her safely established in Westminster, where she directed negotiations with the lowlanders, consulted the angels, and became pregnant every year with a child who died, unseen by Goodwin, shortly after its birth.

These pleasant domestic arrangements, unfortunately, could not be explained to Goodwin's father, who had been trying as he neared his eighty-second birthday to get his affairs in order. In 1692 Lord Wharton had established a trust, still in existence, for distributing Bibles and catechisms 'amongst poor children';[3] and from time to time he had established funds for the support of Nonconformist chapels. By the beginning of 1695, he was ready to deal with Goodwin—the only one of his children not fully provided for—and he was highly incensed when Goodwin still refused to identify his wife or produce his two sons. Since Goodwin would have been disgraced by an official marriage to Mary and since he had never seen Peregrine himself, he continued to pretend that there were compelling and laudable reasons for secrecy, but this time Lord Wharton, rejecting evasions, enforced his demands for information by cutting off Goodwin's allowance. Unable to support his new establishment on his army pay and unwilling to be cut out of his father's will, Goodwin found himself in great difficulties before he was rescued by the angels, who advised him to tell his father that his wife was dead. This stratagem seemed to mollify Lord Wharton. Apparently convinced that Goodwin was not hiding some shameful marriage, he restored Goodwin's allowance and re-admitted him to favour.

In the early months of 1695 while Goodwin was dealing with his family problems, a series of investigations in the House of Commons was uncovering shocking corruption in the army, the government, and the Parliament itself. Before the investigations ended, the Duke of Leeds, Sir John Trevor, and Sir Edward Seymour (all Tories) had been implicated in bribery scandals and driven from power.[4] The investigations were led by Tom Wharton, who had become, as Goodwin conceded with envy, 'the greatest manager in the House of Commons'. Throughout the session, Goodwin supported his brother in the role of faithful lieutenant. He served on two or three committees, including a committee to investigate election fraud, twice acted as teller during important divisions, and in general continued the attacks upon Tory delinquents.[5]

As the session drew towards a close, Goodwin decided, with

the Lord's permission, to volunteer for the summer campaign in the Low Countries, and on 13 April he offered his services to King William. The King, who was deluged with such offers, seemed evasive. Giving no outward sign of having read Goodwin's tracts or of appreciating Goodwin's extraordinary powers, William merely promised to think about the proposal and pointed out, as he had done earlier, that he would need friends in England. By 5 May, after several interviews, it became clear that he had decided to leave Goodwin behind, and Goodwin thought he could detect a 'wilful stubbornness' in William's manner—a determination to oppose his own conscience. Goodwin did not take the rejection lightly. Coupled with the fact that William had failed to back him in a dispute with the Paymaster General over subsistence money for his cavalry troop,[6] it convinced him that William had become depraved—a view shared by the Lord, who declared in an oral revelation of 28 May that William would never return from his campaign on the Continent.

Goodwin's regiment, meanwhile, had been assigned to home duty and sent to Hounslow Heath for summer manœuvres.[7] Goodwin joined it there without enthusiasm. The days had long since passed when a sojourn at Hounslow filled him with plans. His great lowland friends of former days—Queen Penelope, Father Friar, the Duchess of Plymouth, and the Duke of Lorraine—were all gone. Their successors at Hounslow were a breed of faceless politicians whom Mary could not be bothered to name, and most of her negotiations were carried on in places like Brompton with technicians like Jeffrey. While Goodwin was in Hounslow, therefore, he made no attempt to speak with the lowlanders; he simply waited for instructions from Mary, who had been left in Westminster to produce another short-lived daughter. Mary wrote that the lowlanders at Brompton had invited Goodwin to their establishment, but when he returned in mid-July, the invitation was cancelled and the meeting postponed until December.

This routine aggravation was followed on 22 July by a more serious breach of promise, when the Lord announced that He would not destroy King William after all. In the present state of affairs, He told the angels, England and the allies would be 'undone' if William were taken away. Since God's political and military analysis was obviously right and since Goodwin's anger against William had been cooling for two months, Goodwin accepted the drastic change of plan without complaint. The reprieved William, meanwhile, outmanœuvred the French general Villeroi and after a dramatic siege of two months recaptured the fortress city of Namur.

In England, William's victory was immensely popular—a feat to compare with the Boyne or La Hogue. It silenced the critics of the King's Continental strategy and gave an immense advantage to 'Court Whigs' like Goodwin who had consistently supported the war. In the new parliamentary elections, called while enthusiasm was running high, Goodwin was returned from both Cockermouth[8] and Malmesbury; and when he took his seat in the new House, he found himself part of a solid Whig majority—a circumstance which helped to enhance the quality of his parliamentary assignments.

In the new session he was three times appointed as a manager for the Commons in conferences between the two Houses. Twice he helped to argue the position of the Commons on the vital Recoinage Bill, besides serving on the committee that drew up the official statement of the Commons' view; and once he helped to negotiate with the Lords a joint address which asked King William to prevent the Scots from forming an East India Company of their own. By the end of January 1696 he had also served on several special committees, including one to investigate abuses of trade in the West Indies.[9]

But while Goodwin added to his political prestige, his father was nearing the end of what was for the age a remarkably long life.[10] Lord Wharton, who had spent much of that life preparing for death, faced his approaching end calmly. Lucid and methodical as always, he drew up his will on 1 February[11] and in the few days remaining to him said his farewells to his sons and daughters. Towards Goodwin he was especially kind. Officially accepting the story of Goodwin's family, Lord Wharton informed Tom (with Goodwin's permission and in Goodwin's presence) that Goodwin was a widower with two living sons. And on 4 February, the day before he died, he not only gave his blessing to Goodwin (in person) and the two boys (*in absentia*) but 'seemed much afflicted' for the sorrows Goodwin had endured.

Amid the tears of parting, Goodwin forgot his old bitterness and the oral revelations that had once declared his father unjust, hypocritical, and damned. Over the intervening years it had become clear that Lord Wharton, though often difficult, was never hypocritical; he was precisely the faithful and stoical Puritan he pretended to be—impossible to please, perhaps, but as sure of salvation as the Apostles. And to Goodwin, who was beside him at the end, his death put an appropriate seal on a lifetime of charities and stubborn faith. Watching his father slide gently away from a 'foolish world', Goodwin observed with reverence that the old nobleman 'died without a groan'.[12]

On 12 February Lord Wharton was buried in St. Paul's, Wooburn, where a monument still celebrates his devotion to English political liberties and the reformed religion. And on 21 February Goodwin, who had tried briefly to summon his spirit, received further evidence of his concern. With the probate of Lord Wharton's will, Goodwin inherited most of his father's previously unbequeathed property: the town house on Denmark Street (across the way from the Church of St. Giles-in-the-Fields), four houses in nearby Lloyd's Court (now Flitcroft Street), and the contents of the manor houses at Healaugh, Hartforth, and Aske.[13]

Along with the property that Goodwin received from his father's will came the property that had been settled upon him in the days of the Wooburn crisis: a manor in Ireland; the manors of Catterton, Aske, and Hartforth in Yorkshire; Shap Abbey Grange and Rayne Tenement in Westmorland; and Cockermouth Park, Hewthwaite, the Broughton Colliery, and Bowderdale Close in Cumberland.[14] Goodwin had calculated the original settlement at a respectable £900 per year.[15] Now, with the augmentation from his father's will, an earlier gift of a manor in Malmesbury, and some properties once allocated to Lady Wharton's jointure,[16] his income had become respectable indeed—even without his army pay. At his father's death Goodwin was at once transformed from a dependent younger son to an independent landed gentleman.

In Parliament too the change was dramatic. The death of Lord Wharton removed Tom from the Commons and sent him to the House of Lords as the fifth Baron Wharton. There he would continue to serve as a master strategist for the Whig party (along with Somers, Montague, and Russell, his associates in the famous 'Junto') and he would actually increase the number of boroughs and seats in the Commons under his control; but he could no longer lead his former colleagues in person. His numerous duties as manager and tactician were perforce shared among his friends, and some of them fell to Goodwin.

As it happened, Tom left the Commons at a time when a gang of Jacobite assassins was plotting to murder King William. Adding a deadly variation to the usual insurrection-invasion scheme, the plotters intended to waylay William as he returned in his coach from his usual Saturday hunt at Richmond Park, overwhelm his guards, and dispatch him before he could escape. They would then flash a beacon signal across the Channel to Calais where a French invasion force, accompanied by King James, was assembled for a descent upon England. Before the trap was sprung, however, some of the conspirators betrayed the plan to the government, and by 22 February, the hunters had become the hunted. Several were arrested, and a royal proclamation offering £1,000 per fugitive launched a spirited manhunt for the others. Concurrently William raised the militia, recalled several regular regiments from Flanders, and sent Admiral Russell to deploy the fleet before Calais.

Officially informed of the plot by William himself, the two Houses of Parliament drew up a joint address urging the King to take stern measures and promising to support his government against King James and all other enemies 'at home or abroad'.[17] This address, which Goodwin in the Commons and Tom in the House of Lords helped to frame,[18] was quickly followed by another declaration more far reaching and effective—the famous Association. Originating in the Commons, the Association not only bound its signers to support and defend King William, but also declared William the 'rightful and lawful' King of England.[19] In the wave of outrage over the assassination and invasion plot, the declaration was approved by the House without a division in spite of its whiggish language and its implicit repudiation of divine hereditary right.

Writing in his journal sometime later, Goodwin claimed credit for the famous document, recalling that he 'proposed the Association in the House of Commons' and that it afterward 'went through the whole kingdom'. Whether Goodwin was actually the first to propose the Association or whether it was proposed by Sir Rowland Gwyn, as an anonymous Tory pamphleteer asseverated a few years later,[20] cannot now be decided with certainty. The House *Journal* does not say who proposed the measure, and there are no extant parliamentary diaries for the session. It is certain, however, that Goodwin served on the committee which drew up the Association in its final form[21] and that he felt aggrieved when his services were not suitably recognized by William. It is also certain that when the engrossed Association was brought into the Commons, Goodwin (who had not yet chosen between his two constituencies) signed the document twice—once as the member for Cockermouth and once as the member for Malmesbury.[22]

About one thing, at least, Goodwin's memory was perfect: the Association indeed went through the whole kingdom—to all the cities and provincial towns, where copies were signed by thousands of people. Serving as a test of loyalty to the Revolution settlement, the Association strengthened King William's position immensely—and, of course, the position of his Whig ministers. Meanwhile, the trial and execution of some of the conspirators kept the assassination plot before the public, and in early June the excitement was rekindled by the capture of Sir John Fenwick, one of the chief planners of the proposed Jacobite uprising.

That Sir John Fenwick, a major-general under James II and a chronic conspirator, had plotted to raise a rebellion and call in the French army there could be no serious doubt. But the legal case, supported by the testimony of George Porter and Cardell Goodman (two plotters turned King's evidence) and by an incriminating intercepted letter,[23] soon became immensely complicated. Sir John first tried to throw the government into confusion by making a pseudo-confession (an 'Information')[24] which named four of King William's most eminent supporters— Shrewsbury, Russell, Godolphin, and Marlborough—as traffickers with the exiled Court at Saint-Germain; and when this ruse succeeded only in delaying the trial and infuriating the Whigs,[25] Sir John's Jacobite friends bribed Cardell Goodman to flee to France beyond the reach of any summons. Since the Treason Bill, passed during the previous session, demanded two witnesses for legal proof of guilt, the flight of Goodman made

Fenwick immune from ordinary prosecution. He was suddenly placed beyond the reach of the government.

Sir John's triumph, which took place shortly after Parliament reconvened, proved to be very brief. His Whig opponents in the Commons, possessed of an unassailable majority, brought in a bill of attainder.[26] Since Fenwick through bribery and chicane had evaded the judicial processes, they would use the legislative power to take off his head. Understandably, the bill against Fenwick touched off furious debates. Though Fenwick's guilt was clear beyond all but the most ingenious quibbles, the wisdom of destroying him by an act of Parliament was not at all clear. It was better, most Tories argued, that one obnoxious, crafty traitor should escape than that the judicial processes, evolved for the protection of all Englishmen, should be set aside. The history of Parliament, they contended, showed how often attainders, voted in passion, were later reversed, and how dangerous it was to decide matters of life and death by political methods. The Whigs, on the other hand, led by Charles Montague, argued that legalistic rules framed for the guidance of subordinate judicial bodies should not prevent the supreme power in the state—the framers of law—from arriving at justice and protecting the nation against its deadly enemies. Parliament had both a right and a duty, they concluded, to punish Fenwick for the treason he had obviously committed.

During the debates, which brought forth speeches from all the major figures of both parties, Goodwin spoke three times. On 13 November and again on 17 November (when he also served as teller for the *yeas* on the motion to commit the bill),[27] he spoke at considerable length, advocating orderly procedures, defending the attainder process, scoffing at technical objections, and stressing the weight of the evidence.[28] And on 25 November, in the concluding round of debates, he had the honour of saying the last word for his party. Laws framed for the guidance of lower courts, he reiterated in a brief summary speech, were not binding upon the House, which could set aside its own Treason Act and try Fenwick on the basis of common sense and conscience—on the material evidence, which the defence itself had not dared to challenge. As for himself, Goodwin declared, he was convinced of Fenwick's guilt and prepared in his conscience to vote for the attainder.[29]

Though unconvincing to Tories, the speeches of Goodwin and his friends helped to prevent the defection of over-scrupulous members of the Whig majority, who carried the bill by a vote of 189–156 and sent it on to the House of Lords, where after another violent debate it was again passed, this time by the narrow margin of 68–61. A few days later King William approved the attainder and Sir John was officially sentenced to death. On 28 January 1697 he was executed on Tower Hill; and Goodwin, who had helped send him to the block, had the satisfaction of knowing that at least one slippery Jacobite traitor had met the fate he deserved.

Goodwin's part in the conviction of Sir John Fenwick, though dramatic, was much less important than his role in the regular legislative programme of the House. At the beginning of the 1696–97 session (his eleventh session as an MP), Goodwin became Chairman of the prestigious Committee of Privileges and Elections; thereafter he conducted meetings, investigated disputed elections, reported recommendations to the Commons, and served as conference manager when questions of privilege arose between the two Houses.[30] As the session opened, Goodwin was also appointed to the elite, nine-member committee[31] which drew up the official House address to King William—a ringing promise to finance the war until Louis XIV could be forced to conclude 'a safe and honourable peace'.[32]

This declaration came at a time when the failure of the Tory-sponsored National Land Bank and the money shortage caused by recoinage had produced a grave crisis. Along with two other House resolutions—a promise not to debase the coinage and a promise to pay off all post-Revolution deficits—the pronouncement not only helped to restore government credit but also contributed to a radical restructuring of government finance. Before the session was over, the Whig genius Charles Montague and his colleagues had contrived methods for refinancing the war. They consolidated all deficits into one clearly stated account, extended the time of repayment, and created a 'general fund' to liquidate the debt. In addition, they strengthened the Bank of England, authorized the Exchequer to issue notes to the value of £2,000,000, and enacted legislation for completing the recoinage process.[33] In effect, they transformed England into a modern state, complete with government bonds, paper money, and national debt (which then totalled £5,150,400).

In this financial revolution Goodwin, who had supported the original Recoinage Bill, was assigned to oversee the supplemental legislation. On 6 November, therefore, and on several other occasions when the House resolved itself into a committee of the whole to consider a 'bill for the further remedying the ill state of the coin', it was Goodwin, formally designated as 'Colonel Wharton', who replaced the Speaker in the chair and conducted the discussion of such questions as when the undamaged old-style 'hammered' money should be removed from circulation, what price should be established for the purchase of clipped coins, and how the new 'milled' money should be allocated. It was Goodwin who formally reported the bill (approved on 24 November) and who had the honour of carrying it to the House of Lords.[34]

On 30 November Goodwin brought before the Commons a related measure prepared by himself and William Lowndes—'a bill for encouraging persons to bring in their wrought plate to be coined'. This proposal established the rate at which owners of silver plate were to be rewarded for turning their silverware into crowns and shillings.[35] Since the 'Plate' Bill involved a treasury deficit, the discussion of the measure was combined with the general discussion of providing for the deficits caused by recoinage; and Goodwin was appointed to conduct the debates on the combined questions. On 16 December and 22 December, he again took the Speaker's chair when the House resolved itself into a committee of the whole and again he helped to produce significant decisions. The committee agreed that the House should appropriate money to make up all coinage 'deficiencies' and to recompense the owners of plate and that the sum to be raised was £125,000. These decisions, which Goodwin formally reported to the House, were adopted by the Commons as resolutions.[36] Ultimately the bills for buying plate and paying off deficiencies were passed by both Houses and approved by the King.[37]

To Goodwin, who had dealt with Cardinal Wolsey and who had more than £125,000 locked, untouchably, in his closet, his triumphs as a financial expert were not worth writing down in his journal. Nor was he impressed when he was placed on the

most important committee of all—the committee for refinancing
the war (officially, a committee 'to consider . . . the nature of the
deficiencies of parliamentary funds . . . and how the said deficiencies may be best provided for').[38] This committee brought in
the first consolidated statement of what would later be called the
national debt and recommended measures for funding it.[39]
Later, after its measures had been approved, the committee took
up the related problem of strengthening the Bank of England.
Once again its recommendations were adopted, and on 1 April,
King William gave his assent to a final, innovative bill,
innocuously entitled: 'an act for making good the deficiencies of
several funds, therein mentioned; and for enlarging the capital
stock of the Bank of England; and for raising the public
credit'.[40]

   Goodwin's prominent part in fiscal matters completed his rise
to the top of the second echelon of Whig politicians. Only one
step below the Junto itself, Goodwin and such colleagues as Sir
Thomas Littleton, John Methuen, Sir Henry Hobart, and John
Smith headed committees, made motions, and introduced
bills—managed, in short, the legislative programme of their
party. In keeping with such responsibilities, Goodwin worked
diligently throughout the session. On special committees, he
dealt with poverty, unemployment, seditious pamphlets, prison
abuses, criminal sanctuaries, fraud prevention, and marriage
annulment; he worked on a bill for reorganizing the 'Russian
[trading] Company', and once helped to investigate a petition
charging the government with false arrest.[41]

   On a grander scale, Goodwin framed and presented two
major bills: 'a bill for a general naturalization' and 'a bill to
prevent the buying and selling of offices and places of trust'. The
first measure, designed to grant citizenship to Protestant
immigrants driven off the Continent by Louis XIV, survived its
first reading on 22 February 1697;[42] then, like a similar bill of
1694, it ran afoul of Tory prejudices against non-Anglicans and a
general English suspicion of foreigners. To Goodwin's intense
disgust it was rejected on the second reading by the decisive
margin of 168–127.[43]

   Goodwin's anti-corruption bill, designed to root out the
ancient practice of treating public positions as if they were
private property, passed without a division in the House of

Commons,[44] where most MPs had no offices to sell. When Goodwin carried it to the House of Lords, however, the proposal came to grief. As the chief beneficiaries of the patronage system, the Lords were in no hurry to abolish it. Craftily declining to reject the bill outright, they first tried to kill it with amendments, and when that failed, they simply post-poned action until the session ended and the measure auto-matically died.[45] Goodwin was not deceived by what he considered scandalous hypocrisy, but he could do nothing to save his bill.

Although the defeat of his favourite measures rankled, it did not detract from his legislative performance or weaken his position as a party manager—a position clearly symbolized during mid-March when the House went into a committee of the whole for its annual consideration of the Mutiny Bill. Again it was Goodwin who took the Speaker's chair and conducted the discussion; it was Goodwin who read the bill on the floor of the House; and it was Goodwin who carried the approved bill up to the Lords.[46]

Goodwin's achievements did not go unnoticed by the King's ministers, and when rewards were distributed at the end of the session, Goodwin was one of the first to profit. The death of Robert Austen had left a vacancy among the Lords of the Admiralty, and the Duke of Shrewsbury, who managed Whig claims for preferment, succeeded 'without difficulty' in getting the King to award Goodwin the position.[47] On April 22, the *London Gazette* announced the new appointment: 'His Majesty has been pleased to constitute Goodwin Wharton, Esq., one of the Lords Commissioners of the Admiralty. . .'.[48] On the following day, warrants were issued for preparing Goodwin's patent and renewing the patents of his six colleagues, Admiral Edward Russell, Henry Priestman, Sir Robert Rich, Sir George Rooke, Sir John Houblon, and James Kendall.[49]

Along with Goodwin's promotion came rewards for the great Whig chiefs, including Thomas, (now) Lord Wharton, who became Lord Lieutenant of Oxfordshire and official warden of all royal forests and parks in Southern England.[50] Tom's colleagues had tried to get him appointed Secretary of State or Lord Lieutenant of Ireland,[51] but William made other arrange-ments. For once in his life, Goodwin found that he had gained a larger prize than his brother's. His position at the Admiralty, with an annual salary of £1,000, was more lucrative and more prestigious than both of Tom's appointments combined.

Goodwin also found that he had been given a burdensome responsibility. The Lords of the Admiralty were a board of very hard-working executives who supervised naval operations (allocating warships to fleets, squadrons, convoys, and single-vessel patrols) and exercised general control over what a later age would call personnel, construction, maintenance, and supply—managing, in consequence, the most complex industrial organization in England.[52] The Sea Lords met two or three times every weekday in a then-new Admiralty Building[53] and often worked far into the night. In the summer of 1697, Goodwin spent session after session at his 'troublesome' task—issuing orders, hearing complaints, analyzing estimates, weighing strategy and tactics, studying disposition reports, and acting upon the never-ending requests for promotion, reassignment, and special favours.[54]

Naval operations that summer were extensive and frustrating. Although the war on the Continent was winding down, French privateers and attack squadrons under Pointis, Nesmond, and Chateaurenault were as troublesome as ever; the demand for English warships was constant and their success in countering French forays something less than spectacular.[55] In late August, Goodwin saw a chance to intervene in the war personally—to join the not-yet famous Rear Admiral John Benbow in an attack upon Jean Bart, renowned captain of privateers. In late July the Admiralty had assigned Benbow to blockade Dunkirk, where Bart was stationed with a flotilla of eleven ships and where (reports indicated) he was cleaning the hulls of his ships, preparing to run north on the first spring tide. Benbow, with superior forces, including fire-ships, planned to destroy Bart's squadron as it left Dunkirk. Goodwin, as a Lord of the Admiralty, assigned himself to assist in the operation.

Before committing himself to an enterprise as dangerous as fighting Jean Bart, Goodwin discussed the matter with his veteran Admiralty colleague Sir Robert Rich, who favoured the project, and he asked Mary to consult the angels, who declared that 'it was a very honest design'. This advice was corroborated by a vision, which showed French ships burning and which seemed to confirm the strategy of attacking Bart with fire-ships. The only discordant note was Mary's insistence that 'for the sake of the children' Goodwin should make a will—a demand that seemed to show insufficient faith in angels and visions. The implication that he might be killed made Goodwin uneasy, but since it was clear that Mary and Peregrine and Hezekiah, with no claim on his property, would be penniless if he died intestate, he very reluctantly executed a will.

Goodwin's attempt to join Admiral Benbow became a long agony. While being rowed down the Thames to his warship, he encountered an electrical storm so supernaturally violent that it terrified the sailors themselves. Shortly afterward, through pilot error, the ship was almost wrecked against the Red Sand. And after trying unsuccessfully at Dunkirk to find Benbow, who had gone north in unavailing pursuit of Jean Bart,[56] Goodwin and his party were caught in mid-Channel by a gale which threatened to sink the ship. For two days the Captain kept the pitching and rolling vessel at anchor in the Channel, while Goodwin's natural and reasonable fears were augmented by a sense of God's displeasure. Goodwin was haunted too by strange visions which showed Mary, and later Lady Gerard, 'running about in great distraction, half-naked'—bizarre images that seemed to prefigure his own death.

When the storm finally blew itself out, Goodwin returned, shaken, to St. Giles and gave God 'thanks in the church'. Fortunately, his premonitions of death had proved wrong and his reluctantly drawn-up will had been unnecessary. Indirectly, however, Mary's insistence upon a will probably had a significant effect. By forcing Goodwin to provide for Peregrine, Mary had again raised the vexing question of why the boy, now thirteen, could not be seen. Perhaps Goodwin grew pressing about the matter. In any case, after the episode of the will, all references to Peregrine disappeared from Goodwin's journal. Presumably, sometime thereafter, Mary reported the boy's death and explained why Goodwin was not allowed to attend the funeral; and Goodwin, who had begun his journal for Peregrine's instruction, was too dispirited to record the death of the lad, whose passing contravened dozens of bright promises.[57]

In the late summer of 1697, along with Goodwin's other misfortunes, came the collapse of a new series of negotiations with the lowlanders—a series begun in late 1696 when Mary had found 'a new place in Tothill Fields', controlled by an elderly Portuguese duke, assisted by a lowland gentleman named Mr Rich. Both men, Mary learned over a period of several weeks, were willing to give Goodwin treasure and guide him to power in his lowland domain. By June, however, when Goodwin entered into his official duties at the Admiralty, the affair of the lowlanders had developed the classic signs of failure. The Portuguese master of Tothill Fields became chronically ill and peevish, seeing Mary from time to time, but never Goodwin; and Goodwin, now expert in the rhythms of disappointment, found all serious expectations of lowland riches draining away. They were not even revived in early September when Mr Rich, the duke's assistant, put some magical device in Mary's mouth, took hold of her petticoat, and flew with her 'in an instant' from Covent Garden to Tothill Fields. To Goodwin, Mary's experience merely proved that for fourteen years the lowlanders had concealed a resource they now exhibited; and he refused to be diverted by essentially useless feats of magic. All he needed from the lowlanders was a simple meeting and an uncomplicated transfer of treasure. Now, after many delays, these modest goals seemed farther away than ever.

Meanwhile, as his secret projects disintegrated, he acquired the final symbol of social eminence—a country estate within twenty miles of London. He had already improved his urban residence by moving from Westminster into his father's town house at St. Giles. Now, financially strengthened by his salary from the Admiralty,[58] he leased from the Apsley family the charming estate of Richings Park, a mile or so north of Colnbrook in southeastern Buckinghamshire. At the time Goodwin acquired Richings the property included a 'mansion' of some twenty-five or thirty rooms,[59] a number of standard outbuildings (barns, stables, laundry house, and brew house), a summer-house, and a park 'about a mile and a half round'.[60] A few years later, after Richings reverted to the Apsleys,[61] it became a literary shrine, where Allen, Lord Bathurst, entertained Tory immortals like Alexander Pope, John Gay, and Jonathan Swift.[62] In 1697, however, when Goodwin leased the property, he had no thought of entertaining poets—much less Tory poets.

He was concerned with prestige and politics—with King William, who sometimes occupied Windsor Castle some four or five miles away, and with the freeholders of Buckinghamshire. Prestige was not long in coming. The new estate, acquired (coincidentally) just as William was concluding the Peace of Ryswick, helped Goodwin add two more honours to his growing list. He was appointed one of the Justices of the Peace for Buckinghamshire[63]—a position he would hold for the rest of his life—and he would soon be elected Knight of the Shire.

With such consolations from the shabby world of politics and property, Goodwin generally found it possible to forget how pitifully his world had shrunk since the day, for instance, when he and Mary and John Wildman had stopped in Colnbrook to discuss their Northend treasures and decide when Wildman should be admitted to Goodwin's lowland kingdom, or the day when his inner voice had given him Queen Mary Beatrice. It was only occasionally, when he stopped to make a now rare notation in his neglected journal, that he was forced to remember the magnitude of his failures—the losses for which no estate in Buckinghamshire could possibly atone.

21

A Closer Walk

GOODWIN spent the charmed interval of euphoria that followed the Peace of Ryswick helping his Admiralty colleagues transform a wartime navy into a peacetime navy—an intricate task that left little time for celebrating. Enmeshed in business, he did not suspect that the few weeks between the Peace and the parliamentary session of 1697–98 would mark the high point of his secular career. The new session would bring the beginning of the end of Whig political dominance, and Goodwin himself would suffer a near-fatal illness before the session was over.

The troubles of Goodwin's party began with an argument over disarmament. To the taxpayers of England, the end of the war seemed to promise an end to huge military budgets. On economic grounds alone, pressures for a drastic reduction of military forces were formidable, and there were strong political grounds as well. All parties agreed, in principle at least, that standing armies were a threat to civil liberties. Good Tories saw an additional threat in the swarms of contractors, placemen, and money-lenders (mostly Whigs) who profited from the military establishment, while Country Whigs distrusted military men and royal power in general. Even Court Whigs yearned for the days when a few regular battalions sufficed.

Against such instincts stood one simple, ugly fact. Louis XIV, with an immense standing army, remained a clear and present danger. At any moment the ailing King of Spain might die, and Louis was in a position to claim the Spanish throne and the vast Spanish empire on behalf of his grandson—an increase of French power to be prevented at all costs. For England to disband most of its regular regiments in the face of such a nightmare seemed childish folly to King William and his chief ministers. It also seemed folly to Goodwin, who in the hot parliamentary debates, along with such colleagues as Montague and Littleton, 'insisted upon the necessity there was to provide for the security of the kingdom'.[1] Though essentially right,

Goodwin's arguments were wasted. On this issue, the Whig leaders could not control their followers, and the House voted to reduce the army to its 1680 level—to a force of about 7,500 men.

Mercifully, neither Goodwin nor his friends registered the extent of the damage wrought by the split in the Whig party. Content to hold a working majority on other issues, they left long-range worries alone. In spite of his Admiralty duties, Goodwin gave his colleagues in the Commons considerable help, presenting the Navy estimates of 1698 and bringing in, upon the instructions of the House, another ill-fated bill for preventing the sale of government positions. He served, additionally, on a number of committees, with duties that ranged from reviewing finances to reorganizing the militia;[2] and outside of Parliament, as Member for Cockermouth, he appeared before King William at Kensington to present the loyal address of his constituents.[3]

He might have gone on to perform other important duties, but in the middle of the session came disaster. On 25 March 1698, at his home on Denmark Street, he suffered a severe paralytic stroke—'a fit of apoplex'. The violence of the attack baffled his physicians, who despaired at first of saving his life. Though they bled, blistered, and scarified him, they seemed to make no headway against the vicious seizure, and at the end of three days he appeared to be 'past recovery'.[4]

But the despair was premature. Aided by Mary's prayers and the energies that had sustained him at Tobermory and Camaret Bay, Goodwin rallied. On 29 March, his friend James Vernon, Secretary of State, observed that Goodwin had 'passed his great danger';[5] and a news-letter of the same date assured its readers that Colonel Wharton, previously 'given over', was now 'somewhat better'[6]—views echoed two days later by *The Post Boy*, which declared that the 'Honourable Col. Goodwin Wharton', earlier thought to be 'at the point of death', was now 'on the mending hand'.[7]

After surviving the first terrifying onslaught, Goodwin fought a long battle against paralysis. The 'violence of his distemper' rendered his left arm useless[8] and kept him bedridden for several weeks. For a long time, as he later recalled, his physicians thought his condition incurable—an opinion shared by some of his friends, who 'much questioned' whether he would ever recover. As late as 15 May, he was being prayed for in St. Paul's, Covent Garden,[9] and a few days later, when he ventured forth to visit James Vernon, he seemed 'a maimed, weak creature'.[10] Then, gradually, his condition improved. On 17 June and 28 June he attended meetings at the Admiralty, and after mid-July he began to attend more frequently.[11] In late July, backed by his brother Tom, he stood for election in Buckinghamshire, where he was elected Knight of the Shire.[12] By the end of the year, he was making steady progress towards recovery.

As Goodwin looked back later upon his cure, he saw that it was not dramatic enough to rank as a miracle; his paralysis disappeared slowly, and he 'continued under manifold weakness [for] some years'. He perceived, nevertheless, that God had restored him 'wonderfully', after saving him from death and permanent paralysis.

His party, meanwhile, struggled with infirmities of its own. The elections of 1698, though favourable to Goodwin personally, proved disastrous for his friends.[13] The distaste for standing armies and taxes gave Tories and Country Whigs a clear majority, which they used in the ensuing sessions (1698–1701) to drive Junto chiefs and Court Whigs from office and, incidentally, to end Goodwin's hopes of further advancement. This state of affairs, together with his own ill health, meant that in the session of 1698–99, Goodwin served on only two or three minor committees and introduced only one bill.[14] His Tory opponents, meanwhile, in a frenzy of economy and isolationism, further reduced the King's army, dismissing all foreign soldiers (including William's Dutch guards), investigated royal grants, and attacked the wartime ministry.

On 21 December, Goodwin's sister-in-law Lucy Loftus Wharton, Tom's wife, dealt Goodwin (and eventually the whole Wharton family) a blow more serious than any political reverse. After six years of childless marriage, in defiance of many revelations, she bore Tom a son—a new heir to the barony and the Wharton estates. Even Goodwin, now displaced, could not guess that the boy, named Philip after his grandfather, would become a duke, dissipate the vast family fortune, and die a proscribed and alcoholic Jacobite;[15] but Goodwin was unhappy enough, and he was not cheered when King William, Princess

Anne, and the Duke of Shrewsbury became the child's god-parents.[16]

Young Philip's birth was followed a few months later by the death, from smallpox, of Goodwin's sister Mary—Mary Kemeys (widow of William Thomas[17] and wife of Sir Charles Kemeys). Goodwin and Mary, then nicknamed 'Mall', had been close during their motherless childhood at Wooburn,[18] but they had become estranged in the days of Goodwin's feuds with the family. Then, as death thinned the Wharton ranks and as Mary herself lost both children from her first marriage (Anna and Sir Edmond Thomas),[19] she and Goodwin became friends again. During her last illness, she summoned Goodwin to witness her will and bequeathed him as a keepsake a heart-shaped locket set with 'a blue Turkey stone'.[20] Mary, who died on 2 April 1699,[21] chose to be buried at Wooburn rather than in Wales or London, where she had spent most of her life.[22] It was a decision approved by Goodwin, who ultimately chose Wooburn himself.[23]

To Goodwin the losses among the Whartons were partially counterbalanced by the miraculous fertility of Mary Parish, who continued to bear children regularly—though not in supernatural clusters. Her deliveries, moreover, continued to be rapid, painless, and virtually undetectable. In June 1696, for example, she left home about five in the afternoon, gave birth to 'a fine girl', and returned before nine in the evening without arousing the least suspicion among her acquaintances. A week later, to Goodwin's wonderment, 'she again conceived with child'. On 19 March 1697 she delivered twins in an even more noteworthy performance, walking all the way from her house in Westminster to the house of her midwife near St. Anne's, Soho, delivering her children, and then, when the royal guards stopped her sedan chair near Westminster Abbey, walking the rest of the way home down Tothill Street.

Goodwin was fortunate too in the timing of Mary's conceptions. Providentially, she had been delivered of a child in late February 1698 and had conceived again on 2 March, only three and a half weeks before his paralytic stroke. As a result, she was pregnant during the worst days of his incapacity. Later, she proved that his paralysis had not left him sterile. Although she failed to bear a child in 1699, she conceived one—a baby girl born on 9 May 1700; and two years later, a few days before her own seventy-second birthday, she announced to Goodwin the arrival of a son—the last fruit of the 106 conceptions Goodwin had catalogued since 3 August 1683.

Meanwhile, Goodwin's political fortunes continued to deteriorate. In the rancorous parliamentary session of 1698–99, the coalition which had reduced the King's army began attacking the naval administration—particularly the Whig Russell, now Earl of Orford, whose salaries and grants, though strictly legal, were exorbitant. Orford's enemies in the Commons passed what amounted to a vote of censure, and his friends barely defeated (by four votes) a resolution that he should be removed from the Admiralty.[24] Having lost the confidence of the Tory House, the hot-tempered Orford then proceeded to alienate the King by quarreling with Sir George Rooke. When William sided with Rooke, Orford was compelled to recognize defeat; and on 14 May 1699, he went to Kensington and resigned his offices.[25]

Goodwin, Orford's friend and ally, did not wait long to submit his own resignation.[26] Knowing that the Board was to be reconstituted, he resigned his post about a week later. On 25 May, his patent was officially revoked, along with those of Orford, Houblon, Priestman, and Kendall, and a new Board was appointed, headed by the Earl of Bridgwater.[27]

In leaving the Admiralty, Goodwin did not resign his commission in Lord Macclesfield's cavalry regiment, which had survived the drastic post-war demobilization (in part, perhaps, because Goodwin had supported the King in the standing-army debate). Although the regiment was briefly disturbed by a petition alleging that the foreign soldiers dismissed by parliamentary edict had been cheated by their officers, an investigation by the Commons showed the allegations to be false.[28] The regiment emerged unscathed, and Goodwin continued as its second in command at a salary of £400 per year.[29] Although his paralytic stroke ended his hopes of becoming a colonel and a general (as the Lord had promised him in 1694), he remained Lieutenant-Colonel and Captain even after Macclesfield died and the regiment was reorganized under Lord Windsor.[30]

During the two following sessions of Parliament, Goodwin's role, much reduced in the 1698–99 session, continued to shrink. Between Tory malevolence and his own poor health, his committee assignments became few and insignificant.[31] In effect, he was removed from major committees and demoted to the back benches while the Tories attacked his friends, cancelled King William's grants in Ireland, and censured the treaties by which William attempted to avert another general war.

In private life, meanwhile, Goodwin lost his adored mistress, Lady Elizabeth Gerard, who died on 11 March 1700.[32] Their long intrigue had survived Goodwin's illness and a good deal of turmoil within the Gerard family, including a furious lawsuit between Lady Gerard and her only child, Elizabeth, Duchess of Hamilton. (After winning the suit, over property worth £14,000,[33] Lady Gerard cut the Duchess out of her will—leaving her only five shillings.)[34] Goodwin had felt 'a mighty affection' for Lady Gerard, and he was particularly proud of her noble lineage. This was symbolized for the last time on 19 March 1700 when she was buried in St. John the Baptist's Chapel in Westminister Abbey, where she shares the vault of the Cecils.[35]

Whether from sentiment or debility, Goodwin did not replace Lady Gerard with another mistress; he contented himself with his spiritual wife Mary Parish, who stood valiantly by him in his illness and bravely continued her failure-haunted 'commerce' with the lowlanders. These negotiations were stalled by the illness of Mr Rich, who suffered an apoplectic stroke like Goodwin's, and by the machinations of the King of Portugal, who pestered his brother the Duke at Tothill Fields with deputations urging him to come home. For two years, in spite of all her care, Mary could accomplish nothing.

More serious was the silence of the Lord, who failed to speak from the time of Goodwin's stroke until the summer of 1700, when He vouchsafed one brief, non-committal revelation. God delivered his next oral revelation in April 1701, but Goodwin could not understand 'one word'. Finally, on 27 June 1701, Goodwin received a clear and significant message—a definite promise that his business with the lowlanders would be completed on 1 August.

This promise, unfortunately, turned out to be worthless. Though Goodwin's special friend Mr Rich had come to power at Tothill Fields through the death of the Duke of Portugal, he too found himself harassed by Portuguese visitors and unable to deliver treasure. Succeeding promises, delivered to Mary by the archangel Michael, proved equally vain. Finally, instead of treasure, Goodwin received a reprimand for 'want of faith'. In one of the last oral revelations he was ever to receive, he heard the Lord declare, without the usual affectionate preamble:

> Thou canst not believe in Me,
> Then how can I do good to thee.

Against this reproof Goodwin did not venture to argue. 'God help my infirmities,' he wrote humbly in his journal.

While Goodwin's hopes of great wealth dwindled towards a sigh, the fortunes of his political party brightened. Beginning in late 1700, grim events on the Continent proved that King William and his Whig ministers had been right about defence and that their opponents had been suicidally wrong. While England stood by, disarmed and essentially helpless, Carlos II of Spain died; Louis XIV accepted the Spanish Crown on behalf of his grandson and took over the administration of Spanish foreign policy; and French armies expelled Dutch garrisons from the great 'barrier' fortresses in the Spanish Netherlands. Almost too late, the Tory Parliament woke up to the fact that it had been handing Europe over to King Louis.

The final shock wave rolled through England in September 1701 when James II died at Saint-Germain and Louis XIV, in defiance of the Treaty of Ryswick, recognized the thirteen-year-old son of James and Mary Beatrice (the warming-pan baby of 1688) as the legal English king. Thoroughly alarmed at last, the country rallied behind William, and as the loyal addresses came pouring in, William took the opportunity to dissolve his slow-learning Tory Parliament.

The furiously contested election that followed gave the resurgent Whigs a tiny majority. Goodwin was returned for both Cockermouth and Buckinghamshire,[36] where patriotic electors instructed him to 'support the King' and pull down 'the exorbitant power of France'.[37] In the new Parliament, Goodwin again found himself upon the Committee of Privileges and Elections, upon the committee which drafted the official House pledge of support for William, and upon eight or ten minor committees, with duties ranging from investigating maladministration to settling private estates.[38] Outside the Commons, he was appointed Deputy Lieutenant of Buckinghamshire, under his brother Tom, the newly appointed Lord Lieutenant.[39]

During the first few weeks of 1702, Goodwin and his party prospered. On 2 February, however, their hopes were mortally wounded by what seemed at first a trivial accident.[40] At Hampton Court King William, thrown from a stumbling horse, broke his collar-bone. The injury, though apparently slight, refused to heal. Gradually it became apparent, in spite of optimistic bulletins, that William was suffering from inflammation of the lungs and that his frail overworked body would not respond to any treatment then available. As his doctors plied him with useless potions, he grew steadily weaker, until by 7 March it was clear to William himself that he would not survive. The next morning, with a stoical calm worthy of Lord Wharton, he received the Sacrament, said farewell to a few old friends, and finally (to the great admiration of Bishop Burnet, who attended him) died 'in a wonderful tranquillity'.[41]

William's death ended the brief surge of Whig prosperity, for although Queen Anne, William's Tory successor, maintained William's Grand Alliance and resolved to beat the French back across their borders, she chose to employ Tories in the process. After retaining William's last Parliament for a few more weeks, during which she declared war on France, she called a new election and used her influence to secure a Tory majority. Once again Goodwin (re-elected Knight of the Shire for Bucks)[42] found himself part of an embattled minority.

Fortunately, Goodwin had a secret resource—a strong hold on Queen Anne's affections. Goodwin had first become aware of her love in 1688, when as Princess Anne she had seen him at the theatre and found him irresistible. Thereafter, her love had grown steadily, as Goodwin found on his visits to Hampton Court and Kensington, until by the end of 1691 she loved him 'perfectly'.[43] Now he decided to use his advantage to 'counterbalance' her well-known affection for the Marlboroughs; and to make doubly sure of his powers, he had Mary Parish procure a paper inscribed with a magic love formula. This paper, which Goodwin carried religiously, worked very slowly. Not until October was there any sign of progress, and this took the form of a vision which told Goodwin that Anne's husband Prince George was shortly to die, leaving Anne free to marry him.

But while Goodwin waited for the Prince's death, he became

aware that it was Mary Parish who stood in imminent danger. In January 1703 Mary grew desperately ill. Not as dramatic as Goodwin's stroke, Mary's illness was nevertheless terrifying— especially because, at seventy-two, she was in the latter months of pregnancy, and because the Lord kept 'in a manner away', giving her 'no encouragement'. In spite of such ominous signs, Mary managed to recover, and in late February it was Goodwin's turn to be ailing; the chronic weakness that had troubled him since his stroke rendered him unable to fulfil his military duties. On 2 March, therefore, 'by reason of his indisposition', he resigned his commission in Lord Windsor's regiment.[44]

About the same time, Mary was making her very last attempt to get action from the lowlanders—to complete a campaign begun the previous summer. At that time the Lord had driven into the Mediterranean Sea all but three of the Portuguese visitors who infested Tothill Fields, and Mary had persuaded Mr Rich to send Goodwin £14,000 by way of one Mr White. The devious White, however, lent the money out at interest instead of delivering it; and months of delay had ensued while Mr Rich tracked the man down and forced him to call in his loans. Now in March 1703, with the money back in Mr Rich's hands, Mary had only to banish a few more Portuguese. In early April she reported this task accomplished; Mr Rich had been freed from all his guests. Only the fact that she sprained her leg kept her from entering Tothill Fields at once, and in spite of the injury, she made a firm appointment for Goodwin to meet Mr Rich.

The appointment was never kept. On 10 April, Mary suddenly became so ill that she had to be carried upstairs to her bed. From the first, she seemed to realize that the illness was mortal, and for eight days, as Goodwin observed with profound admiration, she displayed an unparalleled resolution. For her death, like her life, could not be a simple affair. Besides undergoing a slow dissolution, she was obliged to conceal the fact that she was on the verge of delivering a child. This she did by 'bending her body' in a way that not only kept the boy from being born but also hid her pregnancy from her nurse and servants. Goodwin would not allow her to be moved from her unusual position; and as her life gradually ebbed away, he was convinced that her strategem had ended the life of the unborn child, which had 'died in her belly'.

For her heroism, Mary was granted a quiet death. Goodwin, attending her, could not perceive that she ever felt pain; and shortly before her last breath, he had a waking vision in which he saw Mary and her child 'refreshing with the Lord'. It was an end in every way fitting for a woman who had communed with spirits and angels, and for a time Goodwin almost forgot his grief in wonder at her passing.

As he left her deathbed, however, he could not help fearing that some trace of her pregnancy might show when she was washed and prepared for burial—that her abdomen might be discolored or that the child might not be cold. Since he was obliged to quit her bedroom, leaving the preparations to her nurse, he could do nothing about his fear except trust in the Lord; and this time the Lord did not fail him. When he cross-examined the nurse, he learned that she had detected nothing strange about Mary's body and that no one entertained the faintest suspicion.

Later, back in Mary's room, alone, Goodwin examined the body himself and found that Mary had been even more heroic than he had supposed. As he verified the fact that there was no sign of pregnancy, it became clear that besides adopting a posture that deceived onlookers, Mary had deliberately starved the child 'to nothing'. For weeks she had been 'pining away', and from the beginning of her last illness she had refused to eat anything. Thus, with the Lord's help, she had made an unborn child vanish and performed the last 'wonderful work' for the partnership.

Goodwin could not, of course, bury his marvellous partner among the Whartons at Wooburn. In death as in life, her social station precluded formal recognition. He could, however, do the next best thing; he could bury her at St. Giles-in-the-Fields, only a stone's throw from his house on Denmark Street. This he did on 20 April, two days after her death. And although the church of St. Giles as Mary knew it was replaced a few years later by the present handsome church, her name (slightly misspelled) still appears in its Parish Register[45]—one of the most fascinating names in a long distinguished list.

Goodwin did further justice to Mary's memory by restoring

to her the title 'best of women', which the Lord had bestowed
upon her in 1687 and which Goodwin had lent to Queen Mary
at the time of her tragic death in 1694. Now, in 1703, as he
reviewed the last prodigies Mary Parish had wrought, he saw
very clearly that she had earned the right to the Lord's high
compliment. 'Best of women dead,' he wrote sadly in his
journal.

Naturally, the death of Mary brought a crisis in Goodwin's
spiritual life. For twenty years, except for the period when he
had relied upon internal revelations, he had consulted Mary on
every spiritual matter. She had been his link with the lowlanders,
the spirits, the angels, and sometimes with God; she had
constructed and described to him a dramatic world in which he
had played the central role. She had made his life significant. In
recent years, of course, the failure of her projects had sometimes
made her miraculous realms remote and unattainable. Goodwin
had managed, nevertheless, by a will to believe that Blaise Pascal
himself might have envied, to keep his threatened kingdoms
from disappearing altogether and had protected an emotional
investment of incalculable value. Now, with Mary's death, he
was 'left alone' (in his own melancholy phrase) to defend his
beleaguered faith and to cope with a final series of reverses—a
last test of his character.

His first disappointment came at the hands of the lowlanders.
Since Mary had finally arranged for his entrance into Tothill
Fields, he naturally hoped that Mr Rich would send for him or
come to St. Giles himself. Nothing of the sort happened; neither
Mr Rich nor any other lowlander 'came near' him. He was
similarly frustrated in the summer when he went to Richings.
Word of Mary's death, he knew, had gone abroad, and it was
only reasonable that the lowlanders in the Hounslow colony—
his neighbours—should get in touch with him directly. This they
failed to do. Though he kept 'hoping to see some of the people',
he could not even hear of them; they remained as silent and
remote as if they had vanished from the earth.

A parallel disappointment occurred when he returned to St.
Giles in September. He had been warned in 1696 that the
treasures in his closet would be stolen if he tried to see them
before he saw his lowland subjects; but since the lowlanders had
defaulted on their appearances, he felt justified in opening his

treasures anyway. These fabulous riches, which had come from Northend, Hounslow, St. James's Park, Red Lion Fields, Ratcliff, and Southampton, represented dozens of expeditions and years of deferred hope. But as Goodwin opened trunk after trunk, he found them empty; the untold wealth 'laid in the closets was there no more'.

Most demoralizing of all was the failure of Mary to reappear. In the crisis of late May 1683, when she had almost bled to death, she had sworn that she would return as a spirit and help Goodwin for the rest of his life—a vow often repeated later. After her death, therefore, while Goodwin waited for the lowlanders, he waited even more anxiously for Mary. But as weeks and then months went by, it gradually became clear that she would never return. About the time he found his treasure trunks empty, he gave up his last hope of seeing her. Like the treasure and Mr Rich, Mary had vanished beyond recall.

As Goodwin faced these irretrievable losses, he called upon two resources that he had almost lost in the disasters of 1688—his visions and his inner voice. Though his voice was only a vestige of the infallible guide that had once directed him, it sometimes helped him with useful hints, and it once produced a short revelation in doggerel verse. His visions, fortunately, though infrequent, were still vivid; and they were all the more precious because they were his last line of defence against despair.

Along with his voice and his visions, there remained the undamaged promise that Queen Anne would marry him—a promise reiterated in early August 1703, when he attended church with the Queen at Windsor Castle. The Queen made no overt advances, however, and by January 1704, Goodwin was almost desperate enough to tell her his great secret—to recount to her the things he had once told her sister Queen Mary and to exhort her, as he had once exhorted King William, to avenge the judicial murders committed by Charles II and James II. But once again his inner voice wisely cautioned him against making hasty declarations. His treatises, once given to Queen Mary and later inherited by William, had now come into the possession of Queen Anne, his voice said. Already apprised of his divine mission, she would come to him in due time.

Although Queen Anne continued to conceal her affection for

Goodwin, she did not conceal her disillusion with the High Tories—the Anglican zealots who seemed more anxious to attack the Dissenters than the French. Although a strong Anglican herself, she found that Marlborough, her General, and Godolphin, her Lord Treasurer, could not wage war against the French with a ministry full of High Tories. Inevitably she began replacing High Tories with moderates, while her ministers relied more and more upon Whig support.[46] Goodwin would not live to see his friends return to power or to see Tom made Earl of Wharton and Lord Lieutenant of Ireland; but in April 1704, with the dismissal of his old enemy Nottingham, he could see that the tide had turned—that Queen Anne would soon be forced to conduct Whig policies with Whigs.

Meanwhile, at his home in Denmark Street, he faced a crisis with his son Hezekiah, who had become his sole responsibility since Mary's death.[47] The boy, now about sixteen, had been brought up under the surname *Knowles* in order to conceal his true identity from the world, and his status had necessarily been equivocal. In the months that followed Mary's death, Goodwin found him 'very rebellious', and in February 1704, the boy ran away, 'mad', to sea. Fortunately, Goodwin's political influence and experience in Admiralty matters enabled him, with God's help, to get Hezekiah back again; and after a few months, he believed he had made great progress in reforming him.

Before he had completed the process, however, he had to deal with his sister Philadelphia, whom the Lord declared to be 'the hardest person upon earth to reclaim'. Philadelphia (who had married another Scotsman, Captain John Ramsay,[48] after the death of Sir George Lockhart) paid Goodwin an extended visit beginning in June 1704; and Goodwin, who remembered only too clearly their escapades as children, still distrusted her sexual morals as well as her general character. Though she was now forty-nine years old, he suspected her of wishing to debauch Hezekiah. It would be no small task, he saw, to reform his 'wicked sister' and thus 'countermine Satan's policy'.

Happily, the very attempt to save Philadelphia brought Goodwin, after an episode of terror, into a state of beatitude—a new and lasting sense of grace. One night as he worried about her, the Lord sent him a horrific vision—a nightmare that encapsulated his worst fears. God, it seemed, had withdrawn totally from the world, removing from Goodwin the very 'light of the hemisphere'. Immersed in absolute blackness, Goodwin woke 'in great agony' to find himself still alone and still in blank darkness. Terrified, he rose from his bed and felt his way to the only available help—a written guarantee against the power of devils. As he clutched this covenant (once given him by the Lord), the idea occurred to him that perhaps his dreadful dream was a duplicate of a vision inflicted on Philadelphia. God, he thought, was helping him reclaim his sister by showing her the hopelessness of a black, abandoned world; and He was sending Goodwin the same vision to show what horrors Philadelphia was suffering.

Soothed by the thought, Goodwin gradually recovered from despair, and before morning he became conscious of God's presence once more, vividly sensing that the Lord had been 'pleased to return'. Soon he was to find that the Lord's return was permanent. As if cleansed by his terror, Goodwin began to experience a new conviction of acceptance—a final emergence from the shadows of conflict and doubt that had clouded the finest of his earlier triumphs. He had begun to learn, as he wrote in his very last journal entry, 'what it was to walk close with God all the day long'.

Goodwin could not have found a better time to achieve a sense of grace. His health had deteriorated further since Mary's death. If the end was not yet clearly in sight, it nevertheless lurked not far away. Now, in God's presence, he could face it courageously. He proved fortunate too in his political concerns. On 2 August 1704 the Duke of Marlborough and Prince Eugene had made the world safe for Whigs by smashing a huge French army at Blenheim, taking thousands of prisoners, and permanently altering the balance of military power. Since Goodwin had spent most of his public life combating Louis XIV and his Jacobite allies, the overwhelming victory at Blenheim served as an appropriate end to his political career.

Before Goodwin could leave what he had once called 'this foolish world,' he had the duty of providing for his 'much reclaimed' son Hezekiah. This he did in a will dated 30 September 1704.[49] Since he had never formally recognized or legitimatized the boy, he could not leave him the hereditary Wharton estates. These went to Tom. He could, however, leave

Hezekiah the town house at St. Giles, the nearby houses on Lloyd's Court, one estate in Cumberland, much movable property (including plate and jewels), about £1,500 in cash and notes, and the arrears of rent due on all the manors. To this handsome bequest, Goodwin added a gift of social prestige. By describing the boy as 'my dear son Hezekiah, lawfully begotten', he provided a public testimonial to the boy's legitimacy and gave him an informal right to the surname *Wharton*.

In the few days remaining to him after making his will, Goodwin also provided Hezekiah with a suitable occupation. Perhaps remembering that his brother Henry had also been wild and rebellious but nevertheless a fine officer, Goodwin got his son a commission in the army. On 20 October 1704, a few days before Goodwin's death, the official warrant was issued, and young Hezekiah, listed as Hezekiah Knowles, became an ensign in Colonel Roger Elliot's infantry regiment.[50]

Blessedly unprophetic—unaware that his son would survive him only seven years[51] and that all of his property, after descending to Tom, would be lost by his scatter-brained nephew Philip—Goodwin died on 25 October 1704,[52] full of hope and trust. Although he had been at odds with his family most of his adult life, he had finally forgiven them all, and in the end he chose to be buried with them at St. Paul's, Wooburn, where he had been christened fifty-one years earlier. Since the family wall monument, ordered by Lord Wharton, was already completed, Goodwin's name could not appear with those of his father, his mother, his stepmother, his grandfather Arthur Goodwin, and his half-brother William. It was enough, however, that his burial was faithfully recorded, on 28 October, and that his body would lie among the Whartons. Having written an autobiography that would reveal his hidden glory, Goodwin had no need of a stone memorial.

ABBREVIATIONS

1. *List of abbreviations commonly used in the citation of book titles and of manuscripts*

Add.	Additional
BL	British Library
Corr.	Correspondence
CSP, Dom.	*Calendar of State Papers, Domestic*
CTB	*Calendar of Treasury Books*
DNB	*Dictionary of National Biography*
HCJ	*Journal of the House of Commons*
HEH	Henry E. Huntington Library
HLJ	*Journal of the House of Lords*
HMC	Historical Manuscripts Commission
HS	Harleian Society
MS, MSS	Manuscript, manuscripts
OED	*Oxford English Dictionary*
PR	Parish Register
PRO	Public Record Office
RCHM	Royal Commission of Historical Monuments
SP	State Papers
VHC	*Victoria History of the Counties of England*

2. *List of Books and Manuscripts cited by Short Titles*

Autobiography	The Autobiography of Goodwin Wharton, BL, Add. MSS 20,006–7.
Burnet	Gilbert Burnet, *Bishop Burnet's History of His Own Time*, ed. Martin Joseph Routh, 2nd edn., 6 vols. (Oxford, 1833).
Carte	Bodleian Library, Carte MSS.
CB	*Complete Baronetage*, ed. G. E. C. [okayne], 5 vols. (Exeter, 1900–6).
Clarendon Corr.	*The Correspondence of Henry Hyde, Earl of Clarendon, and of His Brother Laurence Hyde, Earl of Rochester*, ed. Samuel Singer, 2 vols. (London, 1828).

CP — *The Complete Peerage of England, Scotland, Ireland, Great Britain, and the United Kingdom*, ed. G. E. C. [okayne], rev. edn., 12 vols. (London, 1910–59).

Dalton — *English Army Lists and Commission Registers, 1661–1714*, ed. Charles Dalton, 6 vols. (London, 1892–1904).

E. R. Wharton — E. R. Wharton, *The Whartons of Wharton Hall* (Oxford, 1898).

Evelyn — *The Diary of John Evelyn*, ed. E. S. de Beer, 6 vols. (Oxford, 1955).

Grey, *Debates* — Anchitell Grey, *Debates of the House of Commons from the Year 1667 to the Year 1694*, 10 vols. (London, 1763).

Grey, *Secret History* — Ford Grey, Earl of Tankerville, *The Secret History of the Rye-House Plot and of Monmouth's Rebellion*, 2nd edn. (London, 1754).

Kennett — White Kennett, *A Complete History of England*, 3 vols. (London, 1706).

Langley — Thomas Langley, *The History and Antiquities of the Hundred of Desborough* (London, 1797).

Luttrell — Narcissus Luttrell, *A Brief Historical Relation of State Affairs from September 1678 to April 1714*, 6 vols. (Oxford, 1857).

Macaulay — Thomas Babington Macaulay, 1st Baron Macaulay, *The History of England from the Accession of James the Second*, 6 vols. (London, 1913–15).

Memoirs of TW — *Memoirs of the Life of the Most Noble Thomas, Late Marquess of Wharton* (London, 1715).

Parl. Diary	*The Parliamentary Diary of Narcissus Luttrell, 1691–1693,* ed. Henry Horwitz (Oxford, 1972).
Parl. Hist.	*The Parliamentary History of England*, ed. William Cobbett, 36 vols. (London, 1806–20).
POAS	*Poems on Affairs of State, Augustan Satirical Verse, 1660–1714,* gen. ed. George deF. Lord, 7 vols. (New Haven, Conn., 1963–75).
Rawlinson	Bodleian Library, Rawlinson MSS.
State Trials	*A Complete Collection of State Trials*, ed. T. B. Howell, 21 vols. (London, 1811–26).
Survey of London	Greater London Council, *Survey of London*, vol. i– (London, 1900–).

NOTES

Chapter 1: The Slough of Despond

1. Autobiography, i. 9, 12.
2. For the text of Goodwin's speech, see Carte 109, fol. 396; Grey, *Debates*, vii. 448–9. For Goodwin's comments in 1686, see Autobiography, i. 14.
3. For biographies of Lord Wharton, see Bryan Dale, *The Good Lord Wharton* (London, 1901; 2nd edn., enlarged, 1906), and G. F. Trevallyn Jones, *Saw-Pit Wharton* (Sydney, 1967).
4. For Wooburn Manor and St. Paul's, Wooburn, see Langley, pp. 436–71; John March-Penney, *The Story of Wooburn, Buckinghamshire* (privately printed, 1971); George Lipscomb, *The History and Antiquities of the County of Buckingham*, London, 1847, iii, 633–8; [F. B. Ashley], *Pen and Pencil Sketches by Nemo* (London, 1889), pp. 171–241; *VHC Buckinghamshire*, London, iii, 1925, 105–12; RCHM, *Buckinghamshire*, London, i, 1912, 322–4. Two vital source documents are the will of Arthur Goodwin (1638), with 1642 codicil (Carte 109, fols. 398–9, 402), and the marriage contract (1673) between Thomas Wharton and Anne Lee (Bodleian Library, Add. MS D. 40).
5. Goodwin says that his father spent £40,000 in rebuilding the house (Autobiography, ii. 55).
6. Richard Broke to Lord Wharton, 1 Mar. 1672/3, Rawlinson 50, fol. 237.
7. Autobiography, i. 7; ii. 55–6.
8. E. R. Wharton, p. 44.
9. British Patent Office, *Specifications of Patents, Old Series*, London, 1857, no. 189; no. 189*. See also George Thornbury and Edward Walford, *Old and New London*, London, vi, n.d., 15.
10. Autobiography, i. 9.
11. Ibid. i. 9–10.
12. *Specifications of Patents*, no. 185.
13. For Goodwin's negotiations with Argyll (whence my description of the wreck), see Carte 109, fols. 430–2. For recent theories about the identity of the still-unsalvaged galleon, see Alexander McKee, *From Merciless Invaders* (London, 1963), pp. 270–2; Colin Martin, *Full Fathom Five, Wrecks of the Spanish Armada* (London, 1975), pp. 58, 274; Bryce S. Walker *et al.*, *The Armada* (Alexandria, Va., 1981), p. 152.
14. For a concise history of alchemy, see F. Sherwood Taylor, *The*

Alchemists (New York, 1949); Lynn Thorndike, *A History of Magic and Experimental Science*, New York, viii, 1958, 352–402.

15. Autobiography, i. 9, 10.

16. Ibid. i. 15–16, 118; ii. 27.

17. Rawlinson, 53, fol. 209.

18. Anne Lee was baptized at Spelsbury 24 Aug. 1659 (John Carswell, *The Old Cause*, London, 1954, p. 365).

19. John Wilmot, the famous (2nd) Earl of Rochester, was the half-brother of Anne's father Sir Henry Lee.

20. Autobiography, i. 10–11. For Lord Wharton's negotiations on Goodwin's behalf, see Rawlinson 51, fols. 25, 39, 41, 98, 99, 116; Rawlinson 53, fols. 29, 34, 35, 50, 180, 209.

21. For Goodwin's early difficulties with Lady Wharton, see Autobiography, i. 2, [353]; ii. 27, 28, 30, 43–4.

22. For letters from the boys and their tutors to Lord Wharton, see Rawlinson 49 and 54. For secondary accounts, see Arnold G. Matthews, 'The Wharton Correspondence', *Transactions of the Congregational Historical Society*, London, x, 1927–9, 52–65; John Walter Stoye, *English Travellers Abroad, 1604–1667* (London, 1952), pp. 419–28.

23. Christened 29 June 1662 (PR, St. Giles-in-the-Fields, London).

24. *Memoirs of TW*, p. 21.

25. For the best study of Tom's political career, see Carswell, *Old Cause*, pp. 39–127.

26. For Tom and his horses, see John Philip Hore, *The History of Newmarket and the Annals of the Turf*, London, iii, 1886, 90–370 *passim*; Carte 233, fols. 48, 49, 51, 161, 250, 256; Macaulay, v. 2403; Carswell, *Old Cause*, pp. 46–8. Tom's famous horses included Careless, Willey, Snail, Colchester, and the Wharton Gelding.

27. Tom's entertainment of his friends at Winchendon scandalized the neighbourhood. 'I heare to my Griefe', writes Robert Bennett to Lord Wharton (1 June 1674), 'that Religion is gone from Winchingdon, already. . . . Tis said they have brought the Court into the Country, which these parts have not beene acquainted with' (Rawlinson 51, fol. 96).

28. See 'Of an Elegy Made by Mrs. Wharton on the Earl of Rochester', *The Poems of Edmund Waller*, ed. G. Thorn Drury, 2nd edn., New York, 1901, ii. 89.

29. For Anne's poetry, never collected, see 'Love's Martyr, or Witt above Crowns' (unpublished five-act tragedy), BL, Add. MS 28,693; John Sheffield, Marquis of Normanby (later Duke of Buckingham), *The Temple of Death* (London, 1695), pp. 224–31,

238–52; *The Poetical Works of Philip, the late Duke of Wharton* (1731?), ii. 63–92; Horace Walpole, *A Catalogue of the Royal and Noble Authors of England, Scotland, and Ireland*, London, 1806, iii. 286–7; Edward Young (father of the famous poet), *The Idea of Christian Love* (London, 1688), pp. vii–xxxii; *Ovid's Epistles, Translated by Several Hands* (London, 1712), pp. 160–9.

30. *Autobiography*, i. 307–8.

31. Anne Wharton to Tom Wharton, 1 Apr. 1681, in Walpole, *Catalogue*, iii. 284–5; 10 Apr. 1681, HMC, *Lonsdale*, p. 96.

32. Goodwin says (i. 308) that Anne had a brief love affair with 'Jack How' (John Grubham Howe, 1657–1722), that in her youth she was 'lain with long by her own uncle my Lord Rochester', and that she was seduced 'whilst mighty young' by the Earl of Peterborough. These allegations are hard to evaluate, however, since Goodwin does not say where he got his information. The fact that he added the story of Anne's affairs in a marginal note, probably written in late 1687, after he had begun to receive revelations, makes me suspect that some of the allegations (especially those against Peterborough and Rochester) came from his 'inner voice'.

33. See letters of Gilbert Burnet to Anne Wharton, 14 July 1681 to 15 Jan. 1683, in James Granger, *Letters between the Rev. James Granger . . . and Many of the Most Eminent Literary Men of His Time* (London, 1805), pp. 220–52.

Chapter 2: Mary Tomson Boucher Lawrence Parish

1. For Goodwin's early meetings with Mrs Parish and his 45,000-word account of her life, see *Autobiography*, i. 18–67. Specific page references will not be cited for material drawn from this section.

2. Charles II was born 29 May 1630.

3. My summary of Mrs Parish's life is derived almost exclusively from her own account, as retold by Goodwin. None of her letters seem to have survived, and the public documents that mention her are pitifully few. The problem of finding such documents is complicated by the fact that she seldom dates the events of her life and almost never gives Christian names.

4. The PR of St. Mary's, Turville, shows no trace of any *Tomsons* (*Thomsons* or *Thompsons*) during the relevant period. It does record, however, the marriage of *Mary Cox* (Mrs Parish's maternal grandmother) to *Richard West* on 8 April 1605. (See also *Buckinghamshire Parish Registers, Marriages*, ed. W. P. W. Phillimore and Thomas Gurney, London, vi, 1910, 154.) The PR also records, in an entry for 2 June 1603, the death of one John

Cox, who may very well be Mrs Parish's maternal grandfather, the first husband of Mary Cox. As the PR shows, Richard and Mary West went on to have at least two children of their own—a son, also named Richard, baptized 5 Jan. 1606, and a daughter Agnes, christened 23 Sept. 1609. Agnes died as an infant, but Richard grew up, married, and fathered three daughters whose christenings appear in the Turville PR. Mrs Parish's remarkable stepgrandfather Richard West 'the Elder' (as the PR lists him) was buried at Turville on 31 Dec. 1639.

5. Mrs Parish told Goodwin that she had been brought up a Catholic by her mother, without her father's knowledge; but she did not explain how her mother accomplished this extraordinary feat. It seems likely that Mr Tomson was Catholic and that Mrs Parish 'improved' his religion to make her family more acceptable to Goodwin's aristocratic and anti-Catholic biases.

6. Mary told Goodwin that while she was at Hackney she met the sister of Thomas Osborne, later Earl of Danby, and accompanied the young lady on a visit to France; but this story is apparently false, since Danby's only sister died in 1636 (when Mary Thomson was 6 years old). See Andrew Browning, *Thomas Osborne, Earl of Danby and Duke of Leeds*, Glasgow, i, 1951, 9, 19.

7. In giving 'counsel and advice', Mary explained to Goodwin, 'she would endeavour to avoid the name she hated of fortune-teller—though being but a woman and never having a true friend to take her part . . . she would by rude rascals sometimes be called by that name, though none often dared do it to her face.'

8. A marriage license, recorded in the registry of the Vicar-General of Canterbury, establishes the date of Mary's marriage to Parish, supplies Parish's Christian name, and provides other useful information. The license reads: 'Parish, Thomas, of St. Paul, Covent Garden, gent., widower, about 50, and Mary Lawrence, of St. Sepulchre, London, widow, about 40—at Bow or Bromley, Middlesex. 14 June 1669' (*London Marriage Licences, 1521–1869*, ed. Joseph Foster, London, 1887, p. 1015).

9. The time of Mary's alleged association with Williams can be roughly dated by the fact that it began before Williams was made a baronet (12 Nov. 1674) and apparently continued some time afterwards—'above two years' in all. Mary told Goodwin that she had advised Williams against accepting a title and that she had chided him for taking the oaths of Allegiance and Supremacy when he was in fact a Catholic. For references to Williams— including appointments, honours, and grants—see *CSP, Dom., 1668–69*, pp. 70, 73, 98, 224, 315; *1672–73*, p. 229; [Andrew

Marvell], *A Seasonable Argument to Perswade All the Grand Juries in England to Petition for a New Parliament* (Amsterdam, 1677), p. 10; Luttrell, i. 23; Edward Chamberlayne, *Angliae Notitia* (London, 1687), pt. 1, p. 158; above, pp. 213, 218.

10. No Sir John Tomson (Thompson or Thomson) who could have been Mrs Parish's uncle appears in any of the lists of knights created by Charles II, nor is the name mentioned by astrologers William Lilly and Sir George Wharton in their accounts of prominent English spiritualists and adepts. There is, however, a tantalizing reference to a spiritualist named 'Jo. Tompson' in the diary of Elias Ashmole. In an entry for 27 Sept. 1652, Ashmole says: 'I came to Mr. Jo. Tompson, who dwelt near Dove Bridge; he used a call [i.e. a summons for spirits], and had responses in a soft voice.' See *The Diary and Will of Elias Ashmole*, ed. R. T. Gunther (Oxford, 1927), p. 49 (Old Ashmolean Reprints, ii). For the best modern account of magic in the seventeenth century, see Keith Thomas, *Religion and the Decline of Magic* (London, 1971).

11. The victim in the case, a girl named Partridge, had suffered from seizures, during which 'she would often vomit up toads, pins, nails, frogs, and many other things, to everybody's wonder'—a performance all the more remarkable because she 'hardly ate the least thing whatever'.

12. The distinctive house which Goodwin calls 'King John's Castle' is still extant. Now called 'King John's Palace' and classified as a historical monument, it stands in eastern Colnbrook. According to RCHM, it was built 'in the 16th or early 17th century', with some later additions to south and west wings (RCHM, *Middlesex*, London, 1937, p. 118; see also pl. 27, picture 15). For additional comment, see Michael Robbins, *Middlesex* (London, 1953), p. 336.

Chapter 3: George Whitmore and the Lowlanders

Much of the material and *all* of the direct quotations used in Chapter 3 come from Autobiography, i. 66–79. Specific page references will not be given for material drawn from this section.

1. In the early days of his association with Mary Parish, Goodwin was not careful about recording precise dates. Where such dates can be clearly deduced from the information he gives, they have been supplied without comment.

2. For the death of Henry Glover at the hands of James Lashley, see the Gaol Delivery Register for 6 Dec. 1682, *Middlesex County Records*, ed. John C. Jeaffreson, London, iv, 1892, 188.

3. It surprised Goodwin to find that George, whom he had supposed

immaterial, should be bothered by rain. He learned from Mary, however, that spirits are not insubstantial but merely composed of a more rarified substance than mortals. Thus, although George could pass through solid walls, the task was relatively difficult. Water he found particularly annoying. Upon returning one day from the lowlands through a flood, he looked (Mary said) 'as if he had been cleansing a muddy pond'.

4. Shire Lane was a small street which began at the Strand, where the Courts of Justice now stand, and ran northwest to Lincoln's Inn Fields. See *A Survey of London by John Stow*, ed. Charles L. Kingsford, Oxford, 1908, ii. 22.

5. Goodwin does not tell precisely where in the Temple his room was located; he says only that his chamber was 'four pair of stairs high' and that he sublet it from a gentleman.

6. Goodwin does not explain what a 'black bone' cat is. Perhaps he means a cat barred with streaks of black.

7. Mary's information on the tastes of fairies coincides with that of astrologer William Lilly, who notes, 'The *Fairies* love the Southern Side of Hills, Mountains, Groves.—Neatness and Cleanliness in Apparel, a strict Diet, an upright Life, fervent Prayers unto God' (*Mr. William Lilly's History of His Life and Times, from the Year 1602 to 1681*, London, 1715, p. 103).

8. On 18 Sept. 1683 Goodwin learned that lowlanders are actually the size of ordinary humans and that they make themselves *appear* smaller with a special 'breastplate'—a device 'which contracts the sight from all parts to a point' and thus demagnifies its wearer (Autobiography, i. 100).

9. The failure to pay off the lodgings in Shire Lane led, in late Sept., to a brush with two bailiffs, who tried to seize Mary for debt. Goodwin drew his sword and cut one of the men on the hand before they identified themselves; then he managed to 'accommodate the business' with some money his father had given him (Autobiography, i. 101).

10. For the 'physic garden' at Westminster, maintained by the Society of Apothecaries, see Evelyn, iii. 217 and n. In 1676 the Society began to remove plants from Westminster for a new medical garden at Chelsea (which still flourishes), but in May 1683 the Westminster site provided enough 'stinking aridge' to treat the Queen of the lowlanders.

11. The plant in question, now known as 'stinking orach', or motherwort, was used in treating diseases of the uterus (*OED*).

12. 'Holy Thursday' is another term for Ascension Day, 40 days after Easter.

13. The PR for St. Sepulchre (Guildhall Library, PR 7219, vol. i) records the burial of one *Vincent Lawrence* on 11 Oct. 1668. Since *Vincent* was the only male Lawrence buried at St. Sepulchre's in 1668 and since the date fits with Mary's statement (Autobiography, i. 36) that Lawrence died less than a year before her marriage to Parish (14 June 1669), this entry seems to establish Vincent Lawrence as Mary's second husband. On the other hand, the St. Sepulchre PR shows no *Lawrence* or *Boucher* children on its long, melancholy list of burials during the plague months (1 Nov. 1664 to 1 Feb. 1666). If Mary lost 14 (or any) children during the plague, they were not buried at St. Sepulchre's. An entry in the PR for 25 Mar. 1667 records the burial of Debora, daughter of 'Thomas and Mary Lawrence', but I think the Mary Lawrence involved here is not Mary Tomson Boucher Lawrence.

Chapter 4: Sex and Buried Treasure

For quotations from Goodwin Wharton, see Autobiography, i. 78–98.

1. For Hounslow Heath, see *VHC Middlesex*, London, i, 1969, map between pp.2–3; iii, 1962, 94–5; Robbins, *Middlesex*, pp. 298–301. Heathrow Airport now occupies a small portion of the old Heath. Very likely the entrance to the lowlands, as described by Mary Parish, now lies under the concrete of an airport runway.
2. Goodwin's inn lay just east of the Hounslow parish church, on the site now occupied by the Red Lion hotel and restaurant.
3. Luttrell, i. 260.
4. Goodwin, an inveterate engineer, suggested that a small watertight building should be erected over the entrance to the lowlands, thus preventing floods and making access possible in all weather. The lowlanders were impressed by the scheme, but they never got around to implementing it.
5. The preoccupation with buried treasure derives from a time, before banks and banknotes, when people often buried money and sometimes forgot the exact location or died without revealing it. According to a lively Bucks tradition, Lord Wharton temporarily lost a huge sum he had buried at Wooburn (E. R. Wharton, p. 39).
6. Although Mary Parish and Father Friar were the only adepts who could open the earth above treasure with hazel sticks (or 'rods'), other experts employed such rods in *finding* treasure. In 1634, astrologers William Lilly and John Scott used hazel-wood '*Mosaical* Rods' to locate an irretrievable treasure in the cloister of Westminster Abbey (*Lilly's History*, p. 33).
7. Mary's fall was particularly dangerous, Goodwin says, because she had 'now grown fat and heavy'. Her added pounds, perhaps

the result of good food and regular meals, later became important as camouflage for pregnancy.

8. For Cliveden in the seventeenth century, see Sir Reginald T. Blomfield, *A History of Renaissance Architecture in England, 1500–1800*, London, 1897, ii. 190–1; Lipscomb, *Buckingham*, iii. 296–7.

9. Thomas Wharton to the Earl of Bridgwater, 3 Sept. 1683; Bridgwater to Wharton, 6 Sept. 1683 (Carte 81, fols. 726, 727).

10. Goodwin does not say whether Mary received independent confirmation of her husband's death. He merely relates the story she attributed to George, and notes in the margin that the date of Parish's death was 17 June. I have found no record of the death of a Thomas Parish on or about that date.

Chapter 5: John Wildman and the Angels

For quotations from Goodwin Wharton, see Autobiography, i. 99–121.

1. Luttrell, i. 294–5.

2. Goodwin's older sister Margaret (called 'Pegg' as a child) was married, 26 June 1673, to Major Dunch, who owned 'vast' estates around Pusey, Berkshire. Dunch died (aged 28) 27 Sept. 1679, leaving Margaret with four children (Wharton, Margaret, Major, and Mary). Goodwin considered his 'Sister Dunch' Lord Wharton's favourite daughter. For her education at Wooburn, see Rawlinson 49, fol. 14; for her marriage to Dunch, see *Buckinghamshire PR* v, 1909, 73; for the Dunch genealogy, see *Miscellanea Genealogica et Heraldica*, ed. Joseph J. Howard, 3rd Ser., London, ii, 1898, 44–8; for the Pusey estates, see *VHC Berkshire*, London, iv, 1924, 473–4; for the burial of Major Dunch (11 Oct. 1679), see Pusey PR, PRO, Reading, Berkshire. For later references to Margaret and her children, see above, pp. 202, 213, and below, pp. 355 n. 28, 373 n. 23.

3. According to Thomas Gilbert, who wrote Major Dunch's epitaph, the young man was skilled in languages, humane letters, law, and politics (Elias Ashmole, *The Antiquities of Berkshire*, London, 1723, i. 173–4; Rawlinson 51, fol. 242). Goodwin, however, found Dunch lazy and 'humorsome', uninclined to 'trouble' himself; and it was for this reason that his spirit failed to appear when summoned.

4. Dr Israel Tonge (1621–1680) is known principally as one of the fabricators of the Popish Plot, but he also had interests in alchemy and astrology. Goodwin, who shared Tonge's political and

scientific passions, seems to have known him well (as the attempt to recall his spirit implies). In an extant letter to Lord Wharton, Goodwin says that he has been 'several times Att Dct. Tongues' (Carte 233, fols. 293–4).

5. Goodwin's 'Mr Trott' is either John or Edmund Trott, elder and younger son, respectively, of Sir John Trott, Bt., of Southampton (*CB* iii. 125; *Alumni Oxonienses . . . 1500–1714*, ed. Joseph Foster, Oxford and London, iv, 1892, 1512). One of the two young men was in Paris in 1665 under the guidance of John Panton when Goodwin and Tom were there under the tutelage of Panton's friend Abraham Clifford (letters of Abraham Clifford to Lord Wharton, Rawlinson 49, fol. 160; 54, fols. 45, 57).

6. For a modern biography, see Maurice Ashley, *John Wildman, Plotter and Postmaster* (London, 1947). I am heavily indebted to Ashley for my sketch of Wildman's political career. Unfortunately, Ashley had not read Goodwin's account and hence knew nothing of Wildman's ventures with alchemy, spirits, and lowlanders.

7. 'The Agreement of the People' and 'The Case of the Armie Truly Stated', *The Leveller Tracts 1647–1653*, ed. William Haller and Godfrey Davies (New York, 1944), pp. 64–87; Joseph Frank, *The Levellers* (Cambridge, Mass., 1955), pp. 132–46.

8. Ashley, *Wildman*, pp. 103, 258; will of John Wildman, drawn 14 Oct. 1670, probated 30 May 1712, PRO, Prob 11/527, fols. 91–4.

9. Ashley, *Wildman*, pp. 158–9, 167–71.

10. For seventeenth-century Whig and Tory versions of the Rye House Plot, see Grey, *Secret History*, and [Bishop Thomas Sprat], *A True Account and Declaration of the Horrid Conspiracy against the Late King, His Present Majesty, and the Government* (London, 1685).

11. The report on Goodwin and Wildman is summarized in a letter, dated 12 Mar. 1684, from Roger L'Estrange to Secretary Leoline Jenkins. After writing of various suspicious characters 'come lately to town', L'Estrange says: 'A young man [Goodwin] has lodged two or three months in Vere Street at the house of —— Newel, a tailor and a sergeant of the trained band, a very honest man. He [Goodwin] has never stirred abroad. Nobody knows what he is, only a lass in the house was saying he looked like a woman in man's clothes. He is visited twice or thrice a week by Major [John] Wildman, who stays commonly two or three hours. He [Wildman] leaves his coach and servants in the next street out of sight of the door and neither the lodger nor the visitor is known to any in the house' (*CSP, Dom., Oct. 1683–Apr. 1684*, p. 321).

This short report indicates that Goodwin (who never describes himself) was small and slight, 'like a woman in man's clothes'. It emphasizes the fact that Goodwin (always in danger of being arrested for debt) tried to keep his identity secret.

12. Among the seventeenth-century adepts who claimed communication with angels was 'old *Mr. William Hodges*', who (says William Lilly) could call upon '*Raphael, Gabriel* and *Uriel*'. Unfortunately, Lilly adds, Hodges' personal life 'answered not in Holiness and Sanctity to what it should, having to deal with those holy Angels' *(Lilly's History*, pp. 49–50).

Chapter 6: Delivery and Execution

For quotations from Goodwin Wharton, see Autobiography, i. 121–35.

1. Although Goodwin does not say so, Mr Abab's French must have been as unintelligible as his English. Goodwin himself spoke excellent French (Jacques Le Fevre to Lord Wharton, 6 Oct. 1664, Rawlinson 49, fol. 238); he was tutored in the language from early childhood, and he spent three years in France. He had also mastered Latin (Robert Bennett to Lord Wharton, 9 Feb. 1669, Rawlinson 50, fol. [46]).

2. Wild House (on Wild Street, near Lincoln's Inn Fields) was the residence of the Spanish ambassador, who was allowed to maintain a Catholic chapel. For a description of Wild House in the seventeenth century, see *Survey of London*, v, pt. 2, 93–7.

3. For seventeenth- and early eighteen-century maps and sketches of Somerset House, see John Strype, *A Survey of the Cities of London and Westminster*, London, 1720, Bk. iv, between pp. 108–9; Raymond Needham and Alexander Webster, *Somerset House Past and Present* (New York, 1906), frontispiece; pp. 144, 170. By custom, Somerset House was the property of the English queens.

4. One of Goodwin's few serious errors in dating occurs in his account of the Armstrong episodes (Autobiography, i. 127–8). He places the events in May (1684), whereas they actually took place in June. Apparently he failed to date his notes and then allowed them to get out of order.

5. For Armstrong's arrest, 'trial', and execution, see *DNB*; *CSP, Dom., May 1684–Feb. 1685*, pp. 47–80 *passim*; Luttrell, i. 309–12; *State Trials*, x. 106–24; *Biographia Britannica*, 2nd edn., ed. Andrew Kippis *et al.*, London, i, 1778, 248–56; Burnet, ii. 418–23; Sprat, *True Account*, pp. 140–5; *London Gazette*, 9–12 June, 12–16 June, 19–23 June 1684.

6. Writing in early 1686, when James II was King and Jeffreys Lord Chancellor, Goodwin was cautious in discussing the justice meted out to Armstrong. 'The business I meddle not with,' he wrote, 'but

it was generally said he had very hard measure.' In 1690, however, he was probably as unrestrained as his fellow Whigs when the House reviewed the case and expelled Sawyer (*Parl. Hist.* v. 516–27; *HCJ* x. 284, 289–90, 311, 337).

7. *Biographia Britannica*, i. 253.

8. Burnet, ii. 421. Armstrong left a paper in which he denied participating in any plot to kill the King or to overthrow the government and declared that he died a Christian, a member of the Church of England (*State Trials*, x. 122–4).

Chapter 7: The Exorcists

For quotations from Goodwin Wharton, see Autobiography, i. 135–57.

1. Contemporary maps show two powder mills on the Crane River near Hounslow—one about a mile southwest of the town and the other about a mile and a half almost due west. From Goodwin's account, I assume it was the latter mill that blew up. See Philippa Glanville, *London in Maps* (London, 1972), pl. 19.

2. Goodwin rented the house from Charles Seymour, Duke of Somerset, who (Goodwin says) had bought the property after the death of Nicholson and kept a mistress there.

3. Goodwin had been baffled in two earlier attempts to see his mother—once in early Apr. (at Wooburn) and once in late June at Lincoln's Inn Fields.

4. While Pen Dennis was resting in Mary's bedroom from the fatigue of his journey from Northend, John Wildman came to visit his partners. When Wildman was told 'who was in the next room on the bed, he was ready to leap out of his skin'. Disappointingly, however, Pen Dennis was not allowed to appear to Goodwin and Wildman, or speak in their presence; he could communicate only with Mary.

Chapter 8: Crime and Punishment

For quotations from Goodwin Wharton, see Autobiography, i. 157–208. Beginning on 1 Jan. 1685, Goodwin became more systematic and accurate in taking and dating his notes; from that day forward, his narrative takes on the character of a day-by-day journal.

1. Goodwin identifies only one of his creditors, a physician named Sir Richard Barker. His major debts included one of more than £100 (paid by Lord Wharton), one of 'above £600', and one 'much greater than both these' combined. For Sir Richard Barker, see Peter Le Neve, *Le Neve's Pedigrees of the Knights*, ed. G. W. Marshall (London, 1873), p. 247 (HS Publications, viii).

2. Apparently Goodwin's new lodgings were located on the west side of town, but Goodwin does not say exactly where.

3. For the weekly regimen of prayers, meditations, sermons, and scriptural readings followed by Goodwin and his brother Tom from early 1662 to Oct. 1664, see the schedule drawn up by their tutor Theophilus Gale, Rawlinson 49, fols. 1–3.

4. Goodwin's pea, of course, was the one that belonged to King Byron. Mary's and Wildman's peas were derived from the planting Goodwin had done in the summer of 1683.

5. The Neat Houses (the houses of market gardeners) were in what is now Pimlico; Tothill Fields occupied the area around what is now Vincent Square. See John Rocque, map of 'London in 1741–5' in *Maps of Old London*, ed. G. E. Mitton (London, 1908); *The Diary of Samuel Pepys*, ed. R. C. Latham and W. Matthews, Berkeley, Calif., ii, 1970, 158 and n.

6. Mary received her message about the impending death of Charles II sometime between 22 and 25 Dec. 1684. Charles actually died on 6 Feb. 1685.

7. For a detailed account of the death of Charles II, see Raymond Crawfurd, *The Last Days of Charles II* (Oxford, 1909). Crawfurd (a fellow of the Royal College of Physicians) concludes that Charles did not die of apoplexy, as his doctors mistakenly supposed, but of 'chronic granular kidney (a form of Bright's disease) with uraemic convulsions' (p. 13). For the political context at the time of Charles's death, see Macaulay, i. 422–32.

8. See Luttrell, i. 338.

9. On 1 Jan. 1687 Goodwin learned that Charles had not been saved after all. Ahab, who had reported the supposed event, had mistaken Charles II for another monarch of the same name.

10. The PR for St. Martin's-in-the-Fields, Apr. 1685, shows no burial of infant quintuplets.

Chapter 9: Wildman's Rebellion

For quotations from Goodwin Wharton, see Autobiography, i. 192–225.

1. Primary sources bearing upon John Wildman's involvement in Monmouth's Rebellion include the confession of Robert Cragg (printed in HMC, *12th Report, App. 6, House of Lords*, pp. 392–408, and cited here as *Cragg's Confession*); Grey, *Secret History*, pp. 76–132; the trial of Henry Booth, Lord Delamere (*State Trials*, xi. 509–600); Burnet, iii. 14–57; HMC, *Stopford-Sackville*, i. 22–9; *Miscellaneous State Papers*, ed. Philip Yorke, 2nd Earl of Hardwicke, London, 1778, ii. 315–32; *CSP, Dom., Feb.–Dec. 1685*, pp. 225–426 *passim*; and CTB viii, Pt. 2, 718,

1065, 1098. See also, *London Gazette*, 21 May–9 July 1685; Luttrell, i. 337–69; letters from James II to the Prince of Orange, in Sir John Dalrymple, *Memoirs of Great Britain and Ireland*, 2nd edn., London, ii, 1773, App. Pt. 1, 123–35.

Two twentieth-century accounts of Wildman's part in the plots are Ashley, *Wildman*, pp. 250–60, and William Richard Emerson, *Monmouth's Rebellion* (New Haven, Conn., 1951), pp. 10–32. The most detailed account and analysis is my own, in the original uncut version of my biography of Goodwin Wharton. See HEH MS, HM 49425, Ch. IX and notes.

For the general story of Monmouth's Rebellion, see Macaulay, ii. 517–661; Sir Winston Churchill, *Marlborough*, New York, i, 1933, 203–25; Bryan Little, *The Monmouth Episode* (London, 1956); Peter Earle, *Monmouth's Rebels* (New York, 1977).

2. *Cragg's Confession*, p. 393.
3. Ibid. pp. 393–4.
4. Ibid.
5. Ibid. pp. 395–6.
6. Ibid. p. 396.
7. Testimony of John Jones, *State Trials*, xi. 543.
8. Burnet, iii. 15; Ashley, *Wildman*, p. 256.
9. Testimony of John Jones, *State Trials*, xi. 543–4; *Cragg's Confession*, p. 397.
10. *Cragg's Confession*, pp. 398–9.
11. Ibid. pp. 403–4.
12. *State Trials*, xi. 517–18.
13. *Cragg's Confession*, pp. 400, 403. I should add that I have found no evidence that the horses were actually sent.
14. *CSP, Dom., Feb.–Dec. 1685*, p. 157.
15. Testimony of John Jones, *State Trials*, xi. 546.
16. *Cragg's Confession*, p. 403.
17. *London Gazette*, 4–8 June 1685; Luttrell, i. 346; *CSP, Dom., Feb.–Dec. 1685*, p. 198.
18. For Disney's capture, trial, and execution, see *State Trials*, xi. 465–8; for Monmouth's Proclamation and its effect, see Macaulay, ii. 564; for the response of James II, see Dalrymple, *Memoirs*, ii, App. Pt. 1, 128–9; *London Gazette*, 11–15 June 1685.
19. *Cragg's Confession*, pp. 404–5.
20. *CSP, Dom., Feb.–Dec. 1685*, pp. 225–6.
21. Grey, *Secret History*, pp. 131–2.
22. *Cragg's Confession*, p. 405.
23. *CSP, Dom., Feb.–Dec. 1685*, p. 252.
24. Ibid. pp. 269, 271.

25. Ibid. pp. 277, 278.
26. Luttrell, i. 355.
27. *State Trials*, xi. 509–600.

Chapter 10: God and Lord Wharton

For quotations from Goodwin Wharton, see Autobiography, i. 227–78.

1. The fact that Lord Wharton was 'lame' is noted by Goodwin.

2. For a true copy of Lord Wharton's passport, issued 7 Aug. 1685 and signed by Sunderland, see Carte 81, fol. 731. John Howe, prominent Nonconformist minister, accompanied Lord Wharton's party (Dale, *Good Lord Wharton*, p. 49; *DNB*, s.v. Howe, John, 1630–1705). Apparently Lady Wharton did not go abroad, though Lord Wharton's passport authorized her to do so. She was in London on 7 Jan. 1686, when she sneered at Goodwin's poverty; and Goodwin does not mention her during his adventures with his father in Dover and Germany.

3. Letter, in French, Lord Wharton to unnamed correspondent, n.d., Carte 81, fol. 768.

4. Carte 81, fols. 736–8. This long autobiographical letter, written in Latin and addressed (but not sent) to Alexander, Baron von Spaen, Governor of Mark and Cleves under the Elector of Brandenburg, explains Lord Wharton's *real* reasons for leaving England, though it does not mention his fears about the Monmouth affair.

5. For Tom's refusal to support Monmouth's Rebellion, see *Memoirs of TW*, p. 28. Goodwin says (ii. 44) that his father was actually involved in the conspiracy. This statement, made after Goodwin began having internal revelations, is not supported by any detail and is very likely wrong. It is clear, however, that Lord Wharton, who had been falsely accused in the Farnley Wood affair of 1663, feared another accusation.

6. G. F. Trevallyn Jones, who did not read Goodwin's autobiography, mistakenly says (*Saw-Pit Wharton*, p. 254) that Lord Wharton left England in late December 1685. This four-month error in dating skews Jones's otherwise interesting political analysis of the journey (pp. 253–7). The haste with which Lord Wharton left England (18 Aug. 1685) shows the urgency he felt.

7. Carte 81, fols. 736–8. For the Elector's instructions to Baron von Spaen (letter, 7 June 1686), see Carte 81, fol. 579. In leaving for Emmerich, Lord Wharton did not tell his friends his final destination. On 22 Aug. 1685, Robert Harley wrote to his father Sir Edward that 'Lord Wharton is gone to France' (HMC, *Portland*, iii. 387). In October it was rumoured that Lord

Wharton had died on the Continent (HMC, *Report 7*, *App. and Index*, p. 499b).

8. Dalton, ii. 33.

9. *Memoirs of the Verney Family*, comp. Frances Parthenope, Lady Verney and Margaret Maria, Lady Verney, London, iv, 1899, 353; Seymour Schofield, *Jeffreys of 'The Bloody Assizes'* (London, 1935), pp. 160–1.

10. Verney, iv. 354.

11. *The Ellis Correspondence*, ed. George James Wellbore Agar Ellis, 3rd Baron Dover, London, 1829, i. 40–1; Luttrell, i. 371.

12. Apparently Anne's death was very painful. The poet Robert Gould contrasts it dramatically with the peaceful death of her sister Eleanora, who died in 1691:

> But think (for sure you may remember well)
> Think how her Sister, dear *Urania* [Anne], fell,
> When ev'ry Arte'ry, Fibre, Nerve and Vein
> Were by Convulsions torn, and fill'd with Pain.
> We griev'd that there such Cruelty was shown;
> And shall we murmer because here [in Eleanora's death] was none?

'Mirana, a Funeral Eclogue: To the Memory of that Excellent Lady Eleanora, Late Countess of Abingdon', *The Works of Mr. Robert Gould*, London, 1709, i. 349.

13. In recounting events that occurred after 13 Jan. 1686, Goodwin consistently uses Mary's new name *Lucretia*.

14. Jacques Le Fevre, Goodwin's writing instructor, bears early testimony to Goodwin's writing speed: '. . . being of a quick spirited temper [Le Fevre says] and having many things to write . . . he [Goodwin] makes such haste as no scrivener can write faster. . .' (Letter to Lord Wharton, 6 Oct. 1664, Rawlinson 49, fol. 238).

15. *London Gazette*, 11–15 Mar. 1686; Little, *Monmouth Episode*, p. 236.

16. In describing his journey, Goodwin does not mention the lady at Aix. It was not until 20 Aug. 1686, after the angels had told him of a foreign princess who had fallen in love with him during his travels, that he remembered the adventure.

17. During Lord Wharton's visit with the Elector of Brandenburg, he was given 'a fine set of six horses' (E. R. Wharton, p. 35). Abel Boyer says that while Lord Wharton was abroad he solicited the aid of the Prince of Orange to counter the measures of James II, but I have found no evidence for this uncharacteristic action (*The History of King William the Third*, London, i, 1702, 188).

18. Goodwin Wharton to 'Mr. Phillips' in Vienna, 8 July (NS) 1686, Carte 233, fols. 290–1.

Chapter 11: Visions and Revisions

For quotations from Goodwin Wharton, see Autobiography, i. 278–[354].

1. Grafton Street, destroyed in the 1880s to make way for Shaftesbury Avenue and Charing Cross Road, ran northeast from Gerrard Street to Monmouth Street (*Survey of London*, xxiv. 364, 373–4, fig. 84; Edward Hatton, *A New View of London*, London, 1708, i. 34).

2. In 1686, the encampment on Hounslow Heath lasted from 28 May to 11 Aug. (For a map-diagram of the camp, see *POAS* iv, facing p. 170; see also Dalton, ii. 89–91.) The King's army not only ruined Hounslow as a base of operations for Goodwin, but also lost him possession of the Nicholson house, when the owner, the Duke of Somerset, Colonel of the Queen's Regiment of Dragoons, cancelled Goodwin's lease and used the house himself.

3. *State Trials*, xi. 1165–1316.

4. Goodwin was not allowed to accompany Mary 'to Fish Street' until 18 Oct. 1686, and it is not clear whether he actually went inside the Queen's Head tavern even then or whether he waited, as he says he did on 16 Dec., 'at a house close by'. In any case, he could not accompany Mary down to the tavern cellar, since the toilet there was for women only.

5. Red Lion Square, in Bloomsbury, is all that now remains of the once-extensive Red Lion Fields.

6. After Goodwin's unfortunate speech in 1680, Lord Wharton transferred Goodwin's 'interest' to Henry and William—who were both defeated in the Tory landslide of 1685, William in Westmorland and Henry at Malmesbury (William W. Bean, *The Parliamentary Representation of the Six Northern Counties of England*, Hull, 1890, p. 65). Tom, however, was re-elected as Knight of the Shire for Bucks in a memorable contest (*Memoirs of TW*, pp. 28–30; Browning, *Danby*, i. 367–9).

7. In Dec. 1689 (after Henry's death) Tom helped Goodwin become Knight of the Shire for Westmorland, and in July 1698 he helped Goodwin become Knight of the Shire for Bucks, but Goodwin never comments upon the near fulfilment of his vision.

8. Essex Court, on the west side of the Temple, still survives and flourishes.

9. On 7 Nov. 1686 at St. Giles, Goodwin says, 'two of my sisters (Mrs Carr being one) scolded unreasonably at me . . . and went so

far as to call Lucretia [Mary] whore and witch; for which I pray God forgive them.'

10. In the summer of 1682, Tom and Henry had committed one of the most notorious offences of the age. At Barrington, Somersetshire, after several hours of drinking, the pair broke into the village church in the middle of the night and proceeded to desecrate it outrageously. As the Duke of Leeds said many years later, during a debate in the House of Lords, Tom and Henry 'pissed against a Communion Table' and did their 'other occasions' in the pulpit. They also cut the bell rope, tore up a Bible, and defaced some of the ornaments. This incident, which Tom's political foes never allowed him to forget, was reported to Bishop Robert Frampton, who summoned the pair before him, fined them, and made them deliver abject apologies (*The Life of Robert Frampton*, ed. T. S. Evans, London, 1876, pp. 165–8; Carswell, *Old Cause*, pp. 58–9).

11. For the text of 'Ninnies', see *POAS*, iv. 191–214; for the verses about Tom and one of his brothers (probably Goodwin), see ll. 135–74; for an extended discussion of the dating and other editorial problems, see my uncut biography of Goodwin Wharton, HEH, HM 49425, Ch. XI, n. 41. See also, *The Poems of Charles Sackville, Sixth Earl of Dorset*, ed. Brice Harris (New York and London, 1979), pp. 154–6.

12. Henry appears in 'The Lover's Session' (written sometime before Jan. 1687). Among the prominent lovers, the poem says, is '*Harry Wharton* fresh reaking [*sic*] from *Norfolk*'s lewd *Moll*' (i.e. from Mary, the notorious Duchess of Norfolk). See *Poems on Affairs of State*, London, ii, 1703, 157.

Chapter 12: The Inner Voice

Unless otherwise noted, quotations from Goodwin Wharton are taken from Autobiography, ii. 1–31.

1. Apparently there was a 'dark' (public) passage through the grounds of St. James's Palace, between the Mall and Pall Mall.

2. In Feb. 1687, Tom fought and disarmed John Hollis, Lord Houghton, in a duel. As a gesture of peace, Goodwin wrote Tom a letter on that occasion, but he did not get around to posting it. He brought the letter to Wooburn and showed it to Tom as evidence of his own friendly intentions. For Tom's duel with Lord Houghton (later Duke of Newcastle), see Luttrell, i. 395; *Memoirs of TW*, p. 33.

3. Burnet, *Some Letters* (Rotterdam, 1686), p. 38. Burnet's book, full of anti-Catholic propaganda, was banned from England. The fact that Goodwin read it at Wooburn shows that the Whartons had a

copy nevertheless. For the attempt to suppress the book, see Thomas E. S. Clarke and Helen Charlotte Foxcroft, *A Life of Gilbert Burnet* (Cambridge, 1907), p. 229.

4. On 31 July 1687, Goodwin made a summary of Mary's pregnancies, which then totalled 36. Of these, 23 had occurred since the birth of Hezekiah and Susan on 10 Mar. Mary miscarried of 2 children in May and of 12 in June. At the time Goodwin made the summary chart, she was pregnant with 9 more children, but she lost these on 10 Sept.

5. By 16 Aug. 1687, when James set out on a royal progress, his agents had procured (by my count) 54 addresses of thanks from Dissenting groups. These were published, as Court propaganda, in the *London Gazette*, 4 Apr.–22 Aug.

6. Warrants issued from Windsor, 22 May 1687 (*CSP, Dom., Jan. 1686–May 1687*, p. 430).

7. Both of Letitia's parents were dead. Essex Popham Poulett had died when Letitia was an infant, and Lord Poulett had died in June 1679. Letitia was the granddaughter of Lady Wharton's sister Letitia Carr Popham.

8. Sir William Fermor (2nd Bt. and later 1st Baron Leominster) had been married to Letitia's older sister Catherine, who died in the spring of 1687 (*CB* ii. 143; *CP*, s.v. Leominster).

9. Macaulay (v. 2402) makes three errors in four words when he describes the rearing of Tom Wharton. 'Plays and poems [he writes], hunting and dancing, were proscribed by the austere discipline of his [Tom's] saintly family.' About plays Macaulay was right (see above, Ch. 14, pp. 211–12); about everything else, he was wrong. The Wharton children were not merely allowed to dance, they were required to take lessons (Rawlinson 49, fol. 14). They also hunted with their father's blessing (Autobiography, ii. 47) and read such approved poets as Andrew Marvell and John Milton. Anne Wharton was a poet, of course, as was William, Lord Wharton's youngest son (above, Ch. 14, pp. 215–17).

10. Letitia was married the following spring (12 Apr. 1688) to William Monson (later, 1718, 4th Bt.). Her marriage license lists her as 'Letitia Pawlett, of St. Giles-in-the-Fields, Middlesex, spinster, 22, her parents dead. . .' (*London Marriage Licences*, p. 933). Apparently the marriage was childless; at least, there were no surviving children at the time of Sir William's death, 7 Mar. 1727. Letitia died 25 Apr. 1734 (*CB* i. 39).

11. Alexander was married (1679) to Brilliana Harley, daughter of Sir Edward Harley. In 1688, Brilliana confessed on her deathbed that

only the eldest of her 5 children was sired by Alexander and that the rest were the children of a gentleman named Thomas Rutter. On 11 June 1689 a bill (supported by the Whartons and opposed by the Harleys) was brought before the House of Lords 'for illegitimating four of the children of *Brilliana Popham*, late wife of *Alexander Popham*'. On 26 June, the bill was defeated, leaving the children officially legitimate and capable of inheriting the Popham property (*HLJ* xiv. 240, 254; HMC, *12th Report, App. 6, House of Lords*, pp. 133–4; *Memoirs of TW*, p. 10).

12. The most popular *naturalistic* explanation for the Queen's difficulties in producing healthy children was that the notoriously unfaithful James had given her a venereal disease—a view confirmed in one of Goodwin's revelations, which said that James had given the Queen a 'distemper' (ii. 33).

Chapter 13: Mary Beatrice Anne Margaret Isabel of Este

For Goodwin's account of the Bath episode, 10 Sept.–7 Oct. 1687, see Autobiography, ii. 31–43.

1. Queen Mary Beatrice, whose full name (anglicized) appears in my chapter heading, is also known to English history as Mary of Modena and Mary of Este. For biographies, see Agnes Strickland, *Lives of the Queens of England*, London, ix, 1846; x, 1847, 1–237; Marie Hallé [Martin Haile, pseud.], *Queen Mary of Modena* (London, 1905); Carola Oman, *Mary of Modena* (Bungay, 1962). For letters and other documents, see Marchesa Emilia Campana de Cavelli, *Les Derniers Stuarts* (Paris, 1871), 2 vols.

2. Campana de Cavelli, ii. 140; Oman, pp. 101–2.

3. Campana de Cavelli, ii. 145. Laura, Duchess of Modena, died at Rome on 19 July 1687.

4. For late seventeenth-century Bath, see Dr Thomas Guidott, *A Discourse of Bathe* (London, 1676), *De Thermis Britannicis Tractatus Accesserunt Observationes* (London, 1691), and *The Register of Bath* (London, 1694); Dr Robert Pierce, *Bath Memoirs* (Bristol, 1697); Henry Chapman, *Thermae Redivivae; or the City of Bath Described* (1673), reprinted, along with Guidott's tracts, in *A Collection of Treatises Relating to the City and Waters of Bath* (London, 1725); *The Journeys of Celia Fiennes*, ed. Christopher Morris (London, 1947); Samuel Gale, 'A Tour Through Several Parts of England' [1705] in *Bibliotheca Topographica Britannica*, ed. John Nichols, London, iii, 1790, No. 2, pt. 1, 1–48; John Wood, *An Essay Towards a Description of the City of Bath* (Bath, 1742); *A Description of Bath* (London, 1765),

reprinted in Kingsmead Reprints (Bath, 1969); Richard Warner, *The History of Bath* (Bath, 1801). See also two maps drawn by Joseph Gilmore in 1694 from a survey of 1692. The larger of the two is reproduced (much reduced in scale) in David Gadd, *Georgian Summer* (Bath, 1971), pp. 22–3; the smaller map is reproduced in this volume; see Illustrations.

5. During his Western progress James touched more than 5,000 of his subjects for the 'King's Evil' (*London Gazette*, 19–22 Sept. 1687). In Bath his performance alarmed good Anglicans, since he used the Abbey without Bishop Ken's permission, employed a Catholic assistant, and gave the ceremony a popish flavour (see Thomas Ken to Archbishop Sancroft, 26 Aug. 1687; Edward H. Plumptre, *The Life of Thomas Ken, D.D.*, London, 1889, i. 280–1; Warner, *History of Bath*, p. 257).

6. For a detailed description of the Cross Bath, *c.*1687, complete with schematic diagram, see Guidott, *De Thermis Britannicis*, pp. 11–13. The Cross Bath (completely walled) had a small, irregularly shaped pool measuring about 20 feet across its north (gallery) end, about 24 feet along its sides, and about 12 feet along its south end. Protruding from the centre was a stone column, ringed with a 'bordure' of underwater seats. This column replaced an old cross, which had given the Cross Bath its name.

7. The Queen lodged in the old Abbey House (since destroyed), adjacent to the southwest corner of the Abbey.

8. Francis Charles Turner, *James II* (London, 1948), pp. 335–44; Macaulay, ii. 933–55.

9. Strickland, ix. 198; Campana de Cavelli, ii. 140.

10. Goodwin does not say where his lodgings were located. It is clear, however, that he lived on one of the main thoroughfares (probably Cheap Street) and that his windows overlooked the street.

11. The King's Bath was then open to the street and surrounded by lodging houses (see 1675 drawing, reproduced in Gadd, p. 18, from original now hanging in the Pump Room).

12. *London Gazette*, 15–19 Sept. 1687.

13. In his account of the Bath episode Goodwin does not name his friend, whose identity is established later (Autobiography, ii. 49–50).

14. Born Penelope O'Brien, daughter of Barnabas O'Brien, 5th Earl of Thomond, she was the wife of Henry Mordaunt, 2nd Earl of Peterborough.

15. For Alderman Robert Chapman (1624–1701) and his daughters Mary (1661–1721) and Ann (1668–1705), see Warner, *History of Bath*, pp. 212–13, 264, 325–6; *The Registers of the Abbey*

Church of SS. Peter and Paul, Bath, ed. Arthur J. Jewers, London, i, 1900; ii, 1901 (HS Registers, xxvii, xxviii); will of Robert Chapman 'of the City of Bath Apothecary', drawn 17 Sept. 1700, probated 15 July 1701, PRO, Prob 11/461, fol. 34.

16. Cecilia Gay, daughter of John and Susanna Oliver Gay, was christened 10 Aug. 1668, at the Church of St. Giles, Reading, where her parents were married on 18 Sept. 1667 and where her father was buried on 21 Nov. 1668 (PR for St. Giles, microfilm copy no. 088,342, LDS Genealogical Library, Salt Lake City, Utah). John Gay's will, dated 19 Nov. and probated 24 Dec. 1668 (PRO, Prob 11/328, fol. 331) bequeaths Cecilia £130 in cash and two 'Messuages or Tenements' in 'Lincombe and Whitcombe', Somersetshire. On 27 June 1672, Susanna Gay (Cecilia's mother) married Edward Bushell, later Alderman and Mayor of Bath (*London Marriage Licences, 1521–1869*, p. 226).

17. For Edward Bushell, (*c*.1627–1701), his first wife Hester Chapman Bushell (d. 1671), his second wife Susanna Gay Bushell (*c*.1644–94), and his 5 children, see *Registers of Bath Abbey*, i, ii; Warner, *History of Bath*, pp. 212–13; Pierce, *Bath Memoirs*, pp. 374–6; will dated 20 Mar. 1700, probated 25 July 1701, PRO, Prob 11/461, fol. 8.

18. Goodwin later learned that Mary was to collect £15,000 from Sir John Tomson and find a new nurse for Hezekiah before she died.

19. The spectators' gallery of the Cross Bath was about 20 feet long and 8 feet wide.

20. Sidney, Lord Godolphin was also Commissioner of the Treasury; while at Bath, he conducted considerable Crown business (*CTB* viii, pt. 3, 1532–7).

21. For a biography of the Duchess, see Cyril Hughes Hartmann, *La Belle Stuart* (London, 1924).

22. While Goodwin was trying to avert the Queen's death in Bath, her birthday was formally celebrated in London (Luttrell, i. 414).

23. In spite of Goodwin's revelations, Mary Beatrice lived until 7 May 1718 (NS).

24. For Baber, three times Mayor of Bath, and his wife Elizabeth, see Warner, *History*, pp. 212–13; *Registers of Bath Abbey*, i. 47; ii. 400.

25. For the game of 'lottery', a primitive form of roulette, see Charles Cotton, *The Compleat Gamester*, 3rd edn. (London, 1721), p. 24.

26. For the list of Maids, see Edward Chamberlayne, *Angliae Notitia* (1687), pt. 1, pp. 201–2.

27. Sophia Stuart Bulkeley (*c*.1650–*c*.1716) served as a lady of the bedchamber and eventually followed the Queen into exile. She

died in France about 28 years after Goodwin's voice doomed her to an early death (*DNB*, s.v. 'Lady or Mrs' Sophia Bulkeley; Hartmann, *La Belle Stuart*, pp. 4, 159, 251; Pepys, ix, 1976, 294; Oman, pp. 233–4).

28. For the Duchess of Mazarin, see Cyril Hughes Hartmann, *The Vagabond Duchess* (London, 1926) and Hester Wolferstand Chapman, *Privileged Persons: Four Seventeenth-Century Studies* (London, 1966), pp. 181–246.

29. For William Legge, see Dalton, i. 176; ii. 5; Turner, *James II*, p. 212; Evelyn, v. 182 and n.; HMC, *Dartmouth*, *passim*.

30. Goodwin's account (Autobiography, ii. 40–1) seems to be the only extant record of the Queen's farewell appearances in Bath on 3 Oct. 1687.

31. Less than fifteen months after Mary Beatrice left the Cross Bath she was an exile in France, with the son whom she believed the Cross Bath had helped her to conceive. Meantime, in the summer of 1688, the Earl of Melfort employed Thomas Davis to erect an elegant marble structure in the middle of the pool, with an inscription praising the Trinity and the Cross Bath for her conception. This structure (pictured in Warner, opp. p. 315, and described in Wood, *Description of Bath*, pp. 259–62) replaced the old column of Goodwin's time and linked the Queen's name permanently with the Cross Bath. The inscription that is presently on the east facade of the Cross Bath mistakenly asserts that 'the bath derived its present name from a cross erected in its centre in 1688 to commemorate the birth of a child to Mary, wife of James II, subsequent upon her bathing here.' In fact, however, the name *Cross Bath* antedates Mary Beatrice's visit to Bath by more than 150 years. Melfort's monument was removed in 1787 when the Cross Bath was totally redesigned by Thomas Baldwin. See Charles Robertson, *Bath, an Architectural Guide* (London, 1975), pp. 61–2.

32. Dalton, ii. 121.

33. Goodwin's description establishes the date of the Queen's exit from Bath (Tues., 4 Oct. 1687)—a date unknown to Oman (p. 105) and de Beer (Evelyn, iv. 560 n.). Mary Beatrice arrived at Windsor, 'in very good health', on 6 Oct. (*London Gazette*, 6–10 Oct. 1687).

34. Goodwin later believed that he had misunderstood his revelation and that Cecilia was in fact a virgin.

Chapter 14: Prelude to a Warming Pan

Unless otherwise noted, quotations from Goodwin Wharton are taken from Autobiography, ii. 43–63.

1. *London Gazette*, 10–13 Oct. 1687.
2. No one except Goodwin seems to have recorded the extraordinary events of 14 Oct. The *London Gazette* says nothing about the King's birthday, and Luttrell (i. 416) merely notes that it 'was observed by ringing of bells &c., but noe bonefires [*sic*]'.
3. Now Coram Fields.
4. For Sir Thomas Travell (*c*.1657–1724), see Le Neve, *Knights*, p. 385; *Alumni Oxonienses 1500–1714*, iv, 1892, 1503; Dalton, iii. 354; iv. 286; Alfred B. Beaven, *The Aldermen of the City of London*, London, ii, 1913, 79, 80; *Calendar of Marriage Licences Issued by the Faculty Office*, ed. George E. Cokayne and Edward Alexander Fry (London, 1905), p. 72 (British Record Society, *Index Library*, xxxiii); *Obituary Prior to 1800 . . . Compiled by Sir William Musgrave*, ed. Sir George Armytage, London, vi, 1901, 118 (HS Publications, xlix); *HCJ* xii. 83; xiii. 652; xiv. 10, 38; *Parl. Diary*, p. 506. For his committee assignments in Parliament, see *HCJ* x–xvii *passim*. In 1687 Sir Thomas was a widower; his first wife, Elizabeth Pocock Travell, had died sometime after 1684, leaving him with at least one child, a son named John.
5. Mary Howe Soames, daughter of Sir Gabriel Howe of Wotton under Edge, Gloucestershire, became the second wife of Sir William Soames sometime after the death of his first wife, Beata Pope Soames, in 1679 (*CB* iv. 136; Arthur William Hughes Clarke, *London Pedigrees and Coats of Arms*, London, 1935, p. 200; Rawlinson 50, fol. 57). Sir William died at Malta *en route* to Turkey on 12 June 1686 (HMC, *Downshire*, i. 196, 226). Mary, who had accompanied him, returned to London and took a house on Pall Mall (*CTB* viii, pt. 3, 1654), where she was living when Goodwin began courting her. She again left England on 15 Dec. 1687, thus blighting Goodwin's efforts to seduce her, and on 15 Feb. 1688, Goodwin learned that she had died in Paris. 'And indeed', Goodwin wrote (ii. 71), '. . .she was the sincerest, best woman I almost ever knew, and of a prodigious understanding.'
6. Anne inscribes her unpublished play 'Love's Martyr, or Witt Above Crowns' (BL, Add. MS 28,693) to 'Mrs Mary Howe'. Mary, Anne says (in a long dedication, p. 4), 'alone makes the happynesse of my life. . .'.
7. Goodwin's autobiography (ii. 52–119 *passim*) is a primary source of biographical information about Theodosia, Lady Ivy

(*c*.1627–94), with much detail about her business dealings in 1687–9. Other sources include Le Neve, *Knights*, pp. 143, 387; *State Trials*, x. 555–646; *CSP, Dom., Feb.–Dec. 1685*, p. 266; *HCJ* x. 379, 397–8; HMC, *Ormonde*, N.S., vii. 244; HMC, *Downshire*, i. 278 [called 'Lady Joy']; Richard Lapthorn, *The Portledge Papers*, ed. Russell J. Kerr and Ida C. Duncan (London, 1928), p. 38; and Lady Ivy's will, dated 30 Oct. 1693 and probated 8 Jan. 1694/5, PRO, Prob 11/424, fols. 52–4. Goodwin's notation of 4 Apr. 1694 establishes the approximate date of her death.

8. For Neale—speculator, 'projector', Master of the Mint, and Groom Porter under Charles II and William III—see *DNB*, s.v. 'Neale, Thomas (d. 1699?)'.

9. The transcript of the trial—the second-longest civil action of the age (according to Lord Chief Justice Jeffreys)—is printed in *State Trials*, x. 555–646.

10. Goodwin, who attended the trial, was convinced of her guilt, though he says that 'she had indeed forged but one' of the two indentures in question.

11. Widow of Robert Rich, 5th [26th] Earl of Warwick (*CP*). Goodwin had made some advances towards the Countess shortly before his alliance with Mary Parish (Autobiography, ii. 112).

12. Widow of Randal Mac Donnell, 1st Marquis of Antrim (*CP*).

13. Goodwin says (31 Oct. 1687) that Lady Mary, promised to him by revelation, already loved him, but he did not pursue the affair. For Lady Mary Stuart (1665?–1718), see *The Scots Peerage*, ed. Sir James Balfour Paul, Edinburgh, vi, 1909, 323.

14. Mary Tudor (1673–1726), the 14th and youngest of the illegitimate children of Charles II, was the daughter of Mary ('Moll') Davies, a popular singer and actress on the London stage. See *CP*, s.v. Derwentwater, 2nd Earl; 'Bastards of Charles II', *CP* vi, App. F, 708.

15. In late October, Goodwin yielded the Duchess of Richmond to his friend Alexander Stuart, 20th Earl of Moray, who (Goodwin says) was then courting her.

16. Catherine (or Kathrine) Fraser was the daughter of Sir Alexander Fraser, Bt., principal physician to Charles II. Her mother, Mary Carey Fraser, was dresser to Queen Catherine of Braganza and her older sister, Carey Fraser, was a maid of honour. After the Revolution, Catherine married Charles Scarborough (who held household offices under Queen Anne) and bore three daughters, Henrietta Maria (who became a maid of honour to Queen Anne), Ann, and Elizabeth. For Sir Alexander Fraser of Durris (or Dores),

Scotland (1610?–81), and his family, see *Genealogical Collections Concerning Families in Scotland, Made by Walter Macfarlane, 1750–1751*, ed. James Toshach Clark, Edinburgh, ii, 1900, 323–31 (Scottish History Society, xxxiv); *CB* iv. 293–4; *DNB*, s.v. Sir Alexander Fraizer. For the appointments of Lady Fraser, Carey (later Countess of Peterborough), and Catherine, see *CTB* vi. 86, 173, 191, 456, 457; vii, pt. 1, 659; pt. 2, 1321; Chamberlayne, *Angliae Notitia* (1687), pt. 1, p. 201; *CP*, s.v. Peterborough, 3rd Earl.

17. Catherine Fraser was lodged on the third floor of a new block of buildings designed by Wren and completed in early 1687. This structure, which adjoined the west side of the Banqueting House, included an elegant new apartment for the Queen which was not yet occupied. For descriptions of the building (totally destroyed by the fire of 1698), see *Survey of London*, xiii, pt. 2, 102–6 and pl. 5; George S. Dugdale, *Whitehall through the Centuries* (London, 1950), pp. 80–2 and pl. 41.

18. Goodwin first records the rumour about the Queen's pregnancy on 31 Oct. 1687, but his comment implies that he heard the story a day or two earlier.

19. The Queen's illness was publicly noted on 29 Oct., when she could not attend a dinner for the new Lord Mayor of London (*London Gazette*, 27–31 Oct. 1687; Evelyn, iv. 562–3 and n.).

20. Goodwin seems to have learned about the Queen's confinement and 'blooding' from Catherine Fraser (not from revelation).

21. For the King's campaign to pack a parliament, see James Rees Jones, *The Revolution of 1688 in England* (New York, 1972), pp. 128–75.

22. Petre was appointed on 11 Nov. (*London Gazette*, 10–14 Nov. 1687).

23. No one except Goodwin seems to have recorded James's remarkable series of hunting accidents.

24. Catherine Sedley (1657–1717), the witty but plain daughter of Sir Charles Sedley, had been created Countess of Dorchester on 20 Jan. 1686 and then exiled to Dublin after a sensational court battle (Macaulay, ii. 724–8). She returned, however, in 1687, and by Dec., as Goodwin's account indicates, she was again seeing the King.

25. Dorothy Graham (1652–1701) was the wife of Col. James Graham (see *DNB*), Keeper of the Privy Purse for James II. Goodwin describes her as 'an old acquaintance' and 'one of the King's mistresses'. Goodwin's opinion that she was the King's mistress is obviously shared by the writer of a poem called 'The

Statesman's Almanac' (*POAS* iv. 283). Evelyn, however, calls her 'a most virtuous & excellent Creature' (iv. 69). Evelyn furnishes other information in iii. 345, 529 and n.; iv. 467–8, 558.

26. Goodwin's notes of 19 Nov., 24 Nov., and 12 Dec. 1687 add three 1687 performance dates to those listed in *The London Stage, Part 1, 1660–1700*, ed. William Bird Van Lennep (Carbondale, Ill., 1965), pp. 354–61. Goodwin does *not*, however, record the names of the plays and actors he saw. See also, R. Jordan, 'Some Restoration Playgoers', *Theatre Notebook*, xxxv (1981), 51–7.

27. Ernest Brenneke, Jr., 'Dryden's Odes and Draghi's Music', *PMLA* xlix (1934), 1–36.

28. For Sir Thomas Seyliard, 2nd Bt., see *CB* iii. 218. Goodwin's note of 30 Oct. 1687 establishes within a very few days the date of Margaret's second marriage and amends *CB*, which says the event took place 'in or before 1690'.

29. Autobiography, i. [353]. On 1 Jan. 1688, Goodwin was finally and officially 'discharged' (ii. 65) of all responsibility for seducing his sisters.

30. *DNB*, s.v. Thomas Cole (1627?–97); Walter Wilson, *The History and Antiquities of Dissenting Churches in . . . London*, London, iii, 1810, 79–89; Edmund Calamy, *An Abridgement of Mr. Baxter's History . . . With an Account of the Ministers . . . Ejected after the Restauration of King Charles II*, 2nd edn., London, 1713, ii. 61; Arnold Gwynne Matthews, *Calamy Revised* (Oxford, 1934), p. 125.

31. 'I writ him a letter very long [Goodwin says] to beg him to be at least in charity reconciled to his eldest daughter my sister Carr, whom having suspected to design to marry that gentleman (my Lady Wharton's brother) he had . . . obliged her to quit her right to £3,000 portion, and then would give her none.'

32. Thomas Cole to Lord Wharton, 9 Apr. 1669, Rawlinson 50, fol. 69.

33. The six extant poems in the exchange between Wharton and Wolseley appear in *Poems on Affairs of State . . . Part III* ([London], 1698), pp. 1–21.

34. Ibid. pp. 22–4; reprinted, with commentary, in Brice Harris, *Charles Sackville, Sixth Earl of Dorset* (Urbana, Ill., 1940), pp. 110–11, as well as in Harris's 1979 edn. of *Poems of Dorset*, pp. 22–4.

35. *Memoirs of TW*, p. 10.

36. See the indictment against Wolseley, Gaol Delivery Rolls, 13 Jan. 1688, *Middlesex County Records*, iv. 320. Wolseley was outlawed when he failed to answer the indictment; but in the summer of

1689, he obtained a pardon from King William, over the strenuous objections of Lord Wharton (*CSP, Dom., 1689–90*, pp. 55, 157, 237; *Memoirs of TW*, p. 10). See also, *DNB*, s.v. Robert Wolseley (1649–97); indices and entries in *CSP, Dom.* (1692–98, inclusive); HMC, *Downshire*, i.

37. The King's proclamation, issued 23 Dec. 1687, was later published in the *London Gazette*, 2–5 Jan. 1688.

Chapter 15: The Inglorious Revolution

Unless otherwise noted, quotations from Goodwin Wharton are taken from Autobiography, ii. 65–90.

1. See Evelyn, iv. 552 and n.; Luttrell, i. 407; *CSP, Dom., June 1687–Feb. 1689*, pp. 32–3; Peter Earle, *The Treasure of the Concepción* (New York, 1980). Earle (p. 201) gives a summary of the actual shares of the investors.

2. In an entry for 22 Jan. 1688, Goodwin notes that the Queen is 'now removed just under her [Catherine Fraser's] lodgings'. The Queen's new apartment, designed by Wren and decorated by Antonio Verrio and Grinling Gibbons, had been structurally completed in Jan. 1687 (*Survey of London*, xiii, pt. 2, 102–6).

3. For Cook's attempts to patent his diving invention, see *CTB* viii, pt. 3, 1814.

4. Thomas Herbert (1656–1733), 8th [27th] Earl of Pembroke, was a 'virtuoso', a collector (who bought the Arundel Marbles and acquired most of the pictures at Wilton House), and once President of the Royal Society. He was also a very able politician—a moderate Tory who held many offices under William and Anne (*DNB, CP*). Before acceding to the title, he had served with Goodwin in the Parliament of 1680, and in early 1688 Goodwin promised to share with him a secret in alchemy.

5. Goodwin's entry for Wed., 25 Apr. 1688, establishes the *date* of the third day of Crowne's play—a date unknown to William Van Lennep, editor of *The London Stage*. (See *Part 1, 1660–1700*, p. 363.) Goodwin also attended plays on 8 Mar. and 22 Mar. 1688, but he does not tell what plays he saw.

6. Goodwin's entry for Mon., 14 May 1688, corrects Van Lennep on the *date* of James's attendance at Drury Lane and supplies the fact that the Earl of Arran was in the King's party. See *London Stage, Part 1*, p. 365.

7. Goodwin writes the figure £100,000, but I think he inadvertently added a cypher. The signed agreement between Cook and Goodwin later helped Goodwin defeat Cook in a lawsuit in Jersey (above, pp. 236–7).

8. For a modern, sympathetic account of Penn's political manœuvres on behalf of James II, see Vincent Buranelli, *The King & the Quaker* (Philadelphia, 1962), particularly pp. 112–35.

9. *London Gazette*, 26–30 Apr. 1688.

10. Ibid. 3–7 May 1688. For the crisis of May-June 1688, see Maurice Ashley, *The Glorious Revolution of 1688* (London, 1966), pp. 116–24; John Carswell, *The Descent on England* (New York, 1969), pp. 130–51; Jones, *Revolution of 1688*, pp. 120–7; George Macaulay Trevelyan, *The English Revolution* (London, 1938), pp. 86–93; Macaulay, ii. 990–1039.

11. The petition is reproduced in Macaulay, ii. 997.

12. *London Gazette*, 7–11 June 1688.

13. Luttrell, i. 441.

14. For the Queen's reckoning of her time, see deposition of Sir Charles Scarborough, 'first physician to the king', *State Trials*, xii. 139–40.

15. *London Gazette*, 7–11 June 1688.

16. *State Trials*, xii. 183–434.

Chapter 16: Lilliburlero

Unless otherwise noted, quotations from Goodwin Wharton are taken from Autobiography, ii. 91–104.

1. In July 1687 one Henry Ayscogh patented a device which (the description alleged) enabled divers to 'remain underwater... without any covering over their head or body...'. And in May 1688, Colonel Thomas Colepeper tried unsuccessfully to patent a device which would allow divers to do without 'the help of pipes for air' (*CSP, Dom., June 1687–Feb. 1689*, pp. 57, 201; Autobiography, ii. 86).

2. *London Gazette*, 5–9 July 1688.

3. Ibid. 12–16 July 1688.

4. For summaries of William's problems of July–Oct. 1688, see Ashley, *Glorious Revolution*, pp. 125–37; Carswell, *Descent*, pp. 155–70.

5. Goodwin's account of his legal battle with Osmond Cook is confirmed in Rolls of the Royal Court, Jersey, 24 Aug. and 30 Aug. 1688. In view of Goodwin's patent (his 'Otroy Royall') and the agreement signed by Cook on 1 May 1688 (above p. 225 and p. 356 n. 7), the Court convicted Cook of 'Fraude et mauvaise Foy' and condemned him 'a demander pardon a Dieu au Roy et a la Justice et au dits Srs Wharton et Trafort [Humphrey Trafford, an investor in Cook's expedition]...'. Philippe Le Geyt, a judge in the case and a historian of Jersey legal affairs, viewed the trial as

significant because the King's 'Lettres Patentes' were held superior
to the permission granted by the Governor—a finding which the
Lieutenant Governor did not contest (*Les Manuscrits de P. Le
Geyt, Lieutenant-Bailli de L'Ile de Jersey sur la Constitution, les
Lois et les Usages de cette Ile,* Jersey, iv, 1847, 25). For the
structure of the Court at St. Hélier, see also Philip Falle, *An
Account of the Isle of Jersey* (London, 1694), pp. 102–4.

6. The *Pembroke,* a naval vessel of 22–34 guns, was sunk off
Portland in 1667, in a collision with the *Fairfax* (Sir William Laird
Clowes, *The Royal Navy, a History from the Earliest Times to the
Present,* London, ii, 1898, 436). It was the predecessor of the
Pembroke (also a fifth-rate) which accompanied Goodwin to
Tobermory in 1691.

7. Dalton, i. 178; ii. 88, 185; *CSP, Dom., June 1687–Feb. 1689,*
p. 299; Evelyn, iv. 473 and n.

8. Illegitimate son of James II and Barbara Churchill.

9. Dalton, ii. 170; *Clarendon Corr.* i. 311, 323; ii. 3, 11.

10. Dalton, ii. 49, 76, 89; *CSP, Dom., June 1687–Feb. 1689,* p. 271.

11. The platform from which Ramsey chased Goodwin is still extant.
See Arthur Corney, *Fortifications in Old Portsmouth* (Portsmouth, 1965; reprinted 1973), p. 18 and end-map.

12. PRO, SP 44/338, p. 103. The warrant, dated at Whitehall, 28 Sept.
1688, signed by Sunderland, and given to Zachariah Bourne, 'one
of his Mastie's Messengers in Ordinary', called for the apprehension of 'Goodwin Wharton for High Misdemeanor'.

13. For Goodwin's route, see *Ogilby's Road Maps,* pl. 51.

14. Later (1694) Secretary of the Admiralty.

15. Luttrell, i. 468; News-letter, 11 Oct. 1688, HMC, *Le Fleming,*
p. 214.

16. Letter to John Ellis, 13 Oct. 1688, *Ellis Corr.* ii. 248.

17. *Correspondentie van Willem III en van Hans Willem Bentinck,* ed.
Nicolaas Japikse, 's-Gravenhage, ii, 1928, 626–7; Anthony à
Wood, *The Life and Times of Anthony Wood,* Oxford, iii, 1894,
281–2 (Oxford Historical Society Publications, xxvi); Boyer,
William III, i. 242.

18. Carswell (*Old Cause,* p. 69; *Descent,* p. 189) says that Henry
joined William very shortly after Tom did. Actually, Henry
remained with the royal army until Nov. 24. Then he went over to
William, along with Prince George and the Duke of Ormond
('Autobiography of Dr. George Clark', HMC, *Leyborne-Popham,*
pp. 267–8).

19. For text, music, and history of the song, see *POAS* iv. 309–13;
Carswell, *Old Cause,* pp. 353–9.

20. Burnet, iii. 336.
21. Goodwin saw Bridges at the 'playhouse' (probably Drury Lane) and his account establishes the fact that there were performances (unnoted by Van Lennep) on 29 Oct. and 1 Nov. 1688.
22. For the hearing on the birth of the Prince, 22 Oct. 1688, see *State Trials*, xii. 123–82; *Clarendon Corr.* ii. 195–7.
23. A letter to John Ellis, 13 Nov. 1688, says, 'Though there has been a great noise, as if some men of quality, Mr. Wharton and others, were gone in to the invaders; yet it proves false, for Mr. Wharton was seen since at Court, and other places where he frequents' (*Ellis Corr.* ii. 291).
24. [William Dicconson], *The Life of James II*, London, 1816, ii. 218.
25. The events in Manchester, Nottingham, and York took place on 16, 21, and 22 Nov., respectively. For the affair at York, see *Memoirs of Sir John Reresby*, ed. Andrew Browning (Glasgow, 1936), pp. 527–32.
26. For summaries of the crisis, see Churchill, *Marlborough*, i. 293–302; Ashley, *Glorious Revolution*, pp. 166–8; Carswell, *Descent*, pp. 196–9.
27. Clarendon, who also saw William at Henley, describes some of the business conducted at 'Mr. Whitlock's' (*Clarendon Corr.* ii. 224–5).
28. For the events of 18 Dec. 1688, see Luttrell, i. 489; *Clarendon Corr.* ii. 230–1; Evelyn, iv. 611–12 and n.; Burnet, iii. 358.

Chapter 17: The Second-Best World

Quotations from Goodwin Wharton are taken from Autobiography, ii. 105–40.

1. Dalton, iii. 6. The Earl of Lichfield's regiment became Henry Wharton's Regiment of Foot.
2. *London Gazette*, 14–18 Feb. 1689; Luttrell, i. 502.
3. *London Gazette*, 18–21 Feb. 1689; Luttrell, i. 503; *CSP, Dom.,* 1689–90, pp. 5, 97; Browning, *Danby*, i. 457; Boyer, *William III*, ii, 1702, 89; Kennett, iii. 550.
4. Nottingham to Tom Wharton, 9 Mar. 1689, *CSP, Dom.,* 1689–90, p. 18; Warrant to William Carr 'to be Cursitor Baron', 22 Mar. 1689, PRO, SP 44/338, p. 238; Patent for William Carr, 27 Mar. 1689, Patent Rolls, 1–11 William III, PRO, C 66/3325.
5. Grey, *Debates*, ix. 11, 29, 64.
6. For the election returns of Jan. 1689, see *Parl. Hist.* v. 26–32. Henry chose to sit for Westmorland (*HCJ* x. 13), and the Malmesbury seat was given to his friend Colonel Thomas Talmash. For the Wharton influence at Malmesbury, where Tom

was Lord High Steward, see Henry William Edmund Petty-Fitzmaurice, 6th Marquis of Lansdowne, 'Wiltshire Politicians (*c.*1700)', *Wiltshire Archaeological & Natural History Magazine*, xlvi (Dec. 1932), 64–85; Carswell, *Old Cause*, pp. 74–6, 283–4.

7. For the addresses to William, see *Parl. Hist.* v. 23–6; *The Universal Intelligence*, 26–29 Dec. 1688.

8. For Soho Square in the late seventeenth century, see *Survey of London*, xxxiii. 42–127; xxxiv, pls. 68a, 68b. From the tax records of 1691, the *Survey* (xxxiii. 57) establishes the fact that Sir Thomas (and Goodwin) occupied No. 4. Goodwin's account dates their occupancy from 1 Jan. 1689. The house was renovated in 1726 and demolished in 1800; the present structure, which includes Nos. 4–6, was completed between 1801 and 1804.

9. One of Goodwin's brothers inhabited the Square in 1683 and 1685, but the records do not show which one (ibid. xxxiii. 43–4).

10. *CSP, Dom., 1689–90*, p. 59; Beaven, *Aldermen*, i, 1908, 185; *Parl. Hist.* v. 27; William A. Shaw, *The Knights of England*, London, 1906, ii. 267; Ashley, *Wildman*, pp. 282–99.

11. See Edwin Welch, *Southampton Maps from Elizabethan Times, an Introduction to 24 Facsimiles* (Southampton, 1964), pp. 3, 18–19; map 3 in accompanying portfolio (Southampton Record Series, ix); A. Temple Patterson, *A History of Southampton, 1700–1914*, Southampton, i, 1966, 7–8; *Journeys of Fiennes*, p. 54.

12. *CSP, Dom., June 1687–Feb. 1689*, p. 417.

13. Lady Ivy's extensive properties and some of her debts are detailed in her will, drawn 30 Oct. 1693 and probated 8 Jan. 1694/5, PRO, Prob 11/424.

14. Goodwin's memorial seems to have disappeared. A similar petition, urging reinforcements for Jersey, was delivered to the Privy Council on 26 Feb. 1689 from the 'Royall Court' of Jersey (Acts of the Privy Council, PRO, PC 2/73, p. 20).

15. *CP* dates Jermyn's appointment 1685, but it is clear from *CSP Dom., May 1684–Feb. 1685*, pp. 91, 124, 154, that the appointment was made in the summer of 1684.

16. Charles Gerard, 1st Earl of Macclesfield.

17. The Lely portraits were commissioned by Mary's mother, Anne, Duchess of York (Ernest Law, *The New Guide to the Royal Palace and Gardens of Hampton Court with a New Historical Catalogue of the Pictures*, London, 1898, p. 15).

18. Besides showing that Mary originally planned 16 portraits (not the 12 finally executed) and that she intended to include Dutch ladies, Goodwin's account shows that Mary conceived the project in 1689, not in 1691 as is commonly supposed (e.g. Michael Morris,

3rd Baron Killanin, *Sir Godfrey Kneller and His Times*, London, 1948, p. 19); it also refutes a story (attributed to the Countess of Carlisle) that Mary originated the jealousy-provoking portrait scheme while William was away (at the wars). See Horace Walpole, *Anecdotes of Painting in England*, ed. Ralph N. Wornum, with additions by James Dalaway, London, 1862, ii. 590 n.

18. Goodwin does not say which ladies, besides Queen Mary, he selected. For the 12 ladies actually chosen, see Sir Godfrey Kneller, *The Beauties* (London, 175__?), with 13 plates engraved by John Faber; Law, *New Guide*, pp. 14–20; Charles Henry Collins Baker, *Catalogue of the Pictures at Hampton Court* (Glasgow, 1929), pp. 84–6.

19. Apparently Goodwin retained a faint anxiety on the subject of Mary's speaking from outside the door. On 24 April 1692, he noted that 'the Lord spoke while she was below stairs, which He seldom used [to do].' 'Mem[orandum],' Goodwin added in the margin, 'she [was] not near when the Lord spoke.'

20. Sir John was made a London alderman and knighted during King James's attempt to woo the Dissenters (Beaven, *Aldermen*, i. 7). His will, dated 20 June 1688, probated 8 Jan. 1689, shows extensive property holdings; in it he asks to be buried in Bridgwater (PRO, Prob 11/394). Letitia, who died 7 Oct. 1703, is buried at Wooburn (Langley, p. 460).

21. Anne Bawdon was proposed as a match for Sir John Somers when he was Solicitor-General (between 4 May 1689 and 2 May 1691), but negotiations were broken off (Anon., *Memoirs of the Life of John Lord Somers*, London, 1716, p. 25; William Lewis Sachse, *Lord Somers*, Manchester, 1975, p. 67).

22. Luttrell, i. 519; *DNB*, s.v. Sir George Lockhart. For a summary account of Sir George's property, see *Inquisitionum ad Capellam Domini Regis retornatarum, quae in publicis archivis Scotiae adhuc servantur, abbreviatio*, ed. Thomas Thomson, London, i, 1811, item 1314 (Edinburgh), 24 May 1690.

23. Brief biographies of both sons, George and Philip, appear in *DNB*, which mistakenly dates George's birth 1673, six years before his parents were married. Philip was shot as a Jacobite rebel on 2 Dec. 1715, after the battle at Preston.

24. John Perkins to Anne Wharton, [Feb. 1664], Tom Wharton to Anne Wharton, 3 Apr. 1664, Rawlinson 49, fols. 296–7, 174; Abraham Clifford to Anne Wharton, 18 Nov. 1665, Rawlinson 54, fol. 41.

25. PR, St. Paul's, Wooburn; Langley, p. 461; John Le Neve,

Monumenta Anglicana, 1680–1699 (London, 1718), pp. 106–7. In his will (PRO, Prob 11/396, fol. 121) William leaves small memorial bequests to Tom and Henry Wharton, but nothing to Goodwin.

26. Carte 79, fols. 237, 239; Carte 233, fols. 202–3; George Walter Story, *A True and Impartial History of the Most Material Occurrences in the Kingdom of Ireland during the Two Last Years* (London, 1691), pp. 6–10; Clifford Elliott Walton, *History of the British Standing Army, 1600–1700* (London, 1894), p. 63.

27. Story, *True and Impartial History*, p. 15; Richard Kane, *Campaigns of King William and the Duke of Marlborough*, 2nd edn. (London, 1747), p. 2; Charles Creighton, *A History of Epidemics in Britain*, Cambridge, ii, 1894, 231–2.

28. Carte 79, fol. 261.

29. Some attributed the death of Henry and his friends to 'Irish Usquebaugh' (Boyer, *William III*, ii. 159; *POAS* vi. 428 and n.).

30. Phillip Butler to Tom Wharton, 2 Nov. 1689, Carte 79, fol. 269; Story, *True and Impartial History*, pp. 29, 32; *Diary of Thomas Bellingham*, ed. Anthony Hewitson (Preston, 1908), p. 92. Henry's body, first placed in a vault in Dundalk Church, was shipped home in late 1690 for burial at Winchendon (Col. Richard Brewer to Tom Wharton, 10 Nov. 1690, 2 Jan. 1691, Carte 79, fols. 333–4, 337–8).

31. Story, p. 32.

32. Walton, *History of the British Standing Army*, p. 80.

33. Berners to Tom Wharton, *c.* 1 Nov. 1689, Carte 79, fol. 265.

34. See consolatory letters, George Bradbury to Tom Wharton, 21 Nov. 1689, Carte 79, fol. 279; Frederik Spanheim to Lord Wharton, 21 Mar. 1690, Carte 79, fols. 304–5.

35. Sir John Lowther to Sir Daniel Fleming, 16 Nov. 1689, HMC, *Le Fleming*, p. 265; *HCJ* x. 290.

36. *HCJ* x. 362; Carte 81, fols. 796, [797].

37. *HCJ* x. 348, 365, 391.

Chapter 18: Tobermory and the Counter-Revelation

Quotations from Goodwin Wharton are taken from Autobiography, ii. 139–65.

1. After December 1689, Goodwin's complaints about money—and about his father—decrease dramatically. Although he never explains how his father rescued him, it is clear that by mid-1690 he had attained financial respectability. His worries had been further reduced by the fact that as an MP he could not be arrested for debt.

2. For Mary's problems as Regent during the dramatic summer of 1690, see her letters to William, 19 June–8 Sept., Dalrymple, *Memoirs*, ii, App. Pt. 2, 114–69.

3. Goodwin's information 'of moment' probably concerned some 'tumults' among the tinners of Cornwall. See Nottingham's letters to the Earl of Bath (10 June) and Sir Peter Killigrew (17 June), *CSP, Dom., 1690–91*, pp. 29–30, 34; see also *London Gazette*, 3–7 July 1690.

4. The angels named Charles Talbot, Earl of Shrewsbury, William Lloyd, Bishop of St. Asaph, and Archbishop William Sancroft—a very unlikely team of conspirators.

5. For the arrests, see Evelyn, v. 27; Luttrell, ii. 63–4; and *CSP, Dom., 1690–91*, pp. 28–81 *passim*.

6. Tom Wharton and several other gentlemen offered to raise troops at their own expense (Queen Mary to King William, 10 July 1690, *CSP, Dom., 1690–91*, p. 59; Dalrymple, *Memoirs*, ii, App. Pt. 2, 138).

7. Anchitell Grey, the invaluable parliamentary diarist, missed the 20 Oct. 1690–5 Jan. 1691 session. Goodwin's very brief notation on his own activities is one of the scattered sources of information about the debates.

8. For a full-length biography, see Sir George Reresby Sitwell, *The First Whig* (Scarborough, 1894); see also *DNB*, s.v. William Sacheverell (1638–91).

9. I found no trace of Goodwin's essays, which Mary may have destroyed with many other papers in the summer of 1691 or shortly before her death in December 1694 (Nesca A. Robb, *William of Orange*, New York and London, ii, 1996, App. A, 'Mary's Papers', 559–60). Goodwin himself was convinced, by revelation, that William inherited the papers from Mary and that Anne inherited them from William (above, Ch. 20, p. 296; Ch. 21, p. 323).

10. 'Great wagers', says Luttrell on 16 Mar. (ii. 198), 'have been laid upon the seige [*sic*] of Mons.'

11. *London Gazette*, 2–6 Apr. 1691.

12. Ibid. 6–9 Apr. 1691.

13. For the 1690 campaign in the Hebrides, see Hugh Mackay, *Memoirs of the War Carried on in Scotland and Ireland* (Edinburgh, 1833), pp. 332–59 (Bannatyne Club, xlv); John Mackay, *Life of Lieut.-General Hugh Mackay* (Edinburgh, 1836), pp. 87–93 (Bannatyne Club, liii); James Ferguson, *Two Scottish Soldiers* (Aberdeen, 1888), pp. 11–16; *The Register of the Privy*

Council of Scotland, 3rd Ser., Edinburgh, xv, 1967, 431–2, 514–15, 541, 562; *London Gazette*, 27–30 Oct. 1690.

14. The 'protection' (against impressment by the navy) granted to the Captain and crew of Goodwin's ship *Seventh Son* suggests that William and Mary may have had a financial interest in the project beyond the ordinary Crown percentage. The protection says that the vessel is engaged in 'Wreck Fishing pursuant to a Grant from their Maties wherein their Mats have a share. . .' (PRO, Adm 2/8, p. 225).

15. For the status and orders of the three vessels during the summer of 1691, see Adm 8/2, 1 June, 1 July, 1 Aug., and 1 Sept. 1691; Adm 3/6, pp. 17–18, 27, 77, 85, 140, 200.

16. Goodwin does not name or describe his ships. My information comes from Admiralty documents: PRO, Adm 3/6, pp. 27, 178; Adm 2/8, p. 225. Goodwin's 'Letters of Marque or Reprizall' are dated 23 May 1691, Adm 2/1045, pp. 90–1.

17. The logs of the *Pembroke* (PRO, Adm 51/4285) and the *Conception* (PRO, Adm 51/3796) for July 1691 furnish much vital information about the Tobermory expedition.

18. Log of the *Pembroke*, 2 July.

19. Log of the *Conception*, 2 July.

20. The approximate location of the galleon, near Calve Island, was pointed out to me in 1974 by an inhabitant who had watched the operations of the Royal Navy in the 1950s. The exact location ('about 350 yards from Tobermory pier') was rediscovered in August 1975 by a Navy diving team led by Cdr. John Cratton (Associated Press dispatch, printed 31 Aug. 1975, *Salt Lake City Tribune*; 1 Sept. 1975, *Toronto Globe and Mail*).

21. The Macleans had a stronghold in the small Cairn a'Burgh islands (in the Treshnish Isles), which the pink, operating out of Loch na Keal, probably supplied. See the log of the *Conception*.

22. According to James Macnab, Area Administrative Officer at Tobermory, water temperatures now range from 6° C. in Jan. to 16° in Aug.

23. Cdr. Cratton said, in 1975, that the ship lay under '80 feet of water and 20 feet of mud'. The agent for the 9th Earl of Argyll said, about 1680, that the ship then lay under 48–60 ft of water (Carte 109, fol. 430), depending upon the tides (which now vary by 3.7 m at springs and 1.5 m at neaps).

24. Wrecked on the tiny island of Eilean Rudha an Ridire near the southeast tip of Morven (59° 41′ 12″ N, 5° 41′ 55″ W on present naval charts). The hulk has been explored several times since World War II. As of 19 Nov. 1976, it lay under 15–30 ft of water.

25. *Register of the Privy Council of Scotland*, xv. 432; *London Gazette*, 27–30 Oct. 1690; PRO, Adm 8/2, 13 Nov. 1691.
26. The angels did not protect his captured pink, which was captured in turn by the French *en route* from Liverpool to London. The small vessel may have been named (or renamed) the *Edward and Jane Ketch*. On 23 Sept. 1691, a 'protection' was issued for a master, six men, and two boys to bring the craft 'abt. from Liverpoole' (PRO, Adm 3/6, p. 192).
27. *HCJ* x. 539, 549, 556–7.
28. Ibid. x. 590, 605, 611, 621, 639.
29. Ibid. x. 552.
30. *Parl. Diary*, p. 53.
31. Ibid. p. 61; Grey, *Debates*, x. 199.
32. *Parl. Diary*, pp. 54–5.
33. Ibid. pp. 74–5.
34. Ibid. p. 93.
35. *Parl. Diary*, pp. 186–7; *HCJ* x. 670–1; Leopold von Ranke, *History of England, Principally in the Seventeenth Century*, Oxford, 1875, xi. 178–81.
36. Adam Loftus, 1st Viscount Lisburne, killed at the second siege of Limerick, 15 Sept. 1691 (*CP*). For Lucy's fortune, see *CP*, s.v. Thomas, 1st Earl and Marquis of Wharton.

Chapter 19: The Colonel and the Queen

Quotations from Goodwin Wharton are taken from Autobiography, ii. 162–74.

1. The fact that Goodwin's 1693 Tobermory expedition cost £7,000 and that his friend John, 2nd Baron Stawell, owned a 25-percent share is established in a Chancery suit, Wharton v. Ranelagh, 27 Jan. 1703/4, 17 May 1704, PRO, C 9/173/58.
2. Luttrell, ii. 533, 550; *CSP, Dom., 1692–94*, pp. 160–1; *London Gazette*, 26–29 Sept. 1692.
3. See list of government supporters, Browning, *Danby*, iii, 1951, 183.
4. *Parl. Diary*, p. 291.
5. Ibid. pp. 243–4.
6. Ibid. pp. 252, 255, 257.
7. Ibid. p. 219.
8. Ibid. pp. 243–4; Grey, *Debates*, x. 265–7; Henry Horwitz, *Revolution Politicks: The Career of Daniel Finch, Second Earl of Nottingham* (Cambridge, 1968), p. 136.
9. *Parl. Diary*, p. 244.

10. Goodwin spoke at least 34 times during the complete session (*Parl. Diary*, pp. 216–475 *passim*). For his principal committee assignments, see *HCJ* x. 696, 701, 741, 803, 810, 841.

11. *HCJ* x. 749, 765, 782.

12. *Parl. Diary*, p. 316.

13. Ibid. pp. 274–5.

14. Ibid. p. 295.

15. Ibid. p. 382. For the attack upon Burnet, see Macaulay, v. 2305–7; for the offending tracts, see Gilbert Burnet, *A Pastoral Letter Writ by the Right Reverend Father in God Gilbert, Lord Bishop of Sarum* (London, 1689); William Lloyd, *A Discourse of God's Ways of Disposing of Kingdoms* (London, 1691).

16. *Parl. Diary*, p. 265.

17. Ibid. p. 421.

18. Ibid. p. 438.

19. Ibid. pp. 244, 459.

20. Ibid. pp. 372–3.

21. Ibid. pp. 308, 471.

22. Ibid. pp. 398, 406–7, 416; Grey, *Debates*, x. 374.

23. For the *Dolphin*'s orders, see Sir John Trenchard to the Lords of the Admiralty, 8 May, 12 May 1693, PRO, Adm 1/4080, pp. 329, 341; see also PRO, Adm 3/8, 12 May, 30 May 1693; *CSP, Dom.*, *1693*, pp. 166, 178, 183, 414–15; Nottingham to the Admiralty, 23 June 1693, PRO, Adm 1/4080, p. 440.

24. The *Dolphin* left Tobermory on 1 Aug. 1693 (*CSP, Dom.*, *1693*, p. 260).

25. Apparently Goodwin hoped to salvage one of the Armada galleons wrecked in Ireland. For modern accounts of such wrecks, see McKee, *From Merciless Invaders*, pp. 239–65; Evelyn Hardy, *Survivors of the Armada* (London, 1966), pp. 23–36; Martin, *Full Fathom Five*, pp. 23–224; Walker, *The Armada*, pp. 152–60.

26. Grey, *Debates*, x. 321–2.

27. *HCJ* xi. 37.

28. Dalton, iii. 354. Goodwin was also made captain of a troop.

29. *HCJ* xi. 113, 122, 123, 136.

30. Ibid. xi. 95, 129, 170.

31. Grey, *Debates*, x. 369, 386.

32. *HCJ* xi. 135–6.

33. Sebastien Le Prestre, seigneur de Vauban (1633–1707). Vauban's tower-fortress, now a military museum, is still standing. Among its treasures is a good map of the Battle of Camaret Bay.

34. See *DNB*, s.v. Thomas Tollemache. Contemporary references are too numerous to cite.

35. Like Talmash, Cutts deserves a biography of his own. For brief sketches, see *DNB* and *CP*.

36. John Berkeley, 3rd Baron Berkeley of Stratton (1663–97).

37. Van Almonde's report to the States General, 16/26 June 1694 ('s-Gravenhage, Algemeen Rijksarchief, Eerste Afdeling, States General, 5119 I) furnishes a valuable account of the Camaret operation.

38. Later 2nd Duke of Leeds. Carmarthen's book, *A Journal of the Brest Expedition* (London, 1694), gives a detailed account of the naval action.

39. I have not dealt with the still-vexed question of exactly how and when the French learned the English plans. For contemporary theories about security leaks, see William III to Shrewsbury, 18 June, 1 July 1694, *Private and Original Correspondence of Charles Talbot, Duke of Shrewsbury*, ed. William Coxe (London, 1821), pp. 44–7; Russell to Sir John Trenchard, 6 June 1694, *CSP, Dom., 1694–95*, p. 165; Burnet, iv. 232; Josiah Burchett, *Memoirs of Transactions at Sea during the War with France* (London, 1703), p. 224; Kennett, iii. 664.

40. Vauban to Louis XIV, undated, quoted in Paul de Rapin-Thoyras, *The History of England*, tr. and ed. Nicholas Tindall, 2nd edn., London, iii, 1744, 254 n.

41. Primary sources for the Camaret operation include Autobiography, ii. 172; Carmarthen's *Journal* and van Almonde's letter (noted above); Berkeley to Trenchard, 8 June 1694, *CSP, Dom., 1694–95*, pp. 168–70; report of Talmash to Queen Mary via Capt. Anthony Hammond, Luttrell, iii. 327–8; anon. letter from a naval officer, 'Extracts from a Commissioner's Note Book', *The Naval Miscellany*, ed. Sir John Knox Laughton, [London], ii, 1912, 202–5 (Navy Records Society, xl); report of Capt. Nathaniel Green, *CSP, Dom., 1694–95*, pp. 183–4; and the extant logs of several ships: *Queen* (PRO, Adm 51/751), *Neptune* (Adm 51/3920), *Shoreham* (Adm 51/902), *Charles Galley* (Adm 51/4142), *Monk* (Adm 51/4263). I have given a detailed account of the battle in 'Goodwin Wharton', HEH, HM 49425, Ch. XIX, pp. 36–54.

42. The phrase 'rowed and towed', which applies to all covering ships, comes from the log of the *Charles Galley*.

43. Carmarthen, *Journal*, p. 24.

44. Capt. Green's account, *CSP, Dom., 1694–95*, p. 183.

45. For the disengagement and the casualties on the covering ships, see Carmarthen, *Journal*, pp. 28–32, 41; van Almonde, letter, p. 3; and the logs of the *Monk*, *Shoreham*, and *Charles Galley*. There

are no extant logs for the Dutch ships (*Damiaten*, *Drakenstein*, *Wesep*, and *de Woolff*). The *Wesep* was sunk and its commander, Watercamp, was killed.

46. Perhaps because he was disoriented by the shelling, Goodwin misdates the council of war and credits himself with proposing the attack upon Brest. The report of the council attributes the plan to Talmash (*CSP, Dom.*, *1694–95*, p. 170).

47. Though God officially absolved Goodwin of cowardice, an anonymous Tory wit did not. At Camaret (the satirist wrote) Goodwin found himself wishing for a saw-pit, like the one his father allegedly hid in after the Battle of Edgehill ('The Clubmen of the House of Commons', HEH, Ellesmere MS 8755; *POAS* v. 436–7).

48. Berkeley to Trenchard, 13 June 1694, *CSP, Dom.*, *1694–95*, p. 176.

49. Berkeley to Trenchard, ibid. p. 224; Goodwin Wharton to Trenchard, ibid. pp. 222–3; Trenchard to Berkeley, ibid. pp. 227–8.

50. Berkeley to Trenchard, 17 July 1694, ibid. pp. 229–30.

51. Goodwin's return with dispatches is noted in Luttrell, iii. 346; Lapthorn, *Portledge Papers*, pp. 182–3; *London Gazette*, 19–23 July 1694.

52. *HCJ* xi. 193.

53. Ibid. xi. 194.

Chapter 20: The Ruler of the King's Navy

Unless otherwise indicated, all quotations from Goodwin Wharton come from Autobiography, ii. 175–9.

1. *CP* v. 636.

2. *POAS* iv. 207.

3. For the text of the trust (1692) and its history during the eighteenth and nineteenth centuries, see Dale, *Good Lord Wharton*, pp. 70–115.

4. *Parl. Hist.* v. 881–941; *A Collection of the Debates and Proceedings in Parliament in 1694 and 1695* (London, 1695); *HCJ* xi. 236–333 *passim*; Macaulay, v. 2485–98; *Memoirs of TW*, pp. 23–6; Carswell, *Old Cause*, pp. 81–2; Kennett, iii. 670–85.

5. *HCJ* xi. 201, 216, 253, 259, 273.

6. *CTB* x, pt. 2, 985. Richard (Jones), Earl of Ranelagh, was Paymaster General.

7. Luttrell, iii. 485.

8. Sir Wilfred Lawson unsuccessfully protested the Cockermouth

election, alleging in a petition that Goodwin had used 'Bribery' and 'other undue Practices' (*HCJ* xi. 353–4).

9. For Goodwin's appointments, see *HCJ* xi. 334, 339–40, 362–3, 380, 381, 387, 388, 399.

10. On 8 Oct. 1695 Luttrell (iii. 535) erroneously reported Lord Wharton's death. On 10 Oct. he corrected the report (iii. 536).

11. PRO, Prob 11/430, fols. 181–2.

12. See also William Andrews Clark Library, MS news-letter, dated 6 Feb. and attached to *Post Boy*, 4–6 Feb. 1696: 'Yesterday [5 Feb.] the Right Honorable Phillip [*sic*] Ld Wharton being 83 years of Age dyed at Hamstead where he had been some time to take the Ayre, He behaved himself with great honor in all the Revolutions Yt hapned in His Time, A Great Patron of Religion, True Patriott to his Countrey. . .'. Luttrell (iv. 14) too notes that Lord Wharton died at Hampstead—a fact that Goodwin does not mention.

13. PRO, Prob 11/430, fols. 181–2.

14. For Goodwin's property, see his own will, PRO, Prob 11/481, fols. 132–3.

15. Autobiography, ii. 55–6.

16. Bodleian Library, Add. MS D. 40.

17. *Parl. Hist.* v. 988–9.

18. *HLJ* xv. 679–81; *HCJ* xi. 465–6.

19. For the text of the Association, see *HCJ* xi. 466–7.

20. *England's Enemies Exposed* (London, 1701), p. 12.

21. *HCJ* xi. 466. Sir William Trumball was chairman of the committee.

22. *HCJ* xi. 471, 473.

23. Printed in *The Proceedings against Sir John Fenwick, Bar., upon a Bill of Attainder for High Treason* (London, 1698), pp. 349–50.

24. Printed in *HCJ* xi. 577–9.

25. For Whig strategy, see *Shrewsbury Corr.* pp. 412–18; James Vernon, *Letters Illustrative of the Reign of William III from 1696 to 1708*, ed. George Payne Rainsford James, London, 1841, i. 27–51; Carte 233, fols. 25, 27, 36, 38, 39, 40, 41, 42.

26. *HCJ* xi. 579.

27. *HCJ* xi. 588.

28. *Proceedings*, pp. 51–2, 244–6; *State Trials*, xiii. 572, 688–9.

29. *Proceedings*, pp. 347–8; *State Trials*, xiii. 749.

30. *HCJ* xi. 566–7, 600, 602, 603, 613, 625–6, 690–2, 698–9, 738–9. On 17 Nov. 1696, settling his own double return, Goodwin chose to sit for Cockermouth (xi. 587).

31. *HCJ* xi. 567.

32. Ibid. xi. 568.

33. For a good summary, see Kennett, iii. 722–5.
34. *HCJ*, xi. 576, 584, 585, 589, 591, 593; Luttrell, iv. 139, 141–2, 143. Goodwin also served on the conference committee which rejected the Lords' attempt to amend the bill (*HCJ*, xi. 602, 606, 607).
35. Ibid. xi. 589, 602, 614.
36. Ibid. xi. 629–30, 635, 639.
37. Ibid. xi. 732.
38. Ibid. xi. 616.
39. Ibid. xi. 636–8; Kennett, iii. 723; *Parl. Hist.* v. 1158.
40. *HCJ* xi. 740–1, 752, 753, 759–60, 765.
41. Ibid. xi. 573, 592, 613, 629, 667, 686, 730, 766, 774, 777.
42. Ibid. xi. 697, 714, 715–16. The bill was co-authored by Sir Henry Hobart.
43. *HCJ* xi. 724.
44. Ibid. xi. 667, 681, 686, 706, 713. The bill was co-authored by John Dutton Colt.
45. *HLJ* xvi. 161; *HCJ* xi. 742, 779, 780.
46. *HCJ* xi. 734, 737, 741.
47. Shrewsbury to Somers, 14 Apr. 1697, *Shrewsbury Corr.* p. 478.
48. *London Gazette*, 22–26 Apr. 1697.
49. PRO, SP 44/345, p. 494.
50. *CSP, Dom., 1697*, pp. 123, 125, 126; *London Gazette*, 26–29 Apr. 1697.
51. *Shrewsbury Corr.* pp. 477–8; Vernon, *Letters*, i. 386, 390–1, 399–400, 404–5, 418, 431; Thomas Cecil Nicholson and Arthur Stanley Turberville, *Charles Talbot, Duke of Shrewsbury* (Cambridge, 1930), p. 136; Macaulay, vi. 2744–6.
52. John Ehrman, *The Navy in the War of William III, 1689–1697* (Cambridge, 1953), pp. 551–7; Edward Barzillai Powley, *The Naval Side of King William's War* (Hamden, Conn., 1972), p. 364; *HCJ* xii. 417–18.
53. The building stood on the site of the present Admiralty Old Building. New in 1695, it was demolished and replaced in 1723 (Ehrman, pp. 566–7, with picture facing p. 566).
54. For Goodwin's attendance at meetings during 1697, see Admiralty Minutes, PRO, Adm 3/13.
55. Burchett, *Memoirs*, pp. 355–404.
56. Ibid. pp. 402–3; Benbow to Admiralty, 30 Aug. 1697; news-letter, 31 Aug. 1697, *CSP, Dom., 1697*, pp. 335, 337.
57. It is possible that Mary announced Peregrine's death during the time Goodwin was bedridden with a paralytic stroke (between 25 Mar. and 19 May 1698).

58. By a royal warrant dated 2/12 Aug. 1697, Goodwin's salary was made retroactive to 25 Mar. 1697 (*CTB* xii. 274).

59. Goodwin bought the furniture at Richings and later brought a Chancery suit against one Joseph Devenish, an upholsterer, over the terms of the agreement. Goodwin's complaint involves a room-by-room description of the furnishings and much information about the house itself (PRO, C 9/455/108).

60. David Jacques, 'The Art and Sense of the Scribblerus Club in England, 1715–35', *Garden History: The Journal of the Garden History Society*, iv (Spring 1976), 47–50; *Correspondence between Frances, Countess of Hartford* [sic] *(Afterwards Duchess of Somerset), and Henrietta Louisa, Countess of Pomfret, between the Years 1738 and 1741*, ed. William Bingley, 2nd edn., London, 1806, i. 198, 245–8, 271–3.

61. For the Apsleys and Richings, see *VHC Buckinghamshire*, iii. 290; Lipscomb, *Buckingham*, iv. 517–20; will of Sir Peter Apsley, PRO, Prob 11/410; will of Catherine (Fortray) Apsley, PRO, Prob 11/264.

62. *The Correspondence of Alexander Pope*, ed. George Sherburn, Oxford, 1956, ii. 207, 263, 299, 302 n., 305, 464–5; iii. 120–1, 504 and n.; *The Correspondence of Jonathan Swift*, ed. Harold Williams, Oxford, iii, 1963, 136 and n., 455; iv, 1965, 39, 63.

63. County of Buckingham, *Calendar to the Sessions Records*, ed. William Le Hardy and Geoffrey Ll. Reckitt, Aylesbury, ii, 1936, 456.

Chapter 21: A Closer Walk

Unless otherwise noted, all quotations from Goodwin Wharton come from Autobiography, ii. 179–82.

1. Robert Yard to Sir Joseph Williamson, 10 Dec. 1697, *CSP, Dom., 1697*, p. 507.

2. For Goodwin's naval estimates, see *HCJ* xii. 134; for the anti-corruption bill, see xii. 56, 84, 88, 99, 179; for the finance committee, see xii. 10, 30–2, 53, 86, 94–5; for the Committee of Privileges and Elections, see xii. 1–2; for the militia committee, see xii. 12; and for miscellaneous functions, see xii. 32, 79, 124, 151.

3. *London Gazette*, 24–27 Jan. 1698.

4. Luttrell, iv. 361 (entry for 29 Mar. 1698).

5. Vernon to Shrewsbury, 29 Mar. 1698, Vernon, *Letters*, ii. 28–9.

6. News-letter, 29 Mar. 1698, *CSP, Dom., 1698*, p. 169.

7. *Post Boy*, 29–31 Mar. 1698.

8. Vernon to Shrewsbury, 29 Mar. 1698.

9. *Verney Letters of the Eighteenth Century from the MSS. at*

Claydon House, ed. Margaret Maria, Lady Verney, London, 1930, i. 154.

10. Vernon to Shrewsbury, 19 May 1698, Vernon, *Letters*, ii. 82.

11. Admiralty Minutes, PRO, Adm 3/14.

12. The Bucks election is reported in Luttrell, iv. 408 (entry for 30 July 1698).

13. Even Tom Wharton lost several normally 'safe' boroughs. Somers to Shrewsbury, 16 Aug. 1698, *Shrewsbury Corr.* p. 554; Miles Cooke to Sir Joseph Williamson, 19 Aug. 1698, *CSP, Dom., 1698*, pp. 376–7; Macaulay, vi. 2844–5.

14. *HCJ* xii. 424, 441, 481, 530, 546. The fact that Goodwin was essentially lost to his party during the 1698–99 session and that his loss was significant is shown in the correspondence of Walter Moyle, a Country Whig. What happened to the '*terrible Party*' that dominated the previous session? Moyle asks his friend Anthony Hammond. '*Have they lost their Wisdom with* Goodwin Wharton's *Apoplexy. . . ?*' (Moyle to Hammond, 7 Feb. 1699, in *The Whole Works of Walter Moyle, Esq., That Were Published by Himself*, London, 1727, pp. 14–15).

15. Biographies of Philip, Duke of Wharton, include Lewis Saul Benjamin [Lewis Melville, pseud.], *The Life and Writings of Philip, Duke of Wharton* (London, 1913); E. Beresford Chancellor, *Col. Charteris and the Duke of Wharton* (London, 1925); Mark Blackett-Ord, *Hell-Fire Duke: The Life of the Duke of Wharton* (Windsor, 1983); the 'Life' prefixed to *The Poetical Works of Philip, Late Duke of Wharton*, i. 1–35; *The Life and Writings of Philip, Late Duke of Wharton* (London, 1732), 2 vols.; and sketches in *CP* and *DNB*.

16. Luttrell, iv. 469.

17. Mary and William Thomas were married at St. Paul's, Wooburn, 19 Feb. 1672/3 (PR, St. Paul's; also *Buckinghamshire PRs* v. 72). William died in 1677 (E. R. Wharton, p. 41).

18. Rawlinson 49, fols. 12, 14. Writing to Mary from Caen on 1 Jan. 1664, the ten-year-old Goodwin says, 'I love you very well', and signs himself, 'your afextioned Brother' (fol. 126).

19. Young Edmond, knighted by James II, died sometime before 1693, leaving Anna the heiress apparent to their father's property. During the summer of 1693 Anna was the subject of marriage negotiations between the Whartons and Shrewsbury (Carte 233, fols. 108, 175, 204–5, 218, 246–7). Anna died 23 Aug. 1694 at Pusey, Berkshire, and was buried at Wooburn on 13 Sept. (Anthony à Wood, *Athenae Oxonienses*, 3rd ed., Oxford, iii, 1817, 105). On 23 June 1700, young Sir Edmond, who had been

first buried elsewhere, was reburied at Wooburn (Langley, p. 467).

20. Will dated 27 Mar., probated 6 May 1699, PRO, Prob 11/450/253–4.

21. *Post Boy*, 1–4 Apr. 1699.

22. Mary married Sir Charles Kemeys, 3rd Bt., of Cefn Mabley, Wales, in 1678. Their son Charles, born 23 Nov. 1688, became 4th Bt. at his father's death in Dec. 1702 and died unmarried in 1735, when the baronetage became extinct. Jane Kemeys, Mary's daughter, married Sir John Tynte in 1704. From this marriage descended Charles Theodore Halswell Kemeys-Tynte, who in 1915 got the Wharton barony revived and was called to the House of Lords as 8th Baron Wharton (*CP* xii, pt. 2, 614–15 and App. D, pp. 14–15).

23. Mary's death left only two Wharton sisters, Margaret and Philadelphia: Margaret was then the wife of William, 12th Baron Ross. (Her second husband Sir Thomas Seyliard died in 1692 and she married Lord Ross sometime before Aug. 1695.) Margaret survived three of her four children—Major (bd. 4 Mar. 1684), Margaret (bd. 25 Dec. 1690), Wharton (bd. 25 Sept. 1705). She died in late Feb. 1706 and was buried with her children and first husband at Pusey on 1 Mar. 1706 (Pusey PR, PRO, Reading, Berkshire).

24. *HCJ* xii. 618.

25. *Shrewsbury Corr.* pp. 578–9; *CSP, Dom., 1699–1700*, p. 176; Luttrell, iv. 516; *Post Boy*, 16–18 May 1699.

26. John Ellis to Sir Joseph Williamson, 23 May 1699, *CSP, Dom., 1699–1700*, p. 190.

27. PRO, SP 44/348, pp. 44–5.

28. *HCJ* xii. 650, 681.

29. See *HCJ* xii. 564, 582 for pay scale.

30. Macclesfield died 5 Nov. 1701; the regiment was given to Thomas Windsor, 1st Viscount Windsor, on 10 Mar. 1702 (Dalton, v. 232).

31. *HCJ* xiii. 2, 72, 164–6, 236, 466, 539, 553.

32. *CP* (v. 636) erroneously gives Lady Gerard's death and burial dates as 11 and 19 Jan. 1700. The correct dates are 11 and 19 Mar. 1700. *See Registers of Westminster*, p. 246 and n. *Post Boy*, 12–14 Mar. 1700, notes Lady Gerard's death.

33. Luttrell, iv. 483 (entry for 14 Feb. 1699).

34. PRO, Prob 10/1329; Prob 11/455. Will drawn 13 Jan. 1699, probated 26 Apr. 1700.

35. Her brother the Earl of Macclesfield was buried in the same vault on 14 Nov. 1701 (*Registers of Westminster*, p. 249).

36. *London Gazette*, 11–15, 15–18 Dec. 1701. On 20 Jan. 1702 Goodwin chose to sit for Bucks (*HCJ* xiii. 687).
37. Luttrell, v. 119.
38. Privileges and Elections, *HCJ* xiii. 646; committee for loyal address, xiii. 647; miscellaneous committees, xiii. 752, 764, 768, 778, 779, 782, 783, 808 (two entries), 842, 862.
39. *CSP, Dom., 1700–02*, p. 519.
40. For William's accident, illness, and death, see Burnet, iv. 557–61; Kennett, iii. 835–7; Macaulay, vi. 2998–3006.
41. Burnet, iv. 561.
42. Goodwin's election is reported in *London Gazette*, 23–27 July 1702. The Tory attempt to unseat him, Whigs alleged, involved actionable fraud. 'The Collonel is a Discreet Honourable worthy Gentleman,' wrote John Tutchin, 'and knows well enough how to get satisfaction in this Point' (*The Observator*, ed. Tutchin, London, 5–8 Aug. 1702).
43. Autobiography, ii. 160. When Anne and Queen Mary quarrelled, Goodwin attempted to get the Commons to intercede (*Parl. Diary*, p. 244; Grey, *Debates*, x. 267–8).
44. Luttrell, v. 273.
45. Entry for 20 Apr. 1703 in the register of burials. The name is spelled 'Mary Parris'. For a partial list of famous people buried at St. Giles-in-the-Fields (including Andrew Marvell, Sir Godfrey Kneller, and Sarah Siddons), see Revd Gordon Taylor, 'Saint Giles-in-the-Fields, Its Part in History' (privately produced pamphlet, 1971), p. 13.
46. For the political situation in the spring of 1704, see George Macaulay Trevelyan, *England Under Queen Anne*, London, i, 1930, 328–37.
47. Goodwin does not say how the boy was raised or when he came to live at St. Giles, as he seems to have done. The fact that one Peter Lully, a Flemish music and dancing master lived with Goodwin for a year, beginning (probably) in early 1701, suggests that Hezekiah was brought home about that time (*CSP, Dom., 1702–03*, p. 679).
48. E. R. Wharton, p. 42.
49. PRO, Prob 11/481; will probated 16 Mar. 1705. Goodwin appointed John Harrison, his household steward, as Hezekiah's guardian, but he forgot to appoint an executor. The court therefore appointed Alexander Hall. Hezekiah is described in the probate notations as Hezekiah Wharton, alias Knowles.
50. Dalton, v. 176. On 25 Apr. 1705 Hezekiah was promoted to 'Lieut. of Grendrs.' in the same regiment under the name *Hezekiah*

Wharton, which Dalton (ibid. pp. 176, 177) notes as 'untraced'.

51. A long note appended to Goodwin's will establishes the fact that Hezekiah died, intestate, in 1711 and that Elizabeth Lloyd was appointed on 7 Dec. 1711 to administer his property—the assets remaining from Goodwin's bequests to him.

52. William Andrews Clark Library, MS news-letter attached to copy of the *Post-Man*, 24–26 Oct. 1704. Dated 26 Oct., the letter reads, 'Yesterday [i.e. Wed., 25 Oct.] ye Honble Goodwin Wharton Esqr Knt. of ye Shire for Bucks died. . .'. Luttrell (v. 480) notes Goodwin's death in an entry for 26 Oct., but does not give the date of death. A note appended to Goodwin's journal sometime after 1715 dates his death 26 Oct. On 31 Oct. the Commons officially ordered 'That Mr. Speaker do issue his Warrant to the Clerk of the Crown, to make out a new Writ for the electing a Knight to serve in this present Parliament for the county of *Buckingham*, in the Room of the Honourable *Goodwin Wharton*, Esquire, deceased' (*HCJ* xiv. 393).

INDEX

Note: Peers and peeresses are indexed by title, not by family name. Devils, spirits, and lowlanders are indexed by name under the above categories.

The following abbreviations and short forms are used throughout the index:

GW: Goodwin Wharton
MP: Mary (*née* Tomson) Boucher Lawrence Parish
Lord Wharton: Philip Wharton, 4th Baron Wharton
Lady Wharton: Anne (*née* Carr) Popham, Lady Wharton

T. S. ELIOT
Peter Ackroyd

'Perceptive and assured . . . the fullest and most plausible portrait yet
achieved'
Frank Kermode, *Guardian*

'A major biography . . . the result does justice to the complexity of Eliot's
genius, and builds up a commanding case for the unity of life and work.
We are unlikely to have a better biography of Eliot for many years'
John Carey, *Sunday Times*

0 7474 0182 9   NON-FICTION

BYRON
Frederic Raphael

'I have been reading Byron and most books about him for twenty years,
without feeling that I fully or clearly understood his life, until Frederic
Raphael's *Byron*. It is a very pleasing, quite unacademic book, fizzing with
bad taste, brilliance, and punning wit. It is the only Byron book, written
as it were by an equal, moral without moralising, sharply discriminating in
criticism and warm in affection . . . both exciting and reliable . . . without
a boring page'
Peter Levi, *Guardian*

'I found it so much more readable than other biographies of the great man
of letters and I enjoyed it immensely . . . Raphael brings out the innate
humanity of Byron and the book sparkles'
Spectator

0 7474 0205 1   NON-FICTION

THE CAESARS
Allan Massie

Allan Massie's self-confessed 'enjoyment of the period and characters' certainly shows in this witty account of the lives of the Caesars. As a novelist he is well set to make the imaginative leaps and connections necessary – because of the limited historical documentation surviving from the ancient world – to get to the heart of these remarkable men.

0 7474 0179 9   NON-FICTION

THE LIFE AND DEATH OF MOZART
Michael Levey

'Essential reading for all Mozartians' *The Times*

Mozart's reputation as a composer continues in the ascendant, yet, curiously, our understanding of the man has been clouded: his personality has been seen as irreconcilable with the musical genius. This picture is unsatisfactory and unsatisfying. Michael Levey sees behind that darkened varnish the clear image of a man of immense liveliness and great humanity not at all at odds with the genius we acknowledge in the music. Simply, Michael Levey reveals the real Mozart.

0 7474 0150 0   NON-FICTION

ROMANTIC AFFINITIES

Rupert Christiansen

'Entertainingly anecdotal as well as intelligently documentary, this book offers a large-scale map of Romanticism, not in terms of political creeds or artistic achievement, but in terms of its restlessness, its eccentricities and its human cost . . . the madness of Hölderlin, the pederasty of Byron, the domestic disasters of the Shelleys, the meddlesome energies of Madame de Staël, the macabre and manic performances of Paganini, all make for good stories, and Christiansen recounts them with compulsively enjoyable detail'
TLS

'His portraits are vivid, moving, sometimes funny; together they create a kaleidoscopic picture of an age which to those who lived through it must have seemed every bit as fragmented and confusing as our own'
Spectator

0 7474 0404 6   HISTORY

READS

Brigid Brophy

Brigid Brophy: novelist, critic, biographer, journalist and promoter of – amongst much else – animal rights, Mozart, Firbank, and the Baroque. Her writing is inimitable and incomparable. *READS* captures her spirit in a collection of reviews and essays spanning the whole period of her writing career.

'We read therefore we are. The idea is suggested to me by Brigid Brophy's essays, which constitute one of the strongest proofs of personal identity I have ever come across. If a real person is not here, where is a person to be found? She writes therefore she is, and to receive such an impression, so clearly, is very uncommon indeed'
John Bayley, London Review of Books

0 7474 0275 2   NON-FICTION

CASANOVA

John Masters

Giacomo Casanova's reputation rests largely on his obsession with 'the mystery of exactly what was lurking between any particular woman's legs'. But he was much more than the Great 18th century Lover: lawyer, mathematician, poet, translator, librarian and fluent in several languages, he was described by one contemporary as 'the most civilised man in Europe'. That he was also a con-man, cabalist, spy, revenge-taker and experienced prisoner only enhances his appeal as one who personified the extreme social and moral contradictions of the time.

In chronicling the life of this bastard son of Venetian actors, John Masters has drawn on Casanova's own highly expansive memoirs, unavailable until the 1960s.

0 7474 0388 0   NON-FICTION

HEMINGWAY

Kenneth S. Lynn

'This brilliant biography . . . Hemingway studies will never be the same again'
Daily Telegraph

'Kenneth S. Lynn's magnificent biography . . . Accomplished, revealing and, all in all, profoundly sympathetic'
Times Literary Supplement

Kenneth S. Lynn reveals a man dogged with the fear that he could not support his own myth. Two contemporaries, both female, already sensed this: Zelda Fitzgerald put it tersely – 'No man could be as male as all that' and Gertrude Stein said 'What a book would be the real story of Hemingway, not those he writes, but the confessions of the real Ernest Hemingway'. This is that book: a detective story which tracks down Hemingway's real debts and obsessions. This brilliant biography may appear to be the case against Hemingway, but Hemingway finally emerges as a genuine hero. As Norman Mailer put it: 'he carried a weight of anxiety with him which would have suffocated any man smaller than himself.'

0 7474 0320 1   NON-FICTION

MY LIFE
Isadora Duncan

Born in 1878, Isadora Duncan was one of the most famous dancers of modern times. Variously described as 'eccentric', 'mad', and 'a genius', she was one of the most original artistic personalities of this century. Defying convention from the moment she was born – when, as she frequently remarked, 'Venus was in the ascendant' – she was always a reckless, courageous and dedicated exponent of freedom and love. Her dancing was freestyle, improvised and unique. Dressed in a simple white tunic, she danced her way across America and Europe, found fame and (fickle) fortune, and courted love, disaster, and ultimately tragedy.

Her writing, like her life and her 'Art', is an extraordinary mixture of grace, inspiration and exquisite exaggeration. If she is to be believed – and sometimes it is difficult – she had a 'religious and awe-inspiring' effect on men, she 'discovered the dance', and her life was 'more interesting than any novel and more adventurous than any cinema'.

Her death was as flamboyant as her life. In 1927, shortly after completing this book, she was strangled by her flowing scarf, which had become caught in the wheels of the car in which she was travelling. *Isadora: My Life* first appeared the following year, and was promptly banned.

0 7474 0377 5   NON-FICTION

GUSTAV MAHLER
Alma Mahler

'I lived his life. I had none of my own. He never noticed this surrender of my existence. He was utterly self-centred by nature, and yet he never thought of himself. His work was all in all.'

Both Alma's devotion to Mahler and her own forceful character shine through her recollections of the ten intense years they shared from 1901 to 1911. Her lively account of these last days of the Hapsburg Empire mixes domestic detail with anecdotes of such figures as Richard Strauss, Debussy, Freud and Schoenberg, personal moments with musical analysis – Alma was herself a gifted musician and helped Mahler considerably with his work when he forbade her own. Combined with a large collection of Gustav's letters and sixteen pages of photographs, her memories contribute much to our understanding of one of the most popular composers of recent years.

Edited by the eminent music scholar Donald Mitchell, who also provides the biographical listing, appendix and chronology.

0 7474 0317 1   NON-FICTION

THE MYSTERY OF
WILLIAM SHAKESPEARE
Charlton Ogburn

Could Shakespeare have been the man of Stratford who died in 1616, years after writing his last play, leaving no books, and exciting no tributes from his fellow writers? A man who could barely write his own name, but had twice the vocabulary of Milton; a man who was never referred to as a writer; a mediocre actor, forever in trouble and in debt, whose greatest role was the ghost in his own HAMLET: could this man be Ben Jonson's 'soul of the age'?

Why do we know so little about Shakespeare? Is it because we are looking in the wrong place?

Sigmund Freud wrote, 'The man of Stratford seems to have nothing at all to justify his claims, whereas Oxford has almost everything'.

'Oxford' is Edward de Vere, the seventeenth Earl of Oxford, courtier, patron of the arts, classical scholar, poet, dramatist, sportsman, Italophile and favourite of Elizabeth I. In this brilliant detective story Charlton Ogburn presents the strongest case ever against 'Stratford' and for 'Oxford'. His life time's quest has resulted in a work of enthralling historical reconstruction and imagination.

0 7474 0255 8   NON-FICTION

COUNTRY LIFE
Howard Newby

'Howard Newby has achieved what has long been needed, a single and authoritative telling of village England's economic tale over the past two centuries' Ronald Blythe, *Guardian*

Every age has mythologised the countryside. Our jealously guarded 'heritage' is almost entirely mythical.

With humanity and clarity Howard Newby tells the real story of country life: from the enclosure of the old strip farms to create fields and the first capitalist industry in the world, the effects of the ensuing competition and changes in the law, machinery and farming techniques, to the Napoleonic Wars and the Corn Law, the First World War and Lloyd George's budget, the Second World War and the EEC. It spans the various attempts at unionization and rioting, changing aesthetic perceptions of country living in architecture, literature and painting, and changing patterns of population and movement of labour. All are worked into an extremely readable and moving account of the real heritage of our countryside.

0 7474 0286 8   SOCIAL HISTORY

MARY SHELLEY
Muriel Spark

Fiction's most famous monster was the creation of a nineteen-year-old woman, Mary Shelley. The daughter of famous parents and the wife of a famous man, she made her own mark upon history with the story of a scientist who breathes life into a creature stitched together from corpses. Published in 1818, *Frankenstein* was a best-seller and has haunted the imagination ever since.

At the age of sixteen she eloped with the poet Shelley, accompanied by her step-sister, Claire Clairmont. The young couple's political and social idealism was dogged by hysteria and tragedy.

After only six years of marriage, Shelley was drowned, and Mary faced long, poignant decades of widowhood, attempting to support herself and her son by her writing.

In Muriel Spark's brilliant investigation of Mary Shelley's life and work, biographer and subject are perfectly matched. As Hilary Spurling has written: 'Both are dry, clear and forthright to the point of bluntness, cool and sharp as a mint julep, with something of the same afterkick.'

0 7474 8318 X   BIOGRAPHY

YOUNG BETJEMAN
Bevis Hillier

'If he was England's best-selling poet since Lord Byron, he was also, like Byron, as good value in the flesh as in verse, if not better . . . A delicious volume which takes the late Laureate from birth to marriage'
Sunday Telegraph

'Of my contemporaries who have made a name in the world, I have no hesitation in saying Betjeman was the most unusual, in background, talents, curious erudition and way of life . . . Bevis Hillier has tackled a lot of intricate material remarkably well'
Anthony Powell, *The Times*

'A model of biography, and fascinatingly documented. The chapters on the mass of literary influences that combined to produce Betjeman's unique poetic voice are little masterpieces in themselves. All the personal material is wonderfully rich and unsimplified. It will be hard to wait patiently for volume two'
John Carey, Sunday Times

0 7474 0467 4   BIOGRAPHY

Cardinal now offers an exciting range of quality fiction and non-fiction by both established and new authors. All of the books in this series are available from good bookshops, or can be ordered from the following address:

Sphere Books
Cash Sales Department
P.O. Box 11
Falmouth
Cornwall, TR10 9EN.

Please send cheque or postal order (no currency), and allow 60p for postage and packing for the first book plus 25p for the second book and 15p for each additional book ordered up to a maximum charge of £1.50 in U.K.

B.F.P.O. customers please allow 60p for the first book, 25p for the second book plus 15p per copy for the next 7 books, thereafter 9p per book.

Overseas customers, including Eire, please allow £1.25 for postage and packing for the first book, 75p for the second book and 28p for each subsequent title ordered.